NE능률 영어교과서

대한민국 고등학생 **10명 중**
4.7명이 보는 교과서

영어 고등 교과서 점유율 1위
[7차, 2007 개정, 2009 개정, 2015 개정]

리딩튜터

그동안 판매된
리딩튜터 1,900만 부
차곡차곡 쌓으면 19만 미터

에베레스트
21배 높이

에베레스트 8,848m

190,000m

능률보카

그동안 판매된
능률VOCA 1,100만 부

대한민국 박스오피스
천만명을 넘은 영화
단 28개

VO CA

그래머존

그동안 판매된 450만 부의 그래머존을 바닥에 쭉 ~ 깔면
1000km 서울-부산 왕복가능

서울

부산

GRAMMAR Inside

LEVEL 3

지은이	NE능률 영어교육연구소
선임연구원	김지현
연구원	박효빈, 가민아
영문교열	Curtis Thompson, Angela Lan
디자인	민유화
맥편집	허문희

Let's grow to

NE능률이
미래를
창조합니다.

건강한 배움의 고객가치를 제공하겠다는 꿈을 실현하기 위해
40년이 넘는 시간 동안 열심히 달려왔습니다.

앞으로도 끊임없는 연구와 노력을 통해
당연한 것을 멈추지 않고

고객, 기업, 직원 모두가 함께 성장하는 NE능률이 되겠습니다.

with **workbook**

GRAMMAR
Inside

LEVEL 3

STRUCTURES

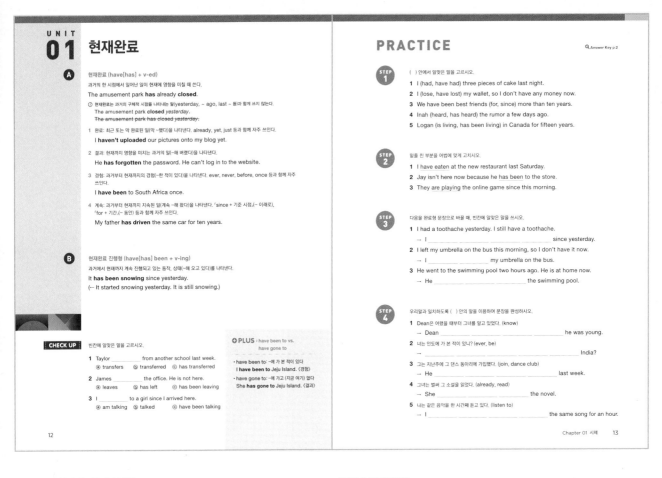

UNIT 01 현재완료

Ⓐ 현재완료 (have[has] + v-ed)
과거의 한 시점에서 일어난 일이 현재에 영향을 미칠 때 쓴다.

The amusement park has already closed.

ⓘ 현재완료는 과거의 구체적 시점을 나타내는 말(yesterday, ~ ago, last ~ 등)과 함께 쓰지 않는다.
The amusement park closed yesterday.
~~The amusement park has closed yesterday.~~

1 완료: 최근 또는 막 완료된 일(막 ~했다)을 나타낸다. already, yet, just 등과 함께 자주 쓰인다.
I haven't uploaded our pictures onto my blog yet.

2 결과: 현재까지 영향을 미치는 과거의 일(~해 버렸다)을 나타낸다.
He has forgotten the password. He can't log in to the website.

3 경험: 과거부터 현재까지의 경험(~한 적이 있다)을 나타낸다. ever, never, before, once 등과 함께 자주 쓰인다.
I have been to South Africa once.

4 계속: 과거부터 현재까지 지속되는 일(계속 ~해 왔다)을 나타낸다. 「since + 기준 시점(~ 이래로)」, 「for + 기간(~ 동안)」 등과 함께 자주 쓰인다.
My father has driven the same car for ten years.

Ⓑ 현재완료 진행형 (have[has] been + v-ing)
과거에서 현재까지 계속 진행되고 있는 동작, 상태(~해 오고 있다)를 나타낸다.

It has been snowing since yesterday.
(← It started snowing yesterday. It is still snowing.)

CHECK UP
빈칸에 알맞은 말을 고르시오.

1 Taylor _____ from another school last week.
ⓐ transfers   ⓑ transferred   ⓒ has transferred

2 James _____ the office. He is not here.
ⓐ leaves   ⓑ has left   ⓒ has been leaving

3 I _____ to a girl since I arrived here.
ⓐ am talking   ⓑ talked   ⓒ have been talking

✚ PLUS : have been to vs. have gone to

· have been to: ~에 가 본 적이 있다 〈경험〉
I have been to Jeju Island.

· have gone to: ~에 가고 (지금 여기) 없다 〈결과〉
She has gone to Jeju Island. 〈결과〉

12

PRACTICE
🔍 Answer Key p-2

STEP 1
( ) 안에서 알맞은 말을 고르시오.

1 I (had, have had) three pieces of cake last night.
2 I (lose, have lost) my wallet, so I don't have any money now.
3 We have been best friends (for, since) more than ten years.
4 Inah (heard, has heard) the rumor a few days ago.
5 Logan (is living, has been living) in Canada for fifteen years.

STEP 2
밑줄 친 부분을 어법에 맞게 고치시오.

1 I have eaten at the new restaurant last Saturday.
2 Jay isn't here now because he has been to the store.
3 They are playing the online game since this morning.

STEP 3
다음을 완료형 문장으로 바꿀 때, 빈칸에 알맞은 말을 쓰시오.

1 I had a toothache yesterday. I still have a toothache.
→ I _____ since yesterday.
2 I left my umbrella on the bus this morning, so I don't have it now.
→ I _____ my umbrella on the bus.
3 He went to the swimming pool two hours ago. He is at home now.
→ He _____ the swimming pool.

STEP 4
우리말과 일치하도록 ( ) 안의 말을 이용하여 문장을 완성하시오.

1 Dean은 어렸을 때부터 그녀를 알고 있었다. (know)
→ Dean _____ he was young.
2 너는 인도에 가 본 적이 있니? (ever, be)
→ _____ India?
3 그는 지난주에 그 댄스 동아리에 가입했다. (join, dance club)
→ He _____ last week.
4 그녀는 벌써 그 소설을 읽었다. (already, read)
→ She _____ the novel.
5 나는 같은 음악을 한 시간째 듣고 있다. (listen to)
→ I _____ the same song for an hour.

GRAMMAR POINT

1 GRAMMAR POINT
해당 Unit에서 배워야 할 핵심 문법들을 명확한 설명과 실용적인 예문으로 체계적으로 정리했습니다.

2 CHECK UP
핵심을 묻는 문제를 통해 Grammar Point에서 배운 내용을 이해했는지 확인할 수 있습니다.

3 PLUS
Grammar Point에서 제시한 핵심 문법 외의 추가 정보를 담았습니다.

PRACTICE

1
Grammar Point에서 학습한 내용을 다양한 유형의 문제를 통해 자연스럽게 익힐 수 있습니다.

2
학교 내신 시험에 자주 등장하는 서술형 쓰기 연습문제를 매 Unit마다 경험할 수 있도록 하였습니다.

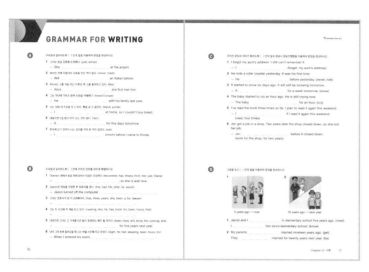

GRAMMAR FOR WRITING

다양한 형태의 쓰기 문제를 풀어봄으로써 Grammar Point를 반복 학습하며 sentence writing의 기초를 마련할 수 있습니다.

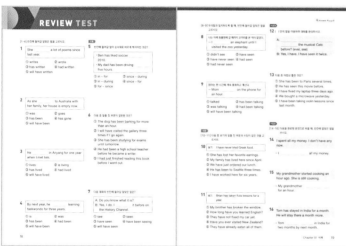

REVIEW TEST

실제 학교 시험과 가장 유사한 유형의 문제들로 구성하여 실전에 대비할 수 있습니다.

고난도 어법 문제와 서술형 문제를 대폭 수록하여 학교 내신 시험의 서술형 주관식 문항에 완벽 대비할 수 있도록 하였습니다.

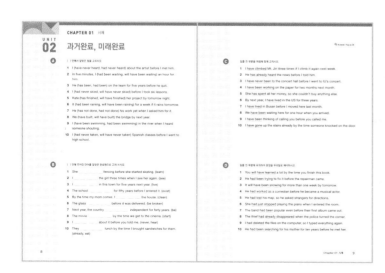

WORKBOOK

각 Unit별 연습문제와 쓰기 문제, Chapter별 Review Test를 수록하였습니다.

더 많은 문제를 풀어봄으로써 문법을 보다 완벽하게 익힐 수 있도록 하였습니다.

CONTENTS

GRAMMAR BASICS

01 문장의 성분

- <u>She</u> <u>studies</u> <u>business</u> <u>in New York</u>.
  주어   동사   목적어   수식어

- <u>He</u> <u>is</u> <u>a popular artist</u> <u>in Tokyo</u>.
  주어 동사   보어   수식어

주어 움직임이나 상태의 주체가 되는 말로, 보통 문장의 맨 앞에 와서 '~은[는, 이, 가]'으로 해석된다. 주어로는 보통 명사나 대명사가 쓰이지만 동명사구나 to부정사구처럼 긴 주어가 쓰이기도 한다.

I want to join a school band.
Reading comic books is one of my hobbies.

동사 주어의 상태나 동작을 나타내는 말로, '~이다[하다]'로 해석된다. 대부분 한 단어로 쓰이지만, 두 단어 이상이 모여 하나의 동사 역할을 하기도 하고, 조동사의 도움을 받아 여러 가지 보충의 의미를 갖기도 한다.

Gabriel **watched** the baseball game.
They **put off** the meeting.
You **may go** home now.

목적어 동사 다음에 오는 말로, 우리말의 '~을[를]'에 해당한다. 보통 목적어로는 명사나 대명사가 쓰이지만, 동명사구나 to부정사구처럼 긴 목적어가 오기도 한다.

I want **some coffee**.
He is trying **to solve the problems**.

보어 주어나 목적어에 대한 정보를 보충 설명해 주는 말이다. 주격 보어는 동사 뒤에서 주어를 보충 설명하고 목적격 보어는 목적어 뒤에서 목적어를 보충 설명한다.

He became **a famous actor**. (he = a famous actor) 〈주격 보어〉
Please leave me **alone**. (me = alone) 〈목적격 보어〉

수식어 문장의 다른 요소들을 꾸며줘서 문장 내용을 풍부하게 만드는 말이다. 형용사처럼 쓰여 명사를 수식할 수도 있고, 부사처럼 쓰여 동사나 형용사, 다른 부사를 수식하기도 한다.

The **handsome** man is my uncle.
I woke up early **in the morning**.

02 문장의 형식

- 1형식: <u>The man</u> <u>ran</u>.
  주어   동사

- 2형식: <u>Andre</u> <u>is</u> <u>a fashion designer</u>.
  주어   동사   보어

- 3형식: <u>Jenny</u> <u>likes</u> <u>snowboarding</u>.
  주어   동사   목적어

- 4형식: <u>Paul</u> <u>sent</u> <u>me</u> <u>a text message</u>.
  주어   동사   간접목적어   직접목적어

- 5형식: <u>My boyfriend</u> <u>calls</u> <u>me</u> <u>an angel</u>.
  주어   동사   목적어   목적격 보어

주어 + 동사 (1형식)

보어나 목적어 없이 주어와 동사만으로 의미가 전달되는 문장이다. 종종 수식어 때문에 문장이 길어지기도 한다.

※ 주요 1형식 동사

be(~에 있다), go, come, walk, work, live, run, shine ...

<u>The sun</u> <u>shines</u>.
주어   동사

<u>We</u> <u>walked</u> <u>all day long yesterday</u>.
주어   동사   (수식어구)

<u>There</u> <u>are</u> <u>a lot of cars</u> <u>on the road</u>.
(수식어구) 동사   주어   (수식어구)

주어 + 동사 + 보어 (2형식)

동사만으로 주어에 대한 충분한 정보를 주지 못할 때 동사 뒤에 주어를 보충 설명해 주는 주격 보어를 쓴다.
보어는 주어의 성질, 상태 등을 설명하며 주로 (대)명사나 형용사를 쓴다. 이때 주어와 보어는 의미상 주술 관계에
있어 '주어 = 주격 보어' 관계가 성립한다.

※ 주요 2형식 동사

상태를 나타내는 동사: be(~이다), keep(~인 채로 있다), remain(여전히 ~이다) ...
감각동사: look, feel, sound, smell, taste ...

<u>My aunt</u> <u>is</u> <u>a director</u>.   <u>The actress</u> <u>looks</u> <u>very beautiful</u>.
주어   동사   보어   주어   동사   보어

주어 + 동사 + 목적어 (3형식)

동사의 동작이 영향을 미치는 대상인 목적어가 필요한 문장으로 목적어 자리에는 주로 명사나 대명사가 오고, 동명사구나 to부정사구, that절과 같은 긴 목적어도 자주 쓰인다. (목적어가 없다면 문장의 의미가 불완전해진다.)

Peter bought a new cell phone.
주어　　동사　　　　목적어

Lily thinks that he likes me.
주어　동사　　　목적어

주어 + 동사 + 간접목적어 + 직접목적어 (4형식)

동사 뒤에 목적어가 두 개 오는 경우가 해당된다. 먼저 '~에게(간접목적어)'가 나오고, 뒤에 '~을[를](직접목적어)'을 쓴다.

※ 주요 4형식 동사

수여동사: give, send, show, teach, tell, bring, buy, make, get, ask ...

My friend gave me this beautiful hairpin.
주어　　　동사　간접목적어　　직접목적어

※ 4형식 문장은 3형식 문장으로 바꿀 수 있다. 이때 간접목적어와 직접목적어 순서를 바꾸고 간접목적어 앞에 전치사를 쓴다.

My friend gave this beautiful hairpin *to* me.
주어　　　동사　　　　목적어　　　　　수식어구

주어 + 동사 + 목적어 + 목적격 보어 (5형식)

목적어 다음에 그 목적어를 보충 설명해 주는 말이 오는 경우가 있는데, 이때 목적어를 보충 설명해 주는 말을 목적격 보어라고 한다. 동사의 종류에 따라 목적격 보어는 명사, 형용사, to부정사, 동사원형 등 다양한 형태가 올 수 있다. 이때 목적어와 목적격 보어는 의미상 주술 관계에 있어 '목적어 = 목적격 보어' 관계가 성립한다.

1 목적격 보어가 명사인 경우

We named the black cat Lucky.
주어　　동사　　　목적어　　　목적격 보어

2 목적격 보어가 형용사인 경우

My brother found the cookie box empty.
주어　　　　동사　　　목적어　　　목적격 보어

3 목적격 보어가 to부정사인 경우

My sister asked me to help her.
주어　　　동사　목적어　목적격 보어

4 목적격 보어가 동사원형인 경우

They saw the boys play soccer.
주어　동사　　목적어　　　목적격 보어

My mom didn't let me go to the concert.
주어　　　동사　　목적어　　　목적격 보어

03 구와 절

- I want <u>a new laptop</u>.
  명사구

- It got cold <u>after the heavy rain stopped</u>.
  부사절

구   **1**   둘 이상의 단어가 모여 문장 내에서 명사, 형용사, 부사의 역할을 한다.

Tom and Jerry, expensive paint, very fast, on the bus, with the actor

2   문장에서의 역할에 따라 명사구, 형용사구, 부사구로 나뉜다.

❶ 명사구: 명사처럼 문장에서 주어, 목적어, 보어로 쓰인다.

The beautiful English poem was written by Byron. 〈주어〉
I bought him **a newly released album**. 〈목적어〉
My daughter is **a gift from God**. 〈보어〉

❷ 형용사구: 형용사처럼 문장에서 명사를 꾸며주는 수식어 또는 보어로 쓰인다.

The bridge **built in the 1800s** is still there.
Our new clerk is **too lazy**.

❸ 부사구: 부사처럼 문장에서 동사나 형용사, 다른 부사, 문장 전체를 꾸며주는 수식어로 쓰인다.

Have you ever stayed **in a small cottage**?
He doesn't like you **very much**.

절   **1**   「주어 + 동사」를 포함한 여러 단어가 모여 문장 내에서 명사, 형용사, 부사의 역할을 한다.

that you are honest, who I like most, if winter comes

2   문장에서의 역할에 따라 명사절, 형용사절, 부사절로 나뉜다.

❶ 명사절: 명사처럼 문장에서 주어, 목적어, 보어로 쓰인다. 절이 주어로 쓰인 경우 가주어 it을 사용하는 경우가 많다.

It is very surprising **that Luke is her son**. 〈주어〉
Did you notice **that he had his hair cut**? 〈목적어〉
The important thing is **that we should finish it by tomorrow**. 〈보어〉

❷ 형용사절: 형용사처럼 문장에서 명사를 꾸며주는 수식어로 쓰인다.

I remember the day **when I first saw him**.

❸ 부사절: 부사처럼 문장에서 동사나 형용사, 다른 부사를 꾸며주는 수식어로 쓰인다.

We should clean the room **before my mother comes back**.

ESSENTIAL RULES OF
ENGLISH GRAMMAR

CHAPTER
01

시제

시제란 동사의 형태 변화를 통해
시간 관계를 표현하는 것을 말한다.

현재완료

A 현재완료 (have[has] + v-ed)

과거의 한 시점에서 일어난 일이 현재에 영향을 미칠 때 쓴다.

The amusement park **has** already **closed**.

ⓘ 현재완료는 과거의 구체적 시점을 나타내는 말(yesterday, ~ ago, last ~ 등)과 함께 쓰지 않는다.
The amusement park **closed** *yesterday*.
~~The amusement park has closed *yesterday*.~~

1 완료: 최근 또는 막 완료된 일(막 ~했다)을 나타낸다. already, yet, just 등과 함께 자주 쓰인다.

I **haven't uploaded** our pictures onto my blog yet.

2 결과: 현재까지 영향을 미치는 과거의 일(~해 버렸다)을 나타낸다.

He **has forgotten** the password. He can't log in to the website.

3 경험: 과거부터 현재까지의 경험(~한 적이 있다)을 나타낸다. ever, never, before, once 등과 함께 자주 쓰인다.

I **have been** to South Africa once.

4 계속: 과거부터 현재까지 지속된 일(계속 ~해 왔다)을 나타낸다. 「since + 기준 시점」(~ 이래로), 「for + 기간」(~ 동안) 등과 함께 자주 쓰인다.

My father **has driven** the same car for ten years.

B 현재완료 진행형 (have[has] been + v-ing)

과거에서 현재까지 계속 진행되고 있는 동작, 상태(~해 오고 있다)를 나타낸다.

It **has been snowing** since yesterday.

(← It started snowing yesterday. It is still snowing.)

 **CHECK UP**   빈칸에 알맞은 말을 고르시오.

1 Taylor _____ from another school last week.
   ⓐ transfers   ⓑ transferred   ⓒ has transferred

2 James _____ the office. He is not here.
   ⓐ leaves   ⓑ has left   ⓒ has been leaving

3 I _____ to a girl since I arrived here.
   ⓐ am talking   ⓑ talked   ⓒ have been talking

➕ PLUS : have been to vs.
              have gone to

• have been to: ~에 가 본 적이 있다
  I **have been to** Jeju Island. 〈경험〉

• have gone to: ~에 가고 (지금 여기) 없다
  She **has gone to** Jeju Island. 〈결과〉

PRACTICE

🔍 Answer Key p.2

 STEP 1

( ) 안에서 알맞은 말을 고르시오.

1 I (had, have had) three pieces of cake last night.

2 I (lose, have lost) my wallet, so I don't have any money now.

3 We have been best friends (for, since) more than ten years.

4 Inah (heard, has heard) the rumor a few days ago.

5 Logan (is living, has been living) in Canada for fifteen years.

STEP 2

밑줄 친 부분을 어법에 맞게 고치시오.

1 I <u>have eaten</u> at the new restaurant last Saturday.

2 Jay isn't here now because he <u>has been</u> to the store.

3 They <u>are playing</u> the online game since this morning.

STEP 3

다음을 완료형 문장으로 바꿀 때, 빈칸에 알맞은 말을 쓰시오.

1 I had a toothache yesterday. I still have a toothache.

　→ I ＿＿＿＿ ＿＿＿＿ ＿＿＿＿ ＿＿＿＿ since yesterday.

2 I left my umbrella on the bus this morning, so I don't have it now.

　→ I ＿＿＿＿ ＿＿＿＿ my umbrella on the bus.

3 He went to the swimming pool two hours ago. He is at home now.

　→ He ＿＿＿＿ ＿＿＿＿ ＿＿＿＿ the swimming pool.

STEP 4

우리말과 일치하도록 ( ) 안의 말을 이용하여 문장을 완성하시오.

1 Dean은 어렸을 때부터 그녀를 알고 있었다. (know)

　→ Dean ＿＿＿＿ ＿＿＿＿ ＿＿＿＿ ＿＿＿＿ he was young.

2 너는 인도에 가 본 적이 있니? (ever, be)

　→ ＿＿＿＿ ＿＿＿＿ ＿＿＿＿ ＿＿＿＿ ＿＿＿＿ India?

3 그는 지난주에 그 댄스 동아리에 가입했다. (join, dance club)

　→ He ＿＿＿＿ ＿＿＿＿ ＿＿＿＿ ＿＿＿＿ last week.

4 그녀는 벌써 그 소설을 읽었다. (already, read)

　→ She ＿＿＿＿ ＿＿＿＿ ＿＿＿＿ the novel.

5 나는 같은 음악을 한 시간째 듣고 있다. (listen to)

　→ I ＿＿＿＿ ＿＿＿＿ ＿＿＿＿ ＿＿＿＿ the same song for an hour.

UNIT 02 과거완료, 미래완료

Ⓐ 과거완료

1 **과거완료(had + v-ed)**

과거의 어느 시점 이전에 완료되었거나, 그 시점까지 지속되었던 일을 나타낼 때 쓴다.

The movie **had** just **started** when I arrived. 〈완료〉

I **had lost** my glasses, so I couldn't read anything. 〈결과〉

She **had** never **traveled** alone before she went to Europe. 〈경험〉

This house **had been** empty for a year before I moved in. 〈계속〉

2 **과거완료 진행형(had been + v-ing)**

과거 이전에 시작하여 과거의 한 시점까지 진행되었던 동작, 상태를 나타낸다.

I **had been waiting** for a month before the test results came.

Ⓑ 미래완료

1 **미래완료(will have + v-ed)**

미래의 특정 시점까지 완료될 동작이나 지속될 상태를 나타낼 때 쓴다.

The soccer game **will have finished** before 8:00 p.m.

By next year I **will have gotten** a job.

2 **미래완료 진행형(will have been + v-ing)**

미래의 특정 시점까지 진행되고 있을 동작, 상태를 나타낸다.

My teacher **will have been teaching** English for ten years next year.

CHECK UP  빈칸에 알맞은 말을 고르시오.

1 Keira _____ her leg, so she couldn't join the game.
ⓐ has injured ⓑ had injured ⓒ will have injured

2 They _____ arguing for an hour before I arrived.
ⓐ has been ⓑ had been ⓒ will have been

3 I'm doing my homework. I _____ it before dinner.
ⓐ have finished ⓑ had finished ⓒ will have finished

4 In ten minutes, I _____ waiting three hours for my turn.
ⓐ has been ⓑ had been ⓒ will have been

➕ PLUS : 대과거(had + v-ed)

과거보다 더 이전에 있었던 일을 나타낼 때 쓴다.

· He told me that he **had lost** his watch the day before.

· I felt better after I **had taken** a nap.

PRACTICE

🔍 Answer Key p.2

( ) 안에서 알맞은 말을 고르시오.

1 Avery (had been, will have been) ill for three days when I visited her.

2 I (had finished, will have finished) the work by the time the boss arrives.

3 We (had been living, will have been living) in China for a year next month.

4 When she came home, her son (has been watching, had been watching) TV.

( ) 안에 주어진 단어를 알맞은 완료형으로 고쳐 쓰시오.

1 I _____ my dinner when the TV news started. (finish)

2 I _____ the movie five times when I see it again. (watch)

3 If he doesn't come tomorrow, he _____ absent from school for five days. (be)

4 We _____ for Mr. Kim for an hour when the phone rang. (wait)

다음을 완료진행형 문장으로 바꿀 때, 빈칸에 알맞은 말을 쓰시오.

1 Ava's mom came home an hour after Ava started chatting online.

→ Ava _____ online for an hour when her mom came home.

2 He started learning French a year ago. Next year will be his third year.

→ He _____ French for three years next year.

우리말과 일치하도록 ( ) 안의 말을 이용하여 문장을 완성하시오.

1 나는 서울로 이사오기 전에는 전주에서 살고 있었다. (live)

→ I _____ _____ _____ in Jeonju before I moved to Seoul.

2 내가 집에 도착했을 때 Eric은 이미 떠났다. (already, leave)

→ Eric _____ _____ _____ when I got home.

3 내가 다시 하와이에 간다면 그곳에 두 번째 가는 것이다. (be)

→ I _____ _____ _____ to Hawaii twice if I go there again.

4 그녀는 은퇴하기 전에 많은 돈을 저축했다. (save)

→ She _____ _____ a lot of money before she retired.

5 Eddie는 다음 달이면 30년 동안 파일럿으로 일하고 있는 셈이 될 것이다. (work)

→ Eddie _____ _____ _____ _____ as a pilot for thirty years next month.

GRAMMAR FOR WRITING

A 우리말과 일치하도록 ( ) 안의 말을 이용하여 문장을 완성하시오.

1 그녀는 방금 공항에 도착했다. (just, arrive)

→ She _____ at the airport.

2 Will은 전에 이탈리아 사람을 만난 적이 없다. (never, meet)

→ Will _____ an Italian before.

3 Alice는 그를 처음 만난 이후로 쭉 그를 좋아하고 있다. (like)

→ Alice _____ she first met him.

4 그는 작년에 가족과 함께 유럽을 여행했다. (travel Europe)

→ He _____ with his family last year.

5 나는 집에 내 지갑을 두고 와서, 빵을 살 수 없었다. (leave, purse)

→ I _____ at home, so I couldn't buy bread.

6 내일이면 5일 동안 비가 오는 것이 된다. (rain)

→ It _____ for five days tomorrow.

7 한국에 오기 전까지 나는 김치를 먹어 본 적이 없었다. (eat)

→ I _____ kimchi before I came to Korea.

B 우리말과 일치하도록 ( ) 안에 주어진 단어를 바르게 배열하시오.

1 Diana는 병에서 방금 회복되어서 지금은 건강하다. (recovered, has, illness, from, her, just, Diana)

→ _____, so she is well now.

2 Jason은 파일을 저장한 후 컴퓨터를 껐다. (the, had, file, after, he, saved)

→ Jason turned off the computer _____.

3 그녀는 변호사가 된 지 3년째이다. (has, three, years, she, been, a, for, lawyer)

→ _____.

4 그는 두 시간째 저 책을 읽고 있다. (reading, two, he, has, book, for, been, hours, that)

→ _____.

5 내년이면 그녀는 그 가게를 5년 동안 운영하는 셈이 될 것이다. (been, have, will, store, the, running, she)

→ _____ for five years next year.

6 내가 그의 방에 들어갔을 때 그는 여덟 시간째 자고 있었다. (eight, he, had, sleeping, been, hours, for)

→ When I entered his room, _____.

C 주어진 문장과 의미가 통하도록 ( ) 안의 말과 완료나 완료진행형을 이용하여 문장을 완성하시오.

1 I forgot my aunt's address. I still can't remember it.

→ I _____. (forget, my aunt's address)

2 He rode a roller coaster yesterday. It was his first time.

→ He _____ before yesterday. (never, ride)

3 It started to snow six days ago. It will still be snowing tomorrow.

→ It _____ for a week tomorrow. (snow)

4 The baby started to cry an hour ago. He is still crying now.

→ The baby _____ for an hour. (cry)

5 I've read the book three times so far. I plan to read it again this weekend.

→ I _____ if I read it again this weekend.
(read, four times)

6 Jen got a job in a shop. Two years later the shop closed down, so she lost her job.

→ Jen _____ before it closed down.
(work for the shop, for two years)

D 그림을 보고 ( ) 안의 말을 이용하여 문장을 완성하시오.

1

5 years ago → now

2

19 years ago → next year

1 Jacob and I _____ in elementary school five years ago. (meet)

I _____ him since elementary school. (know)

2 My parents _____ married nineteen years ago. (get)

They _____ married for twenty years next year. (be)

REVIEW TEST

[1-4] 빈칸에 들어갈 알맞은 말을 고르시오.

1

> She _____ a lot of poems since last year.

① writes   ② wrote
③ has written   ④ had written
⑤ will have written

2

> As she _____ to Australia with her family, her house is empty now.

① was   ② goes
③ has been   ④ has gone
⑤ will have been

3

> He _____ in Anyang for one year when I met him.

① lives   ② is living
③ has lived   ④ had lived
⑤ will have lived

4

> By next year, he _____ learning taekwondo for three years.

① is   ② was
③ has been   ④ had been
⑤ will have been

빈출

5 빈칸에 들어갈 말이 순서대로 바르게 짝지어진 것은?

> · Ben has liked soccer _____ 2010.
> · My dad has been driving _____ five hours.

① in – for   ② since – during
③ in – during   ④ since – for
⑤ for – since

6 다음 중 밑줄 친 부분이 잘못된 것은?

① The dog has been barking for more than an hour.
② I will have visited the gallery three times if I go again.
③ She has been studying for exams until tomorrow.
④ He had been a high school teacher before he became a writer.
⑤ I had just finished reading this book before I went out.

7 다음 대화의 빈칸에 들어갈 알맞은 말은?

> A: Do you know what it is?
> B: Yes, I do. I _____ it before on the History Channel.

① see   ② seen
③ have seen   ④ have been seeing
⑤ will have seen

[8-9] 우리말과 일치하도록 할 때, 빈칸에 들어갈 알맞은 말을 고르시오.

8

> 나는 어제 동물원에 갈 때까지 코끼리를 본 적이 없었다.
> → I _____ an elephant until I visited the zoo yesterday.

① didn't see　　② have seen
③ have never seen　④ had seen
⑤ had never seen

9

> 엄마는 한 시간째 계속 통화하고 계신다.
> → Mom _____ on the phone for an hour.

① talked　　② has been talking
③ was talking　④ had been talking
⑤ will have been talking

[10-11] 다음 중 보기의 밑줄 친 부분과 쓰임이 같은 것을 고르시오.

10

> 보기　I have never tried Greek food.

① She has lost her favorite earrings.
② My family has lived here since April.
③ We have just ordered our lunch.
④ He has been to Seattle three times.
⑤ I have worked here for six years.

11

> 보기　Brian has taken flute lessons for a year.

① My brother has broken the window.
② How long have you learned English?
③ They have not fixed my car yet.
④ Have you ever visited New Zealand?
⑤ They have already eaten all of them.

12 ( ) 안의 말을 이용하여 대화를 완성하시오.

> A: _____ _____ _____
> _____ the musical *Cats* before? (ever, see)
> B: Yes, I have. I have seen it twice.

13 다음 중 어법상 틀린 것은?

① She has been to Paris several times.
② He has seen this movie before.
③ I have fixed my laptop three days ago.
④ We bought a microwave yesterday.
⑤ I have been taking violin lessons since last month.

[14-16] 다음을 완료형 문장으로 바꿀 때, 빈칸에 알맞은 말을 쓰시오.

14

> I spent all my money. I don't have any now.
> → I _____ all my money.

15

> My grandmother started cooking an hour ago. She is still cooking.
> → My grandmother _____ for an hour.

16

> Tom has stayed in India for a month. He will stay there a month more.
> → Tom _____ in India for two months by next month.

[17-18] 어법상 <u>틀린</u> 부분을 찾아 바르게 고치시오.

17 He has gone to bed before I came. So I couldn't see him.

18 If I see him once more, I have seen him three times.

[19-21] 우리말과 일치하도록 ( ) 안에 주어진 단어를 바르게 배열하시오.

19 너는 전에 스파게티를 만들어 본 적이 있니?
(you, cooked, spaghetti, before, have, ever)

→ _____ ?

20 나는 열 살 때부터 안경을 쓰고 있다.
(glasses, I, wearing, been, have, since)

→ _____
I was ten.

21 내가 그녀의 방에 들어갔을 때 그녀는 자신의 지갑을 찾고 있던 중이었다.
(been, had, purse, for, her, she, looking)

→ _____
when I entered her room.

22 다음 중 어법상 옳은 것은? (2개)

① I was sick since last Friday.
② Ron has been waiting for her call for an hour.
③ I have seen Zoe at the park yesterday.
④ When I got there, she had already left.
⑤ He has been sleeping when I visited him.

[23-24] 우리말과 일치하도록 ( ) 안의 말을 이용하여 문장을 완성하시오.

23 Julie는 출장으로 브라질에 간 적이 세 번 있다.
(be, Brazil)

→ Julie _____
three times on business.

24 만약 그 컴퓨터가 한 번 더 고장 난다면, 네 번째 고장나는 것이다. (break down, four times)

→ If the computer breaks down once more, it _____ .

25 우리말과 일치하도록 주어진 조건에 맞게 문장을 완성하시오.

우리가 도착했을 때 그 콘서트는 이미 시작했다.

〈조건〉 1. already, start, arrive를 이용할 것
2. 접속사 when을 쓸 것

→ The concert _____
_____ .

26 다음 중 어법상 옳은 것을 모두 고르면?

① It has been raining yesterday.

② I have eaten dinner when you called.

③ I will have lived in Seoul for three years next month.

④ I didn't know you had done your homework.

⑤ We have never met each other since we graduated.

27 다음 중 어법상 옳은 것으로 바르게 짝지어진 것은?

> a. Dad has lost his key when I got home.
> b. He has won twelve trophies since 2011.
> c. After she had hurt her leg, she left the stadium.
> d. By next year she has been teaching math for thirty years.
> e. I had been studying English before I moved to Canada.

① a, b, c ② a, c, d

③ a, d, e ④ b, c, e

⑤ b, d, e

28 다음 중 어법상 옳은 것의 개수는?

> · Have you ever had a scary dream?
> · We will have finished the project by next week.
> · I had seen Ronald last week.
> · The machine had been working for several years before it was broken.
> · My English teacher has lived in New Zealand before she came to Korea.

① 1개 ② 2개 ③ 3개

④ 4개 ⑤ 5개

[29-31] 밑줄 친 부분이 어법상 옳은지 판단하고, 틀리면 바르게 고치시오.

29 By the time you arrive tonight, the guests <u>have left</u>.

(O / X) _____

30 He <u>had drawn</u> more than one hundred portraits before he died in 1990.

(O / X) _____

31 The show <u>has just finished</u> when we turned on the TV.

(O / X) _____

[32-33] 어법상 틀린 부분을 찾아 바르게 고치시오.

32 I have been learning how to swim for last year. I think I have mastered it by next year. (2개)

33 It was not my first game of tennis. I have played many times before I played you. Next year, I will play tennis for three years. (2개)

LET'S REVIEW

주요 예문을 다시 한번 확인하고, 우리말과 일치하도록 빈칸을 채우시오.

- I **haven't uploaded** our pictures onto my blog yet.
  나는 우리 사진들을 아직 내 블로그에 올리지 않았다. **Unit 01 - A**

- He **has forgotten** the password. He can't log in to the website.
  그는 비밀번호를 잊어버렸다. 그는 그 웹 사이트에 로그인할 수 없다. **Unit 01 - A**

- I ¹_____ to South Africa once. 나는 남아프리카 공화국에 한 번 가 본 적이 있다. **Unit 01 - A**

- My father ²_____ the same car for ten years.
  우리 아빠는 같은 차를 10년 동안 운전해 오셨다. **Unit 01 - A**

- It ³_____ since yesterday. 어제부터 눈이 내리고 있다. **Unit 01 - B**

- The movie **had** just **started** when I arrived. 내가 도착했을 때 영화가 막 시작했다. **Unit 02 - A**

- I ⁴_____ my glasses, so I couldn't read anything.
  나는 내 안경을 잃어버려서, 아무것도 읽을 수가 없었다. **Unit 02 - A**

- She ⁵_____ never _____ alone before she went to Europe.
  그녀는 유럽에 가기 전에 혼자 여행해 본 적이 전혀 없었다. **Unit 02 - A**

- This house **had been** empty for a year before I moved in.
  내가 이사오기 전에 이 집은 일 년 동안 비어 있었다. **Unit 02 - A**

- I ⁶_____ for a month before the test results came.
  시험 결과가 나오기 전에 나는 한 달 동안 기다리고 있었다. **Unit 02 - A**

- By next year I ⁷_____ **gotten** a job. 내년쯤이면 나는 취직해 있을 것이다. **Unit 02 - B**

- My teacher ⁸_____ **teaching** English for ten years next year.
  우리 선생님은 내년이면 십 년 동안 영어를 가르쳐 오신 셈이 될 것이다. **Unit 02 - B**

🔍 **Answers**

¹ have been   ² has driven   ³ has been snowing   ⁴ had lost   ⁵ had, traveled
⁶ had been waiting   ⁷ will have   ⁸ will have been

ESSENTIAL RULES OF
ENGLISH GRAMMAR

CHAPTER
02

조동사

조동사란 본동사의 기본 의미에 능력, 허가,
추측, 의무, 충고, 요청 등의 의미를 더해주는
동사이다.

can, may, must, should

A   **can + 동사원형**

Noah **can[is able to]** speak five languages. (능력: ~할 수 있다 / = be able to)

ⓘ 두 개의 조동사는 연이어 쓸 수 없으므로, 조동사 다음에는 반드시 be able to를 쓴다.

     I **will be able to** go to Europe next year. (~~I will can~~)

Can I borrow your notebook for a day? (허가: ~해도 된다)

That **can't** be Ruby. She is in LA now. (강한 부정적 추측: ~일 리가 없다)

He **could[was able to]** swim when he was ten. (과거의 능력: ~할 수 있었다)

Could you wait a moment, please? (정중한 요청: ~해 주시겠어요?)

B   **may + 동사원형**

You've finished your homework. You **may** go out to play. (허가: ~해도 된다)

The rumor **may[might]** be true. (불확실한 추측 · 가능성: ~일지도 모른다)

C   **must + 동사원형**

They **must[have to]** work from 9:00 a.m. to 6:00 p.m. every day.
(의무: ~해야 한다 / = have to)

ⓘ must(의무)의 부정: must not vs. don't have to

     You **must not** tell a lie in court. (금지: ~해서는 안 된다)

     You **don't have to** bring your camera. (~할 필요가 없다 / = don't need to, need not)

She **must** be tired after her long trip. (강한 추측: ~임에 틀림없다)

D   **should + 동사원형**

You **should** obey the school rules. (의무 · 충고: ~해야 한다, ~하는 것이 좋다)

CHECK UP   빈칸에 알맞은 말을 고르시오.

1 Dean runs 100 m in eleven seconds. _____ you beat him?

   ⓐ Can   ⓑ May   ⓒ Should

2 Emily lives in a very big house. She _____ be rich.

   ⓐ must   ⓑ cannot   ⓒ is able to

3 Your hair is too long. You _____ get a haircut.

   ⓐ might   ⓑ must not   ⓒ should

PRACTICE

🔍 Answer Key p.3

STEP 1

( ) 안에서 알맞은 말을 고르시오.

1 The floor is wet. You (may, should) be careful.

2 He stayed up late last night. He (must, cannot) be tired.

3 Tricia is absent today. She (might, has to) be sick.

4 (Should, Could) you ask Ted to come to my house, please?

STEP 2

두 문장의 의미가 같도록 빈칸에 알맞은 말을 쓰시오.

1 I have a headache. Can I leave early today?

→ I have a headache. _____ I leave early today?

2 Penguins are birds, but they are not able to fly.

→ Penguins are birds, but they _____ _____.

3 She must do her homework by herself.

→ She _____ _____ do her homework by herself.

STEP 3

우리말과 일치하도록 어법상 틀린 부분을 찾아 바르게 고치시오.

1 우리는 아침에 일찍 떠날 필요가 없다.

→ We must not leave early in the morning.

2 그가 지금 집에 있을 리가 없다.

→ He should not be at home now.

3 너는 내일 병원에 가야 한다.

→ You can go to the hospital tomorrow.

STEP 4

우리말과 일치하도록 ( ) 안의 말을 이용하여 문장을 완성하시오.

1 내 아들은 자전거를 탈 수 있다. (ride)

→ My son _____ _____ _____ _____ a bike.

2 너는 비행기가 이륙하기 전에 안전벨트를 매야만 한다. (have, fasten)

→ _____ _____ _____ _____ your seat belt before the plane takes off.

3 Dan이 회의에 올지도 모른다. (come)

→ Dan _____ _____ to the meeting.

4 너는 우리 계획에 대해 아무에게도 말하면 안 된다. (tell, anyone)

→ You _____ _____ _____ about our plan.

had better, ought to, used to, 조동사 + have v-ed

A **had better + 동사원형:** ~하는 게 좋겠다 (축약형: 'd better)

You **had better** eat more vegetables.

ⓘ had better의 부정형: had better not
  You **had better not** be late for class.

B **ought to + 동사원형:** ~해야 한다

You **ought to** turn off your cell phone during class.

ⓘ ought to의 부정형: ought not to
  You **ought not to** waste your time.

C **used to + 동사원형:** ~하곤 했다(과거의 습관 / = would), ~이었다(과거의 상태)

When he was a child, he **used to** go swimming every summer. 〈과거의 습관〉
= When he was a child, he **would** go swimming every summer.

The TV **used to** be in my room. 〈과거의 상태〉

ⓘ 과거의 상태를 나타낼 때는 would를 쓸 수 없다.

D **조동사 + have v-ed:** 과거의 일에 대한 추측, 후회, 유감 등을 나타낸다.

Daniel **can't have finished** his report already. (과거의 일에 대한 강한 의심: ~이었을 리가 없다)

She **may[might] have read** the book already. (과거의 일에 대한 약한 추측: ~이었을지도 모른다)

He **must have been** to Paris. (과거의 일에 대한 강한 추측: ~이었음에 틀림없다)

I **should have studied** harder. (과거의 일에 대한 후회나 유감: ~했어야 했다)

CHECK UP 빈칸에 알맞은 말을 고르시오.

1 You'd better _____ to your parents.
  ⓐ listen   ⓑ listening   ⓒ to listen

2 I _____ work at a magazine company, but I don't anymore.
  ⓐ had better   ⓑ ought to   ⓒ used to

3 You missed a great speech. You _____ it.
  ⓐ should have heard   ⓑ may have heard   ⓒ must have heard

PRACTICE

🔍 Answer Key p.3

STEP 1

( ) 안에서 알맞은 말을 고르시오.

1 I ought to (memorize, memorizing) the poem by tomorrow.

2 You (had not better, had better not) wear those muddy shoes in the house.

3 She is not here. She (may have gone, should have gone) out for lunch.

4 We used (to go, to going) to school together when we were young.

STEP 2

빈칸에 알맞은 말을 보기에서 골라 쓰시오. (단, 한 번씩만 쓸 것)

보기	ought to	had better	used to

1 I _____ keep a diary. But I don't keep one anymore.

2 He has just fallen asleep. You _____ not wake him up.

3 You _____ listen to what Mom says.

STEP 3

우리말과 일치하도록 어법상 틀린 부분을 찾아 바르게 고치시오.

1 그녀가 그 공포 영화를 봤을 리가 없다.

→ She can have seen the horror movie.

2 강 근처에 공장이 있었지만 지금은 그곳에 없다.

→ There would be a factory near the river, but it's not there anymore.

3 너는 온라인 게임을 너무 많이 해서는 안 된다.

→ You ought to not play online games too much.

4 나는 내 지갑을 식당에 두고 왔을지도 모른다.

→ I should have left my wallet in the restaurant.

STEP 4

우리말과 일치하도록 ( ) 안의 말을 이용하여 문장을 완성하시오.

1 너는 이번 기회를 놓쳐서는 안 된다. (miss)

→ You _____ _____ _____ _____ this chance.

2 나는 긴 곱슬머리를 가졌었다. (have)

→ I _____ _____ _____ long curly hair.

3 나는 오늘 우산을 가져왔어야 했다. (bring)

→ I _____ _____ _____ my umbrella today.

4 너는 그의 충고를 따르는 게 좋겠다. (better, take one's advice)

→ You _____ _____ _____ _____ .

GRAMMAR FOR WRITING

A 우리말과 일치하도록 ( ) 안의 말을 이용하여 문장을 완성하시오.

1 이 스마트폰은 Lucy의 것임에 틀림없다. (smartphone, be)

→ _____ Lucy's.

2 그는 벌써 집에 갔을지도 모른다. (go, home)

→ He _____ already.

3 그가 그렇게 비싼 자전거를 샀을 리가 없다. (buy)

→ He _____ such an expensive bike.

4 너는 우리와 함께 콘서트에 갔어야 했다. 그것은 정말 굉장했다. (go)

→ You _____ to the concert with us. It was really great.

5 너는 너무 많은 커피를 마시지 않는 것이 좋겠다. (better, drink)

→ You _____ too much coffee.

6 너는 오늘 숙제를 끝낼 필요는 없다. (have, finish)

→ You _____ your homework today.

7 내 충고를 따르면 너는 돈을 절약할 수 있을 것이다. (will, able, save)

→ You _____ money if you take my advice.

B 우리말과 일치하도록 ( ) 안에 주어진 단어를 바르게 배열하시오.

1 그녀는 어제 아팠음에 틀림없다. (been, must, have, yesterday, ill, she)

→ _____.

2 너는 운전할 때 안전벨트를 착용해야 한다. (seat belt, you, wear, your, should)

→ _____ when you drive.

3 그 가게는 일요일에 열지도 모른다. (might, store, open, the, be)

→ _____ on Sundays.

4 제게 괜찮은 식당을 추천해 주시겠어요? (restaurant, you, recommend, could, good, a)

→ _____ to me?

5 나는 주말에 야구 경기를 보곤 했다. (used, watch, baseball, to, I, games)

→ _____ on the weekends.

6 복도에서 큰 소리를 내서는 안 된다. (ought, not, make, loud, to, noises, you)

→ _____ in the hallway.

C 보기에서 알맞은 조동사를 골라 ( ) 안의 말과 함께 써서 문장을 완성하시오. (단, 한 번씩만 쓸 것)

[1-4]

보기	can't	be able to	had better	may

1 You look tired. You _____ for a while. (rest)

2 You studied hard. You will _____ well on the test. (do)

3 It _____ Jeremy's address. He doesn't live there. (be)

4 I want to play outside, Mom. _____ out now? (go)

[5-8]

보기	can't	should	must	would

5 She had a runny nose yesterday. She _____ a cold. (catch)

6 You are very late. You _____ earlier. (leave)

7 Emily _____ Joel. He was in Sydney last week. (see)

8 I _____ the piano a lot when I was young, but I don't play it now. (play)

D 그림을 보고 보기의 조동사와 ( ) 안의 말을 이용하여 문장을 완성하시오. (단, 한 번씩만 쓸 것)

보기	have to	should	can

1 These suitcases are heavy. _____ one of them? (carry)

2 Look at the traffic sign. You _____ here. (turn right)

3 I'm feeling sick. I _____ so much. (eat)

[1–3] 빈칸에 들어갈 알맞은 말을 고르시오.

1

| She ought _____ to you. |

① apologize　　② to apologize
③ apologizing　　④ apologizes
⑤ apologized

2

| The road is wet. It _____ last night. |

① must rain　　② has to rain
③ had to rain　　④ must have rained
⑤ should have rained

3

| She _____ be Jasmine's sister. They look very different. |

① cannot　　② had better not
③ should not　　④ ought not to
⑤ is not able to

4 빈칸에 들어갈 말로 알맞지 <u>않은</u> 것은?

| You have a fever. You _____ go to see a doctor. |

① must　　② should
③ used to　　④ ought to
⑤ had better

[5–6] 다음 중 어법상 <u>틀린</u> 것을 고르시오.

5 ① Can I use your scissors?
② He has to wear a suit to the party.
③ He must have spent all his money.
④ The gym used to be on the corner.
⑤ He will can speak Japanese fluently.

6 ① Could you repeat it one more time?
② You had not better bite your nails.
③ I may have put the key on the table.
④ A learner ought to ask many questions.
⑤ She must be disappointed with you.

[빈출]

7 다음 중 두 문장의 의미가 같지 <u>않은</u> 것은?

① As a child, I used to go camping.
　→ As a child, I would go camping.
② You can use my correction pen.
　→ You may use my correction pen.
③ You should take notes during class.
　→ You ought to take notes during class.
④ You must not smoke in this building.
　→ You don't have to smoke in this building.
⑤ Jake can solve the math problem.
　→ Jake is able to solve the math problem.

[8-9] 다음 우리말을 영어로 바르게 옮긴 것을 고르시오.

8

> 그가 그 일을 벌써 끝냈을 리가 없다.

① He can't have finished the work already.
② He must not have finished the work already.
③ He may not have finished the work already.
④ He should not have finished the work already.
⑤ He ought not to have finished the work already.

9

> 그는 새 안경을 살 필요가 없다.

① He must not buy new glasses.
② He should not buy new glasses.
③ He ought not to buy new glasses.
④ He doesn't have to buy new glasses.
⑤ He had better not buy new glasses.

서술형
[10-11] 빈칸에 공통으로 들어갈 조동사를 쓰시오.

10 · She _____ be happy because she got the job.
· Every student _____ wear a school uniform.

11 · I _____ go surfing every weekend before I moved here.
· There _____ be an old house here.

빈출

12 밑줄 친 부분의 의미가 나머지 넷과 다른 것은?

① I must get up early in the morning.
② You must be back home by nine.
③ You must run to catch the train.
④ His car must be very expensive.
⑤ She must brush her teeth after each meal.

13 다음 중 어법상 옳은 것은?

① It might is cloudy tomorrow morning.
② She used to working for the company.
③ They are not able understand English.
④ Jim may have gone home after work.
⑤ He have to go to the dentist this afternoon.

서술형
[14-15] 주어진 문장과 의미가 통하도록 빈칸에 알맞은 말을 쓰시오.

14 I am certain that she forgot about the appointment with us.

→ She _____ _____ about the appointment with us.

15 We had five dogs, but now we don't have any.

→ We _____ _____ have five dogs.

16 다음 중 어느 빈칸에도 들어갈 수 <u>없는</u> 것은?

> · It ___ⓐ___ rain later. Bring an umbrella.
> · James broke a glass again. He ___ⓑ___ have been more careful.
> · She has just had breakfast. She ___ⓒ___ be hungry already.

① may　　　　② can't
③ is able to　　④ should
⑤ might

17 다음 중 보기의 밑줄 친 부분과 의미가 같은 것은?

> 보기　It <u>may</u> snow tonight.

① <u>May</u> I ask you a question?
② You <u>may</u> borrow my science book.
③ He <u>may</u> like the yellow T-shirt.
④ You <u>may</u> not use my cell phone.
⑤ You <u>may</u> take a break now.

서술형

[18-20] 우리말과 일치하도록 알맞은 조동사와 ( ) 안의 말을 이용하여 문장을 완성하시오.

18 여기에 중국 음식점이 있었다. (be)

→ There _____ a Chinese restaurant here.

19 형이 내 야구 모자를 가져갔을지도 모른다. (take)

→ My brother _____ my baseball cap.

20 아직 이른 시간이니 너는 서두를 필요 없다. (hurry)

→ It is still early, so you _____
_____.

서술형

[21-22] 빈칸에 알맞은 조동사를 써서 대화를 완성하시오.

21 A: Can I eat this slice of pizza?
B: Of course. But your hands are dirty. You _____ _____ wash them first.

22 A: I think I saw Joe at the amusement park last Saturday.
B: She _____ have been there. She said she spent all weekend studying for an exam.

서술형

[23-25] 우리말과 일치하도록 ( ) 안에 주어진 단어를 바르게 배열하시오.

23 나는 부모님 말씀을 들었어야 했다.
(my parents, have, to, I, should, listened)

→ _____.

24 너는 밖에서 놀지 않는 게 좋겠다. 날씨가 매우 춥다.
(not, play, better, you, had, outside)

→ _____
It's very cold.

25 너는 도서관에서 큰 소리로 이야기해서는 안 된다.
(loudly, not, ought, you, to, talk)

→ _____
in the library.

26 다음 중 어법상 옳은 것을 모두 고르면?

① You should get there by noon.

② He could be able to jump rope very well.

③ You had better go to bed early.

④ I have not to make dinner. We will eat out.

⑤ My mother used to pick me up from school every day.

27 다음 중 어법상 옳은 것으로 바르게 짝지어진 것은?

a. She can't have said that.
b. I must wear a tie at my workplace.
c. Could you give me a ride to the station?
d. I should wear a helmet yesterday.
e. There would be a large desk in my room.

① a, b, c   ② a, c, d
③ a, c, e   ④ b, c, d
⑤ b, c, e

28 다음 중 어법상 옳은 것의 개수는?

· He won't able to get the ticket.
· You must not tell lies to your friends.
· This book might be helpful to you.
· You had not better send messages late at night.
· She must be very beautiful when she was young.

① 1개   ② 2개   ③ 3개
④ 4개   ⑤ 5개

[29-31] 밑줄 친 부분이 어법상 옳은지 판단하고, 틀리면 바르게 고치시오.

29 You not ought to do such things.

(O / X) _____

30 You have to keep it a secret. You must not tell anyone else.

(O / X) _____

31 I have a flight to catch. I have better go now.

(O / X) _____

[32-33] 어법상 틀린 부분을 찾아 바르게 고치시오.

32 Phillip had a stomachache yesterday. He must eat some spoiled food. (1개)

33 Yesterday it snowed heavily, but I didn't wear my boots. My socks got wet, and I caught a cold. I should dress warmly yesterday. (1개)

LET'S REVIEW

주요 예문을 다시 한번 확인하고, 우리말과 일치하도록 빈칸을 채우시오.

- Noah **can**[^{1}_____] speak five languages. Noah는 5개 국어를 말할 수 있다. **Unit 01 - A**
- That ^{2}_____ be Ruby. She is in LA now.
  저 사람이 Ruby일 리 없다. 그녀는 지금 LA에 있다. **Unit 01 - A**
- **Could** you wait a moment, please? 조금만 기다려 주시겠어요? **Unit 01 - A**

- You've finished your homework. You ^{3}_____ go out to play.
  너는 숙제를 끝냈다. 너는 놀러 나가도 된다. **Unit 01 - B**
- The rumor **may**[**might**] be true. 그 소문이 사실일지도 모른다. **Unit 01 - B**

- They **must**[**have to**] work from 9:00 a.m. to 6:00 p.m. every day.
  그들은 매일 오전 9시부터 오후 6시까지 일해야 한다. **Unit 01 - C**
- She ^{4}_____ be tired after her long trip. 그녀는 긴 여행 후 피곤한 것임에 틀림없다. **Unit 01 - C**

- You **should** obey the school rules. 너는 학교 규칙을 따라야 한다. **Unit 01 - D**

- You ^{5}_____ eat more vegetables. 너는 채소를 더 먹는 게 좋겠다. **Unit 02 - A**

- You **ought** ^{6}_____ turn off your cell phone during class.
  너는 수업 중에 휴대 전화를 꺼야 한다. **Unit 02 - B**

- When he was a child, he ^{7}_____ go swimming every summer.
  그가 아이였을 때 그는 여름마다 수영하러 가곤 했다. **Unit 02 - C**

- Daniel ^{8}_____ his report already. Daniel이 보고서를 벌써 끝냈을 리가 없다. **Unit 02 - D**
- She **may**[**might**] **have read** the book already. 그녀는 그 책을 이미 읽었을지도 모른다. **Unit 02 - D**
- He ^{9}_____ to Paris. 그는 파리에 가 본 적이 있음에 틀림없다. **Unit 02 - D**
- I ^{10}_____ harder. 나는 더 열심히 공부했어야 했다. **Unit 02 - D**

🔍 Answers

^{1} is able to ^{2} can't[cannot] ^{3} may[can] ^{4} must ^{5} had better ^{6} to ^{7} used to / would

^{8} can't have finished ^{9} must have been ^{10} should have studied

ESSENTIAL RULES OF
ENGLISH GRAMMAR

CHAPTER
03

수동태

수동태는 주어가 동사의 영향을 받거나
동작을 당하는 것을 표현한다.

UNIT 01 수동태의 의미와 형태

A

수동태: 「be + v-ed」 형태로, 행위의 영향을 받는 대상에 초점을 둘 때 사용한다.

Shakespeare **wrote** *Romeo and Juliet*. 〈능동태: 행위자에 초점을 둠〉

Romeo and Juliet **was written** by Shakespeare. 〈수동태: 행위의 대상에 초점을 둠〉

ⓘ 수동태를 쓰지 않는 동사

happen, disappear 등 목적어가 없는 자동사나 resemble, lack 등 상태를 나타내는 타동사, 소유를 나타 내는 have 등은 수동태로 쓰지 않는다.

All the files **disappeared** from the computer.

~~All the files were disappeared from the computer.~~

Mike **resembles** his father.

~~His father is resembled by Mike.~~

B

행위자의 생략

행위자가 막연한 일반인일 때 또는 분명하지 않거나 중요하지 않을 때 「by + 행위자」는 생략한다.

French **is spoken** in Monaco.

A lot of people **were killed** in the war.

C

수동태의 여러 형태

1 미래형: will be + v-ed

The meeting **will be held** in December.

2 진행형: be동사 + being + v-ed

The elevator **is being repaired**. You can't use it now.

3 완료형: have[has, had] been + v-ed

The flight **has been canceled** because of the storm.

4 조동사가 있는 문장의 수동태: 조동사 + be + v-ed

This book **must be returned** by next Wednesday.

CHECK UP 빈칸에 알맞은 말을 고르시오.

1 These earrings _____ by my sister.

　ⓐ make　　　ⓑ made　　　ⓒ were made

2 The sun _____ above the sea a few minutes ago.

　ⓐ rises　　　ⓑ rose　　　ⓒ was risen

3 This sweater should _____ in cold water.

　ⓐ wash　　　ⓑ be washed　　　ⓒ been washed

PRACTICE

🔍 Answer Key p.5

( ) 안에서 알맞은 말을 고르시오.

1 The radio (invented, was invented) by Nikola Tesla.

2 Kirk (resembles, is resembled by) a cartoon character.

3 A famous designer (made, was made) my wedding dress.

4 The basketball game is (be shown, being shown) on TV.

5 A new idea had (suggested, been suggested) by Tim at the meeting.

밑줄 친 부분을 어법에 맞게 고치시오.

1 The problem is be discussed by the staff now.

2 The actor was disappeared without a trace.

3 My favorite soap opera will shown after the advertisements.

4 Alice punished for being late for class this morning.

STEP 3

다음 문장을 수동태로 바꿔 쓰시오.

1 People all around the world play soccer.

→ Soccer _____ .

2 They will deliver the package within three days.

→ The package _____ .

3 Tourists are destroying the beautiful island.

→ The beautiful island _____ .

STEP 4

우리말과 일치하도록 ( ) 안의 말을 이용하여 문장을 완성하시오.

1 부상당한 그 선수는 병원으로 옮겨졌다. (take)

→ The injured player _____ _____ to the hospital.

2 그 당시에 이 집은 지어지는 중이었다. (build)

→ This house _____ _____ _____ at that time.

3 암 치료법을 찾기 위해서 많은 연구가 행해져 왔다. (do)

→ A lot of research _____ _____ _____ to find a cure for cancer.

4 그 콘서트 표는 온라인으로 미리 살 수 있다. (can, buy)

→ Tickets for the concert _____ _____ _____ online in advance.

UNIT 02 4형식, 5형식 문장의 수동태

A 4형식 문장의 수동태

- 간접목적어와 직접목적어를 각각 주어로 하여 두 가지 형태의 수동태 문장을 만들 수 있다.
- 직접목적어가 문장의 주어가 될 때 대부분의 수여동사는 간접목적어 앞에 전치사 to를 쓰나 make, buy 등은 for를 쓴다.

A Canadian teaches us English at school.
→ We **are taught** English by a Canadian at school.
→ English **is taught to** us by a Canadian at school.

ⓘ make, buy 등의 동사는 간접목적어가 주어인 수동태로는 쓰지 않는다.
My friend **bought** me the pretty mug.
→ The pretty mug **was bought for** me by my friend.
→ I was bought the pretty mug by my friend.

B 5형식 문장의 수동태

1 목적격 보어가 그대로 쓰이는 경우

We elected Julian to be our leader.
→ Julian **was elected to be our leader**.

His good looks made the actor popular.
→ The actor **was made popular** by his good looks.

2 목적격 보어가 바뀌는 경우

1) 지각동사의 목적격 보어로 쓰인 동사원형은 수동태 문장에서 현재분사나 to부정사로 바뀐다.
I saw Maria read a travel guide.
→ Maria **was seen reading[to read]** a travel guide by me.

2) 사역동사는 make만 수동태로 쓰이며, 이때 목적격 보어로 쓰인 동사원형은 수동태 문장에서 to부정사로 바뀐다.
My mom made me learn taekwondo.
→ I **was made to learn** taekwondo by my mom.

 **CHECK UP** 빈칸에 알맞은 말을 고르시오.

1 A thank-you card was sent _____ my teacher.
ⓐ to　　　　ⓑ for　　　　ⓒ of

2 Neil was seen _____ baseball with his friends yesterday.
ⓐ play　　　　ⓑ playing　　　　ⓒ being played

PRACTICE

Answer Key p.5

STEP 1

( ) 안에서 알맞은 말을 고르시오.

1 The recipe for seafood spaghetti was given (to, for) me by Tony.

2 A model plane was bought (to, for) my son for his birthday.

3 The baby was seen (play, playing) with the robots.

4 We were made (work, to work) on the project as a group.

STEP 2

밑줄 친 부분을 어법에 맞게 고치시오.

1 He was heard shout, "I didn't do it!"

2 A cup of coffee was made me by the barista.

3 A surprising story was told him by his parents.

4 The noisy students were made stand in the back of the classroom.

STEP 3

다음 문장을 수동태로 바꿔 쓰시오.

1 The boy's rude attitude made the old man angry.

→ The old man _____ .

2 I saw the artist paint the beautiful scenery.

→ The artist _____ .

3 My mom made me help my brother with his homework.

→ I _____ .

4 My grandfather taught me Chinese.

→ Chinese _____ .

→ I _____ .

STEP 4

우리말과 일치하도록 ( ) 안의 말을 이용하여 문장을 완성하시오.

1 우리의 검은 고양이는 Lucky라고 불린다. (call)

→ Our black cat _____ _____ _____ .

2 학생들은 그 책을 읽게 시켜졌다. (make, read)

→ Students _____ _____ _____ _____ the book.

3 그 가방은 삼촌이 나에게 사주신 것이다. (buy)

→ The bag _____ _____ _____ by my uncle.

4 아이들이 밖에서 큰 소리로 웃는 것이 들렸다. (hear, laugh)

→ The children _____ _____ _____ loudly outside.

주의해야 할 수동태

A 동사구의 수동태

동사만 「be + v-ed」의 형태로 바꾸고, 나머지 부분은 하나의 단어처럼 취급하여 같이 붙여 쓴다.

We carried out the project in secret.
→ The project **was carried out** in secret (by us).

B 목적어가 that절인 문장의 수동태

「It + be동사 + v-ed + that ~」의 형태로 쓴다. that절의 주어를 수동태 문장의 주어로 할 때, that절의 동사는 to부정사로 바뀐다.

People say that the movie is worth watching.
→ **It is said that** the movie is worth watching.
→ The movie **is said to be** worth watching.

C by 이외의 전치사를 쓰는 수동태

- be covered with: ~로 덮여 있다
- be pleased with: ~로 기뻐하다
- be satisfied with: ~에 만족하다
- be crowded with: ~로 붐비다
- be disappointed with[at]: ~에 실망하다
- be worried about: ~에 대해 걱정하다
- be interested in: ~에 흥미가 있다
- be filled with: ~로 가득 차다(= be full of)
- be known to: ~에게 알려지다
- be surprised at: ~에 놀라다
- be composed of: ~로 구성되다
- be made of[from]: ~로 만들어지다

The room **was filled with** colorful balloons for the party.
I **am worried about** the result of the math exam.

CHECK UP 빈칸에 알맞은 말을 고르시오.

1 The lost dog _____ my brother.
ⓐ looked after by   ⓑ was looked after   ⓒ was looked after by

2 It _____ that smoking is a bad habit.
ⓐ is think   ⓑ thought   ⓒ is thought

3 James is interested _____ traditional Korean music.
ⓐ by   ⓑ in   ⓒ at

PRACTICE

🔍 Answer Key p.5

STEP 1

( ) 안에서 알맞은 말을 고르시오.

1 The boy (was laughed, was laughed at) by his friends.

2 All my family was pleased (to, with) my sister's success.

3 The movie was boring. I was disappointed (with, of) it.

4 The homeless (are taken care, are taken care of) by the volunteers.

STEP 2

다음 문장을 주어진 말로 시작하는 수동태로 바꿔 쓰시오.

1 They reported that the police arrested the murderer.

→ It _____.

2 The speeding truck ran over the dog.

→ The dog _____.

3 Some people believe that blood type affects personality.

→ Blood type _____.

STEP 3

빈칸에 알맞은 말을 보기에서 골라 쓰시오. (단, 한 번씩만 쓸 것)

보기		with	about	of	to

1 The purse is made _____ artificial leather.

2 The song is known _____ people all around the world.

3 The books on the top shelf were covered _____ thick dust.

4 Many people are worried _____ the high cost of gasoline.

STEP 4

우리말과 일치하도록 ( ) 안의 말을 이용하여 문장을 완성하시오.

1 물은 산소와 수소로 구성되어 있다. (compose)

→ Water _____ _____ _____ oxygen and hydrogen.

2 인터넷이 우리의 삶을 더 편하게 해 주었다고 말해진다. (say)

→ _____ _____ _____ _____ the internet has made our lives easier.

3 우리 역사 선생님은 많은 학생들에게 존경받는다. (look up to)

→ My history teacher _____ _____ _____ _____ _____ many students.

4 그는 경기의 최종 점수에 실망했다. (disappoint)

→ He _____ _____ _____ the final score of the game.

GRAMMAR FOR WRITING

A 우리말과 일치하도록 ( ) 안의 말을 이용하여 문장을 완성하시오.

1 한글은 세종 대왕에 의해 창제되었다. (create)

→ Hangeul _____ King Sejong the Great.

2 그 서류들은 비밀로 유지되어야 한다. (must, keep)

→ The documents _____ secret.

3 그 웹 사이트는 업데이트되고 있어서 지금 사용할 수 없다. (update)

→ The website _____, so you can't use it now.

4 그 도둑이 나의 집에 들어가는 것이 이웃에 의해 목격되었다. (see, enter)

→ The thief _____ my house by my neighbor.

5 Esther는 다섯 살에 발레를 배우게 되었다. (make, learn)

→ Esther _____ ballet at the age of five.

6 그 계란 샌드위치는 오늘 아침에 우리 아빠를 위해 만들어졌다. (make, my dad)

→ The egg sandwich _____ this morning.

7 그 배우는 매년 천만 달러 이상을 번다고 믿어진다. (believe, earn)

→ The actor _____ more than $10 million every year.

B 우리말과 일치하도록 ( ) 안에 주어진 단어를 바르게 배열하시오.

1 그 퍼즐은 아직 풀리지 않았다. (solved, the, puzzle, been, has, not)

→ _____ yet.

2 우리는 다음 학기를 위한 새 교과서를 받았다. (given, the, were, textbooks, new)

→ We _____ for next semester.

3 나는 Bill이 우리 반 회장으로 뽑힐 것임을 확신한다. (class president, be, Bill, elected, our, will)

→ I'm sure that _____.

4 Dan은 그 회사에서 새 직책에 만족하고 있다. (new, is, position, Dan, with, his, satisfied)

→ _____ at the company.

5 내가 휴가 갔을 때 내 강아지들은 내 여동생에 의해 보살펴졌다.
(puppies, were, my, care, sister, my, of, by, taken)

→ _____ when I went on vacation.

6 이 반지는 청혼할 때 내 남자친구가 나에게 주었다.
(to, ring, given, me, by, my, this, boyfriend, was)

→ _____ when he proposed.

C 다음 문장을 주어진 말로 시작할 때 빈칸에 알맞은 말을 쓰시오.

1 Hip-hop has influenced his musical style.

→ His musical style _____ by hip-hop.

2 Our boss put off his business trip because of his illness.

→ Our boss's business trip _____ because of his illness.

3 My father made me bring his fishing rod.

→ I _____ my father's fishing rod by him.

4 They are building a long bridge that will connect the two islands.

→ A long bridge that will connect the two islands _____.

5 I will give you a ten-minute break from now on.

→ A ten-minute break _____ from now on.

6 You should bake the apple pie for forty minutes.

→ The apple pie _____ for forty minutes.

7 People say that good art makes us creative thinkers.

→ It _____ good art makes us creative thinkers.

D 그림을 보고 보기에 주어진 말을 이용하여 문장을 완성하시오. (단, 현재시제로 쓸 것)

보기	fill	compose	interest

1 This band _____ three members: Chris, Alex, and Mia.

2 He _____ joining a ski camp during the vacation.

3 The restaurant _____ customers at dinnertime.

REVIEW TEST

[1–5] 빈칸에 들어갈 알맞은 말을 고르시오.

1

> Yesterday's baseball game _____ because of the rain.

① cancels   ② canceled
③ canceling   ④ was canceled
⑤ were canceled

2

> Rainbows can often _____ in this village.

① see   ② be seen
③ be seeing   ④ have seen
⑤ being seen

3

> I was made _____ with my right hand by my parents when I was young.

① write   ② wrote
③ to write   ④ writing
⑤ to writing

4

> The blue dress was made _____ me by a fashion designer.

① by   ② to   ③ for
④ of   ⑤ with

5

> Guam is known _____ many people as a resort island.

① in   ② to   ③ for
④ at   ⑤ of

[6–8] 다음 중 어법상 틀린 것을 고르시오.

6
① My wallet suddenly disappeared.
② The actor is resembled by my little brother.
③ The washing machine is being repaired.
④ The problem has been solved by Tom.
⑤ You will be paid $15 an hour for the work.

7
① The job offer was turned down by Ray.
② The old man was seen enter the room.
③ The gray sweater was bought for him by his girlfriend.
④ Every room in this hotel is cleaned every day.
⑤ The children were made to stay quiet during the ceremony.

8
① He is always worried about money.
② This tea table is made of oak wood.
③ Jessica is interested in knitting.
④ The castle is crowded to many people.
⑤ The garden was covered with snow.

빈출

[9-10] 빈칸에 공통으로 들어갈 말을 고르시오.

9

- A movie was shown _____ the children by their parents.
- We were made _____ help him with his work.

① by ② to ③ for
④ at ⑤ with

10

- Dana is pleased _____ her new dress.
- They were satisfied _____ the good service at the restaurant.

① by ② to ③ for
④ at ⑤ with

서술형

[11-13] ( ) 안의 말을 이용하여 문장을 완성하시오.

11 The museum _____ on the site of a former school now. (build)

12 Having breakfast is said _____ good for your health. (be)

13 The couple was heard _____ last night by neighbors. (fight)

14 두 문장의 의미가 같도록 할 때, 빈칸에 들어갈 알맞은 말은?

People believe that artists are more creative than most people.
→ _____ that artists are more creative than most people.

① It believes ② People to believe
③ It is to believe ④ It is believed
⑤ People are believed

서술형 **빈출**

[15-17] 다음 문장을 주어진 말로 시작할 때 빈칸에 알맞은 말을 쓰시오.

15 My girlfriend made me this card for Christmas.

→ This card _____ by my girlfriend for Christmas.

16 They haven't fixed my laptop yet.

→ My laptop _____ yet.

17 My father gave me some money for the school trip.

→ Some money _____ by my father for the school trip.

18 다음 우리말을 영어로 바르게 옮긴 것은? (2개)

> 나의 상사는 진정한 리더라고 일컬어진다.

① My boss is said to be a true leader.
② My boss is said being a true leader.
③ It is said my boss to be a true leader.
④ It is said that my boss be a true leader.
⑤ It is said that my boss is a true leader.

서술형
[19-21] 우리말과 일치하도록 ( ) 안의 말을 이용하여 문장을 완성하시오.

19 학생들은 운동장의 쓰레기를 줍도록 시켜졌다.
(make, pick up)

→ Students _____
trash in the playground.

20 그의 새 앨범이 올해 말에 나올 것이다.
(will, release)

→ His new album _____
at the end of this year.

21 그녀의 방은 그녀가 가장 좋아하는 아이돌 그룹 사진으로 가득 차 있다. (fill)

→ Her room _____ pictures
of her favorite idol group.

22 다음 중 어법상 옳은 것은?

① The book is said that is boring.
② The road is rebuilt yesterday.
③ Your order will be delivered tomorrow.
④ Tim was seen jog this morning.
⑤ This pizza was made Sam by me.

서술형
[23-24] 우리말과 일치하도록 ( ) 안에 주어진 단어를 바르게 배열하시오.

23 그 사슴은 트럭에 치여 다리를 다쳤다.
(was, over, by, the deer, the truck, run)

→ _____, and
its leg was hurt.

24 안전을 위해 당신의 비밀번호는 3개월마다 변경되어야 한다.
(changed, be, your, should, password)

→ For safety, _____
every three months.

서술형
25 우리말과 일치하도록 주어진 조건에 맞게 문장을 완성하시오.

> 요가는 몸과 정신 둘 다에 좋다고 말해진다.

〈조건〉 1. It으로 시작할 것
2. say, yoga, good을 이용할 것

→ _____
for both the body and the mind.

26 다음 중 어법상 옳은 것을 모두 고르면?

① The house has been building for six months.
② The paper will be sign by my boss.
③ The room was filled with a coffee aroma.
④ That funny video was posted by Zoe.
⑤ Nicole is said to be the best singer in her town.

27 다음 중 어법상 옳은 것으로 바르게 짝지어진 것은?

a. The car is being repair by Tom.
b. Our victory must be celebrated.
c. Jimmy was made cleaning his room by his father.
d. The sneakers were given to me for my birthday.
e. It is said that Jonathan speaks five languages.

① a, b, c
② a, c, d
③ a, d, e
④ b, c, e
⑤ b, d, e

28 다음 중 어법상 옳은 것의 개수는?

· Two cats were had by me when I was a kid.
· I haven't been invited to the party yet.
· *The Harry Potter* series is composed of seven books.
· A security camera will be placed on every floor.
· This beautiful scarf was bought to my mother by me.

① 1개
② 2개
③ 3개
④ 4개
⑤ 5개

[29-31] 밑줄 친 부분이 어법상 옳은지 판단하고, 틀리면 바르게 고치시오.

29 The last slice of pizza <u>was given for</u> my sister.

(O / X) _____

30 People all over the world <u>were surprised to</u> the discovery.

(O / X) _____

31 Paul <u>was seen help</u> the old lady by his colleagues.

(O / X) _____

[32-33] 어법상 틀린 부분을 찾아 바르게 고치시오.

32 We had a football game last night. The game was greatly enjoy by all of the students. (1개)

33 A few days ago, I had a big fight with my brother. Today, I was made saying sorry to him by my mom. (1개)

LET'S REVIEW

주요 예문을 다시 한번 확인하고, 우리말과 일치하도록 빈칸을 채우시오.

- *Romeo and Juliet* [1]_____ by Shakespeare.
  "로미오와 줄리엣"은 셰익스피어에 의해 쓰였다. **Unit 01 - A**

- French **is spoken** in Monaco. 모나코에서는 프랑스어가 사용된다. **Unit 01 - B**

- The meeting **will** [2]_____ **held** in December. 그 회의는 12월에 개최될 것이다. **Unit 01 - C**

- The elevator [3]_____ repaired. 그 엘리베이터는 수리되는 중이다. **Unit 01 - C**

- The flight **has been canceled** because of the storm. 폭풍 때문에 그 항공편이 취소되었다. **Unit 01 - C**

- This book **must** [4]_____ by next Wednesday.
  이 책은 다음 주 수요일까지 반납되어야 한다. **Unit 01 - C**

- English **is taught** [5]_____ us by a Canadian at school.
  영어는 학교에서 한 캐나다인에 의해 우리에게 가르쳐진다. **Unit 02 - A**

- Julian **was elected to be our leader**. Julian이 우리 대표로 선출되었다. **Unit 02 - B**

- Maria **was seen** [6]_____ a travel guide by me.
  Maria가 관광 안내서를 읽는 것이 나에게 목격되었다. **Unit 02 - B**

- I **was made** [7]_____ taekwondo by my mom.
  나는 엄마에 의해 태권도를 배우게 되었다. **Unit 02 - B**

- The project **was carried out** in secret (by us).
  그 프로젝트는 (우리에 의해) 비밀리에 수행되었다. **Unit 03 - A**

- [8]_____ **that** the movie is worth watching. 그 영화는 볼 가치가 있다고 말해진다. **Unit 03 - B**

- I [9]_____ the result of the math exam. 나는 수학 시험 결과가 걱정된다. **Unit 03 - C**

Answers

[1] was written   [2] be   [3] is being   [4] be returned   [5] to   [6] reading[to read]   [7] to learn
[8] It is said   [9] am worried about

ESSENTIAL RULES OF
ENGLISH GRAMMAR

CHAPTER
04

부정사

부정사는 다른 동사와는 달리 수, 인칭에 따라
형태가 변하지 않는다. 부정사에는 원형부정
사와 to부정사가 있다.

UNIT 01 명사적 용법의 to부정사

A 명사적 용법의 to부정사

to부정사가 명사처럼 문장에서 주어, 목적어, 보어 역할을 한다.

1 주어 역할

To learn a new language is fun.

2 목적어 역할

Tony decided **to tell** the truth to his parents.

3 보어 역할

The chef's plan is **to open** his own restaurant.

B 가주어와 가목적어 it

to부정사가 주어로 쓰이거나, 5형식 문장에서 목적어로 쓰인 경우 보통 가주어나 가목적어 it을 쓰고 to부정사는 뒤로 보낸다.

1 가주어 it

It is exciting **to travel** to new places.

2 가목적어 it

I found **it** interesting **to keep** a blog.

C 의문사 + to-v

의문사 what, who(m), when, where, how가 to부정사 앞에 쓰여 '무엇을[누구를, 언제, 어디서, 어떻게] ~할지'의 의미를 나타낸다. 「의문사 + to부정사」는 보통 「의문사 + 주어 + should + 동사원형」으로 바꿔 쓸 수 있다.

He showed me **how to use** the robot vacuum cleaner.
      = how I should use

CHECK UP   빈칸에 알맞은 말을 고르시오.

1 Her advice was _____ my writing short and simple.

  ⓐ make   ⓑ made   ⓒ to make

2 It can be dangerous _____ a lot of weight in a short time.

  ⓐ lose   ⓑ to lose   ⓒ losing

3 The map made _____ a lot easier to find the way.

  ⓐ it   ⓑ that   ⓒ this

4 He hasn't decided yet where _____ during the trip.

  ⓐ stay   ⓑ to stay   ⓒ staying

PRACTICE

🔍 Answer Key p.6

STEP 1

( ) 안에서 알맞은 말을 고르시오.

1 His plan is (travel, to travel) around Europe by train.

2 The internet makes (it, that) convenient to get information.

3 I don't know what (wearing, to wear) to the Christmas party.

4 She made it a rule (exercise, to exercise) every morning.

STEP 2

두 문장의 의미가 같도록 빈칸에 알맞은 말을 쓰시오.

1 To learn how to cook is very interesting.

→ _____ is very interesting _____ _____ how to cook.

2 My boss told me when I should start the project.

→ My boss told me _____ _____ _____ the project.

3 To clean the garden by myself is impossible.

→ _____ is impossible _____ _____ the garden by myself.

STEP 3

보기에서 알맞은 의문사를 골라 ( ) 안의 말과 to부정사를 함께 써서 문장을 완성하시오.

보기	how	where	what

1 I have a lot of things to do. I don't know _____ first. (do)

2 Juan is a cook. He taught me _____ Mexican food. (cook)

3 I don't know _____ for my summer vacation. Do you have any recommendations? (go)

STEP 4

우리말과 일치하도록 ( ) 안의 말을 이용하여 문장을 완성하시오.

1 내 꿈은 건축가가 되는 것이다. (be, architect)

→ My dream _____ _____ _____ _____ _____.

2 스키 캠프에 가는 것은 재미있었다. (fun, go)

→ It _____ _____ _____ _____ to the ski camp.

3 그는 언제 그것을 끝내야 하는지 내게 말해주지 않았다. (finish)

→ He didn't tell me _____ _____ _____ it.

4 나는 눈 때문에 제시간에 도착하는 것이 불가능하다는 것을 알았다. (impossible, arrive)

→ I found _____ _____ _____ _____ on time because of the snow.

UNIT 02 형용사적 용법, 부사적 용법의 to부정사

A 형용사적 용법의 to부정사

to부정사가 명사를 수식하거나, 「be to-v」의 형태로 주어를 설명한다.

1 (대)명사 수식

Winter is *the best time* **to go** on a safari in Africa.

ⓘ 수식 받는 명사가 to부정사에 이어지는 전치사의 의미상 목적어가 될 때는 전치사를 반드시 같이 쓴다.
The child needed *someone* **to play with**. (→ ~ play with someone)

2 be to-v 용법

The new service **is to begin** next month. 〈예정〉

The man **was not to be** seen anywhere. 〈가능〉

You **are to upload** your file by tomorrow. 〈의무〉

The baby **was to become** the next king. 〈운명〉

If you **are to pass** the exam, you must study harder. 〈의도〉

B 부사적 용법의 to부정사

to부정사가 동사, 형용사, 부사를 수식한다.

I eat breakfast **to stay** healthy. 〈목적: ~하기 위해서〉

ⓘ '목적'의 의미를 강조하기 위해 to-v 내신 in order to-v를 쓰기도 한다.
Many people come here **in order to live** a better life.

The shy girl grew up **to be** an actress. 〈결과: 결국 ~했다〉

I'm so sorry **to change** my mind. 〈감정의 원인: ~해서〉

To hear him sing, you would think he was a professional singer. 〈조건: ~한다면〉

You must be a fool **to believe** his lies. 〈판단의 근거: ~하다니〉

The new machine is convenient **to use**. 〈형용사 수식: ~하기에〉

CHECK UP 빈칸에 알맞은 말을 고르시오.

1 They were tired, so they were looking for a bench _____.
ⓐ sitting   ⓑ to sit   ⓒ to sit on

2 My parents _____ Paris next week.
ⓐ visiting   ⓑ to visit   ⓒ are to visit

3 I went to the library _____ some history books.
ⓐ borrow   ⓑ borrowing   ⓒ to borrow

PRACTICE

🔍 Answer Key p·7

 STEP 1

( ) 안에서 알맞은 말을 고르시오.

1 The bird is making a nest (to live, to live in).

2 The little boy grew up (became, to become) a good soccer player.

3 Mom turned on the light (wake, to wake) up my brother.

4 You must smile if you (are to make, are to making) a good impression.

 STEP 2

어법상 틀린 부분을 찾아 바르게 고치시오.

1 The children needed some toys to play.

2 I don't have anything doing at home.

3 You must be Joe's close friend know him so well.

4 The couple was in love, but they were never to seeing each other again.

 STEP 3

밑줄 친 부분에 유의하여 문장을 우리말로 해석하시오.

1 The actor is happy <u>to be</u> so famous.

2 We know that love <u>is not to be bought</u>.

3 Now is the best time <u>to call</u> your parents.

4 Jenny must be brave <u>to travel</u> around the world alone.

 STEP 4

우리말과 일치하도록 ( ) 안의 말을 이용하여 문장을 완성하시오.

1 책을 읽어야 할 많은 이유가 있다. (reason, read)

→ There are ＿＿＿＿＿ ＿＿＿＿＿ ＿＿＿＿＿ ＿＿＿＿ books.

2 Sandra는 내일 서울에 도착할 예정이다. (be, arrive in)

→ Sandra ＿＿＿＿ ＿＿＿＿ ＿＿＿＿ ＿＿＿＿ Seoul tomorrow.

3 그에게서 연락을 받는다면 나는 기쁠 것이다. (hear from)

→ I would be glad ＿＿＿＿ ＿＿＿＿ ＿＿＿＿ .

4 그가 그 시험에 합격했다는 것을 듣고 나는 매우 기뻤다. (very, happy, hear)

→ I ＿＿＿＿ ＿＿＿＿ ＿＿＿＿ ＿＿＿＿ ＿＿＿＿ that he
passed the exam.

to부정사의 의미상의 주어, 시제, 태

A **to부정사의 의미상의 주어:** to부정사가 뜻하는 동작이나 상태의 주체이다.

1 for + 목적격: 보통 to부정사의 의미상의 주어는 「for + 목적격」을 사용한다.

It is *difficult* **for me** to wake up early. I'm not a morning person.

2 of + 목적격: 사람에 대한 주관적 평가를 나타내는 형용사(kind, polite, rude, cruel, careless, nice, foolish, silly, generous, brave 등)와 함께 쓰이면 「of + 목적격」을 사용한다.

It was *kind* **of him** to give us a ride to the airport.

B **to부정사의 시제**

1 단순부정사: 「to-v」의 형태로 to부정사의 시제가 문장의 시제와 같을 때 쓴다.

Ron *seems* **to be** rich.

(← It *seems* that Ron **is** rich now.)

2 완료부정사: 「to have v-ed」의 형태로 to부정사의 시제가 문장의 시제보다 앞설 때 쓴다.

Ron *seems* **to have been** rich.

(← It *seems* that Ron **was** rich.)

C **to부정사의 수동태**

1 단순형: to be v-ed

The actor didn't expect **to be given** the award.

2 완료형: to have been v-ed

Sue is proud **to have been selected** as the winner.

 빈칸에 알맞은 말을 고르시오.

1 It is difficult _____ to read an English newspaper.

ⓐ me   ⓑ for me   ⓒ of me

2 She seems _____ a lot of novels when she was young.

ⓐ read   ⓑ to be read   ⓒ to have read

3 John hates _____ the same thing several times.

ⓐ tell   ⓑ to be told   ⓒ to have told

PRACTICE

Answer Key p.7

STEP 1

( ) 안에서 알맞은 말을 고르시오.

1 It was easy (for us, of us) to win the soccer game yesterday.

2 It was rude (to him, of him) to make such a joke.

3 He seems (to lose, to have lost) a lot of weight in the past year.

4 Do children need (to punish, to be punished) when they behave badly?

STEP 2

( ) 안의 말을 이용하여 문장을 완성하시오.

1 It is possible _____ to memorize the script in an hour. (he)

2 It was careless _____ to forget our appointment. (you)

3 It was smart _____ to ask for help in that situation. (she)

4 It is essential _____ to bring my laptop to the meeting. (I)

STEP 3

두 문장의 의미가 같도록 to부정사를 이용하여 빈칸에 알맞은 말을 쓰시오.

1 I am sorry that I made the same mistake again.

→ I am sorry _____ the same mistake again.

2 I was happy that I was invited to the party.

→ I was happy _____ to the party.

3 It seemed that she was disappointed with the result.

→ She seemed _____ with the result.

4 It seemed that he had been told to correct his bad habit.

→ He seemed _____ to correct his bad habit.

STEP 4

우리말과 일치하도록 ( ) 안의 말을 이용하여 문장을 완성하시오.

1 나는 더 많은 월급을 받고 싶다. (pay)

→ I want _____ _____ _____ a higher salary.

2 그가 네게 먼저 사과한 것은 아주 예의 발랐다. (polite, apologize)

→ It was very _____ _____ _____ _____ _____ to you first.

3 우리가 그 일을 오늘 끝내는 것은 중요하다. (important, finish)

→ It is _____ _____ _____ _____ _____ the work today.

4 그녀는 의사였던 것처럼 보인다. (seem, be)

→ She _____ _____ _____ _____ a doctor.

UNIT 04 목적격 보어로 쓰이는 부정사

A to부정사가 목적격 보어

want, expect, tell, ask, allow, order, advise 등은 목적격 보어로 to부정사를 취한다.

I *want* you **to answer** my question honestly.

He *told* me **to wear** comfortable shoes when hiking.

B 원형부정사가 목적격 보어

1 지각동사

see, watch, look at, listen to, hear, feel + 목적어 + 원형부정사: ~가 …하는 것을 보다, 듣다, 느끼다

I *saw* Susie **leave** in the middle of the concert.

I *heard* my brother **cry** in his room.

ⓘ 지각동사는 분사도 목적격 보어로 취할 수 있다.

I *saw* him **walking** down the street.

I *heard* my nickname **called** from a distance.

2 사역동사

make, let, have + 목적어 + 원형부정사: ~가 …하게 하다

My teacher *made* us **think** about our future job.

My parents didn't *let* me **go** on a trip with my friends.

David *had* his son **wash** his car.

ⓘ 목적어와 목적격 보어가 수동의 관계일 때는 목적격 보어로 과거분사를 쓴다.

David *had* his car **washed**.

ⓘ help는 to부정사와 원형부정사 모두 목적격 보어로 취할 수 있다.

I *helped* the old lady (**to**) **buy** a train ticket.

ⓘ get은 사역의 의미를 갖지만 목적격 보어로 to부정사를 취한다.

Mom *got* me **to make** my bed every morning.

빈칸에 알맞은 말을 고르시오.

1 The doctor told me _____ a vitamin pill every day.

ⓐ take   ⓑ taking   ⓒ to take

2 We felt the floor _____ for a few seconds.

ⓐ shake   ⓑ shaken   ⓒ to shake

3 My brother let me _____ his new bag.

ⓐ borrow   ⓑ borrowing   ⓒ to borrow

PRACTICE

🔍 Answer Key p.7

 STEP 1

( ) 안에서 알맞은 말을 고르시오.

1 My sister allowed me (wear, to wear) her clothes.

2 When I saw her (dance, danced), I fell in love with her.

3 My father made me (write, to write) in my diary before bed.

4 They had their new house (paint, painted).

5 I've never heard Arabic (speak, spoken).

STEP 2

( ) 안의 말을 이용하여 문장을 완성하시오.

1 Mom never lets me _____ expensive clothes. (buy)

2 My teacher asked me _____ after class. (stay)

3 I saw Keeran _____ the guitar at the rehearsal. (play)

4 His parents wanted him _____ an astronaut. (become)

5 I had my tooth _____ out yesterday. (pull)

STEP 3

어법상 틀린 부분을 찾아 바르게 고쳐 쓰시오.

1 Did you see Dave to hit the home run?

2 The owner of the bookstore had it renovating.

3 My sister helped me choosing the furniture.

4 I got my secretary change my flight.

5 I won't make him to give up this chance.

STEP 4

우리말과 일치하도록 ( ) 안의 말을 이용하여 문장을 완성하시오.

1 나는 그들이 밖에서 떠드는 소리를 들었다. (hear, make noises)

→ I _____ _____ _____ _____ outside.

2 이 지도는 내가 그 가게로 가는 길을 찾도록 도와주었다. (help, find)

→ This map _____ _____ _____ the way to the store.

3 부모님은 내가 고양이를 갖는 것을 허락하지 않으셨다. (let, have)

→ My parents _____ _____ _____ a cat.

4 나의 아빠는 나에게 망치를 가져오라고 말씀하셨다. (tell, bring)

→ My dad _____ _____ _____ _____ a hammer.

UNIT 05 to부정사 구문, 독립부정사

A to부정사를 이용한 구문

1 too ~ to-v: 너무 ~해서 …할 수 없다(= so ~ that + 주어 + can't)

She is **too young to travel** abroad alone.

→ She is **so young that she can't travel** abroad alone.

The puzzle was **too difficult for me to solve**.

→ The puzzle was **so difficult that I couldn't solve** it.

2 ~ enough to-v: …할 만큼 충분히 ~하다(= so ~ that + 주어 + can)

The purse is **small enough to fit** into a pocket.

→ The purse is **so small that it can fit** into a pocket.

The weather is **good enough for children to play** on the beach.

→ The weather is **so good that children can play** on the beach.

B 독립부정사

to부정사를 이용한 관용 표현으로, 문장 전체를 수식한다.

- to begin with: 우선, 먼저
- to tell the truth: 사실대로 말하면
- so to speak: 말하자면
- to be sure: 확실히
- to make matters worse: 설상가상으로
- strange to say: 이상한 이야기지만
- to make a long story short: 간단히 말해서
- to be frank (with you): 솔직히 말해서

To begin with, I will tell you how the system works.
To tell the truth, I lost your phone number.
To make matters worse, the lights went out.

CHECK UP 빈칸에 알맞은 말을 고르시오.

1 Brian is _____ to say hello to strangers.

　ⓐ so shy　　　ⓑ too shy　　　ⓒ shy enough

2 The child is _____ to ride the roller coaster.

　ⓐ so tall　　　ⓑ to tall　　　ⓒ tall enough

3 _____ a long story short, she had her son run the family business.

　ⓐ Make　　　ⓑ Made　　　ⓒ To make

PRACTICE

🔍 Answer Key p.7

STEP 1

( ) 안에서 알맞은 말을 고르시오.

1 (To tell, Telling) the truth, I didn't read the book.

2 (To be, Being) frank with you, I knew the result before you told me.

3 The last question was too difficult for me (answer, to answer).

4 The singer's performance was (good enough, enough good) to satisfy me.

STEP 2

밑줄 친 부분을 어법에 맞게 고치시오.

1 James is too busy <u>cook</u> dinner every day.

2 I was <u>enough</u> scared to call for help.

3 Your voice is <u>enough good</u> to join the choir.

4 Strange <u>say</u>, he looks like a thief.

STEP 3

두 문장의 의미가 같도록 to부정사를 이용하여 문장을 완성하시오.

1 The coffee is so bitter that I can't drink it.

→ The coffee is _____ .

2 The dog is so smart that it can guide the blind.

→ The dog is _____ the blind.

3 This car is so old that it can't drive on the highway.

→ This car is _____ .

4 This animated film is so interesting that adults can enjoy it.

→ This animated film is _____ .

STEP 4

우리말과 일치하도록 ( ) 안의 말을 이용하여 문장을 완성하시오.

1 확실히, 그는 네 생각에 동의하지 않는다. (sure)

→ _____ _____ _____ , he doesn't agree with your idea.

2 너는 그 시험에 합격할 수 있을 만큼 충분히 똑똑하다. (smart, pass)

→ You are _____ _____ _____ _____ the exam.

3 설상가상으로, 그는 치통으로 음식을 먹을 수가 없었다. (make, matters)

→ _____ _____ _____ _____ , he couldn't eat due to a toothache.

4 그 산은 너무 위험해서 하이킹을 갈 수 없다. (dangerous, go)

→ The mountain is _____ _____ _____ _____ hiking on.

GRAMMAR FOR WRITING

A 우리말과 일치하도록 ( ) 안의 말을 이용하여 문장을 완성하시오.

1 그는 그녀가 공원에서 자전거 타는 것을 보았다. (see, ride a bike)

→ He _____ at the park.

2 그가 그 제안을 받아들인 것은 매우 현명했다. (wise, accept)

→ It was very _____ the offer.

3 우리 모두는 의지할 누군가가 필요하다. (someone, depend on)

→ We all need _____ .

4 사실대로 말하면, 나는 그녀의 첫 번째 노래가 이것보다 더 좋았다. (tell, truth)

→ _____ , I liked her first song better than this one.

5 내 컴퓨터는 곧 수리되어야 한다. 너무 느리다. (need, repair)

→ My computer _____ soon. It is too slow.

6 이 탑은 수백 년 전에 지어졌다고 믿어진다. (believe, to, build)

→ This tower _____ hundreds of years ago.

7 그는 그의 전공을 선택하기 전에 그것에 대해 많은 생각을 했던 것처럼 보인다. (seem, think)

→ He _____ a lot about his major before he chose it.

B 우리말과 일치하도록 ( ) 안에 주어진 단어를 바르게 배열하시오.

1 그녀를 웃게 하는 것은 그에게 어려운 일이었다. (laugh, him, for, difficult, to, make, her)

→ It was _____ .

2 나는 그의 마음을 바꾸는 것이 불가능하다는 것을 알게 되었다. (to, his, it, change, impossible, mind)

→ I found _____ .

3 엄마는 나에게 패스트푸드를 먹지 말라고 하셨다. (me, to, told, not, eat, fast food)

→ Mom _____ .

4 그 커플은 내년에 결혼할 예정이다. (to, married, is, the, be, couple)

→ _____ next year.

5 우리는 그곳에 도착하고 나서 어디에 머물지 결정할 것이다. (decide, to, will, where, we, stay)

→ _____ after we get there.

6 내가 그 대학에 합격했다는 것을 알고 우리 부모님은 매우 기뻐하셨다.
(my, pleased, parents, very, know, to, were)

→ _____ that I had been accepted to the college.

C 주어진 문장과 의미가 통하도록 부정사를 이용하여 문장을 완성하시오.

1 I told him to move the heavy boxes, and he did it.

→ I got _____.

2 I hope that you can go there instead of me.

→ I want _____.

3 She said that I should put on sunscreen.

→ She advised _____.

4 When my mom painted the wall, I gave her a hand.

→ I helped my mom _____.

5 The film was very sad, so I cried a lot.

→ The sad film made _____.

6 My brother said that I could wear his new jacket.

→ My brother let _____.

7 He was surprised that she gave him a birthday present.

→ He didn't expect her _____.

D 그림을 보고 상자 안의 말과 to부정사를 이용하여 문장을 완성하시오.

1

how, train dogs

2

hot, wear shorts

3

sick, get out of bed

1 The trainer showed me _____.

2 The weather is _____ these days.

3 Jacob was _____ yesterday.

REVIEW TEST

[1–4] 빈칸에 들어갈 알맞은 말을 고르시오.

1

| It was not easy _____ this hotel. |

① find   ② found
③ to find   ④ to finding
⑤ for finding

2

| My cat needs a bed _____. |

① lie   ② lie on
③ to lie   ④ lying on
⑤ to lie on

3

| My teacher advised me _____ positively. |

① think   ② thinking
③ to think   ④ to thinking
⑤ thought

4

| I watched the children _____ out of the school building. |

① come   ② to come
③ to coming   ④ to came
⑤ be come

`빈출`

[5–6] 빈칸에 들어갈 말로 알맞지 <u>않은</u> 것을 고르시오.

5

| It was _____ of you to say that. |

① polite   ② rude   ③ kind
④ nice   ⑤ impossible

6

| My parents _____ me go there. |

① let   ② had   ③ made
④ got   ⑤ helped

[7–8] 다음 중 어법상 틀린 것을 고르시오.

7
① I don't like to speak in public.
② My father taught me how to ski.
③ He is looking for a house to live in.
④ It's important for you reply to his email.
⑤ I will have my hair cut tomorrow.

8
① My father got me to help him.
② She heard him turn on the TV.
③ My brother had me to bring his book.
④ My sister helped me choose the bag.
⑤ I asked her not to make a lot of noise.

`빈출`

9 다음 중 보기의 밑줄 친 부분과 쓰임이 같은 것은?

| 보기 | I decided <u>to wear</u> my lucky red shirt to the big game. |

① She grew up <u>to be</u> a great pianist.
② The new machine is difficult <u>to use</u>.
③ He planned <u>to run</u> the marathon.
④ I am looking for someone <u>to help</u> me.
⑤ He must be foolish <u>to refuse</u> the offer.

10 다음 중 두 문장의 의미가 같지 <u>않은</u> 것은?

① No one could be seen on the street.
→ No one was to be seen on the street.

② You must finish this project by Sunday.
→ You are to finish this project by Sunday.

③ It seems that he waited for a long time.
→ He seems to wait for a long time.

④ He went on a diet to fit into the jeans.
→ He went on a diet in order to fit into the jeans.

⑤ He is so tall that he can reach the ceiling.
→ He is tall enough to reach the ceiling.

11 다음 중 영어를 우리말로 <u>잘못</u> 옮긴 것은?

① We are to leave Paris tonight.
→ 우리는 오늘 밤에 파리를 떠날 예정이다.

② He hasn't decided where to go.
→ 그는 어디로 갈지 정하지 않았다.

③ It can be unfortunate to win the lottery.
→ 복권에 당첨되는 것이 불행할 수도 있다.

④ I went to the store to buy some milk.
→ 나는 우유를 좀 사기 위해 상점에 갔다.

⑤ She is too young to watch this movie.
→ 그녀는 이 영화를 보기에 충분히 어리다.

서술형

12 두 문장의 의미가 같도록 빈칸에 알맞은 말을 쓰시오.

It seems that he got lost on the way.
→ He seems _____ lost on the way.

13 다음 중 밑줄 친 부분을 <u>잘못</u> 고친 것은?

① My mom let me <u>played</u> games online.
→ play

② She got me <u>bringing</u> her a magazine.
→ bring

③ I heard two men <u>to fight</u> outside.
→ fight

④ I'll help you <u>moving</u> the chair.
→ move

⑤ The rain made me <u>felt</u> sad.
→ feel

서술형

[14-16] ( ) 안의 말을 이용하여 문장을 완성하시오.

14 She heard her son _____ in the room. (sing)

15 She had her secretary _____ a table at a restaurant. (reserve)

16 The dog behaves badly, so it needs _____. (train)

[17-18] 다음 중 밑줄 친 부분이 어법상 옳은 것을 고르시오.

17 ① She refused <u>to received</u> the prize.

② My computer needed <u>to repair</u>.

③ He was <u>so shy to ask</u> her out.

④ I am lucky <u>to have been given</u> the offer.

⑤ He is <u>enough well</u> to leave the hospital.

18
① There aren't enough seats to sit.
② The brave boy grew up being a soldier.
③ Do you know how to playing chess?
④ He found it hard to make new friends.
⑤ He went to the cafeteria have a snack.

22 다음 중 빈칸에 for를 쓸 수 없는 것은?
① It's necessary _____ him to see a dentist.
② It's important _____ me to learn English.
③ It's common _____ babies to cry often.
④ It's generous _____ him to share his food.
⑤ It's dangerous _____ children to play with knives.

서술형

[19-21] 우리말과 일치하도록 ( ) 안의 말을 이용하여 문장을 완성하시오.

19 마침내 아버지는 내가 휴대 전화를 갖는 것을 허락하셨다. (let, have)

→ Finally, my father _____ _____ _____ a cell phone.

서술형

[23-25] 우리말과 일치하도록 ( ) 안에 주어진 단어를 바르게 배열하시오.

23 그를 농구로 이기는 것은 내게 불가능하다.
(impossible, me, beat, him, is, for, it, to)

→ _____ at basketball.

20 내 상사는 어렸을 때 가난했던 것 같다.
(seem, be, poor)

→ My boss _____ _____ _____ _____ _____ when he was young.

24 그 식당은 큰 파티를 열 수 있을 정도로 충분히 넓다.
(hold, to, the, enough, large, restaurant, is)

→ _____ a big party.

21 그 물은 너무 뜨거워서 목욕할 수 없다.
(hot, take a bath)

→ The water is _____ _____ _____ _____ _____ _____ in.

25 엄마는 나에게 잠자는 개를 건들지 말라고 말씀하셨다.
(me, not, touch, Mom, told, to)

→ _____ the sleeping dog.

26 다음 중 어법상 <u>틀린</u> 것을 모두 고르면?

① It was nice to meet old friends.
② It is not easy for me talk first.
③ Dad got me eat more vegetables.
④ I found it very difficult to exercise every day.
⑤ The leaders of the countries are to meet next week.

27 다음 중 어법상 옳은 것으로 바르게 짝지어진 것은?

> a. The baby seems to be very happy.
> b. He didn't know what to say for a moment.
> c. She helped children crossing the road safely.
> d. It was rude of you laugh at her when she made a mistake.
> e. Jay seems to have studied hard last night.

① a, b, c   ② a, b, e
③ a, c, e   ④ b, c, d
⑤ b, d, e

28 다음 중 어법상 옳은 것의 개수는?

> • I heard Ava to shout at her friend.
> • I stopped by a market to buy a drink.
> • This movie is too violent for you watch.
> • Our teacher wanted us to bring a family photo.
> • I hoped to be chosen as a member of the soccer team.

① 1개   ② 2개   ③ 3개
④ 4개   ⑤ 5개

[29-31] 밑줄 친 부분이 어법상 옳은지 판단하고, 틀리면 바르게 고치시오.

29 I didn't expect <u>be asked</u> about my family in the interview.

(O / X) _____

30 My parents made me <u>to decide</u> what I wanted to do for summer vacation.

(O / X) _____

31 <u>To make a long story short</u>, they got married and had a son.

(O / X) _____

[32-33] 어법상 <u>틀린</u> 부분을 찾아 바르게 고치시오.

32 Mom is happy to have a new vacuum cleaner. It is very convenient using. (1개)

33 I went to the beach with my friends today. The weather was enough warm to swim. We had a great time and promised come back again. (2개)

LET'S REVIEW

주요 예문을 다시 한번 확인하고, 우리말과 일치하도록 빈칸을 채우시오.

- Tony decided **to tell** the truth to his parents. Tony는 그의 부모님께 사실을 말하기로 결심했다. **Unit 01 - A**

- **It** is exciting [1]_____ to new places. 새로운 장소들을 여행하는 것은 신이 난다. **Unit 01 - B**

- He showed me [2]_____ the robot vacuum cleaner.
  그는 나에게 로봇 진공청소기를 어떻게 사용하는지를 보여주었다. **Unit 01 - C**

- Winter is the best time **to go** on a safari in Africa.
  겨울은 아프리카에 있는 사파리로 가기에 가장 좋은 시기이다. **Unit 02 - A**

- I eat breakfast **to stay** healthy. 나는 건강을 유지하기 위해 아침을 먹는다. **Unit 02 - B**

- It is difficult [3]_____ to wake up early. 일찍 일어나는 것은 나에게 어렵다. **Unit 03 - A**

- It was kind [4]_____ to give us a ride to the airport.
  그가 우리를 공항에 태워다 준 것은 친절했다. **Unit 03 - A**

- Ron seems [5]_____ rich. Ron은 부자였던 것처럼 보인다. **Unit 03 - B**

- The actor didn't expect **to be given** the award. 그 배우는 그 상을 받을 것을 예상하지 못했다. **Unit 03 - C**

- I want you [6]_____ my question honestly.
  나는 네가 내 질문에 정직하게 대답하길 원한다. **Unit 04 - A**

- My teacher made us [7]_____ about our future job.
  우리 선생님은 우리가 우리의 미래 직업에 대해 생각하도록 하셨다. **Unit 04 - B**

- She is [8]_____ **to travel** abroad alone.
  그녀는 너무 어려서 혼자 해외로 여행을 갈 수 없다. **Unit 05 - A**

- [9]_____, the lights went out. 설상가상으로, 전등이 나갔다. **Unit 05 - B**

Answers

[1] to travel   [2] how to use / how I should use   [3] for me   [4] of him   [5] to have been
[6] to answer   [7] think   [8] too young   [9] To make matters worse

ESSENTIAL RULES OF
ENGLISH GRAMMAR

CHAPTER
05

동명사

동명사는 v-ing 형태로 문장에서 명사
역할을 한다.

01 동명사의 역할

A

동명사의 역할: 문장에서 주어, 보어, 목적어 역할을 한다.

Learning languages takes time and effort. 〈주어〉

One of my hobbies is **shopping** online. 〈보어〉

Subin enjoys **watching** American dramas. 〈동사의 목적어〉

The girl is afraid of **talking** to strangers. 〈전치사의 목적어〉

ⓘ 동명사의 부정은 동명사 바로 앞에 not을 붙인다.

My boss thought about **not attending** the meeting.

B

동명사의 의미상의 주어

동명사의 주어가 문장의 주어와 다르거나 일반인이 아닌 경우 동명사 앞에 소유격이나 목적격을 써서 동명사의 행위 주체를 나타낸다.

Do you mind **my[me]** turning off the TV? 〈끄는 사람은 'I'〉

cf. Do you mind turning off the TV? 〈끄는 사람은 'you'〉

C

동명사의 시제

1 단순형(v-ing): 동명사의 시제가 문장의 시제와 같을 때 쓴다.

David is good at **repairing** electrical goods.

2 완료형(having v-ed): 동명사의 시제가 문장의 시제보다 앞설 때 쓴다. (단순형을 쓰기도 한다.)

I am sorry for **having lost[losing]** your science textbook.

D

동명사의 수동태

1 단순형 수동태(being v-ed): 동명사가 수동의 의미이고, 동명사의 시제가 문장의 시제와 같을 때 쓴다.

I don't like **being ignored**.

2 완료형 수동태(having been v-ed): 동명사가 수동의 의미이고, 동명사의 시제가 문장의 시제보다 앞설 때 쓴다. (단순형 수동태를 쓰기도 한다.)

The thief is afraid of **having been seen[being seen]**.

CHECK UP 빈칸에 알맞은 말을 고르시오.

1 _____ is one of the best kinds of exercise.

ⓐ Swim ⓑ Swimming ⓒ To swimming

2 He was angry about _____ being late again.

ⓐ she ⓑ her ⓒ for her

3 Peter didn't mind _____ waiting for an hour.

ⓐ keep ⓑ to keep ⓒ being kept

PRACTICE

Answer Key p.8

STEP 1

( ) 안에서 알맞은 말을 고르시오.

1 (Drink, Drinking) enough water is good for your skin.

2 We didn't mind (he, his) joining our music club.

3 My mom loves (drinking, having drunk) coffee every morning.

4 He regrets (telling not, not telling) the truth.

5 He didn't like (elected, being elected) class president.

STEP 2

( ) 안의 말을 이용하여 문장을 완성하시오.

1 I am happy about _____ to the party. (invite)

2 _____ too many sweets is not good for your health. (eat)

3 The kids were excited about _____ their uncle's house. (visit)

4 I am sorry for _____ my promise. (not, keep)

STEP 3

두 문장의 의미가 같도록 빈칸에 알맞은 말을 쓰시오.

1 I am sorry that I missed your baseball game.

→ I am sorry for _____ _____ your baseball game.

2 Would you mind if I closed the door?

→ Would you mind _____ _____ the door?

3 He is proud that he is involved in the dance club.

→ He is proud of _____ _____ in the dance club.

STEP 4

우리말과 일치하도록 ( ) 안의 말을 이용하여 문장을 완성하시오.

1 살을 빼는 것은 내가 생각했던 것보다 더 어려웠다. (lose, weight)

→ _____ _____ _____ more difficult than I thought.

2 나는 내 고향에 돌아가지 않을 생각이다. (go)

→ I am thinking of _____ _____ back to my hometown.

3 우리는 그가 아파서 걱정했다. (be, sick)

→ We were worried about _____ _____ _____.

4 그녀는 무례한 대접을 받았던 것에 대해 항의했다. (treat)

→ She complained of _____ _____ _____ rudely.

UNIT 02 동명사 vs. to부정사

A 동명사만 목적어로 취하는 동사

enjoy, keep, mind, avoid, finish, quit, stop, give up, consider, suggest, deny, admit 등
We *enjoyed* **watching** the air show.

B to부정사만 목적어로 취하는 동사

want, wish, hope, expect, plan, refuse, promise, agree, decide 등
He *promised* **to give** me my money back.

C 동명사와 to부정사를 모두 목적어로 취하는 동사

1 의미 차이가 거의 없는 경우: like, love, hate, begin, start, continue 등
My sister *likes* **baking[to bake]** in her free time.

2 의미 차이가 있는 경우: forget, try, remember 등

- forget[remember] v-ing: ~한 것을 잊다[기억하다] 〈과거〉
- forget[remember] to-v: ~할 것을 잊다[기억하다] 〈미래〉
- try v-ing: (시험 삼아) ~해 보다
- try to-v: ~하려고 노력하다

I *forgot* **bringing** my cell phone. (→ I brought it.)
I *forgot* **to bring** my cell phone. (→ I didn't bring it.)
Try **typing** something in English.
She *tried* **to fix** the computer.

D 주요 동명사 구문

- go v-ing: ~하러 가다
- look forward to v-ing: ~하기를 고대하다
- on[upon] v-ing: ~하자마자
- be busy v-ing: ~하느라 바쁘다
- be worth v-ing: ~할 가치가 있다
- spend + 시간[돈] + (on) v-ing: ~하는 데 시간[돈]을 쓰다
- prevent[keep] + 목적어 + from v-ing: ~가 …하는 것을 막다
- feel like v-ing: ~하고 싶어지다
- be used to v-ing: ~하는 것에 익숙하다
- cannot help v-ing: ~하지 않을 수 없다
- There is no v-ing: ~할 수 없다

I *feel like* **going** to the movies tonight.

CHECK UP 빈칸에 알맞은 말을 고르시오.

1 Avoid _____ outside when the sun is too strong.
ⓐ stay ⓑ staying ⓒ to stay

2 The government plans _____ more trees.
ⓐ plant ⓑ planting ⓒ to plant

PRACTICE

🔍 Answer Key p.9

STEP 1

( ) 안에서 알맞은 말을 고르시오.

1 I gave up (running, to run) marathons.

2 He didn't remember (meeting, meet) me before.

3 I'm looking forward to (hear, hearing) about your trip.

4 In the end, Mike decided not (changing, to change) his plan.

5 Don't forget (turning, to turn) off the computer when you're not using it.

STEP 2

( ) 안의 말을 이용하여 문장을 완성하시오.

1 People began _____ about the service. (complain)

2 The actor refused _____ the question. (answer)

3 I still remember _____ you for the first time in Paris. (see)

4 He spends his weekends _____ TV. (watch)

STEP 3

빈칸에 알맞은 말을 보기에서 골라 적절한 형태로 바꿔 쓰시오.

보기	hear	become	listen	start

1 Harry enjoys _____ to different kinds of music.

2 She is considering _____ her own business.

3 I hope _____ a world-famous actor.

4 Upon _____ the news, I called my mom.

STEP 4

우리말과 일치하도록 ( ) 안의 말을 이용하여 문장을 완성하시오.

1 그녀는 온라인으로 옷을 사는 것을 그만두었다. (stop, buy)

→ She _____ _____ clothes online.

2 더 많은 과일과 채소를 먹으려고 노력해라. (try, eat)

→ _____ _____ _____ more fruit and vegetables.

3 그 도시는 언제라도 방문할 가치가 있다. (worth, visit)

→ The city _____ _____ _____ at any time.

4 그는 도서관에 그 책을 반납한 것을 기억한다. (remember, return)

→ He _____ _____ _____ to the library.

5 그는 폭설 때문에 외출할 수 없었다. (prevent, from)

→ The heavy snow _____ _____ _____ _____ out.

GRAMMAR FOR WRITING

A 우리말과 일치하도록 ( ) 안의 말을 이용하여 문장을 완성하시오.

1 나는 그가 내 생일 파티에 오는 것을 꺼리지 않는다. (mind, come)

→ _____ to my birthday party.

2 그녀는 그에게서 돈을 빌린 것을 기억한다. (remember, borrow money)

→ She _____ from him.

3 나는 식물에 물 준 것을 잊어버렸고, 다시 물을 주었다. (forget, water)

→ I _____ the plants and watered them again.

4 나는 그의 숙제를 돕기로 약속했다. (promise, help)

→ I _____ him with his homework.

5 그는 그의 실수에 대해 처벌받을까 봐 두려워했다. (be afraid of, punish)

→ He _____ for his mistakes.

6 그녀는 컴퓨터 게임 하는 것을 그만두었다. (stop, play)

→ She _____ computer games.

7 커피 대신에 차를 (시험 삼아) 마셔보는 게 어때? (try, drink tea)

→ Why don't you _____ instead of coffee?

B 우리말과 일치하도록 ( ) 안에 주어진 단어를 바르게 배열하시오.

1 그는 그녀의 농담에 웃지 않을 수 없었다. (laughing, could, not, at, help, he)

→ _____ her joke.

2 날씨를 예측하는 것은 어렵다. (weather, predicting, the, is, difficult)

→ _____ .

3 나는 숙제를 끝내지 못한 것이 걱정된다. (not, finishing, about, homework, worried, my)

→ I am _____ .

4 모든 사람들은 다른 이들에게 사랑받는 것을 좋아한다. (by, all, loved, like, being, people, others)

→ _____ .

5 그는 시험에서 부정행위를 했던 것을 부인했다. (denied, he, the, on, cheated, having, exam)

→ _____ .

6 Mark는 시골에서 양육된 것을 자랑스러워한다. (of, raised, having, been, proud, Mark, is)

→ _____ in the countryside.

C 주어진 문장과 의미가 통하도록 ( ) 안의 말을 이용하여 문장을 완성하시오.

1 I planned to visit David this morning. But I forgot.

→ I _____ David this morning. (forget, visit)

2 They usually go to the cinema on weekends. They enjoy it.

→ They _____ on weekends. (enjoy, go)

3 He asked her to take a walk with him. But she refused.

→ She _____ with him. (refuse, take)

4 She spends too much time chatting online. I am worried about it.

→ I am worried about _____ chatting online.
(she, spend)

5 If you take my advice, you won't make the same mistake again.

→ My advice will _____ you from _____ the same
mistake again. (prevent, make)

D 그림을 보고 상자 안의 말을 이용하여 기숙사 규칙에 관한 문장을 완성하시오.

1

sing or speak loudly

2

lock the door

3

have pets

Dormitory Rules

1 Please avoid _____. It can disturb others.

2 Remember _____, even if you leave your
room only for a few minutes.

3 _____ is not allowed. Do not bring any pets
into the dormitory.

REVIEW TEST

[1-4] 빈칸에 들어갈 알맞은 말을 고르시오.

1

Chris decided _____ his job. He will study marketing instead.

① quit　　　　　② will quit
③ quitting　　　④ to quit
⑤ to quitting

2

He avoided _____ a mistake by checking twice.

① make　　　　② making
③ to make　　　④ being made
⑤ to be made

3

Tim hates _____ like a child even though he is only ten.

① treat　　　　② treating
③ to treat　　　④ being treated
⑤ be treating

4

His illness kept him from _____ to work.

① go　　　　　② going
③ to go　　　　④ went
⑤ being gone

[5-6] 다음 중 어법상 옳은 것을 고르시오.

5　① Shop online is not always cheaper.
　② We avoided to stand in the sun.
　③ This is a video about he dancing.
　④ This play is worth to watch again.
　⑤ I'm sure of having left my purse here.

6　① Recycling can save our environment.
　② Kate is good at play the flute.
　③ Did you finish to use the bathroom?
　④ I felt like to eat something sweet.
　⑤ He hates calling a liar by his friends.

7　다음 우리말을 영어로 바르게 옮긴 것은?

우리는 에너지를 낭비하지 않도록 노력해야 한다.

① We must try wasting not energy.
② We must try not wasting energy.
③ We must not try to waste energy.
④ We must try not to waste energy.
⑤ We must try to waste not energy.

서술형

[8-9] 밑줄 친 부분을 어법에 맞게 고치시오.

8　I am proud of <u>she</u> winning first prize at the English speech contest.

9　Jenny was angry about <u>not inviting</u> to his birthday party.

[10-11] 빈칸에 들어갈 말로 알맞지 <u>않은</u> 것을 고르시오.

10

We _____ to keep the secret.

① hoped　　② planned
③ agreed　　④ promised
⑤ considered

11

He _____ visiting the museum.

① likes　　② enjoys
③ avoids　　④ wants
⑤ hates

[12-13] 다음 중 어법상 <u>틀린</u> 것을 고르시오.

12 ① He forgot meeting me at the party.
② He tried to eat less for dinner.
③ Remember calling me tomorrow.
④ She likes watching horror movies.
⑤ We went surfing last weekend.

13 ① He denied having taken my book.
② She is good at making me smile.
③ I'm angry about having been told lies.
④ I got tired of watching the same show.
⑤ He suggested changing not our plan.

[14-16] ( ) 안의 말을 이용하여 문장을 완성하시오.

14 I forgot _____ my smartphone this morning, so I couldn't answer your call. (bring)

15 I didn't feel well this morning. I felt like _____ in bed all morning. (stay)

16 Stop _____ games and do your homework. (play)

17 빈칸에 들어갈 말이 순서대로 바르게 짝지어진 것은?

· People expect _____ a lot of seafood here.
· Jonathan is not used _____ with chopsticks.

① eating – eating
② to eat – to eat
③ to eat – eating
④ eating – to eating
⑤ to eat – to eating

[18-19] 우리말과 일치하도록 ( ) 안에 주어진 단어를 바르게 배열하시오.

18 그는 내가 또 늦은 것에 화가 나 있다.
(late, my, angry, being, about, again)

→ He is _____ .

19 오랜 습관을 그만두는 것은 어렵다.
(old, habits, giving, difficult, is, up)

→ _____ .

20 우리말과 일치하도록 주어진 조건에 맞게 문장을 완성하시오.

그 남자는 그 돈을 훔쳤던 것을 부인했다.

〈조건〉 1. deny, steal, money를 이용할 것
2. 훔친 행위가 부인한 행위보다 앞서 일어났음을 명확히 표현할 것

→ The man _____ .

21 주어진 문장과 의미가 통하도록 빈칸에 알맞은 말을 쓰시오.

· He is sick.
· I am worried about it.

→ I am worried about _____ sick.

22 다음 중 밑줄 친 부분을 잘못 고친 것은?

① He promised be on time, but he was late.   → to be
② His album is worth buy. He sings well.
→ buying
③ I gave up study abroad because of my illness.   → studying
④ Do you mind turn down the volume?
→ to turn
⑤ She refused work overtime.
→ to work

[23-25] 우리말과 일치하도록 ( ) 안의 말을 이용하여 문장을 완성하시오.

23 그 도둑은 체포될까 봐 두려웠다.
(be afraid of, arrest)

→ The thief _____ .

24 오늘 밤 Elizabeth를 만날 것을 기억해라.
(remember, meet)

→ _____ Elizabeth tonight.

25 그것이 제대로 작동하지 않으면, (시험 삼아) 다른 방법을 사용해 보자. (try, use)

→ If it doesn't work, let's _____
_____ a different method.

26 다음 중 어법상 옳은 것을 모두 고르면?

① No one likes being laughed at.
② I was busy to clean the house.
③ I'd like to go swimming.
④ I spent all of my money buy a new computer.
⑤ Do you mind me ask you a few questions?

27 다음 중 어법상 옳은 것으로 바르게 짝지어진 것은?

> a. My sister is not used to ride a bike.
> b. I tried to finish the work on my own.
> c. I cannot help to have chocolates when I'm feeling down.
> d. Mom says washing the dishes is not difficult at all.
> e. Jim is still angry about having been made fun of by his classmates.

① a, b, c
② a, b, e
③ a, c, d
④ b, c, e
⑤ b, d, e

28 다음 중 어법상 옳은 것의 개수는?

> · I stopped worrying about my future.
> · Would you mind opening the window?
> · The bad weather prevented me from arriving on time.
> · I avoided to meet him because I had lost his favorite book.
> · Swimming is one of the best activities to do on a hot summer day.

① 1개
② 2개
③ 3개
④ 4개
⑤ 5개

[29-31] 밑줄 친 부분이 어법상 옳은지 판단하고, 틀리면 바르게 고치시오.

29 He suggested eating out tonight.

(O / X) _____

30 Lucy hoped receiving an invitation to the party.

(O / X) _____

31 I am looking forward to hear good news from you soon.

(O / X) _____

[32-33] 어법상 틀린 부분을 찾아 바르게 고치시오.

32 He forgot turning off the light when he went out. The light has been on all night. (1개)

33 The musical *Miss Saigon* is coming to Korea next week. It is a love story with beautiful songs and dances. I guarantee it is worth to see! (1개)

LET'S REVIEW

주요 예문을 다시 한번 확인하고, 우리말과 일치하도록 빈칸을 채우시오.

- **Learning** languages takes time and effort. 언어를 배우는 것은 시간과 노력이 든다.   **Unit 01 - A**

- Do you mind ¹_____ turning off the TV? 내가 TV를 꺼도 될까?   **Unit 01 - B**

- I am sorry for ²_____ your science textbook.
  네 과학 교과서를 잃어버려서 미안해.   **Unit 01 - C**

- I don't like ³_____. 나는 무시당하는 것을 좋아하지 않는다.   **Unit 01 - D**

- The thief is afraid of **having been seen**. 그 도둑은 목격되었을까 봐 두려워한다.   **Unit 01 - D**

- We enjoyed ⁴_____ the air show. 우리는 에어쇼 보는 것을 즐겼다.   **Unit 02 - A**

- He promised ⁵_____ me my money back.
  그는 나에게 내 돈을 돌려줄 것을 약속했다.   **Unit 02 - B**

- My sister likes **baking[to bake]** in her free time.
  내 여동생은 여가 시간에 빵 굽는 것을 좋아한다.   **Unit 02 - C**

- I forgot ⁶_____ my cell phone. 나는 내 휴대 전화를 가져온 것을 잊었다.   **Unit 02 - C**

- I forgot ⁷_____ my cell phone. 나는 내 휴대 전화를 가져올 것을 잊었다.   **Unit 02 - C**

- Try ⁸_____ something in English. 영어로 뭔가를 타이핑해 보아라.   **Unit 02 - C**

- She tried **to fix** the computer. 그녀는 컴퓨터를 고치려고 노력했다.   **Unit 02 - C**

- I feel like ⁹_____ to the movies tonight. 나는 오늘 밤에 영화를 보러 가고 싶다.   **Unit 02 - D**

Q Answers

¹ my[me]   ² having lost / losing   ³ being[to be] ignored   ⁴ watching   ⁵ to give   ⁶ bringing
⁷ to bring   ⁸ typing   ⁹ going

ESSENTIAL RULES OF
ENGLISH GRAMMAR

CHAPTER

06

분사

분사란 동사에 **-ing**나 **-ed**를 붙여
형용사처럼 쓰이는 말이다.

현재분사 vs. 과거분사

A 현재분사 vs. 과거분사

1 현재분사(v-ing): 능동(~하는)과 진행(~하고 있는)의 의미를 가진다.

Look at the **sleeping** baby. Isn't she cute?

2 과거분사(v-ed): 수동(~된)과 완료(~한)의 의미를 가진다.

Don't touch the **broken** glass.

B 분사의 역할

1 명사 수식: 보통 명사 앞에서 수식하나, 분사가 다른 어구와 함께 쓰여 길어질 경우 명사 뒤에서 수식한다.

The sitcom has an **interesting** story line. 〈명사 앞에서 수식〉

I got an email **written** in English. 〈명사 뒤에서 수식〉

2 보어 역할

She sat **watching** the TV show. 〈주격 보어〉

He heard his name **called** from a distance. 〈목적격 보어〉

3 동사구의 일부로 쓰인 분사

1) 진행형(be + v-ing): I was **reading** a comic book then.

2) 완료형(have[has, had] + v-ed): I have **seen** him before.

3) 수동태(be + v-ed): The furniture was **delivered** the next day.

C 감정을 느끼게 하는 v-ing vs. 감정을 느끼는 v-ed

- exciting(흥분하게 하는) – excited(흥분한)
- surprising(놀라게 하는) – surprised(놀란)
- boring(지루한) – bored(지루해하는)
- amusing(재미있는) – amused(재미를 느낀)
- satisfying(만족스러운) – satisfied(만족한)
- shocking(충격적인) – shocked(충격을 받은)

The soccer game was **exciting**.

I was **excited** during the soccer game.

 **CHECK UP** 빈칸에 알맞은 말을 고르시오.

1 He is planning to buy some _____ furniture.

ⓐ use   ⓑ using   ⓒ used

2 The kids sat _____ with some toys.

ⓐ play   ⓑ playing   ⓒ played

3 It was _____ news to me.

ⓐ shock   ⓑ shocking   ⓒ shocked

PRACTICE

🔍 Answer Key p.10

 STEP 1

( ) 안에서 알맞은 말을 고르시오.

1 She added some pork to the (boiling, boil) water.

2 They got into the boat (renting, rented) for their trip.

3 The baby lay (smiling, smiled) in the stroller.

4 Suddenly, I heard someone (shouting, shouted) outside.

STEP 2

( ) 안의 말을 이용하여 문장을 완성하시오.

1 The manager had the table _____ pink. (paint)

2 I was careful not to wake up the _____ dog. (sleep)

3 Mark knows a man _____ a Chinese restaurant. (run)

4 I felt _____ when I heard the news. (depress)

STEP 3

우리말과 일치하도록 보기에서 알맞은 말을 골라 적절한 형태로 바꿔 쓰시오.

보기	lock	amaze	bore

1 그 긴 회의에 모두가 지루해했다.

→ Everyone was _____ with the long meeting.

2 그 소년은 놀라운 재능을 가지고 있다.

→ The boy has an _____ talent.

3 우리는 잠긴 문을 열 열쇠가 필요하다.

→ We need a key to open the _____ door.

STEP 4

우리말과 일치하도록 ( ) 안의 말을 이용하여 문장을 완성하시오.

1 그는 나에게 패션에 관한 재미있는 책 한 권을 보내줬다. (interest)

→ He sent me _____ _____ _____ about fashion.

2 그녀는 클래식 음악에 관심이 있는 몇몇 사람을 만났다. (some people, interest)

→ She met _____ _____ _____ in classical music.

3 그는 수학 시험 결과에 실망한 것처럼 보였다. (look, disappoint)

→ He _____ _____ with his math exam results.

4 그들은 그들의 차가 눈에 덮여 있는 것을 발견했다. (cover)

→ They found _____ _____ _____ with snow.

UNIT 02 분사구문

「접속사 + 주어 + 동사」를 분사로 줄여 쓴 구문으로, 문맥에 따라 다양한 의미를 나타낸다.

Ⓐ 분사구문 만들기

부사절의 주어가 주절과 같을 때, 부사절의 접속사와 주어를 생략하고 동사를 v-ing 형태로 바꾼다.

Because I felt tired, I stayed at home all day.

→ **Feeling** tired, I stayed at home all day.

ⓘ 분사구문의 부정은 분사 앞에 not을 붙인다.
Not knowing Jamie's phone number, I couldn't call him.
(← As I didn't know ...)

Ⓑ 분사구문의 의미

1 시간: ~할 때(when, as), ~하는 동안(while), ~하고 나서(after)

Leaving your house, you should lock the door.

(← When you leave your house, you should lock the door.)

2 동시동작: ~하면서(as)

I ate popcorn **watching** the movie.

(← I ate popcorn as I watched the movie.)

3 이유: ~ 때문에(because, as, since)

Sitting at the back of the classroom, I couldn't hear the teacher well.

(← Because I sat at the back of the classroom, I couldn't hear the teacher well.)

4 조건: ~하면(if)

Turning right, you'll find the flower shop.

(← If you turn right, you'll find the flower shop.)

5 양보: ~이지만(though, although)

Although being old, my grandmother goes jogging every day.

(← Although she is old, my grandmother goes jogging every day.)

cf. 분사구문이 나타내는 뜻을 분명히 하기 위해 접속사를 밝히는 경우도 있다. 특히 양보의 분사구문은 접속사를 주로 남겨 둔다.

CHECK UP   빈칸에 알맞은 말을 고르시오.

1 _____ for the train, I dropped my cell phone.
ⓐ Rushing   ⓑ To rush   ⓒ Rushed

2 _____ any money, I couldn't buy the bag.
ⓐ Not have   ⓑ Having not   ⓒ Not having

3 _____ sick, I didn't go to the swimming pool.
ⓐ Be   ⓑ Being   ⓒ Been

PRACTICE

🔍 Answer Key p.10

STEP 1

( ) 안에서 알맞은 말을 고르시오.

1 (Feel, Feeling) cold, I put on a thick coat.

2 I read a magazine (waited, waiting) for my turn.

3 (Being not, Not being) rich, he couldn't buy a new car.

4 (Turning off, To turn off) the alarm, I went back to sleep.

STEP 2

밑줄 친 부분을 분사구문으로 바꿔 쓰시오.

1 <u>If you take this bus</u>, you'll get to city hall.

→ _____, you'll get to city hall.

2 <u>When he fell down the stairs</u>, he hurt his arm.

→ _____, he hurt his arm.

3 <u>As I didn't know what to buy</u>, I called my mom.

→ _____, I called my mom.

STEP 3

보기의 접속사를 이용하여, 밑줄 친 부분을 「접속사 + 주어 + 동사」의 형태로 바꿔 쓰시오. (단, 한 번씩만 쓸 것)

보기	because	while	if

1 <u>Turning left</u>, you'll find the bank on your right.

→ _____, you'll find the bank on your right.

2 <u>Traveling in Europe</u>, I met a lot of interesting people.

→ _____, I met a lot of interesting people.

3 <u>Not having enough time</u>, she couldn't eat breakfast.

→ _____, she couldn't eat breakfast.

STEP 4

우리말과 일치하도록 ( ) 안의 말을 이용하여 문장을 완성하시오.

1 커피를 마시면서 그녀는 소설을 읽었다. (coffee)

→ _____ _____, she read a novel.

2 배가 고파서 그는 닭 한 마리를 몇 분 만에 다 먹었다. (hungry)

→ _____, he ate a whole chicken in a few minutes.

3 저희 웹 사이트를 방문하시면, 더 많은 정보를 보실 수 있습니다. (visit, website)

→ _____ _____ _____, you can see more information.

4 그의 일을 마치지 못해서 그는 집에 갈 수 없었다. (finish, work)

→ _____ _____ _____, he couldn't go home.

여러 가지 분사구문

A 완료형 분사구문(having v-ed): 부사절의 시제가 주절의 시제보다 앞선 경우에 쓴다.

Having learned this before, I can explain it.

(← Because I learned this before, ...)

B 수동 분사구문(being[having been] v-ed): being이나 having been은 생략 가능하다.

(Being) Asked to make a speech, he became nervous.

(← Because he was asked to make a speech, ...)

(Having been) Bitten by that dog, I am afraid of it now.

(← Because I was bitten by that dog, ...)

C 주어가 있는 분사구문: 부사절의 주어가 주절의 주어와 다를 경우 분사구문을 만들 때 분사 앞에 주어를 남겨 둔다.

It being Christmas Eve, all the restaurants are full of people.

(← Because it is Christmas Eve, ...)

D 접속사를 생략하지 않은 분사구문: 의미를 분명히 하기 위해 접속사를 쓰기도 한다.

While answering the phone, I heard the doorbell ring.

E 숙어처럼 쓰이는 분사구문

- generally speaking: 일반적으로 말해서
- strictly speaking: 엄밀히 말해서
- frankly speaking: 솔직히 말해서
- considering: ~을 감안하면
- judging from: ~로 판단하건대
- speaking of: ~ 이야기가 나와서 말인데

Generally speaking, children don't like this kind of spicy food.

F with + (대)명사 + 분사: ~가 …한[된] 채로

She studies better **with music playing**.

With her arms crossed, she complained about the service.

CHECK UP 빈칸에 알맞은 말을 고르시오.

1 _____ in Paris, he can speak French fluently.

ⓐ Being lived　　ⓑ Having lived　　ⓒ Having been lived

2 _____ no lights, he couldn't see anything.

ⓐ Being　　　　ⓑ Having been　　ⓒ There being

PRACTICE

🔍 Answer Key p.10

 STEP 1

( ) 안에서 알맞은 말을 고르시오.

1 (Permitting weather, Weather permitting), we will go hiking.

2 (Judging, Judged) from her clothes, she must be an athlete.

3 (Accepting, Accepted) by the university, she was very happy.

STEP 2

밑줄 친 부분을 분사구문으로 바꿔 쓰시오.

1 <u>Since there is a lot of snow</u>, I won't drive my car.

→ _____, I won't drive my car.

2 <u>Because he was chosen to be the team captain</u>, he was excited.

→ _____, he was excited.

3 <u>As he was run over by a car</u>, he is in the hospital now.

→ _____, he is in the hospital now.

STEP 3

우리말과 일치하도록 밑줄 친 부분을 어법에 맞게 고치시오.

1 집에 혼자 남겨져서 내가 그 식물에 물을 주어야 했다.

→ <u>Leaving</u> home alone, I had to water the plant.

2 프로젝트를 끝낸 후, 그녀는 직장을 그만두었다.

→ After <u>finish</u> the project, she quit her job.

3 일반적으로 말해서 한국 음식은 건강하다.

→ <u>Generally speak</u>, Korean food is healthy.

4 나는 방에 불이 꺼진 채로 TV를 봤다.

→ I watched TV <u>with the lights turning off</u> in the room.

STEP 4

우리말과 일치하도록 ( ) 안의 말을 이용하여 문장을 완성하시오.

1 그의 나이를 감안하면 그는 매우 성숙하다. (consider, age)

→ _____ _____ _____, he is very mature.

2 그녀는 다리를 꼰 채 앉아 있었다. (with, cross)

→ She sat _____ _____ _____ _____.

3 그의 지갑을 잃어버렸기 때문에 그는 경찰서로 갔다. (lose)

→ _____ _____ his wallet, he went to the police station.

GRAMMAR FOR WRITING

A 우리말과 일치하도록 분사와 ( ) 안의 말을 이용하여 문장을 완성하시오.

1 끓는 물을 항상 조심해라. (boil)

→ Always be careful with _____.

2 그는 그 결과에 만족하지 않았다. (satisfy)

→ _____ with the results.

3 어젯밤 늦게까지 공부해서 나는 지금 졸리다. (study)

→ _____ late last night, I am sleepy now.

4 왼쪽으로 돌면, 너는 호텔 두 개를 발견할 것이다. (turn)

→ _____, you will find two hotels.

5 그는 그의 눈을 감은 채로 버스에 앉아 있었다. (with, close)

→ He was sitting on the bus _____.

6 돈이 전혀 없어서 나는 쇼핑하러 가지 않았다. (have, any money)

→ _____, I didn't go shopping.

7 큰 글자로 적혀 있어서 그 간판은 알아채기 쉽다. (write)

→ _____ in large letters, the sign is easy to notice.

B 우리말과 일치하도록 ( ) 안에 주어진 단어를 바르게 배열하시오.

1 Judy는 한 남자가 산책하는 것을 보았다. (a walk, saw, a, taking, man)

→ Judy _____.

2 날이 추워서 나는 히터를 켰다. (it, cold, I, being, turned)

→ _____ on the heater.

3 그의 억양으로 판단하건대 그는 영국 출신이다. (from, judging, his, accent)

→ _____, he is from England.

4 축구를 하다가 그는 부상당했다. (got, while, football, he, playing)

→ _____ injured.

5 그는 그의 아버지가 쓰신 이메일을 읽고 있다. (written, by, an, father, email, his)

→ He is reading _____.

6 숙제를 끝낸 뒤에 나는 영화를 보러 외출했다. (finished, my, out, homework, having, went, I)

→ _____ for a movie.

C 주어진 문맥과 일치하도록 ( ) 안의 말을 이용하여 빈칸에 알맞은 말을 쓰시오.

1 Ted got worse grades than he expected. (disappoint)

    a. Ted's grades were _____.

    b. Ted was _____ with his grades.

2 Mia is going to Hawaii next week. She thinks that it will be fun. (excite)

    a. Mia thinks it will be _____ to go to Hawaii.

    b. Mia is very _____ about going to Hawaii.

3 The musical has a funny story line. I laughed a lot while watching it. (amuse)

    a. I was _____ by the musical.

    b. The musical was _____ to me.

4 Emily often goes to the art gallery. She likes art. (interest)

    a. Emily is _____ in art.

    b. Art is _____ to Emily.

5 Nate watched a movie. He liked the ending. (satisfy)

    a. Nate was _____ with the ending.

    b. The ending was _____ to Nate.

D 그림을 보고 보기에서 알맞은 말을 골라 분사를 이용하여 문장을 완성하시오.

| 보기 | lie on the bed | play on a swing | his arms/fold |

1 The girl _____ _____ _____ _____ is my daughter.

2 _____ _____ _____ _____, Brad read a book.

3 The man sat on the sofa with _____ _____ _____.

REVIEW TEST

[1–5] 빈칸에 들어갈 알맞은 말을 고르시오.

1

Who is the boy _____ at you?

① wave
② waving
③ waved
④ being waved
⑤ having been waved

2

They were _____ at the election results.

① surprise
② surprising
③ surprised
④ to surprise
⑤ to surprising

3

The ending of the action movie was _____.

① shock
② shocking
③ shocked
④ to shock
⑤ to shocking

4

_____ an only child, he often feels lonely.

① Be
② Being
③ Been
④ To being
⑤ Having been

5

_____ the exam, Joanna took after-school classes.

① Fail
② Failed
③ To fail
④ Being failed
⑤ Having failed

빈출

[6–7] 밑줄 친 부분의 쓰임이 나머지 넷과 다른 것을 고르시오.

6 ① Don't touch the sleeping dog.
② She is writing an email to her friend.
③ His hobby is collecting stamps.
④ Do you know the girl standing over there?
⑤ I smelled something burning in the kitchen.

7 ① Being young, she is energetic.
② Being a good writer takes time.
③ Being excited, I talked too much.
④ Being ill, he didn't go to work.
⑤ Being tired, she couldn't clean the house.

[8–9] 다음 중 어법상 틀린 것을 고르시오.

8 ① He left the office with the light turned on.
② I know the woman wearing a red hat.
③ They were shocked by the news.
④ I saw a crying girl on the street.
⑤ She had her bike stealing yesterday.

9
① Having traveled many countries, he knows a lot about different cultures.
② Not having a job, he worries about money.
③ After finishing my homework, I ate dinner.
④ Strictly speaking, it is not your fault.
⑤ Having raised in a city, I don't know country life well.

10 다음 중 어법상 옳은 것은?
① James is interesting in cooking.
② I'll tell you some surprised news.
③ The man stood over there is my uncle.
④ I fixed my broken computer last week.
⑤ She was satisfying with the game scores.

서술형
[11-13] ( ) 안의 말을 이용하여 문장을 완성하시오.

11 With my car _____, I went into the store. (park)

12 She played the guitar _____ by her fans. (surround)

13 Do you know the boy _____ basketball with Liam? (play)

서술형
14 우리말과 일치하도록 어법상 틀린 부분을 찾아 바르게 고치시오.

> 그녀의 성격으로 판단하건대, 그녀는 꿈을 포기하지 않을 것이다.
> → Judged from her character, she will not give up her dream.

15 다음 중 보기의 밑줄 친 부분과 의미가 같은 것은?

보기	Not having eaten all day, he was very hungry.

① When he had eaten all day
② If he hadn't eaten all day
③ As he hadn't eaten all day
④ Because he had eaten all day
⑤ Though he hadn't eaten all day

서술형
[16-17] 밑줄 친 부분을 분사구문으로 바꿔 쓰시오.

16 Because I didn't know where to get a taxi, I went to the information desk.

→ _____,
I went to the information desk.

17 As he was given lots of homework, he has no time to watch TV tonight.

→ _____,
he has no time to watch TV tonight.

18 밑줄 친 부분을 「접속사 + 주어 + 동사」로 잘못 옮긴 것은?

① <u>Arriving at the museum</u>, I called Jason.
→ When I arrived at the museum

② <u>Having seen him once</u>, I know his face.
→ As I saw him once

③ <u>Placed in the fridge</u>, the water is cold.
→ Because it placed in the fridge

④ <u>Being generous</u>, he helped the poor.
→ Because he was generous

⑤ <u>Going straight</u>, you'll see the place.
→ If you go straight

22 빈칸에 들어갈 말이 순서대로 바르게 짝지어진 것은?

> · The lecture was really _____.
> · He was _____ during the class.

① bore – bore
② boring – boring
③ boring – bored
④ bored – boring
⑤ bored – bored

서술형

[19-21] 우리말과 일치하도록 ( ) 안의 말을 이용하여 문장을 완성하시오.

19 그 실수를 한 번 했기 때문에 나는 다시는 (그 실수를) 하지 않을 것이다. (make, mistake)

→ _____ _____ _____
_____ once, I won't make it
again.

서술형

[23-24] 우리말과 일치하도록 ( ) 안에 주어진 단어를 바르게 배열하시오.

23 밖에 주차되어 있는 빨간 차는 엄마의 것이다.
(car, the, outside, red, parked)

→ _____ is my
mom's.

24 나는 무엇인가가 내 다리를 때리는 것을 느꼈다.
(hitting, my, I, something, leg, felt)

→ _____ .

20 나는 그 식당이 그날 닫힌 것을 알게 되었다.
(find, restaurant, close)

→ I _____ _____ _____
_____ for the day.

서술형

25 두 문장이 같은 뜻이 되도록 주어진 조건에 맞게 문장을 완성하시오.

〈조건〉 1. 분사구문을 이용할 것
2. 분사구문이 5단어가 되도록 할 것

Because it was too cold outside, we
decided not to go mountain climbing.

→ _____ , we
decided not to go mountain climbing.

21 이 약을 먹으면 곧 나을 거야. (take, medicine)

→ _____ _____ _____ ,
you will get well soon.

26 다음 중 어법상 <u>틀린</u> 것을 모두 고르면?

① The results were disappointing to me.
② The rising sun gave us some warmth.
③ Be nervous, I made a terrible mistake.
④ When cleaning the house, you should open the window.
⑤ The kids run in the garden are my children.

27 다음 중 어법상 옳은 것으로 바르게 짝지어진 것은?

> a. I think this book is very amused.
> b. Listening to the radio, I checked my email.
> c. The shocking news was reported today.
> d. Have you ever seen the man talking to Jeremy?
> e. I want to see a picture taking during the event.

① a, b, c   ② a, c, d
③ b, c, d   ④ b, c, e
⑤ b, d, e

28 다음 중 어법상 옳은 것의 개수는?

> · Who is the girl waiting outside?
> · Being rich, he feels satisfied with his wealth.
> · It being dark, we decided to go back to the hotel.
> · Many critics said the movie was somewhat bored.
> · Knowing not his address, I couldn't send him the invitation.

① 1개   ② 2개   ③ 3개
④ 4개   ⑤ 5개

[29-31] 밑줄 친 부분이 어법상 옳은지 판단하고, <u>틀리면</u> 바르게 고치시오.

29 A bridge <u>connected</u> two towns is being built.

(O / X) _____

30 <u>Cooking</u> too long, the vegetables don't taste good.

(O / X) _____

31 <u>Having finishing</u> my homework, I played computer games.

(O / X) _____

[32-33] 어법상 <u>틀린</u> 부분을 찾아 바르게 고치시오.

32 I told a lie to my mom with my fingers crossing. (1개)

33 There was a big fire in the village. Many houses were damaging and several people died. Be asleep, they couldn't escape from the fire. (2개)

LET'S REVIEW

주요 예문을 다시 한번 확인하고, 우리말과 일치하도록 빈칸을 채우시오.

- Look at the ¹_____ baby. Isn't she cute? 자고 있는 아기를 봐. 귀엽지 않니? **Unit 01 - A**

- Don't touch the **broken** glass. 깨진 유리를 만지지 마. **Unit 01 - A**

- He heard his name ²_____ from a distance.
  그는 멀리서 그의 이름이 불리는 것을 들었다. **Unit 01 - B**

- I was ³_____ during the soccer game. 나는 축구 경기 동안 신이 났다. **Unit 01 - C**

- **Not** ⁴_____ Jamie's phone number, I couldn't call him.
  Jamie의 전화번호를 몰라서 나는 그에게 전화할 수 없었다. **Unit 02 - A**

- **Leaving** your house, you should lock the door. 집을 나설 때, 너는 문을 잠가야 한다. **Unit 02 - B**

- ⁵_____ this before, I can explain it.
  전에 이것을 배웠기 때문에 나는 이것을 설명할 수 있다. **Unit 03 - A**

- **Being asked** to make a speech, he became nervous.
  연설을 해달라는 요청을 받아서 그는 초조해졌다. **Unit 03 - B**

- ⁶_____ **bitten** by that dog, I am afraid of it now.
  그 개에게 물렸기 때문에 나는 이제 그것이 무섭다. **Unit 03 - B**

- ⁷_____ **being** Christmas Eve, all the restaurants are full of people.
  크리스마스이브여서 모든 식당들이 사람들로 가득하다. **Unit 03 - C**

- **While answering** the phone, I heard the doorbell ring.
  전화를 받는 동안, 나는 초인종이 울리는 것을 들었다. **Unit 03 - D**

- ⁸_____, children don't like this kind of spicy food.
  일반적으로 말해서, 아이들은 이런 종류의 매운 음식을 좋아하지 않는다. **Unit 03 - E**

- She studies better ⁹_____ **music playing**.
  그녀는 음악을 튼 채로 공부를 더 잘한다. **Unit 03 - F**

🔍 Answers

¹ sleeping   ² called   ³ excited   ⁴ knowing   ⁵ Having learned / Because I learned
⁶ Having been   ⁷ It   ⁸ Generally speaking   ⁹ with

CHAPTER
07

비교

비교는 형용사나 부사의 기본 형태에 '-er',
'-est'를 붙이거나 'more', 'most'를 앞에
붙여 대상의 성질, 상태, 수량, 정도를 비교
하는 것을 말한다.

UNIT 01 원급, 비교급, 최상급

A

as + 형용사/부사의 원급 + as: ~만큼 …한[하게]

The musical was **as good as** I expected.

My girlfriend likes video games **as much as** I do.

ⓘ A not as ~ as B: A는 B만큼 ~하지 않다

　　He is **not as rich as** his parents.

B

비교급 + than: ~보다 더 …한[하게]

비교급 형태: 보통 원급에 -(e)r을 붙이고, 2음절 단어 중 -ful, -less, -ous 등으로 끝나는 것과 3음절 이상의 단어 앞에는 more를 붙인다.

Adrian is **taller than** his older brother.

Words are **more powerful than** a sword.

ⓘ much, even, far, a lot 등은 비교급 앞에서 '훨씬'의 의미로 쓰여 비교급을 강조한다.

　　The students are **much** *smarter* than I thought.

C

the + 최상급 + in[of]: ~에서 가장 …한[하게]

최상급 형태: 보통 원급에 -(e)st를 붙이고, 2음절 단어 중 -ful, -less, -ous 등으로 끝나는 것과 3음절 이상의 단어 앞에는 most를 붙인다.

It is **the most popular** song **in** Korea. <in + 장소나 범위를 나타내는 단수명사>

I am **the oldest** (girl) **of** all my cousins. <of + 비교의 대상이 되는 명사>

ⓘ the + 최상급 + (that +) 주어 + have ever v-ed: 지금까지 ~한 것 중 가장 …한

　　She is **the smartest** girl (**that**) **I have ever met**.

빈칸에 알맞은 말을 고르시오.

1 The actor is not as _____ as his father.

　　ⓐ famous　　　　　ⓑ more famous　　　　　ⓒ most famous

2 Tomorrow I will go to school _____ than usual.

　　ⓐ early　　　　　ⓑ earlier　　　　　ⓒ earliest

3 This hotel is _____ cheaper than that one.

　　ⓐ much　　　　　ⓑ many　　　　　ⓒ very

4 She is the _____ of all our group members.

　　ⓐ popular　　　　　ⓑ more popular　　　　　ⓒ most popular

PRACTICE

🔍 Answer Key p·11

 STEP 1

( ) 안에서 알맞은 말을 고르시오.

1 This sofa is as (soft, softer) as that one.

2 The street was (very, even) more crowded than usual.

3 My sister spends (more, most) money shopping than me.

4 This is the (more boring, most boring) book I've ever read.

STEP 2

밑줄 친 부분을 어법에 맞게 고치시오.

1 James is <u>careful than</u> his twin brother.

2 The exhibition was <u>so</u> better than I expected.

3 Tiffany is <u>the younger</u> girl in our dance club.

4 The question was <u>as not difficult</u> as I thought.

STEP 3

주어진 문장과 의미가 통하도록 ( ) 안의 말을 이용하여 빈칸에 알맞은 말을 쓰시오.

1 The red box is 10 kg. The green box is 12 kg. (heavy)

→ The red box is _____ _____ _____ as the green box.

2 The T-shirt is $20. The silk blouse is $30. (expensive)

→ The silk blouse is _____ _____ _____ the T-shirt.

3 Mina can lift the 40 kg weight. Karen can lift the 35 kg weight. Helen can lift the 50 kg weight. (strong)

→ Helen is _____ _____ _____ the three.

STEP 4

우리말과 일치하도록 ( ) 안의 말을 이용하여 문장을 완성하시오.

1 나는 그녀만큼 많은 책을 읽지는 않는다. (many)

→ I don't read _____ _____ _____ _____ she does.

2 그녀의 가방은 내 것보다 훨씬 더 무겁다. (far, heavy)

→ Her bag is _____ _____ _____ mine.

3 나는 바지가 치마보다 더 편하다고 생각한다. (comfortable)

→ I think pants are _____ _____ _____ a skirt.

4 세계에서 가장 큰 도시는 어디입니까? (big)

→ What is _____ _____ _____ _____ the world?

5 그것은 내가 지금까지 본 것 중 가장 무서운 영화이다. (scary, movie)

→ That is _____ _____ _____ _____

_____ _____ .

여러 가지 비교구문

A 배수사 + as + 원급 + as: ~의 몇 배로 …한[하게](= 배수사 + 비교급 + than)

This pen is **three times as cheap as** that one.

(= This pen is **three times cheaper than** that one.)

B as + 원급 + as possible: 가능한 한 ~한[하게](= as + 원급 + as + 주어 + can)

I'll be back **as soon as possible**.

(= I'll be back **as soon as I can**.)

C 비교급 + and + 비교급: 점점 더 ~한[하게]

Sadly, his condition is getting **worse and worse**.

The reality show is getting **more and more interesting**.

D the + 비교급, the + 비교급: 더 ~할수록 더 …하다

The more one has, **the more** one wants.

E one of the + 최상급 + 복수명사: 가장 ~한 … 중 하나

Health is **one of the most important things** in life.

F 원급과 비교급을 이용한 최상급 표현

Mount Everest is **the highest** mountain in the world. 〈the + 최상급〉

→ Mount Everest is **higher than any other** mountain in the world.
  〈비교급 + than any other + 단수명사〉

→ **No** (**other**) mountain in the world is **as high as** Mount Everest.
  〈부정 주어 ~ as + 원급 + as〉

→ **No** (**other**) mountain in the world is **higher than** Mount Everest.
  〈부정 주어 ~ 비교급 + than〉

CHECK UP 빈칸에 알맞은 말을 고르시오.

1 The black bag is _____ as expensive as the white one.

ⓐ three   ⓑ three times   ⓒ third

2 He drove _____.

ⓐ fast and fast   ⓑ fast and faster   ⓒ faster and faster

3 The higher I went up the mountain, _____ the air was.

ⓐ the fresh   ⓑ the fresher   ⓒ the freshest

4 Einstein is one of the _____ scientists in history.

ⓐ famous   ⓑ more famous   ⓒ most famous

PRACTICE

Answer Key p.12

STEP 1

( ) 안에서 알맞은 말을 고르시오.

1 He eats (two, twice) as much as his sister.

2 London is one of the biggest (city, cities) in Europe.

3 The older the actor gets, (the good, the better) he looks.

4 (Many and many, More and more) people gathered in the square.

5 You should leave here (as early as can, as early as possible).

STEP 2

두 문장의 의미가 같도록 빈칸에 알맞은 말을 쓰시오.

1 He pushed the button as hard as he could.

→ He pushed the button _____.

2 As you practice more, you'll be able to dance better.

→ _____ you practice, _____ you'll be able to dance.

3 He is the bravest man in our town.

→ He is _____ in our town.

STEP 3

보기의 문장과 의미가 같도록 빈칸에 알맞은 말을 쓰시오.

보기	He is the funniest boy in his class.

1 He is _____ _____ _____ _____ in his class.

2 No other boy in his class is _____ _____ _____ him.

3 No other boy in his class is _____ _____ him.

STEP 4

우리말과 일치하도록 ( ) 안의 말을 이용하여 문장을 완성하시오.

1 내 배낭은 그녀의 것보다 세 배 더 무겁다. (heavy)

→ My backpack is _____ _____ _____ _____ hers.

2 더 자면 잘수록 나는 더 피곤했다. (much, tired)

→ _____ _____ I slept, _____ _____ _____ I was.

3 그 드라마는 점점 더 흥미진진해지고 있다. (exciting)

→ The drama is getting _____ _____ _____.

4 불국사는 한국에서 가장 큰 절 중 하나이다. (big, temple)

→ Bulguksa is _____ _____ _____ _____ _____ in Korea.

GRAMMAR FOR WRITING

A 우리말과 일치하도록 ( ) 안의 말을 이용하여 문장을 완성하시오.

1 KTX는 한국에서 다른 어느 기차보다 더 빠르다. (fast, other, train)

→ The KTX is _____ in Korea.

2 더 많이 연습할수록 너는 피아노를 더 잘 연주하게 될 것이다. (much, good)

→ _____ you practice, _____ you will play the piano.

3 가능한 한 빨리 그 책을 내게 보내라. (soon, possible)

→ Send me the book _____.

4 그 잡지는 평소보다 세 배 더 두껍다. (thick)

→ The magazine is _____ usual.

5 권투는 세상에서 가장 위험한 스포츠 중 하나이다. (dangerous, sport)

→ Boxing is _____ in the world.

6 1월은 일 년 중 가장 추운 달이다. (cold, month)

→ January is _____ the year.

7 Freddie는 점점 더 자신감 있어졌다. (confident)

→ Freddie became _____.

B 우리말과 일치하도록 ( ) 안에 주어진 단어를 바르게 배열하시오.

1 그는 나만큼이나 낚시하러 가는 것을 좋아한다. (as, I, do, fishing, go, much, as)

→ He loves to _____.

2 그 호텔은 우리 집만큼 편하지 않았다. (home, my, hotel, comfortable, not, as, the, was, as)

→ _____.

3 우리 고양이가 점점 더 무거워지고 있다. (getting, heavier, cat, is, and, my, heavier)

→ _____.

4 그 노트북 컴퓨터는 내가 생각했던 것보다 훨씬 더 쌌다.
(a, thought, cheaper, than, laptop, was, the, lot, I)

→ _____.

5 그의 학교의 어느 소년도 준호보다 더 빨리 달리지 않는다.
(boy, in, than, Junho, no, runs, his, faster, school)

→ _____.

6 Brown 선생님은 내가 만난 선생님 중 가장 재미있는 분이시다.
(I, have, met, the, ever, teacher, funniest)

→ Mr. Brown is _____.

C 주어진 문장과 의미가 같도록 빈칸에 알맞은 말을 쓰시오.

1 This question is not as difficult as that one.

→ That question is _____ than this one.

2 Your hair is three times longer than mine.

→ Your hair is _____ as mine.

3 Monday is the busiest day of the week for me.

→ Monday is _____ than _____ of the week for me.

→ No other day of the week is _____ as Monday for me.

→ No other day of the week is _____ than Monday for me.

4 Eric's dog is the largest dog in my neighborhood.

→ Eric's dog is _____ than _____ in my neighborhood.

→ _____ in my neighborhood is _____ as Eric's dog.

→ _____ in my neighborhood is _____ than Eric's dog.

D 세 야구 선수의 프로필을 보고 ( ) 안의 말을 이용하여 문장을 완성하시오.

Age: 18
Height(cm): 183
Weight(kg): 83
Ball Speed(km/h): 150

Liam

Age: 17
Height(cm):185
Weight(kg): 79
Ball Speed(km/h): 144

Noah

Age: 16
Height(cm):178
Weight(kg): 83
Ball Speed(km/h): 142

Henry

1 Liam is _____ Henry. (heavy)

2 Liam is _____ pitcher of the three. (fast)

3 Noah is _____ player. (light, other)

4 No other player is _____ Henry. (short)

5 Noah is older than Henry, but _____ Liam. (young)

6 No other player is _____ Noah. (tall)

[1–5] 빈칸에 들어갈 알맞은 말을 고르시오.

1

Peter speaks as _____ as I do.

① slowly
② more slowly
③ most slowly
④ the more slowly
⑤ the most slowly

2

Angel Falls is _____ waterfall in the world.

① tall
② taller
③ tallest
④ the taller
⑤ the tallest

3

The higher the price, _____ the service.

① good
② better
③ best
④ the better
⑤ the best

4

No student in our class is _____ than Joan.

① intelligent
② intelligenter
③ intelligentest
④ more intelligent
⑤ most intelligent

5

This theater is _____ as big as that one.

① five
② fifth
③ the fifth
④ five time
⑤ five times

[6–7] 다음 중 어법상 틀린 것을 고르시오.

6
① He sleeps so more than his wife.
② He is nicer than any other boy.
③ No other singer is as good as her.
④ He speaks English better than me.
⑤ February is the shortest month of the year.

7
① It is getting warmer and warmer.
② Rebecca walked as quietly as possible.
③ The earlier you go to bed, the earlier you'll get up.
④ He is one of the closest friend of mine in school.
⑤ It is the most boring play I've ever watched.

빈출

8 표의 내용과 일치하지 않는 것은?

	Ethan	Oliver	Logan
Age	14	16	16
Height	165 cm	168 cm	170 cm
Weight	60 kg	68 kg	63 kg

① Ethan is younger than Oliver.
② Logan is the tallest.
③ Oliver is not as tall as Ethan.
④ Logan is heavier than Ethan.
⑤ Oliver is as old as Logan.

9 다음 중 어법상 옳은 것은?

① Her hair is three as long as yours.
② The movie is getting bad and bad.
③ It is the nicest car I've ever driven.
④ She was very smarter than I thought.
⑤ Yesterday was one of the luckiest day of my life.

10 다음 중 밑줄 친 부분을 잘못 고친 것은?

① Her hands are as smaller as a child's.
→ small

② His illness was so more serious than I thought. → far

③ The snow is getting heavy and heavy.
→ heavy and heavier

④ Who is most popular singer in Cuba?
→ the most popular

⑤ He bought three as much food as I did. → three times

서술형 빈출
[11-13] 두 문장의 의미가 같도록 빈칸에 알맞은 말을 쓰시오.

11 No girl in the world is as beautiful as my girlfriend.

→ My girlfriend is _____ _____
_____ girl in the world.

12 When you pay more, you get more.

→ _____ _____ you pay,
_____ _____ you get.

13 She walked as quietly as she could.

→ She walked as quietly as _____.

14 빈칸에 들어갈 말로 알맞지 않은 것은?

| The roller coaster was _____ scarier than I expected. |

① much   ② far
③ even   ④ very
⑤ a lot

서술형
[15-16] 주어진 문장과 의미가 통하도록 ( ) 안의 말을 이용하여 문장을 완성하시오.

15
· Julie runs 100 m in fifteen seconds.
· Amy runs 100 m in eighteen seconds.

→ Amy doesn't run _____ _____
_____ Julie. (fast)

16
· Keeran gets up at 7:00 a.m.
· Sam gets up at 6:30 a.m.
· Aiden gets up at 7:10 a.m.

→ Sam gets up _____ _____
any of the other boys. (early)

17 다음 중 어느 빈칸에도 들어갈 수 없는 것은?

| · Ron spends three times ⓐ money than Jim.
· They are the ⓑ comfortable jeans in my closet.
· Incheon Bridge is ⓒ longest bridge ⓓ Korea. |

① in   ② as
③ the   ④ more
⑤ most

18 다음 우리말을 영어로 잘못 옮긴 것은?

> 나에게는 나의 가족이 가장 중요하다.

① My family is the most important thing to me.
② Nothing is as important to me as my family.
③ Nothing is not as important as my family to me.
④ Nothing is more important to me than my family.
⑤ My family is more important to me than any other thing.

22 다음 중 두 문장의 의미가 같지 않은 것은?

① I'll call you as often as possible.
　→ I'll call you as often as I can.
② My dog is not as heavy as yours.
　→ My dog is heavier than yours.
③ No girl in our club is as kind as her.
　→ No girl in our club is kinder than her.
④ The Nile is the longest river in the world.
　→ The Nile is longer than any other river in the world.
⑤ My dad is the best dad in the world.
　→ My dad is better than any other dad in the world.

서술형

[19-21] 우리말과 일치하도록 ( ) 안의 말을 이용하여 문장을 완성하시오.

19 오늘은 일 년 중 가장 더운 날 중 하나이다. (hot)

→ Today is ＿＿＿＿＿＿＿＿＿＿
of the year.

서술형

[23-25] 우리말과 일치하도록 ( ) 안에 주어진 단어를 바르게 배열하시오.

23 그녀는 그 일을 가능한 한 빨리 끝내려고 노력했다.
(possible, work, as, as, finish, the, soon)

→ She tried to ＿＿＿＿＿＿＿＿＿＿
＿＿＿＿＿＿＿＿＿＿＿＿＿ .

20 스마트폰은 점점 더 유용해지고 있다. (useful)

→ Smartphones are getting ＿＿＿＿＿
＿＿＿＿＿＿＿＿＿＿＿＿＿ .

24 이것은 내가 지금껏 먹어본 것 중 가장 맛있는 케이크이다. (I, most, had, have, ever, delicious, cake, the)

→ This is ＿＿＿＿＿＿＿＿＿＿
＿＿＿＿＿＿＿＿＿＿＿＿＿ .

21 그 일은 내가 생각했던 것보다 더욱 더 힘들었다.
(even, hard)

→ The work was ＿＿＿＿＿＿＿＿
I thought.

25 더 연습하면 할수록 너는 노래를 더 잘할 것이다.
(the, better, more, practice, the, you)

→ ＿＿＿＿＿＿＿＿＿＿＿＿＿
you'll sing.

26 다음 중 어법상 틀린 것을 모두 고르면?

① He is better in math than me.

② I am much smart than my brother.

③ This movie is as not exciting as the last one.

④ Please let me know the result as soon as possible.

⑤ The younger you are, the more easy you learn a foreign language.

27 다음 중 어법상 옳은 것으로 바르게 짝지어진 것은?

a. My sister is the tallest in her class.

b. Her bag is twice as bigger as mine.

c. The older you get, the wiser you become.

d. My new laptop is very faster than the old one.

e. English grammar is not as difficult as Spanish grammar.

① a, b, c　　　② a, b, e

③ a, c, e　　　④ b, c, d

⑤ b, c, e

고난도

28 다음 중 어법상 옳은 것의 개수는?

• Mia looks most happy than last week.

• It is the sweetest candy I've ever had.

• The sooner you start, the sooner you finish.

• He always complains that he is not as lucky as others.

• No other student in our class is as funnier as Andrew.

① 1개　　② 2개　　③ 3개

④ 4개　　⑤ 5개

서술형

[29-31] 밑줄 친 부분이 어법상 옳은지 판단하고, 틀리면 바르게 고치시오.

29 Jamie is <u>one of the famousest teenage actors</u> in the world.

(O / X) _____

30 This hotel is <u>twice as expensive as the</u> other one.

(O / X) _____

31 I like seafood pasta <u>best than any other dish</u> in the restaurant.

(O / X) _____

서술형　고난도

[32-33] 어법상 틀린 부분을 찾아 바르게 고치시오.

32 One of the kittens is getting bigger as bigger. Now, it is twice as biggest as the others. (2개)

33 Christmas is coming. The downtown is most crowded than usual. People go shopping to buy Christmas presents and celebrate the holiday. (1개)

LET'S REVIEW

주요 예문을 다시 한번 확인하고, 우리말과 일치하도록 빈칸을 채우시오.

- The musical was **as good as** I expected. 그 뮤지컬은 내가 기대했던 만큼 훌륭했다. **Unit 01 - A**

- Adrian is ¹_____ his older brother. Adrian은 그의 형보다 키가 더 크다. **Unit 01 - B**

- Words are ²_____ a sword. 말은 칼보다 더 강력하다. **Unit 01 - B**

- It is ³_____ **popular** song **in** Korea. 그것은 한국에서 가장 인기 있는 노래이다. **Unit 01 - C**

- This pen is ⁴_____ **as cheap as** that one. 이 펜은 저것보다 세 배 더 싸다. **Unit 02 - A**

- I'll be back **as soon as** ⁵_____. 나는 가능한 한 빨리 돌아올 것이다. **Unit 02 - B**

- Sadly, his condition is getting ⁶_____.
  슬프게도, 그의 상태가 점점 더 나빠지고 있다. **Unit 02 - C**

- **The more** one has, ⁷_____ one wants. 더 많이 가질수록 더 많이 원한다. **Unit 02 - D**

- Health is ⁸_____ **the most important things** in life.
  건강은 인생에서 가장 중요한 것 중 하나이다. **Unit 02 - E**

- Mount Everest is **the highest** mountain in the world. 에베레스트산은 세계에서 가장 높은 산이다.

  → Mount Everest is **higher than** ⁹_____ mountain in the world.
    에베레스트산은 세계의 다른 어떤 산보다 더 높다.

  → **No (other)** mountain in the world is **as high as** Mount Everest.
    세계의 어떤 산도 에베레스트산만큼 높지 않다.

  → **No (other)** mountain in the world is **higher than** Mount Everest.
    세계의 어떤 산도 에베레스트산보다 더 높지 않다. **Unit 02 - F**

Q Answers

¹ taller than   ² more powerful than   ³ the most   ⁴ three times   ⁵ possible[I can]
⁶ worse and worse   ⁷ the more   ⁸ one of   ⁹ any other

ESSENTIAL RULES OF
ENGLISH GRAMMAR

CHAPTER
08

접속사

접속사는 단어와 단어, 구와 구, 절과 절을
연결한다.

UNIT
01 종속 접속사

A **시간을 나타내는 접속사:** when(~할 때), while(~하는 동안), as(~함에 따라, ~할 때), until[till](~까지), since(~한 이래로), every time(~할 때마다), as soon as(~하자마자)

When I was a child, I wanted to be a police officer.

While you were out, your friend called several times.

As time goes by, I love him even more.

We will not order food **until[till]** he comes.

Jeff and I have known each other **since** we were five.

Every time[Each time, Whenever] I call him, he isn't home.

As soon as you see her, tell her that I am looking for her.

① 시간을 나타내는 부사절에서는 현재시제로 미래를 나타낸다.
   I'll wait here until your class **is** over.

B **이유를 나타내는 접속사:** because[since, as](~ 때문에)

I have read all the *Harry Potter* books **because** I'm a big fan of them.

Since[As] the weather was bad, the flight was delayed.

C **조건을 나타내는 접속사:** if(만일 ~라면), unless(~하지 않으면 / = if ~ not)

If you work late tonight, I'll wait for you.

Unless the test is difficult, we can all pass.

= **If** the test is **not** difficult, …

① 조건을 나타내는 부사절에서는 현재시제로 미래를 나타낸다.
   If you **turn** left, you'll see the sign.

D **양보를 나타내는 접속사:** though[although, even though](비록 ~하지만), even if(만약 ~할지라도)

Though[Although, Even though] he's good at math, he can't solve the problem.

Even if you don't want to do your homework, you must.

CHECK UP 빈칸에 알맞은 말을 고르시오.

1 I'll ask him about this question when he _____ back.
   ⓐ come ⓑ comes ⓒ will come

2 _____ I didn't have time, I skipped breakfast this morning.
   ⓐ As ⓑ If ⓒ Until

PRACTICE

Q Answer Key p.13

STEP 1

( ) 안에서 알맞은 말을 고르시오.

1 Mom will be happy when she (will hear, hears) the news.

2 Please wait here (until, since) I come back.

3 (As, Although) it was rush hour, there was a lot of traffic.

4 His family was poor (when, as soon as) he was young.

STEP 2

밑줄 친 부분을 어법에 맞게 고치시오.

1 I have lived in this city <u>till</u> I was born.

2 I won't talk to her again unless she <u>will say</u> sorry to me.

3 <u>Unless</u> you don't leave now, you'll miss the beginning of the movie.

STEP 3

빈칸에 알맞은 말을 보기에서 골라 쓰시오. (단, 한 번씩만 쓸 것)

보기	though	as	while	if

1 _____ the singer grows older, she becomes more and more popular.

2 Will you have a cup of tea _____ you wait for him?

3 _____ she is very old, she still acts like a young person.

4 _____ I miss the school bus, I'll have to walk to school.

STEP 4

우리말과 일치하도록 ( ) 안의 말을 이용하여 문장을 완성하시오.

1 나는 그녀가 나에게 말할 때까지 결과를 알지 못할 것이다. (tell)

→ I won't know the results _____ _____ _____ _____ .

2 그는 이 노래를 들을 때마다 운다. (hear)

→ _____ _____ _____ _____ this song, he cries.

3 만약 그가 오지 않더라도 나는 신경쓰지 않을 것이다. (come)

→ _____ _____ _____ _____ _____ , I won't mind.

4 비록 시간이 거의 없었지만, 그는 그 일을 마쳤다. (have, little)

→ _____ _____ _____ _____ _____ , he finished the work.

5 그 쇼가 시작하자마자 나에게 알려줘. (show, start)

→ _____ _____ _____ _____ _____ , let me know.

UNIT
02
짝으로 이루어진 접속사, 간접의문문

(A) 짝으로 이루어진 접속사

1 both A and B: A와 B 둘 다

Both my husband **and** I enjoyed the trip.

2 either A or B: A와 B 둘 중 하나

Either you **or** Bob will be the team leader.

3 neither A nor B: A도 B도 아닌

The dessert was **neither** delicious **nor** healthy.

4 not only A but also B: A뿐만 아니라 B도(= B as well as A)

This laptop is **not only** slim **but also** light.

= This laptop is light **as well as** slim.

(B) 간접의문문

1 의문사가 있는 경우: 의문사 + 주어 + 동사

I don't know. + What is his name?

→ I don't know **what his name is**.

① 의문사가 주어일 때는 의문문 그대로 「의문사 + 동사」의 어순으로 쓴다.
Tell me. + Who told you the news?
→ Tell me **who told** you the news.

① 주절의 동사가 think, believe, guess, suppose 등인 경우 의문사를 맨 앞에 둔다.
Do you think? + Who will win this game?
→ **Who** *do you think* **will** win this game?

2 의문사가 없는 경우: if[whether](~인지 아닌지) + 주어 + 동사

I'm not sure. + Will she like my present?

→ I'm not sure **if[whether] she will like** my present.

| CHECK UP | 빈칸에 알맞은 말을 고르시오.

1 You have to learn either Japanese _____ German.

ⓐ and   ⓑ or   ⓒ nor

2 I don't know _____.

ⓐ who like   ⓑ who Eli likes   ⓒ who does Eli like

3 Please tell me _____ he will come to the meeting.

ⓐ if   ⓑ which   ⓒ what

➕ PLUS : 짝으로 이루어진 접속사를
쓸 경우 동사의 수 일치

1. both A and B: 복수 취급
   Both he *and* I **are** able to swim.

2. either A or B / neither A nor B:
   B에 동사의 수 일치
   Neither he *nor* I **am** a student.

3. not only A but also B / B as
   well as A: B에 동사의 수 일치
   Not only Tom *but also* I **am**
   interested in hip hop music.

PRACTICE

🔍 Answer Key p.13

( ) 안에서 알맞은 말을 고르시오.

1 (Both, Either) Linda and I laughed a lot when we watched the movie.

2 I will visit my uncle's house either on Saturday (or, nor) Sunday.

3 Not only Ron (but also, and also) I couldn't stand the noise.

4 I don't know when (the movie starts, does the movie start).

다음 두 문장을 보기에 주어진 접속사를 이용하여 한 문장으로 쓰시오.

보기	both ~ and	either ~ or	neither ~ nor

1 Alice has been to Europe. I have been to Europe too.

→ _____ Alice _____ I have been to Europe.

2 My father doesn't drink. He doesn't smoke either.

→ My father _____ drinks _____ smokes.

3 They sell pizza and spaghetti. You can order one of them.

→ You can order _____ pizza _____ spaghetti.

다음 두 문장을 한 문장으로 쓰시오.

1 Do you think? + Who will be the next president?

→ _____

2 Can you tell me? + How much is this hat?

→ _____

3 Do you know? + Who lives next door?

→ _____

4 I'd like to know. + Does Harry have a girlfriend?

→ _____

우리말과 일치하도록 ( ) 안의 말을 이용하여 문장을 완성하시오.

1 Liam과 나는 둘 다 안경을 쓴다. (wear)

→ _____ _____ _____ _____ glasses.

2 그 음식은 맛있었을 뿐만 아니라 저렴했다. (delicious)

→ The food was cheap _____ _____ _____ _____ .

3 너는 그가 그 돈을 왜 훔쳤다고 생각하니? (think, steal)

→ _____ _____ _____ _____

_____ the money?

GRAMMAR FOR WRITING

A 우리말과 일치하도록 ( ) 안의 말을 이용하여 문장을 완성하시오.

1 나는 그녀의 이메일 주소가 무엇인지 모른다. (email address)

→ I don't know _____.

2 내가 거실을 청소하고 있는 동안, 남편은 설거지를 했다. (clean the living room)

→ _____, my husband did the dishes.

3 그 학교의 시설과 선생님들 둘 다 훌륭하다. (the facilities)

→ _____ at the school are excellent.

4 Andy뿐만 아니라 나도 파일럿이 되기를 원한다. (well, want, be)

→ _____ a pilot.

5 나는 누가 나에게 이 소포를 보냈는지 모른다. (parcel)

→ I don't know _____ to me.

6 그 쇼핑몰은 크지도 않았고 붐비지도 않았다. (big, crowded)

→ The shopping mall was _____.

7 네가 5분 안에 오지 않으면 우리는 너 없이 출발할 것이다. (come)

→ _____ in five minutes, we will leave without you.

B 우리말과 일치하도록 ( ) 안에 주어진 단어를 바르게 배열하시오.

1 너는 성공의 열쇠가 무엇이라고 생각하니? (is, do, you, what, key, the, think)

→ _____ to success?

2 나는 돈이 전혀 없어서 그 셔츠를 사지 못했다. (have, money, I, since, any, didn't)

→ _____, I couldn't buy the shirt.

3 그 은행을 지나자마자 우회전하세요. (as, you, pass, soon, bank, the, as)

→ _____, turn right.

4 비록 그는 화가 났지만, 우리에게 그의 감정을 보여주지 않았다. (angry, was, though, he)

→ _____, he didn't show us his feelings.

5 내 여동생은 그녀의 방이나 부엌 중 한 곳에 있다. (in, kitchen, or, the, her, either, room, in)

→ My sister is _____.

6 네가 만약 내 책을 읽고 싶다면, 내가 너에게 언제든지 빌려줄 수 있다.

(you, read, my, if, to, books, want)

→ _____, I can lend them to you anytime.

C 다음 두 문장을 보기에 주어진 접속사를 이용하여 한 문장으로 바꿔 쓰시오. (단, 한 번씩만 쓸 것)

보기	neither ~ nor	if	although	since
	when	both ~ and	either ~ or	

1 Henry wants to learn kung fu and taekwondo. But he can do only one.

→ Henry can learn _____.

2 She was sixty-five years old. She wrote her first novel then.

→ She was sixty-five years old _____.

3 It rained heavily. So we didn't go fishing.

→ _____, we didn't go fishing.

4 He was very tired. But he answered all my questions.

→ _____, he answered all my questions.

5 Can you tell me? Is the restaurant open on Sundays?

→ Can you tell me _____?

6 Zoey likes to learn new languages. I like to learn new languages too.

→ _____.

7 My bag is not in my room. It is not in the living room either.

→ My bag is _____.

D 그림을 보고 보기 1에 주어진 접속사와 보기 2에 주어진 말을 이용하여 문장을 완성하시오. (단, 한 번씩만 쓸 것)

보기 1		if	while	because	not only ~ but also

보기 2	wait for the food	want something to drink	be hungry	pizza/hamburgers

1 Jessica and I entered a restaurant _____.

2 We ordered _____.

3 The waiter asked us _____.

4 We took pictures _____.

REVIEW TEST

[1-3] 빈칸에 들어갈 알맞은 말을 고르시오.

1

> It's very cold outside. You'd better wear _____ a coat or a jacket.

① both ② either
③ neither ④ not only
⑤ but also

2

> _____ I like most Japanese food, I don't eat sushi.

① As ② When
③ Since ④ If
⑤ Though

3

> I want to know _____ this train goes to Seoul.

① if ② unless
③ that ④ so
⑤ what

4 두 문장의 의미가 같도록 할 때, 빈칸에 들어갈 말이 순서대로 바르게 짝지어진 것은?

> • _____ her speech is not long, I will be able to ask some questions.
> • _____ her speech is long, I will be able to ask some questions.

① As – If ② If – If
③ If – Unless ④ Unless – If
⑤ Unless – Unless

[5-6] 다음 중 밑줄 친 부분이 어법상 옳은 것을 고르시오.

5

① I don't know <u>where is he from</u>.
② Do you guess <u>when</u> she came here?
③ Tell me <u>if he will come</u> tonight.
④ I wonder <u>who the window broke</u>.
⑤ <u>Where can you tell me</u> the bank is?

6

① If it <u>snows</u> tomorrow, I won't go out.
② <u>Either</u> Jayden nor I speak Japanese.
③ Neither Ava <u>and</u> I was late for school.
④ He is not only kind <u>and also</u> gentle.
⑤ I've been there both in winter <u>but</u> in summer.

7 다음 두 문장을 한 문장으로 바꾼 것 중 잘못된 것은?

① I don't know. + When does the shop open?
→ I don't know when the shop opens.
② Do you think? + Who will win the race?
→ Who do you think will win the race?
③ Please tell me. + Where is the bakery?
→ Please tell me where the bakery is.
④ I want to know. + How old is this tree?
→ I want to know how old this tree is.
⑤ I wonder. + Is he interested in art?
→ I wonder that he is interested in art.

빈출

[8-9] 밑줄 친 접속사의 의미가 나머지 넷과 다른 것을 고르시오.

8
① If you turn left, you can see my office.
② The game will be canceled if it rains.
③ If I am late, you don't have to wait.
④ Do you know if he knows the truth?
⑤ He will cut himself if he isn't careful.

9
① She has created five movies since she became a director.
② We'll stay home since it is raining outside.
③ He usually eats at home since he likes cooking.
④ Since it was getting late, they decided to go home.
⑤ Since I had a few minutes until the bus came, I wandered around.

서술형 빈출

[10-11] 두 문장의 의미가 같도록 빈칸에 알맞은 말을 쓰시오.

10
If you don't study hard, you won't pass the exam.

→ _____ you study hard, you won't pass the exam.

11
He is good at history as well as math.

→ He is good at _____ math _____ history.

12 다음 중 보기의 밑줄 친 접속사와 의미가 같은 것은?

보기 | As time went by, he felt better.

① He came in as I was watching TV.
② As it was cold, I turned on the heater.
③ As I was taking a walk, I saw him jogging.
④ As we climbed higher, the air grew colder.
⑤ My plane was delayed as the weather was bad.

서술형

[13-15] 우리말과 일치하도록 ( ) 안의 말을 이용하여 문장을 완성하시오.

13
너는 디저트로 아이스크림이나 케이크 둘 중 하나를 먹을 수 있다. (ice cream, cake)

→ You can eat _____ for dessert.

14
그에게 무슨 일이 일어났는지 나에게 말해주겠니? (happen)

→ Can you tell me _____?

15
너는 집에 도착하자마자 손을 씻어라. (soon, get home)

→ _____, wash your hands.

16 두 문장의 의미가 같도록 할 때, 빈칸에 들어갈 알맞은 말은?

> Every time I am on a plane, I get sick.
> → _____ I am on a plane, I get sick.

① As
② Though
③ Since
④ While
⑤ Whenever

17 다음 중 어법상 틀린 것은?

① He never calls me until I call him first.
② I haven't seen him since I moved here.
③ Every time I call the shop, the line is busy.
④ Unless you don't have a ticket, you can't go in.
⑤ Even if you're angry, don't shout at me.

서술형

[18-20] 다음 두 문장을 간접의문문을 이용하여 한 문장으로 쓰시오.

18 Do you think? Who knows the answer?

→ _____ the answer?

19 I wonder. Does Carl have a pet?

→ I wonder _____.

20 I'm not sure. When can I visit Korea?

→ I'm not sure _____.

서술형

[21-23] 빈칸에 공통으로 들어갈 접속사를 쓰시오.

21
- I felt hungry _____ I didn't have lunch.
- He has lived in that house _____ he was born.

22
- I wonder _____ she will like my present.
- _____ he comes back, I'll tell him the truth.

23
- _____ I have a test tomorrow, I can't go to the movies tonight.
- _____ she grows older, she becomes wiser.

서술형

24 우리말과 일치하도록 ( ) 안에 주어진 단어를 배열하시오.

엄마도 나도 쇼핑하는 것을 좋아하지 않는다.
(go, Mom, nor, I, like, to, neither, shopping)

→ _____.

서술형

25 우리말과 일치하도록 주어진 조건에 맞게 문장을 완성하시오.

누가 그 그림을 훔쳤는지 아무도 모른다.

〈조건〉 1. nobody, know, steal을 이용할 것
2. 시제에 유의하여 4단어로 쓸 것

→ _____ the painting.

26 다음 중 어법상 **틀린** 것을 모두 고르면?

① As I get older, I become more mature.
② I have lived in Seoul as I was six.
③ I'll call you when I'll arrive there.
④ Every time he calls me by my nickname, I get angry.
⑤ Even if I don't like him, I should do the project with him.

27 다음 중 어법상 옳은 것으로 바르게 짝지어진 것은?

a. Neither I nor my friends was late.
b. I will go home unless you stop laughing at me.
c. While she was out, her younger brother broke her computer.
d. I want to know if he likes me.
e. Not only you but also Jinny have similar problems.

① a, b, c   ② a, c, d
③ b, c, d   ④ b, c, e
⑤ b, d, e

28 다음 중 어법상 옳은 것의 개수는?

· Tell me who told you the story.
· Why do you suppose is he so angry?
· She asked me if I had been to Paris.
· Since I had not cleaned my room, I could not go to the party.
· I have been to all his concerts though I'm a big fan of him.

① 1개   ② 2개   ③ 3개
④ 4개   ⑤ 5개

[29-31] 밑줄 친 부분이 어법상 옳은지 판단하고, **틀리면** 바르게 고치시오.

29 My teacher as well as my parents <u>wants</u> me to go to college.

(O / X) _____

30 Unless it <u>will rain</u> tomorrow, we can go to the theme park.

(O / X) _____

31 <u>Although</u> he hurt his foot, he finished the race.

(O / X) _____

[32-33] 어법상 **틀린** 부분을 찾아 바르게 고치시오.

32 Both my sister and I am able to speak French since we lived in France when we were young. (1개)

33 My uncle is going to travel abroad for a month. I don't know where will he visit on his trip. (1개)

LET'S REVIEW

주요 예문을 다시 한번 확인하고, 우리말과 일치하도록 빈칸을 채우시오.

- [1]_____ you were out, your friend called several times.
  네가 나가 있는 동안 네 친구가 몇 번 전화했다. **Unit 01 - A**

- **As** time goes by, I love him even more. 시간이 흐름에 따라, 나는 그를 더욱 더 사랑한다. **Unit 01 - A**

- **Since[As]** the weather was bad, the flight was delayed.
  날씨가 나빠서 항공편이 지연되었다. **Unit 01 - B**

- **If** you work late tonight, I'll wait for you.
  만약 네가 오늘 밤 늦게까지 일한다면, 나는 너를 기다릴 것이다. **Unit 01 - C**

- [2]_____ the test is difficult, we can all pass.
  시험이 어렵지 않으면, 우리는 모두 통과할 수 있다. **Unit 01 - C**

- [3]_____ he's good at math, he can't solve the problem.
  비록 그가 수학을 잘하지만, 그는 그 문제를 풀 수 없다. **Unit 01 - D**

- **Even if** you don't want to do your homework, you must.
  숙제를 하고 싶지 않더라도 너는 해야만 한다. **Unit 01 - D**

- [4]_____ my husband **and** I enjoyed the trip. 내 남편과 나 둘 다 그 여행을 즐겼다. **Unit 02 - A**

- [5]_____ you **or** Bob will be the team leader.
  너나 Bob 둘 중 한 명이 팀장이 될 것이다. **Unit 02 - A**

- The dessert was **neither** delicious [6]_____ healthy.
  그 후식은 맛있지도 건강에 좋지도 않았다. **Unit 02 - A**

- This laptop is [7]_____ slim **but also** light. 이 노트북은 얇을 뿐만 아니라 가볍다. **Unit 02 - A**

- I don't know **what his name is.** 나는 그의 이름이 무엇인지 모른다. **Unit 02 - B**

- I'm not sure [8]_____ **she will like** my present.
  나는 그녀가 내 선물을 좋아할지 확신이 없다. **Unit 02 - B**

Q Answers

[1] While   [2] Unless   [3] Though[Although, Even though]   [4] Both   [5] Either   [6] nor
[7] not only   [8] if[whether]

ESSENTIAL RULES OF ENGLISH GRAMMAR

CHAPTER

09

관계사

대명사 또는 부사의 역할을 하면서 절을
이끌어 앞의 명사나 대명사에 연결하는 말로,
관계대명사와 관계부사가 있다.

UNIT 01 관계대명사

관계대명사: 「접속사 + 대명사」의 역할을 하며, 관계대명사가 이끄는 절은 형용사처럼 선행사를 수식한다.

I saw *the horror movie*. + You recommended *it* yesterday.

I saw the horror movie [**that** you recommended yesterday].

선행사	사람	사물/동물	사람/사물/동물	선행사 포함
주격	who	which	that	what
소유격	whose	whose	whose	–
목적격	who(m)	which	that	what

① 선행사가 〈사람 + 사물〉, 〈사람 + 동물〉이거나 최상급, 서수사, the only, the very, all, every, -thing으로 끝나는 부정대명사 등을 포함한 경우 주로 that을 쓴다.
It was *the very concert* **that** I wanted to go to.

A 주격 관계대명사: who, which, that

I like a man **who[that]** has a sense of humor.

He knows an online shop **which[that]** rents snowboard equipment.

B 소유격 관계대명사: whose

Andy is a boy **whose** goal is to be a world-famous actor.

Please pass me the book **whose** cover is red.

C 목적격 관계대명사: who(m), which, that

The woman **who(m)[that]** you saw wasn't my teacher.

I have lost the fashion magazine **which[that]** you lent me.

D 관계대명사 what: 그 자체가 the thing(s) that[which]의 의미로, 선행사를 포함한다.

Tim saved the child from the fire. **What** he did was brave.
        = The thing that[which]

빈칸에 알맞은 말을 고르시오.

1 I know a boy _____ lived in Hawaii for five years.
  ⓐ who   ⓑ whose   ⓒ which

2 The mirror _____ we bought had a wooden frame.
  ⓐ who   ⓑ that   ⓒ what

3 I really liked _____ she gave to me for my birthday.
  ⓐ which   ⓑ that   ⓒ what

PRACTICE

🔍 Answer Key p.14

( ) 안에서 알맞은 말을 고르시오.

1 (That, What) made me angry was her rude attitude.

2 She was the only girl (that, which) got a perfect score on the test.

3 The information (which, what) I found on the internet was wrong.

4 He gave me a teddy bear (which, whose) face was very cute.

5 What is the name of the boy (whom, which) we met yesterday?

어법상 틀린 부분을 찾아 바르게 고치시오.

1 I met a young couple who dream was to live in a traditional house.

2 The performance what the singer gave last night was fantastic.

3 Brian didn't understand that the teacher said in English.

4 He saw an old friend which used to go to elementary school with him.

다음 두 문장을 관계대명사를 이용하여 한 문장으로 쓰시오.

1 I have a parrot. Its feathers are very colorful and attractive.

→ _____

2 The newspaper was wet. It was delivered this morning.

→ _____

3 The reporter interviewed a woman. She won first prize in a contest.

→ _____

STEP 4

우리말과 일치하도록 ( ) 안에 주어진 단어를 바르게 배열하시오.

1 나는 나와 취미가 같은 남자 친구가 있다. (the, a, whose, is, same, boyfriend, hobby)

→ I have _____ as mine.

2 달 위를 걸은 첫 번째 사람은 누구입니까? (first, the, walked, on, the, man, that, moon)

→ Who is _____ ?

3 책 가격을 비교해 주는 웹 사이트는 유용하다. (the, compares, the, prices, website, which)

→ _____ of books is useful.

관계부사: 「접속사 + 부사(구)」의 역할을 하며, 관계부사가 이끄는 절은 형용사처럼 선행사를 수식한다.

I still remember *the day*. + We first met *on the day*.

→ I still remember the day [**when** we first met].

A   **when:** 시간을 나타내는 명사(time, day, year 등)가 선행사가 된다.

This is *the time* **when** my favorite talk show is on.
             = at which

B   **where:** 장소를 나타내는 명사(place, town, house 등)가 선행사가 된다.

Jim forgot *the place* **where** he parked his car.
           = in which

C   **why:** 이유를 나타내는 reason이 선행사가 된다.

Lower prices are *the reason* **why** I prefer online stores.
                  = for which

D   **how:** 방법을 나타내는 way가 선행사가 된다. 단, 선행사 the way와 관계부사 how는 함께 쓰지 않는다.

This is **how** I solved the problem.
This is **the way** I solved the problem.
~~This is the way how I solved the problem.~~

CHECK UP   빈칸에 알맞은 말을 고르시오.

1 I remember the day _____ I first flew in a plane.
     ⓐ when   ⓑ where   ⓒ why

2 This is the house _____ I used to live.
     ⓐ why   ⓑ where   ⓒ how

3 That is the reason _____ he acts like that.
     ⓐ when   ⓑ why   ⓒ how

➕ PLUS : 선행사나 관계부사의 생략

선행사가 place, time, reason일 때 선행사나 관계부사 중 하나가 생략될 수 있다.

This is **the place where** I was born.

⌈ This is **where** I was born.
⌊ This is **the place** I was born.

PRACTICE

🔍 Answer Key p.14

STEP 1

( ) 안에서 알맞은 말을 고르시오.

1 2020 was the year (when, how) I met my girlfriend.

2 A lot of foreigners want to know (the way how, how) kimchi is made.

3 This is the factory (where, when) my father worked a few years ago.

4 Do you know the reason (where, why) Ethan isn't in class today?

STEP 2

두 문장의 의미가 같도록 빈칸에 알맞은 관계부사를 쓰시오.

1 I saw the house in which Michael Jackson had lived.

 → I saw the house _____ Michael Jackson had lived.

2 This is the way he solved the difficult puzzle.

 → This is _____ he solved the difficult puzzle.

3 Do you know the day on which the pop art exhibition will be held?

 → Do you know the day _____ the pop art exhibition will be held?

4 He didn't know the reason for which his name wasn't on the list.

 → He didn't know the reason _____ his name wasn't on the list.

STEP 3

다음 두 문장을 관계부사를 이용하여 한 문장으로 쓰시오. (단, 선행사나 관계부사를 생략하지 말 것)

1 Tomorrow is the day. The shopping mall will start its big sale then.

 → _____

2 I don't know the reason. My grades are lower than I expected for that reason.

 → _____

3 The video clip shows the way. Rice cakes are cooked in this way.

 → _____

STEP 4

우리말과 일치하도록 ( ) 안의 말을 이용하여 문장을 완성하시오.

1 그는 나에게 그가 전화하지 않은 이유를 말했다. (reason)

 → He told me _____ _____ _____ he didn't call me.

2 당신이 제 컴퓨터를 어떻게 고쳤는지 저에게 설명해 주세요. (fix)

 → Please explain to me _____ _____ _____ my computer.

3 나는 처음 내 새 차를 운전했던 그날을 잊을 수 없다. (day)

 → I can't forget _____ _____ _____ I first drove my new car

4 여기가 내 선글라스를 산 그 가게이다. (store)

 → This is _____ _____ _____ I bought my sunglasses.

UNIT 03 주의해야 할 관계사

A 관계대명사의 생략

1 목적격 관계대명사의 생략: 목적어로 쓰인 관계대명사는 생략할 수 있다.

I couldn't believe the story (**that[which]**) he told me.

2 「주격 관계대명사 + be동사」의 생략: 「주격 관계대명사 + be동사」는 뒤에 형용사구[분사구]가 올 때 생략할 수 있다. 이때 형용사구[분사구]가 앞의 선행사를 수식한다.

The girl [(**who is**) wearing the school uniform] is my sister.

B 전치사 + 관계대명사

관계대명사가 전치사의 목적어로 쓰일 때, 전치사는 관계대명사 앞이나 관계사절 끝에 올 수 있다. 전치사가 관계대명사 앞에 쓰인 경우에는 관계대명사를 생략할 수 없다.

Tell me about the man **with whom** you fell in love.

Tell me about the man **whom** you fell in love **with**.

ⓘ 전치사 뒤에 목적격 관계대명사 who 또는 that을 쓸 수 없으며, 이때는 전치사가 관계사절 끝에 와야 한다.

Tell me about the man **who[that]** you fell in love **with**.

~~Tell me about the man with who[that] you fell in love.~~

C 관계사의 계속적 용법: 선행사에 부가적인 설명을 덧붙일 때 사용하며, 관계사 앞에 콤마(,)를 붙인다.

1 관계대명사의 계속적 용법: who와 which만 가능하며, 「접속사 + 대명사」로 바꿔 쓸 수 있다. (that은 계속적 용법으로 쓸 수 없다.)

I learned about Bach, **who**(= and he) is called the father of classical music.

I bought a new laptop, **which**(= but it) is not as fast as I expected.

ⓘ 계속적 용법으로 쓰인 관계대명사 which는 앞 문장 전체를 선행사로 취할 수 있다.

*I got an A on the math exam, **which**(= and it) made my parents happy.*

ⓘ 계속적 용법의 관계대명사는 생략할 수 없다.

~~The fan, I bought yesterday, is out of order.~~

2 관계부사의 계속적 용법: when과 where만 가능하며, 「접속사 + 부사」로 바꿔 쓸 수 있다.

I went to the festival, **where**(= and there) I had a great time.

빈칸에 알맞은 말을 고르시오.

1 She visited the country from _____ her mother came.
ⓐ which   ⓑ that   ⓒ where

2 He has two cats, _____ have blue eyes.
ⓐ who   ⓑ which   ⓒ that

122

PRACTICE

🔍 Answer Key p-15

STEP 1

( ) 안에서 알맞은 말을 고르시오.

1 This is an island on (which, that) many types of rare birds live.

2 The girl (sitting, is sitting) beside me is my best friend, Clara.

3 My sister wore my skirt without asking me, (which, what) made me angry.

4 Tomorrow, we are going to the valley, (when, where) we'll swim and go fishing.

STEP 2

다음 문장에서 생략할 수 있는 부분을 ( )로 묶으시오. (생략할 수 있는 부분이 없으면 X표 하시오.)

1 I'll give you some tips which will help you find the answer.

2 These are the pictures of the earth which were taken from space.

3 She is the woman that I told you about a few days ago.

4 Look at those cute koalas that are eating the leaves.

5 My grandfather lives in Rome, where he was born.

STEP 3

두 문장의 의미가 같도록 관계사를 이용하여 빈칸에 알맞은 말을 쓰시오.

1 I sent a text message to Katie, but she didn't reply.

 → I sent a text message to Katie, _____.

2 My family went camping near the river, and there we slept for one night.

 → My family went camping near the river, _____

3 He made a lot of cartoons, and they are still loved by many children.

 → He made a lot of cartoons, _____.

STEP 4

우리말과 일치하도록 ( ) 안의 말을 이용하여 문장을 완성하시오.

1 강 선생님은 우리 학교의 모두가 좋아하는 선생님이다. (everyone)

 → Ms. Kang is _____ _____ _____ in my school likes.

2 어제 나는 면으로 만들어진 파자마를 구입했다. (make, cotton)

 → Yesterday I bought pajamas _____ _____ _____.

3 그가 지난번에 당신이 말했던 요리사인가요? (talk)

 → Is he the cook about _____ _____ _____ last time?

4 나는 방송국에서 일했는데, 거기서 나의 아내를 만났다. (meet)

 → I worked at a TV station, _____ _____ _____ my wife.

UNIT 04 복합관계사

A 복합관계대명사: 「관계대명사 + -ever」의 형태로, 명사절과 양보의 부사절을 이끈다.

복합관계대명사	whoever	whichever	whatever
명사절 (주어/목적어)	anyone who (~하는 누구나)	anything which (~하는 어느 것이나)	anything that (~하는 무엇이나)
양보의 부사절	no matter who (누가 ~할지라도)	no matter which (어느 것을[이] ~할지라도)	no matter what (무엇을[이] ~할지라도)

Whoever gives the correct answer first will get a free gift.

= Anyone who

Whoever wins the World Cup, it will be fun to watch.

= No matter who

ⓘ 사람인 선행사를 포함하는 복합관계대명사가 목적어 역할을 할 때 whomever를 쓰기도 한다.
  Whomever you meet, be confident.
  = No matter whom

B 복합관계부사: 「관계부사 + -ever」 형태로, 시간, 장소의 부사절이나 양보의 부사절을 이끈다.

복합관계부사	whenever	wherever	however
시간, 장소의 부사절	any time (that) / at any time (~할 때마다)	at any place (that) (~하는 곳은 어디든지)	–
양보의 부사절	no matter when (언제 ~하더라도)	no matter where (어디서 ~하더라도)	no matter how (아무리 ~하더라도)

Take a seat **wherever** you like.
          = at any place that

Wherever the criminal goes, the police will find him.

= No matter where

CHECK UP 빈칸에 알맞은 말을 고르시오.

1 _____ my mom cooks is very delicious.
  ⓐ Whoever   ⓑ Whatever   ⓒ Wherever

2 _____ comes, don't open the door.
  ⓐ Whenever   ⓑ Wherever   ⓒ Whoever

3 He takes his laptop _____ he goes.
  ⓐ whatever   ⓑ wherever   ⓒ however

➕ PLUS : 복합관계형용사

whatever, whichever는 뒤에 오는 명사를 수식하는 형용사의 역할을 하기도 한다.

You may order **whichever** food on the menu you prefer.

PRACTICE

🔍 Answer Key p.15

STEP 1

( ) 안에서 알맞은 말을 고르시오.

1 (Where, Wherever) I go in the house, my dog follows me.

2 It is your birthday. You can invite (whomever, whatever) you like.

3 (How, However) dangerous each scene was, the movie star was not afraid.

4 (Whichever, Wherever) item you buy from this table, you'll get a 10% discount

STEP 2

빈칸에 알맞은 말을 보기에서 골라 쓰시오.

보기	whenever however whoever

1 _____ hard he tried, he couldn't beat his rival.

2 We can meet to have an interview _____ you are available.

3 I will welcome _____ you pick to join our study group.

STEP 3

두 문장의 의미가 같도록 빈칸에 알맞은 말을 쓰시오.

1 No matter where the musician played the guitar, people gathered.

→ _____ the musician played the guitar, people gathered.

2 You can call me at any time you need my advice.

→ You can call me _____ you need my advice.

3 I will give a reward to anyone who finds my dog.

→ I will give a reward to _____ finds my dog.

4 The journalist wrote down anything that the sports star did.

→ The journalist wrote down _____ the sports star did.

STEP 4

우리말과 일치하도록 ( ) 안의 말을 이용하여 문장을 완성하시오.

1 오디션을 보는 누구나 이 노래를 불러야 할 것이다. (audition)

→ _____ _____ will have to sing this song.

2 무슨 일이 일어나더라도, 그는 그의 마음을 바꾸지 않을 것이다. (happen)

→ _____ _____ , he won't change his mind.

3 네가 아무리 화가 나더라도, 폭력을 사용해서는 안 된다. (be, angry)

→ _____ _____ _____ _____ , you must not use violence.

4 내가 Ben을 만날 때마다, 그는 그의 고양이에 대해 이야기한다. (meet)

→ _____ _____ _____ _____ , he talks about his cat.

GRAMMAR FOR WRITING

A 우리말과 일치하도록 관계사와 ( ) 안의 말을 이용하여 문장을 완성하시오.

1 너는 Noah와 이야기하고 있는 저 소녀를 아니? (talk)

→ Do you know the girl with _____?

2 나는 Emma가 내가 그녀를 위해 산 것을 좋아하길 바란다. (what, for)

→ I hope that Emma will like _____.

3 나는 우유를 더 부었고, 그것이 그 빵을 더 부드럽게 만들었다. (make, softer)

→ I had added more milk, _____.

4 Olivia는 거짓말쟁이다. 그녀가 무슨 말을 하더라도, 나는 그녀를 믿을 수 없다. (say)

→ Olivia is a liar. _____, I can't believe her.

5 아무리 열심히 노력해도, 나는 수학에서 좋은 점수를 받을 수 없었다. (hard, try)

→ _____, I couldn't get a good grade in math.

6 나는 그 예술가가 이 그림을 그린 방식에 놀랐다. (artist, paint)

→ I was amazed at _____ this picture.

7 나는 주말을 해변에서 보냈는데, 그곳에서 나는 파도타기를 즐겼다. (enjoy, surfing)

→ I spent the weekend at the beach, _____.

B 우리말과 일치하도록 ( ) 안에 주어진 단어를 바르게 배열하시오.

1 아인슈타인은 내가 가장 존경하는 과학자이다. (is, admire, the, Einstein, scientist, I)

→ _____ the most.

2 나는 영화를 만드는 것이 꿈이었던 한 남자를 안다. (man, dream, films, whose, to, make, was, a)

→ I know _____.

3 우리 아버지는 LED 모니터를 만드는 회사에서 일하신다. (makes, that, a company, LED monitors)

→ My father works for _____.

4 나는 네가 어제 나에게 이야기했던 그 책의 제목을 잊어버렸다. (about, you, told, me, yesterday, that)

→ I forgot the title of the book _____.

5 지금이 네가 너의 직업에 대해 생각해야 할 때이다. (about, the, should, is, you, time, think, when)

→ Now _____ your career.

6 공항 앞에 서 있는 그 소녀들은 한국 배우를 기다리고 있었다.
(front, the, of, girls, airport, standing, in, the)

→ _____ were waiting for a Korean actor.

C 다음 두 문장을 보기에 주어진 관계사를 이용하여 한 문장으로 쓰시오.

| 보기 | whose | that | when | where | why | how |

1 I don't understand the reason. He is upset with me for that reason.

→ I don't understand the reason _____.

2 This is the playground. I used to play soccer with friends there.

→ This is the playground _____.

3 I remember the day. We went on a field trip then.

→ I remember the day _____.

4 Amy is interested in politics. It seems that she is the only one.

→ It seems that Amy is the only one _____.

5 I have a friend. His ambition is to win the championship.

→ I have a friend _____.

6 He explained to me the way. His company makes money in that way.

→ He explained to me _____.

D 그림을 보고 보기에 주어진 말과 알맞은 관계사를 이용하여 문장을 완성하시오.

| 보기 | I/holding | hat is purple | grilling some meat | we/spent the last weekend |

1 This is the camping site _____.

2 The man _____ is my dad.

3 The woman _____ is my mom.

4 The dog _____ is my pet Max.

REVIEW TEST

[1–5] 빈칸에 들어갈 알맞은 말을 고르시오.

1

People _____ eat a lot of fast food tend to be unhealthy.

① whom   ② that
③ which   ④ what
⑤ whose

2

Amy is the classmate with _____ I share my dormitory room.

① who   ② that
③ which   ④ whom
⑤ whose

3

The tall building has several elevators, _____ are very fast.

① who   ② whose
③ that   ④ which
⑤ what

4

Santorini is the island _____ I've always wanted to go.

① when   ② where
③ why   ④ how
⑤ what

5

_____ wins the race will receive the gold medal.

① Whoever   ② Whatever
③ Whenever   ④ Wherever
⑤ However

[6–7] 다음 중 어법상 <u>틀린</u> 것을 고르시오.

6 ① I want to marry a man who I can trust.
② I can't believe what happened to me.
③ He is the tallest man that I've ever met.
④ She is the clever girl I talked about the other day.
⑤ What you buy in this shop, you'll get a 30% discount.

7 ① This is the way how I made a decision.
② There was a time when salt was more valuable than gold.
③ She liked the boy whose hobby was taking pictures.
④ A café that sells good coffee is near here.
⑤ Whoever calls, tell them I'm sleeping.

8 다음 밑줄 친 부분과 바꿔 쓸 수 있는 것은?

No matter who talks to Luke, he won't listen. He never listens to anyone.

① Whoever   ② Whomever
③ Whichever   ④ Whatever
⑤ However

빈출

9 빈칸에 들어갈 말이 순서대로 바르게 짝지어진 것은?

> I ate dinner in a restaurant _____ air conditioner was broken. It was too hot there, _____ annoyed me.

① that – that
② who – which
③ whose – that
④ whose – which
⑤ whom – which

13 밑줄 친 that의 쓰임이 옳은 것은?

① This novel is that I've wanted to read.
② Is there anything that I can do for you?
③ Yesterday I visited the museum, that was closed.
④ Sue is my co-worker with that I'm doing the project.
⑤ He introduced me to a man that job is selling cars.

10 다음 우리말을 영어로 바르게 옮긴 것은?

> 나는 Sarah에게 이메일을 보냈는데, 그녀는 답장을 보내지 않았다.

① I sent an email to Sarah, whom didn't answer me.
② I sent an email to Sarah, what didn't answer me.
③ I sent an email to Sarah, that didn't answer me.
④ I sent an email to Sarah, which didn't answer me.
⑤ I sent an email to Sarah, who didn't answer me.

서술형

[14-17] 두 문장의 의미가 같도록 빈칸에 알맞은 관계사를 쓰시오.

14 Boston is the city in which my father went to college.

→ Boston is the city _____ my father went to college.

서술형

[11-12] 다음 문장에서 생략할 수 있는 부분을 찾아 쓰시오.

11 I visited the house which Beethoven actually lived in.

15 The thing that I like about her is that she has a warm heart.

→ _____ I like about her is that she has a warm heart.

12 Cars that are made in Korea are very popular all over the world.

16 Every time my favorite singer is on TV, I can't take my eyes off him.

→ _____ my favorite singer is on TV, I can't take my eyes off him.

17 I often visit this bookstore, and it has a lot of foreign books.

→ I often visit this bookstore, _____ has a lot of foreign books.

서술형
[18-20] 다음 두 문장을 관계사를 이용하여 한 문장으로 쓰시오.

18 The store is closed today. It sells my favorite type of bags.

→ _____
_____

19 They didn't say the reason. The game was canceled for that reason.

→ _____
_____

20 I saw a building. Its roof collapsed.

→ _____
_____

서술형
[21-22] 우리말과 일치하도록 복합관계사와 ( ) 안의 말을 이용하여 문장을 완성하시오.

21 내가 아무리 빨리 달렸어도, Eric을 따라잡을 수는 없었다. (fast)

→ _____, I couldn't catch up with Eric.

22 그녀는 그녀의 친구들을 만날 때마다 그녀의 아들에 대해 이야기한다. (meet)

→ _____, she talks about her son.

빈출
23 다음 중 밑줄 친 부분을 생략할 수 <u>없는</u> 것은?

① I like the skirt <u>that</u> you're wearing.
② I don't know the man <u>who is</u> sitting behind me.
③ This is the building in <u>which</u> my father works.
④ The woman <u>whom</u> Alice is talking to is her secretary.
⑤ A fortune cookie is a dessert <u>that is</u> served in Chinese restaurants.

서술형
24 우리말과 일치하도록 ( ) 안에 주어진 단어를 배열하시오.

네가 나중에 후회할 일은 어떤 것이든 하지 마라.
(regret, will, that, you, anything, later)

→ Don't do _____.

서술형
25 우리말과 일치하도록 주어진 조건에 맞게 문장을 완성하시오.

나는 베니스로 여행을 갔는데, 그곳에서 내 오랜 친구를 만났다.

〈조건〉 1. an old friend of mine을 이용할 것
2. 관계부사를 쓸 것

→ I traveled to Venice, _____
_____.

26 다음 중 어법상 옳은 것을 모두 고르면?

① Have you found the hat which you lost?
② Please call me wherever you are.
③ I want to know about the people with who I work.
④ Do you know the girl whom Tom is talking to?
⑤ Hitler, that was born in Germany, was one of the worst dictators in the world.

27 다음 중 어법상 옳은 것으로 바르게 짝지어진 것은?

a. I can meet whomever I want.
b. I will visit Guam, which my uncle lives.
c. The girl is talking to Tom is my cousin.
d. Whatever I choose to do, my mother always supports me.
e. I won't eat in a restaurant whose staff is not kind.

① a, b, c   ② a, b, d
③ a, d, e   ④ b, c, e
⑤ c, d, e

28 다음 중 어법상 옳은 것의 개수는?

· Whoever breaks the rules should be punished.
· I want to live in a place where the weather is nice.
· Missy talked about her sister with whom she lives.
· Can I get back the umbrella that I lent you yesterday?
· Robert wrote a novel, that was a huge success.

① 1개   ② 2개   ③ 3개
④ 4개   ⑤ 5개

[29-31] 밑줄 친 부분이 어법상 옳은지 판단하고, 틀리면 바르게 고치시오.

29 <u>That</u> I wanted to do was to go to bed.

(O / X) _____

30 A crowd follows <u>wherever</u> the actress goes.

(O / X) _____

31 The coach didn't find out the reason <u>which</u> the players fought.

(O / X) _____

[32-33] 어법상 틀린 부분을 찾아 바르게 고치시오.

32 On my way to Korea, my flight was delayed, that forced me to spend the night at the airport. (1개)

33 Barcelona is the city what I want to visit the most. I would especially like to go to the Sagrada Familia, who is one of the world's most famous buildings. (2개)

LET'S REVIEW

주요 예문을 다시 한번 확인하고, 우리말과 일치하도록 빈칸을 채우시오.

- I like a man [1]_____ has a sense of humor.

  나는 유머 감각이 있는 남자를 좋아한다. **Unit 01 - A**

- Andy is a boy [2]_____ goal is to be a world-famous actor.

  Andy는 세계적으로 유명한 배우가 되는 것이 목표인 소년이다. **Unit 01 - B**

- I have lost the fashion magazine [3]_____ you lent me.

  나는 네가 나에게 빌려준 패션 잡지를 잃어버렸다. **Unit 01 - C**

- Tim saved the child from the fire. **What** he did was brave.

  Tim은 그 아이를 불에서 구했다. 그가 한 일은 용감했다. **Unit 01 - D**

- This is the time [4]_____ my favorite talk show is on.

  지금은 내가 가장 좋아하는 토크 쇼 하는 시간이다. **Unit 02 - A**

- Jim forgot the place **where** he parked his car. Jim은 그의 차를 세워 둔 곳을 잊었다. **Unit 02 - B**

- Lower prices are the reason [5]_____ I prefer online stores.

  더 저렴한 가격이 내가 온라인 매장을 선호하는 이유이다. **Unit 02 - C**

- This is [6]_____ I solved the problem. 이것이 내가 그 문제를 푼 방법이다. **Unit 02 - D**

- I couldn't believe the story (**that**[**which**]) he told me.

  나는 그가 내게 말한 이야기를 믿을 수 없었다. **Unit 03 - A**

- The girl (**who is**) wearing the school uniform is my sister.

  교복을 입고 있는 여자아이는 내 여동생이다. **Unit 03 - A**

- Tell me about the man **with whom** you fell in love. 네가 사랑에 빠진 그 남자에 대해 말해 줘. **Unit 03 - B**

- I bought a new laptop, [7]_____ is not as fast as I expected.

  나는 새 노트북을 샀는데, 내가 기대했던 것만큼 빠르지 않다. **Unit 03 - C**

- [8]_____ wins the World Cup, it will be fun to watch.

  누가 월드컵에서 이기더라도, 지켜보는 것은 재미있을 것이다. **Unit 04 - A**

- Take a seat **wherever** you like. 네가 원하는 곳 어디든지 앉아라. **Unit 04 - B**

🔍 **Answers**

[1] who[that]   [2] whose   [3] which[that]   [4] when[at which]   [5] why[for which]   [6] how[the way]

[7] which   [8] Whoever[No matter who]

ESSENTIAL RULES OF
ENGLISH GRAMMAR

CHAPTER

10

가정법

가정법은 실제로 일어나지 않았거나 앞으로
일어나지 않을 것 같은 일에 대한 가정이나
소망을 표현한다.

UNIT 01

가정법 과거, 가정법 과거완료, 혼합 가정법

A

가정법 과거: If + 주어 + 동사의 과거형, 주어 + would[could, might] + 동사원형

'만일 ~라면 …할 텐데'의 의미로, 현재 사실에 반대되거나 실현 가능성이 없는 일을 가정할 때 쓴다.

If I **knew** her problem, I **could help** her.
(← As I don't know her problem, I can't help her.)

If I **had** a million dollars, I **would buy** a yacht.

ⓘ 가정법 과거에서 if절의 be동사는 인칭/수에 관계없이 were를 쓴다.
  If I **were** you, I would finish my homework before going out.

B

가정법 과거완료: If + 주어 + had v-ed, 주어 + would[could, might] + have v-ed

'만일 ~였다면 …했을 텐데'의 의미로, 과거 사실과 반대되는 가정을 할 때 쓴다.

If I **had reserved** the ticket online, I **would have gotten** a discount.
(← As I didn't reserve the ticket online, I didn't get a discount.)

C

혼합 가정법: If + 주어 + had v-ed, 주어 + would[could, might] + 동사원형

'만일 ~였다면 …할 텐데'의 의미로, 과거에 실현되지 못한 일이 현재까지 영향을 미칠 때 쓴다.

If he **had not moved** to another city, I **could see** him now.
(← As he moved to another city, I can't see him now.)

CHECK UP 빈칸에 알맞은 말을 고르시오.

1 If I were rich, I _____ in a bigger apartment.
  ⓐ lived   ⓑ would live   ⓒ would have lived

2 If I had not been so busy, I _____ to meet him.
  ⓐ went   ⓑ would go   ⓒ would have gone

3 If it hadn't snowed last night, there _____ so many accidents.
  ⓐ won't be   ⓑ wouldn't be   ⓒ hadn't been

➕ PLUS : 단순 조건문 vs. 가정법 과거

• 단순 조건문: 실제로 발생 가능한 일을 가정할 때 쓰인다.
  If he **joins** us for dinner, **make** space for him.
  (그가 저녁을 함께 먹을지 알 수 없음)

• 가정법 과거: 현재 사실의 반대나 실현 불가능한 일을 가정할 때 쓰인다.
  If he **joined** us for dinner, I **would make** space for him.
  (그가 저녁을 함께 먹을 가능성이 희박함)

PRACTICE

🔍 Answer Key p.16

STEP 1

( ) 안에서 알맞은 말을 고르시오.

1 If I (am, were) born again, I would become a drummer.

2 If you take the survey, you (will, would) get a $10 gift card.

3 If I had not eaten the burger, I (would be, would have been) hungry now.

4 If I (didn't tell, hadn't told) the truth, he wouldn't have forgiven me.

STEP 2

밑줄 친 부분을 어법에 맞게 고치시오.

1 What <u>do you say</u> if you were in my position?

2 If I spoke foreign languages well, I <u>had</u> a better job.

3 If he hadn't stopped playing the violin, he <u>would have been</u> a great violinist now.

4 If I <u>have not bought</u> that coat, I could have saved enough money for the trip.

STEP 3

주어진 문장과 의미가 통하도록 빈칸에 알맞은 말을 쓰시오.

1 My grandparents don't live near here, so I don't see them often.

→ If my grandparents _____ near here, I _____ them often.

2 As we didn't have enough money, we couldn't go to see the movie.

→ If we _____ enough money, we _____ to see the movie.

3 As Mia did her homework, she can play outside now.

→ If Mia _____ her homework, she _____ outside now.

STEP 4

우리말과 일치하도록 ( ) 안의 말을 이용하여 문장을 완성하시오.

1 내가 너라면, 수업에 더 집중할 것이다. (be, pay)

→ If I _____ you, I _____ _____ more attention to the lesson.

2 내가 만약 종이와 펜이 있었더라면, 그 가수에게 사인을 요청했을 텐데. (have, ask)

→ If I _____ _____ a pen and paper, I _____ _____ _____ the singer for an autograph.

3 내가 어젯밤에 더 일찍 잤다면, 지금 피곤하지 않을 텐데. (go, be)

→ If I _____ _____ to bed earlier last night, I _____ _____ tired now.

UNIT 02 I wish, as if, It's time + 가정법

A **I wish + 가정법**

1 I wish + 가정법 과거: I wish + 주어 + 동사의 과거형

'~라면 좋을 텐데'의 의미로, 현재의 일에 대한 유감이나 아쉬움을 표현한다.

I've never had my own room. **I wish** I **had** my own room.

(← I'm sorry I don't have my own room.)

2 I wish + 가정법 과거완료: I wish + 주어 + had v-ed

'~했더라면 좋을 텐데'의 의미로, 과거의 일에 대한 유감이나 아쉬움을 표현한다.

My grades are bad. **I wish** I **had studied** harder for the exams.

(← I'm sorry I didn't study harder for the exams.)

B **as if + 가정법**

1 as if + 가정법 과거: as if + 주어 + 동사의 과거형

'마치 ~인 것처럼'의 의미로, 현재 사실과 반대되는 내용을 가정할 때 쓴다.

Julie explains the concept **as if** she **were** a teacher.

(← In fact, Julie is not a teacher.)

2 as if + 가정법 과거완료: as if + 주어 + had v-ed

'마치 ~였던 것처럼'의 의미로, 과거 사실과 반대되는 내용을 가정할 때 쓴다.

Jake talks **as if** he **had lived** in New York for a long time.

(← In fact, Jake didn't live in New York for a long time.)

C **It's time + 가정법:** It's time + 주어 + 동사의 과거형

'~할 때이다'의 의미로, 마땅히 해야[했어야] 할 일에 대한 재촉이나 유감을 표현한다.

It's time you **went** to bed. It's very late.

CHECK UP 빈칸에 알맞은 말을 고르시오.

1 I wish I _____ to Brian at the party yesterday.
ⓐ apologize ⓑ apologized ⓒ had apologized

2 He talks as if he _____ a doctor. In fact, he is not a doctor.
ⓐ were ⓑ have been ⓒ has been

3 I gave you enough time to think. It's time you _____ a decision.
ⓐ will make ⓑ made ⓒ had made

PRACTICE

🔍 Answer Key p.16

 STEP 1

( ) 안에서 알맞은 말을 고르시오.

1 Tony has gone to Tokyo to study. I wish he (is, were) with us now.

2 I missed an important meeting. I wish I (attended, had attended) the meeting.

3 Eli talks as if he (made, had made) the cake himself, but his mom actually made it.

4 It's time I (will go, went) home. It's very dark outside.

STEP 2

주어진 문장과 의미가 통하도록 빈칸에 알맞은 말을 쓰시오.

1 I'm sorry that the weather is not nice today.

→ I wish _____ today.

2 I'm sorry that I didn't listen to my mother then.

→ I wish _____ my mother then.

3 In fact, Kate is not an expert on the environment.

→ Kate talks as if _____ .

4 In fact, it was not his fault.

→ He feels as if _____ .

STEP 3

( ) 안의 말을 이용하여 가정법 문장을 완성하시오.

1 My mom gets sick often. I wish she _____ healthier. (be)

2 I wish I _____ more money before I traveled to Asia. (save)

3 Ted talks as if he _____ a lot of actors personally, but he doesn't. (know)

4 My dog is eating as if he _____ anything all day, but he actually ate a lot. (not, eat)

STEP 4

우리말과 일치하도록 ( ) 안에 주어진 단어를 바르게 배열하시오.

1 내가 어렸을 때 좀 더 활발했더라면 좋을 텐데. (I, had, wish, I, been, active, more)

→ _____ when I was young.

2 우리 오빠는 가끔 자신이 나의 아버지인 것처럼 행동한다. (father, as, were, if, he, my)

→ My brother sometimes behaves _____ .

3 이제 타인에 대한 불평을 멈출 때이다. (time, you, is, stopped, it, complaining)

→ _____ about others.

UNIT 03 주의해야 할 가정법

A Without[But for]

'~가 없(었)다면'의 의미로, 가정법의 if절을 대신하는 구문이다. 가정법 과거와 과거완료에 모두 쓰인다.

Without[But for] love, life **would be** meaningless.

(← If it were not for love, …)

Without[But for] his goal, we **would have lost** the soccer game.

(← If it had not been for his goal, …)

B 접속사 if를 생략한 가정법 문장

if절의 동사가 were, had일 때 접속사 if를 생략할 수 있으며, 이때 주어와 동사의 위치가 바뀐다.

Were I a magician, I would fly home.

(← If I were a magician, …)

Had I known about that ski camp, I would have gone.

(← If I had known about that ski camp, …)

C if절을 대신하는 어구

부정사구, 주어, 부사구에 가정의 의미가 함축되어 가정법의 if절을 대신해서 쓰일 수 있다.

It would be silly **to argue about that**. 〈부정사구〉

(← … if we argued about that.)

A good friend would forgive you for making such a mistake. 〈주어〉

(← If he/she were a good friend, he/she would forgive you …)

With your help, I could finish the project earlier. 〈부사구〉

(← If you helped me, …)

CHECK UP 빈칸에 알맞은 말을 고르시오.

1 _____ your umbrella, I would have gotten wet.

ⓐ With ⓑ But ⓒ Without

2 _____ rich, I would buy a new sports car.

ⓐ I were ⓑ Were I ⓒ If were I

3 _____ not helped him, he would have given up on the project.

ⓐ I had ⓑ Had I ⓒ If had I

PRACTICE

Answer Key p.16

STEP 1

( ) 안에서 알맞은 말을 고르시오.

1 (Without, But) for the rain, we would have arrived on time.

2 (It were not for, Were it not for) oxygen, we could not live.

3 It would be nice (take a nap, to take a nap) for an hour every day.

STEP 2

두 문장의 의미가 같도록 if를 생략하여 빈칸에 알맞은 말을 쓰시오.

1 If it were warmer, we could eat lunch in the park.

→ _____ _____ _____ , we could eat lunch in the park.

2 If it were not for the internet, our lives would be very different.

→ _____ _____ _____ , our lives would be very different.

3 If it had not been for my teacher's advice, I would have given up on my goal.

→ _____ _____ _____ , I would have given up on my goal.

STEP 3

주어진 문장과 의미가 통하도록 if절을 대신하는 어구를 써서 문장을 완성하시오.

1 It would be fun if I made friends in a foreign country.

→ It would be fun _____ _____ _____ in a foreign country.

2 If he were a wise man, he would not do such a thing.

→ _____ _____ _____ would not do such a thing.

3 If my brother had helped me, I could have finished my homework on time.

→ _____ _____ _____ _____ , I could have finished my homework on time.

STEP 4

우리말과 일치하도록 ( ) 안에 주어진 단어를 바르게 배열하시오.

1 우리 부모님의 지원이 없다면, 나는 해외에서 공부할 수 없을 텐데. (parents', my, without, support)

→ _____ , I wouldn't be able to study abroad.

2 그의 부상이 없었더라면, 그는 마라톤 선수가 될 수 있었을 텐데. (injury, had, for, his, it, been, not)

→ _____ , he could have been a marathoner.

3 영국인이라면 그 단어를 사용하지 않을 텐데. (word, British, not, use, a, that, would, person)

→ _____ .

GRAMMAR FOR WRITING

A 우리말과 일치하도록 ( ) 안의 말을 이용하여 문장을 완성하시오.

1 내가 건강하다면, 긴 여행을 갈 수 있을 텐데. (take)

→ If I _____ healthy, I _____ a long trip.

2 네 전화가 없었다면, 나는 일찍 일어나지 못했을 것이다. (without, phone call)

→ _____, I would not have woken up early.

3 Stacy가 도와줬다면, 나는 그 시험에 통과할 수 있었을 텐데. (with, help)

→ _____, I could have passed the exam.

4 만약 내가 중국어를 잘했더라면, Tao와 더 친한 친구가 될 수 있었을 텐데. (speak, be)

→ If I _____ Chinese well, I _____ closer friends with Tao.

5 어젯밤에 눈이 오지 않았다면, 우린 오늘 등산을 갈 텐데. (snow, go)

→ If it _____ last night, we _____ mountain climbing today.

6 Amy는 마치 어젯밤에 나쁜 꿈을 꾼 것처럼 보이지만, 그렇지 않았다. (have)

→ Amy looks _____ a bad dream last night, but she didn't.

B 우리말과 일치하도록 ( ) 안에 주어진 단어를 바르게 배열하시오.

1 Tony는 마치 인생에 대해 다 아는 것처럼 이야기한다. (as, if, he, talks, knew)

→ Tony _____ all about life.

2 우리가 휴식을 취해야 할 때이다. 우리는 온종일 열심히 일했다. (is, break, we, it, time, took, a)

→ _____. We have worked very hard all day.

3 네 가족이라면 저 상황에서 너를 비난하지 않을 텐데. (family, not, your, blame, would, you)

→ _____ in that situation.

4 하루에 더 많은 시간이 있으면 좋을 텐데. (would, to, have, it, be, nice)

→ _____ more hours in a day.

5 내가 슈퍼히어로라면, 곤경에 처한 사람들을 도울 수 있을 텐데. (were, superhero, I, I, help, a, could)

→ _____ people in trouble.

6 그녀의 아름다운 목소리가 아니었더라면, 이 노래는 인기가 없었을 것이다.
(been, voice, it, her, not, had, for, beautiful)

→ _____, this song wouldn't have been popular.

C 주어진 문장과 의미가 통하도록 빈칸에 알맞은 말을 쓰시오.

1 As I don't play the electric guitar well, I can't join the band.

→ If I _____ the electric guitar well, I _____ the band.

2 As I didn't have enough time, I couldn't answer all the questions on the exam.

→ If I _____ enough time, I _____ all the questions on the exam.

3 I'm sorry that I wasn't honest from the beginning.

→ I wish _____ honest from the beginning.

4 In fact, Olivia didn't see a ghost.

→ Olivia looks as if she _____ a ghost.

5 Because Dean played very well, we won the soccer game.

→ If Dean _____ very well, we _____ the soccer game.

6 I'm sorry that I can't speak English well.

→ I wish _____ English well.

D 그림을 보고 상자 안의 말을 이용하여 가정법 문장을 완성하시오.

1	2	3
have an umbrella	can ride it	study harder

1 It is raining hard! I wish I _____.

2 The line for the roller coaster is so long. If there were less people, we _____ sooner.

3 She got a bad score. If she _____, she would have gotten a better score.

REVIEW TEST

[1-5] 빈칸에 들어갈 알맞은 말을 고르시오.

1

| If I _____ you, I would forgive him for his mistake. |

① am　　　　　　② were
③ had been　　　④ have been
⑤ would have been

2

| If my computer had not been broken, I _____ my homework. |

① finish　　　　　② can finish
③ have finished　④ had finished
⑤ could have finished

3

| If you had exercised more regularly, you _____ much healthier now. |

① will be　　　　② am
③ were　　　　　④ would be
⑤ would have been

4

| I wish I _____ my cousins last summer vacation. |

① visit　　　　　　② visited
③ had visited　　　④ would visit
⑤ would have visited

5

| _____ you, I would not give up on my studies. |

① I am　　　　　② Am I
③ I were　　　　④ Were I
⑤ If were I

[6-7] 다음 중 어법상 틀린 것을 고르시오.

6　① It's time you got out of bed.
　② I wish I could whistle well.
　③ Nick talks as if he had lived in Africa.
　④ I had known his situation, I could have helped him.
　⑤ Without my friends, my life would be boring.

7　① If I had a sister, I could go shopping with her.
　② I wish I hadn't eaten too much.
　③ If it had not rained, the sports day would not have been postponed.
　④ He acts as if nothing had happened between us.
　⑤ If I had brought my purse this morning, I would have had it now.

8 빈칸에 들어갈 말로 알맞지 않은 것은?

| _____ my glasses, I couldn't see anything. |

① Without　　　② But
③ But for　　　④ Were it not for
⑤ If it were not for

142

빈출

[9-10] 다음 우리말을 영어로 바르게 옮긴 것을 고르시오.

9

내가 그 약을 먹었다면, 지금 훨씬 나을 텐데.

① If I took the medicine, I would feel much better now.
② If I took the medicine, I would have felt much better now.
③ If I had taken the medicine, I would feel much better now.
④ If I had taken the medicine, I would have felt much better now.
⑤ If I had taken the medicine, I feel much better now.

10

어렸을 때 부모님의 조언을 들었더라면 좋을 텐데.

① I wish I listen to my parents' advice when I was young.
② I wish I didn't listen to my parents' advice when I was young.
③ I wish I listened to my parents' advice when I was young.
④ I wish I had listened to my parents' advice when I was young.
⑤ I wish I hadn't listened to my parents' advice when I was young.

11 우리말과 일치하도록 할 때, 빈칸에 들어갈 알맞은 말은?

Bella는 마치 발레리나인 것처럼 춤춘다.
→ Bella dances as if she _____ a ballerina.

① is
② were
③ has been
④ had been
⑤ will be

[12-13] 두 문장의 의미가 같도록 할 때, 빈칸에 들어갈 알맞은 말을 고르시오.

12

If you had helped me, I could have finished the job sooner.
→ _____ your help, I could have finished the job sooner.

① To
② With
③ Without
④ But
⑤ But for

13

It would be fun if we saw the movie together.
→ It would be fun _____ the movie together.

① see
② to see
③ to seeing
④ saw
⑤ having seen

서술형

[14-16] 우리말과 일치하도록 ( ) 안의 말을 이용하여 문장을 완성하시오.

14 내 집이 학교와 더 가까우면 좋을 텐데.
(wish, house, be)

→ I _____ _____ _____
_____ closer to my school.

15 내가 너라면, 그에게 그 돈을 빌려줄 텐데. (be)

→ _____ _____ _____,
I would lend him the money.

16 그 보안 카메라가 없었다면, 그 도둑은 잡히지 않았을 것이다. (the security camera)

→ _____ _____ _____
_____, the thief wouldn't have been arrested.

17 다음 우리말을 영어로 잘못 옮긴 것은?

> 그 의사의 치료가 없었다면, 그는 죽었을 것이다.

① With the doctor's treatment, he would have died.

② Without the doctor's treatment, he would have died.

③ But for the doctor's treatment, he would have died.

④ Had it not been for the doctor's treatment, he would have died.

⑤ If it had not been for the doctor's treatment, he would have died.

서술형
[18-20] 주어진 문장과 의미가 통하도록 빈칸에 알맞은 말을 쓰시오.

18 As I don't have a car, I can't pick you up from the airport.

→ If I _____ a car, I _____ you up from the airport.

19 Because they had fastened their seat belts, they weren't seriously injured.

→ If they _____ their seat belts, they _____ seriously injured.

20 I'm sorry that I didn't read a lot of books when I was young.

→ _____ when I was young.

서술형
[21-23] 우리말과 일치하도록 ( ) 안에 주어진 단어를 바르게 배열하시오.

21 정직한 사람이라면 그런 말을 하지 않을 것이다.
(not, honest, an, person, say, would)

→ _____ such a thing.

22 여행 안내서가 없었다면, 나는 그 랜드마크들을 찾을 수 없었을 것이다. (a, I, have, travel guide, found, without, could, not)

→ _____ those landmarks.

23 우리는 집에 갈 시간이다. 벌써 10시이다.
(went, it's, we, home, time)

→ _____ .
It's already ten o'clock.

24 다음 중 어느 빈칸에도 들어갈 수 없는 것은?

> • Luke behaves as if he ⓐ rich.
> • A good friend ⓑ always be with you in your tough times.
> • I am really busy. I wish I ⓒ more time to relax.
> • If I had known about the play, I would ⓓ seen it.

① would   ② had   ③ were
④ have   ⑤ been

서술형
25 우리말과 일치하도록 주어진 조건에 맞게 문장을 완성하시오.

> 그가 나에게 부탁을 했더라면, 나는 그를 도와주었을 텐데.

〈조건〉 1. ask를 이용할 것
        2. if를 생략할 것

→ _____ , I would have helped him.

26 다음 중 어법상 옳은 것을 모두 고르면?

① Were I there, I would have seen it.

② It's time you cleaned your room. It's very dirty.

③ If I know her phone number, I would have called her.

④ Without science, we would see many things differently.

⑤ If you had finished your homework, you could go to the party now.

27 다음 중 어법상 옳은 것으로 바르게 짝지어진 것은?

a. Without her help, I would have failed.

b. If I had not spent all my money, I could buy this dress now.

c. If I have had more time, I could have studied more.

d. It would be great meet him at the party.

e. Jim talks as if he were a computer expert.

① a, b, d   ② a, b, e

③ b, c, d   ④ b, c, e

⑤ b, d, e

고난도

28 다음 중 어법상 옳은 것의 개수는?

· If I were you, I would not go out late at night.

· But for his last-minute goal, we would have lost the game.

· Had it not been for your advice, I could not have finished the project.

· Andy talks as if he had helped me to finish the work.

· If I woke up early yesterday, I would have had a breakfast.

① 1개   ② 2개   ③ 3개

④ 4개   ⑤ 5개

서술형

[29-31] 밑줄 친 부분이 어법상 옳은지 판단하고, 틀리면 바르게 고치시오.

29 If I had bought a ticket, I <u>could have gone</u> to the concert.

(O / X) _____

30 Kimberley is angry with me. I wish I <u>have not lost</u> her cell phone.

(O / X) _____

31 <u>With your support</u>, I could continue my studies.

(O / X) _____

서술형 고난도

[32-33] 어법상 틀린 부분을 찾아 바르게 고치시오.

32 It's time I go on a diet. My jeans are too tight now. (1개)

33 My grandfather passed away a few months ago. He was a great man, and I loved him very much. I wish I showed my love to him more when he was alive. (1개)

LET'S REVIEW

주요 예문을 다시 한번 확인하고, 우리말과 일치하도록 빈칸을 채우시오.

- If I **knew** her problem, I [1]_____ her.
  내가 그녀의 문제를 안다면, 그녀를 도울 수 있을 텐데.   **Unit 01 - A**

- If I [2]_____ **reserved** the ticket online, I **would have gotten** a discount.
  내가 온라인으로 표를 예매했다면, 할인을 받을 수 있었을 텐데.   **Unit 01 - B**

- If he **had not moved** to another city, I [3]_____ him now.
  그가 다른 도시로 이사 가지 않았더라면, 나는 지금 그를 볼 수 있을 텐데.   **Unit 01 - C**

- I've never had my own room. [4]_____ I **had** my own room.
  나는 한 번도 내 방을 가져본 적이 없다. 내 방이 있다면 좋을 텐데.   **Unit 02 - A**

- My grades are bad. **I wish** I [5]_____ harder for the exams.
  내 성적이 나쁘다. 내가 시험공부를 더 열심히 했더라면 좋을 텐데.   **Unit 02 - A**

- Julie explains the concept [6]_____ she **were** a teacher.
  Julie는 마치 선생님인 것처럼 그 개념을 설명한다.   **Unit 02 - B**

- Jake talks **as if** he [7]_____ in New York for a long time.
  Jake는 마치 뉴욕에서 오랫동안 살았던 것처럼 이야기한다.   **Unit 02 - B**

- **It's time** you **went** to bed. It's very late. 너는 자야할 시간이다. 많이 늦었다.   **Unit 02 - C**

- [8]_____ love, life **would be** meaningless. 사랑이 없다면, 삶은 무의미할 것이다.   **Unit 03 - A**

- **Were I** a magician, I would fly home. 내가 마법사라면, 나는 집으로 날아갈 텐데.   **Unit 03 - B**

- It would be silly [9]_____ **argue about that.**
  그것에 대해 논쟁한다면 어리석은 일일 것이다.   **Unit 03 - C**

Q Answers

[1] could help   [2] had   [3] could see   [4] I wish   [5] had studied   [6] as if   [7] had lived

[8] Without[But for, If it were not for, Were it not for]   [9] to

ESSENTIAL RULES OF
ENGLISH GRAMMAR

CHAPTER
11

일치와 화법

일치는 수와 시제에 맞추어 동사를 변형시키는
것이고, 화법은 말을 전달하는 방법을 말한다.

수의 일치

A 단수 취급하는 경우

1 each, every, -thing, -one, -body

Every student in our school **has** a locker.

Something **is** wrong with my car. It makes a noise whenever I brake.

2 (복수형의) 학과명, 국가명

Mathematics **is** a subject that many students hate.

The Philippines **consists** of about 7,100 islands.

3 시간, 거리, 금액, 무게

Five kilometers **is** not a short distance to walk.

Fifty dollars **is** a lot of money for students.

4 동명사구나 명사절이 주어인 경우

Smoking cigarettes **is** a bad habit.

Where Jessica went **is** unknown. She didn't tell anyone.

B 복수 취급하는 경우

1 (both) A and B

Julie and I **were** born in 2008.

　① A and B가 하나의 개념을 나타내는 경우, 단수 취급한다.
　　Slow and steady **wins** the race.

2 the + 형용사(~한 사람들)

The blind **are** able to read by using their hands.

3 a number of + 복수명사(많은 ~)

A number of people **were** waiting at the bank.

　① 「the number of + 복수명사」는 '~의 수'라는 의미이고, 단수 취급한다.
　　The number of owls **is** decreasing each year.

CHECK UP 빈칸에 알맞은 말을 고르시오.

1 Learning a foreign language _____ a lot of time.
　ⓐ take　　　ⓑ takes　　　ⓒ taking

2 A number of students in my school _____ glasses.
　ⓐ wear　　　ⓑ wears　　　ⓒ is wearing

PRACTICE

Answer Key p.18

( ) 안에서 알맞은 말을 고르시오.

1 (Is, Are) there anyone here who saw the movie *Frozen*?

2 Statistics (is, are) a branch of mathematics.

3 A number of people (was, were) injured in the airplane crash.

4 Both the doctor and nurse (come, comes) to examine me every morning.

어법상 틀린 부분을 찾아 바르게 고치시오.

1 Economics are a popular major in many universities.

2 Everyone were jumping for joy when the Korean team scored a goal.

3 A lot of people think that the old is wiser than the young.

4 Three kilometers are too far for him to run.

( ) 안의 말을 이용하여 문장을 완성하시오.

1 Curry and rice _____ my favorite dish these days. (be)

2 The United States of America _____ a lot of famous landmarks. (have)

3 The number of obese children _____ increasing. (be)

4 Eight dollars _____ to be a good price for the book. (seem)

우리말과 일치하도록 ( ) 안의 말을 이용하여 문장을 완성하시오.

1 누군가가 내 자리에 앉아 있다. 나는 그에게 비켜 달라고 할 것이다. (someone, sit)

→ _____ _____ _____ in my seat. I'll tell him to move.

2 물리학은 자연의 법칙에 관한 연구이다. (physics, be)

→ _____ _____ the study of the laws of nature.

3 Connor가 말한 것은 사실이 아니었다. (what, say)

→ _____ _____ _____ _____ not true.

4 판타지 소설을 읽는 것은 재미있다. (fantasy novels)

→ _____ _____ _____ _____ fun.

UNIT 02 시제의 일치

A 시제 일치의 원칙

주절의 시제	종속절의 시제
현재	모든 시제
과거	현재 → 과거
	현재완료, 과거 → 과거완료
	will → would, can → could, may → might, must → must[had to]

I *think* that Aria **is** in Europe on business.
I *think* that Aria **was** in Europe on business.
I *think* that Aria **will be** in Europe on business.

I *knew* that Joe **worked** at an animation company.
I *knew* that Joe **had worked** at an animation company.
I *knew* that Joe **would work** at an animation company.

B 시제 일치의 예외

1 과학적 사실, 일반적 진리, 속담 등은 주절의 시제와 상관없이 현재시제를 쓴다.

My teacher said that the moon **goes** around the earth.
My mom said that time **is** money.

2 역사적 사실은 주절의 시제와 상관없이 과거시제를 쓴다.

Lucas read that Columbus **discovered** America in 1492.

3 과거의 상황이 현재에도 지속될 때는 주절이 과거시제여도 종속절에 현재시제를 쓰기도 한다.

Chris said that he **checks** his email twice a day.

 **CHECK UP** 빈칸에 알맞은 말을 고르시오.

1 The teacher said that the sports day _____ postponed.
ⓐ will be   ⓑ is   ⓒ would be

2 We learned that light _____ faster than sound.
ⓐ travels   ⓑ traveled   ⓒ had traveled

3 The article said that Princess Diana _____ in 1997.
ⓐ die   ⓑ died   ⓒ has died

150

PRACTICE

Q Answer Key p.18

STEP 1

( ) 안에서 알맞은 말을 고르시오.

1 Brian said that he (has lost, had lost) his math textbook.

2 Julie told me she (will study, would study) more after graduation.

3 Even the child understood that five times two (is, was) ten.

4 We learned that the Joseon Dynasty (was, had been) founded in 1392.

STEP 2

( ) 안의 말을 이용하여 문장을 완성하시오.

1 The teacher said that hot air _____ lighter than cold air. (be)

2 The book said that Captain Cook _____ Australia in 1770. (discover)

3 I heard that Alexander Graham Bell _____ the telephone. (invent)

4 Jay discovered that Korea _____ four seasons. (have)

STEP 3

문장의 주절을 과거시제로 바꿀 때, 빈칸에 알맞은 말을 쓰시오.

1 Nobody knows why Mason is absent from school.

→ Nobody knew why Mason _____ absent from school.

2 I think that Evelyn will attend the meeting.

→ I thought that Evelyn _____ the meeting.

3 In school, we learn that Antarctica is the coldest place on Earth.

→ In school, we learned that Antarctica _____ the coldest place on Earth.

4 Do you know that email was invented in the 1970s?

→ Did you know that email _____ invented in the 1970s?

STEP 4

우리말과 일치하도록 ( ) 안의 말을 이용하여 문장을 완성하시오.

1 그 아이들은 물은 0°C에서 언다고 배웠다. (freeze)

→ The children learned that _____ _____ at 0°C.

2 나는 한국 전쟁이 1950년에 일어났다고 들었다. (break out)

→ I heard that the Korean War _____ _____ in 1950.

3 우리 영어 선생님은 항상 연습이 완벽을 만든다고 말씀하셨다. (practice, make)

→ My English teacher always said that _____ _____ perfect.

4 Wyatt는 휴가 동안 일본에 갈 것이라고 말했다. (will)

→ Wyatt said that _____ _____ _____ to Japan during the vacation.

UNIT 03 화법

직접화법은 다른 사람이 한 말을 따옴표로 묶어서 그대로 전달하는 것이고, 간접화법은 다른 사람이 한 말을 전달자의 입장에 맞게 바꿔서 전달하는 것이다.

A 평서문의 간접화법 전환

① 전달동사를 바꾼다. (say[said] → say[said], say to[said to] → tell[told])
② 주절의 콤마와 인용 부호를 없애고 접속사 that을 쓴다. (that은 생략 가능)
③ 인용 부호 안의 인칭대명사는 전달자에 맞춰서 바꾸고, 동사와 부사도 시제에 맞춰 바꾼다.

Jay said to me, "I won't change my decision." 〈직접화법〉
→ Jay **told** me **(that) he wouldn't** change **his** decision. 〈간접화법〉

B 의문문의 간접화법 전환

1 의문사가 있는 경우: ask (+ 목적어) + 의문사 + 주어 + 동사

Zoe said to me, "Why do you need a hammer?" 〈직접화법〉
Zoe **asked** me **why I needed** a hammer. 〈간접화법〉

ⓘ 의문사가 주어인 경우에는 「의문사 + 동사」의 어순을 그대로 쓴다.
Brian said to us, "Who took my science textbook?"
→ Brian asked us **who had taken his** science textbook.

2 의문사가 없는 경우: ask (+ 목적어) + if[whether] + 주어 + 동사

Harry said to me, "Do you like Greek food?" 〈직접화법〉
→ Harry **asked** me **if[whether] I liked** Greek food. 〈간접화법〉

C 명령문의 간접화법 전환: tell[ask, order, advise, ...] + 목적어 + to-v

Gary said to me, "Change your password regularly." 〈직접화법〉
→ Gary **told** me **to change my** password regularly. 〈간접화법〉

ⓘ 부정 명령문의 경우 to-v 앞에 not을 붙인다.
My teacher said to us, "Don't cheat on the exam."
→ My teacher ordered us **not to cheat** on the exam.

빈칸에 알맞은 말을 고르시오.

1 Dean asked me _____ I had seen the play *Hamlet*.
 ⓐ that ⓑ if ⓒ what

2 I asked Terry _____ me some money.
 ⓐ lend ⓑ lending ⓒ to lend

➕ PLUS : 화법 전환에 따라 변하는 부사(구)

간접화법으로 바꿀 때, 말하는 시점이나 장소가 다른 경우 부사(구)를 현재의 시점에 맞춰 바꿔 쓴다.
now → then / today → that day /
tomorrow → the next day,
the following day / yesterday →
the day before, the previous day /
ago → before / here → there /
this → that / these → those

PRACTICE

Q **Answer Key p.18**

STEP 1

( ) 안에서 알맞은 말을 고르시오.

1 Jenny (said, told) me that she would help me with the work.

2 I asked him (why he had called, why had he called) me last night.

3 A stranger asked me (that, if) there was a police station nearby.

4 My parents advised me (not to go, to not go) out alone late at night.

STEP 2

다음을 간접화법으로 바꿀 때, 빈칸에 알맞은 말을 쓰시오.

1 Paul said, "My business is in trouble."

→ Paul _____ in trouble.

2 The woman said to me, "I fell in love with you at first sight."

→ The woman _____ at first sight.

3 Brian said to us, "Have you seen the musical *The Lion King*?"

→ Brian _____ the musical *The Lion King*.

4 The doctor said to me, "You will get well soon."

→ The doctor _____ well soon.

5 Mom said to us, "Who broke the vase on the table?"

→ Mom _____ on the table.

6 The doctor said to him, "Drink eight glasses of water a day."

→ The doctor _____ of water a day.

7 She said to the children, "Don't run in the hall."

→ She _____ in the hall.

STEP 3

우리말과 일치하도록 ( ) 안의 말을 이용하여 문장을 완성하시오.

1 엄마는 내게 언제 내가 집에 오는지 물어보셨다. (get)

→ Mom asked _____ _____ _____ _____ home.

2 아버지는 나에게 항상 정직하라고 말씀하셨다. (be)

→ My father told _____ _____ _____ honest all the time.

3 Harry가 나에게 요리에 관심이 있는지 물었다. (be)

→ Harry asked me _____ _____ _____ interested in cooking.

4 Tim은 Sarah에게 그녀가 휴대 전화를 어디서 샀는지 물었다. (buy)

→ Tim asked _____ _____ _____ _____ _____ her cell phone.

GRAMMAR FOR WRITING

A 우리말과 일치하도록 ( ) 안의 말을 이용하여 문장을 완성하시오.

1 두 시간은 낮잠을 자기에 충분한 시간이다. (enough time)

→ _____ for a nap.

2 어머니는 경험이 최고의 스승이라고 말씀하셨다. (experience, be)

→ My mother _____ the best teacher.

3 Sarah와 Brad는 같은 학교에 다닌다. (go)

→ _____ to the same school.

4 선생님께서 나에게 왜 수업에 늦었는지 물어보셨다. (late)

→ My teacher _____ for class.

5 Mike는 내게 공포 영화를 좋아하는지 물었다. (like)

→ Mike _____ horror movies.

6 우리는 물이 지구 표면의 약 70%를 덮고 있다고 배웠다. (learn, cover)

→ We _____ about 70% of the earth's surface.

7 나는 마카오가 1999년에 중국에 반환되었다고 들었다. (be returned)

→ I heard that Macau _____ to China in 1999.

B 우리말과 일치하도록 ( ) 안에 주어진 단어를 바르게 배열하시오.

1 네가 그것을 좋아하는지 아닌지는 또 다른 문제이다. (you, or, whether, like, it, not, is)

→ _____ another matter.

2 홈런 공을 모으는 게 내 취미이다. 나는 벌써 다섯 개를 가지고 있다. (home run, collecting, balls, is)

→ _____ my hobby. I already have five.

3 그들은 그들의 일정을 변경하고 싶다고 말했다. (wanted, they, said, that, change, they, to)

→ _____ their schedule.

4 나는 버스에 내 쇼핑백을 두고 내렸다는 것을 깨달았다. (left, I, that, had, realized, I)

→ _____ my shopping bag on the bus.

5 내 선생님께서 우리에게 떠들지 말라고 지시하셨다. (us, ordered, to, teacher, make, my, not)

→ _____ any noise.

6 일반적으로 말해서, 젊은이들은 노인들보다 더 빨리 달린다. (run, the, old, young, than, the, faster)

→ Generally speaking, _____.

154

C 인용 부호(" ") 안의 말을 빈칸에 알맞은 형태로 바꿔 쓰시오.

1 "Life is short, but art is long."

→ Someone told me _____.

2 "Do you have medicine for a headache?"

→ Emily asked me _____.

3 "I found my cell phone in the bathroom."

→ My brother told me _____.

4 "Don't blame me for the accident."

→ Jake told me _____.

5 "Blue jeans were invented in America in 1873."

→ The book said _____.

6 "The earth rotates once a day."

→ Our class learned _____.

7 "When did you see the strange man with a moustache?"

→ The policeman asked me _____.

D 그림을 보고 보기에서 알맞은 말을 골라 ( ) 안의 말과 함께 써서 문장을 완성하시오. (단, 한 번씩만 쓸 것)

보기	each	every	a number of

1 The play was sold out. _____ taken in the theater. (seat, be)

2 Three people are playing a card game. _____ three cards. (player, have)

3 Look at the long line! _____ waiting to get the singer's autograph. (fan, be)

REVIEW TEST

[1–5] 빈칸에 들어갈 알맞은 말을 고르시오.

1

The man knew that someone _____ watching him.

① is   ② are
③ was   ④ were
⑤ have been

2

Did you know that Harvard University _____ founded in 1636?

① be   ② is
③ was ·   ④ has been
⑤ had been

3

I didn't know that Canberra _____ the capital city of Australia.

① be   ② is
③ will be   ④ has been
⑤ had been

4

He asked me _____ there was a convenience store nearby.

① that   ② what
③ as   ④ unless
⑤ whether

5

Dad told me _____ the battery of the laptop.

① check   ② checked
③ checking   ④ to check
⑤ had checked

[6–7] 다음 중 어법상 틀린 것을 고르시오.

6

① What Tim suggested was a good idea.
② Each question has five choices.
③ Both Mia and I want to be great dancers.
④ Two hours are enough time for me to read this book.
⑤ The old are more likely to vote than the young.

7

① Mathematics is difficult but interesting.
② Every restaurant on this street is good.
③ Ivy said that she would go shopping with her sister.
④ The couple asked me to come to their wedding.
⑤ He read that pine trees stayed green all year long.

빈출

8 다음을 간접화법으로 바르게 전환한 것은?

My teacher said to us, "Don't speak during the test."

① My teacher told us don't speak during the test.
② My teacher told us don't to speak during the test.
③ My teacher told us not speak during the test.
④ My teacher told us not speaking during the test.
⑤ My teacher told us not to speak during the test.

빈출

[9-11] 빈칸에 들어갈 말이 순서대로 바르게 짝지어진 것을 고르시오.

9

- A number of buildings _____ destroyed by the flood.
- The number of blood donations _____ decreasing.

① was – is
② was – are
③ were – is
④ were – are
⑤ be – are

10

- Learning about other cultures _____ very fun.
- The rich _____ not always happier than the poor.

① is – is
② is – are
③ are – is
④ are – are
⑤ be – are

11

- Thirty dollars for a meal _____ expensive for students.
- _____ there anyone here who can speak Spanish?

① is – Is
② is – Are
③ are – Is
④ are – Are
⑤ be – Are

12 다음 중 어법상 옳은 것은?

① She ordered us don't touch the wall.
② Henry and I am going to the movies.
③ It is often said that hunger was the best sauce.
④ Two days are a long time for me to be without a cell phone.
⑤ Sue asked me if I had met Jane the previous night.

서술형

[13-15] ( ) 안의 말을 이용하여 문장을 완성하시오.

13 In science class, I discovered that gas _____ when it is heated. (expand)

14 I learned that the steam engine _____ invented by an English inventor. (be)

15 Physics _____ the scientific study of matter and energy. (be)

16 다음 중 간접화법의 전환이 잘못된 것은?

① He said to me, "What are you doing?"
→ He asked me what I was doing.
② Drew said to me, "Don't tell anyone."
→ Drew told me not to tell anyone.
③ Eric said, "I will lose weight."
→ Eric said that he would lose weight.
④ She said to us, "Has anyone seen my cell phone?"
→ She asked us if had anyone seen her cell phone.
⑤ Ava said to me, "What is your hobby?"
→ Ava asked me what my hobby was.

[17-19] 다음을 간접화법으로 바꿔 쓰시오.

17 My secretary said to me, "Someone called you several times."

→ _____

_____

18 My professor said to me, "Study marketing abroad."

→ _____

_____

19 The waiter asked me, "How do you like your steak?"

→ _____

_____

[20-22] 우리말과 일치하도록 ( ) 안의 말을 이용하여 문장을 완성하시오.

20 모든 나라는 그들만의 독특한 음식을 가지고 있다. (every, country)

→ _____ its own unique food.

21 그 글에서 나는 지구가 태양 주위를 일년에 한 바퀴 돈다는 것을 읽었다. (go, around)

→ In the article, I read that the earth _____ once a year.

22 선생님께서 나에게 내가 소설 읽기를 좋아하는지 물으셨다. (ask, like)

→ My teacher _____ reading novels.

[23-24] 우리말과 일치하도록 ( ) 안에 주어진 단어를 바르게 배열하시오.

23 나는 그가 세계적으로 유명한 배우가 될 것이라고 생각했다. (would, thought, that, I, be, he)

→ _____ a world-famous actor.

24 Jamie는 나에게 아무에게도 그의 비밀을 말하지 말라고 부탁했다. (secret, not, his, to, tell)

→ Jamie asked me _____ to anyone.

25 우리말과 일치하도록 주어진 조건에 맞게 문장을 완성하시오.

아픈 사람들은 그곳에서 간호사들에 의해 돌봐진다.

〈조건〉 1. 「the + 형용사」를 쓸 것
2. sick, take care of를 이용할 것

→ _____ by the nurses there.

26 다음 중 어법상 옳은 것을 모두 고르면?

① Each desk in the library have a lamp.
② Exercising too much is not good for your health.
③ Next lesson, we will learn how the Second World War ends.
④ The number of students in each class are twenty.
⑤ My mother asked me who had broken her perfume bottle.

27 다음 중 어법상 옳은 것으로 바르게 짝지어진 것은?

> a. I asked which team does he support.
> b. Tony said he was going to marry Amy.
> c. Sophie and I are going to a concert tonight.
> d. Politics is a subject that is relevant to our lives.
> e. Twenty dollars are enough to buy a T-shirt here.

① a, b, c   ② a, b, e
③ a, c, e   ④ b, c, d
⑤ b, c, e

28 다음 중 어법상 옳은 것의 개수는?

> • Everything in this country captures my eyes.
> • In class, I learned that cold air was heavier than warm air.
> • Three kilograms is not heavy for adults to carry.
> • My sister said she would move to Busan next year.
> • In this movie, the dead rises from graves.

① 1개   ② 2개   ③ 3개
④ 4개   ⑤ 5개

[29-31] 밑줄 친 부분이 어법상 옳은지 판단하고, 틀리면 바르게 고치시오.

29 The Netherlands <u>have</u> many great tourist attractions.

(O / X) _____

30 I think that Matt <u>was</u> much taller than me last year.

(O / X) _____

31 Because of the heavy snow, a number of students <u>was</u> late for class.

(O / X) _____

[32-33] 어법상 틀린 부분을 찾아 바르게 고치시오.

32 I was invited to Oliver's house. He asked me I liked Italian food. (1개)

33 After I changed schools, I was often late for class. One day, my teacher got angry and told me don't be late again. (1개)

LET'S REVIEW

주요 예문을 다시 한번 확인하고, 우리말과 일치하도록 빈칸을 채우시오.

- Every student in our school **has** a locker. 우리 학교의 모든 학생은 사물함이 있다. **Unit 01 - A**

- Mathematics [1]_____ a subject that many students hate.

  수학은 많은 학생이 싫어하는 과목이다. **Unit 01 - A**

- Five kilometers [2]_____ not a short distance to walk.

  5킬로미터는 걷기에 짧은 거리가 아니다. **Unit 01 - A**

- Smoking cigarettes [3]_____ a bad habit. 담배를 피는 것은 나쁜 습관이다. **Unit 01 - A**

- Julie and I [4]_____ born in 2008. Julie와 나는 2008년에 태어났다. **Unit 01 - B**

- The blind [5]_____ able to read by using their hands.

  시각 장애인들은 그들의 손을 이용해서 읽을 수 있다. **Unit 01 - B**

- A number of people [6]_____ waiting at the bank.

  은행에서 많은 사람들이 기다리고 있었다. **Unit 01 - B**

- I knew that Joe **had worked** at an animation company.

  나는 Joe가 애니메이션 회사에서 일했다는 것을 알고 있었다. **Unit 02 - A**

- My mom said that time [7]_____ money. 엄마는 시간이 돈이라고 말씀하셨다. **Unit 02 - B**

- Lucas read that Columbus **discovered** America in 1492.

  Lucas는 Columbus가 1492년에 아메리카를 발견했다고 읽었다. **Unit 02 - B**

- Jay said to me, "I won't change my decision."

  Jay는 나에게 "나는 내 결정을 바꾸지 않을 거야."라고 말했다.

  → Jay **told** me **(that) he wouldn't** change **his** decision.

  Jay는 나에게 그가 그의 결정을 바꾸지 않을 거라고 말했다. **Unit 03 - A**

- Zoe said to me, "Why do you need a hammer?" Zoe는 나에게 "너는 왜 망치가 필요하니?"라고 말했다.

  → Zoe [8]_____ me **why** _____ a hammer.

  Zoe는 나에게 내가 왜 망치가 필요한지 물었다. **Unit 03 - B**

- Harry **asked** me [9]_____ **I liked** Greek food.

  Harry는 나에게 그리스 음식을 좋아하는지 물었다. **Unit 03 - B**

- Gary **told** me **to change my** password regularly.

  Gary는 나에게 정기적으로 내 비밀번호를 바꾸라고 말했다. **Unit 03 - C**

Q Answers

[1] is   [2] is   [3] is   [4] were   [5] are   [6] were   [7] is   [8] asked, I needed   [9] if[whether]

160

CHAPTER

12

기타 구문

영어에서는 특정 부분에 대한 강조나 명료한
정보 전달을 목적으로 특이한 문장 구조가
쓰이기도 한다.

UNIT 01 강조, 부정구문, 병렬

A 강조

1 do에 의한 강조: 강조하는 동사 앞에 do[does, did]를 쓰고, 뒤에는 동사원형이 온다.

I don't remember his name, but I **do** remember his face.

2 「It is[was] ~ that ...」에 의한 강조: 강조하고자 하는 부분을 It is[was]와 that 사이에 놓으며, '···한 것은 바로 ~이다[였다]'의 의미이다.

Tom saw Julie at the theater yesterday.

→ **It was** Tom **that** saw Julie at the theater yesterday. 〈주어 강조〉

→ **It was** Julie **that** Tom saw at the theater yesterday. 〈목적어 강조〉

→ **It was** at the theater **that** Tom saw Julie yesterday. 〈부사구 강조〉

→ **It was** yesterday **that** Tom saw Julie at the theater. 〈부사 강조〉

Who wrote the novel?

→ Who **was it that** wrote the novel? 〈의문사 강조〉

B 부정구문

1 부분 부정: 「not + all[every, always]」 형태로 '모두[항상] ~인 것은 아니다'의 의미이다.

Not all of the members agreed to the new plan.

2 전체 부정: no, none, never, neither는 '아무도[결코, 둘 다] ~ 않다'의 의미이다.

None of the students were in the classroom. 〈all의 전체 부정〉
Neither of us can play the guitar. 〈both의 전체 부정〉

C 병렬: 등위 접속사(and, but, or 등)나 상관 접속사(both A and B, [n]either A [n]or B, not only A but also B 등)에 의해 연결되는 말은 동일한 문법 형태와 구조를 가져야 한다.

Bob is **smart**, **kind**, *and* **funny**.
I like *neither* **reading** books *nor* **watching** movies.
Hunter is *not only* **handsome** *but also* **intelligent**.

CHECK UP 빈칸에 알맞은 말을 고르시오.

1 My brother doesn't believe in ghosts, but I _____ in them.
ⓐ do believe   ⓑ does believe   ⓒ am believe

2 His voice was husky, attractive, and _____.
ⓐ low   ⓑ lower   ⓒ lowness

3 Anthony and I don't have a car. _____ of us has a car.
ⓐ One   ⓑ Both   ⓒ Neither

162

PRACTICE

Q Answer Key p.19

STEP 1

( ) 안에서 알맞은 말을 고르시오.

1 I (do know, does know) how to drive, but I don't have a car.

2 I'm good at not only making speeches but also (writing, to write) essays.

3 Jessica likes neither singing nor (listening, to listen) to music.

STEP 2

밑줄 친 부분을 강조하여 쓸 때, 빈칸에 알맞은 말을 쓰시오.

1 Hal <u>studied</u> very hard, but he failed the exam.

→ Hal _____ very hard, but he failed the exam.

2 <u>Brian</u> gave me this teddy bear on my birthday.

→ It _____ gave me this teddy bear on my birthday.

3 <u>Who</u> revealed the secret?

→ Who was _____ the secret?

STEP 3

주어진 문장과 의미가 통하도록 빈칸에 알맞은 말을 쓰시오.

1 A lot of news articles are true. But some news articles are not true.

→ Not _____ news articles are true.

2 I don't like fast food. My boyfriend doesn't like fast food either.

→ _____ my boyfriend nor I like fast food.

3 The hair shop opens on Sundays, but only the first and third Sunday of each month.

→ The hair shop does not _____ open on Sundays.

STEP 4

우리말과 일치하도록 ( ) 안에 주어진 단어를 바르게 배열하시오.

1 내가 그 목걸이를 찾은 것은 바로 욕실에서였다. (that, was, bathroom, it, in, the)

→ _____ I found the necklace.

2 우리 중 누구도 전에 해외에 가 본 적이 없다. (us, have, of, abroad, been, none)

→ _____ before.

3 모든 소녀가 다 인형 놀이를 좋아하는 것은 아니다. (not, likes, girl, play, to, every)

→ _____ with dolls.

4 Harry는 스키 타는 것뿐만 아니라 스노보드 타는 것도 좋아한다.
(only, snowboarding, not, but, also, skiing)

→ Harry likes _____ .

도치, 생략, 동격

A

도치

1 장소나 방향의 부사(구)가 문장 앞으로 나오는 경우의 도치: 부사(구) + 동사 + 주어

In the Trevi Fountain were a lot of coins.

(← A lot of coins were in the Trevi Fountain.)

ⓘ 주어가 대명사인 경우에는 보통 「주어 + 동사」의 어순이다.

Here he comes.

2 부정의 부사가 앞에 나올 경우의 도치: 조동사나 be동사가 있는 문장은 「부정의 부사(hardly, never, rarely, little 등) + 조동사[be동사] + 주어」, 일반동사가 있는 문장은 「부정의 부사 + do[does, did] + 주어 + 동사원형」의 어순으로 쓴다.

Hardly have I seen such an exciting soccer game.

(← I have hardly seen such an exciting soccer game.)

Never did I imagine seeing you here. What a small world!

(← I never imagined seeing you here.)

3 so[neither, nor] + 동사 + 주어: '~도 또한 그렇다[그렇지 않다]'의 의미로 「so + 동사 + 주어」는 긍정문 뒤에, 「neither[nor] + 동사 + 주어」는 부정문 뒤에 쓰며, 일반동사를 받을 때는 do[does, did]를 쓴다.

A: I am afraid of spiders.   B: **So am I.**

A: I don't like cold weather.   B: **Neither do I.**

B

생략: 반복되거나 없어도 의미 파악이 가능한 부분은 종종 생략된다.

1 반복되는 어구의 생략

Please help me if you can (**help me**)!

Do as I told you to (**do**).

2 부사절의 「주어 + be동사」 생략: 부사절과 주절의 주어가 같고 동사가 be동사인 경우 「주어 + be동사」는 생략 가능하다.

Though (**she was**) wrong, she didn't know it.

C

동격: 명사의 의미를 보충하거나 바꿔 말하기 위해 콤마 뒤에 다른 명사를 둘 수 있는데, 이때 두 명사의 관계를 동격이라고 한다.

I'm going to *Vancouver*, **a city in Canada**.

John, **my younger brother**, doesn't eat any meat.

 빈칸에 알맞은 말을 고르시오.

1 Hardly _____ such heavy rain.

ⓐ I have seen   ⓑ have I see   ⓒ have I seen

2 A: I run a blog.   B: So _____.

ⓐ do I   ⓑ I do   ⓒ I am

PRACTICE

🔍 Answer Key p.19

STEP 1

( ) 안에서 알맞은 말을 고르시오.

1 In the backyard (a tree house was, was a tree house).

2 A: I don't have a girlfriend.   B: Neither (I do, do I).

3 Hardly (I could understand, could I understand) what he was saying.

STEP 2

다음 문장을 주어진 말로 시작할 때 빈칸에 알맞은 말을 쓰시오.

1 A famous Italian restaurant is around the corner.

　→ Around the corner _____.

2 Caleb rarely comes to meetings on time.

　→ Rarely _____ to meetings on time.

3 I have never seen such a handsome man.

　→ Never _____ such a handsome man.

STEP 3

다음 문장에서 생략할 수 있는 부분을 ( )로 묶으시오.

1 Minsu is an actor just like his father is an actor.

2 When I was young, I didn't like vegetables.

3 You can leave now if you have to leave now.

4 Though she was sick, Julie went to the farewell party.

STEP 4

우리말과 일치하도록 ( ) 안에 주어진 단어를 바르게 배열하시오.

1 해바라기 위에 나비 한 마리가 앉았다. (a, sat, butterfly)

　→ On a sunflower _____.

2 내가 금메달을 딸 것이라고는 꿈에도 결코 생각 못했다. (dream, of, did, I, winning)

　→ Never _____ the gold medal.

3 파리에서 가장 높은 구조물인 에펠탑은 아름답다. (in, the, structure, Paris, tallest, beautiful, is)

　→ The Eiffel Tower, _____, _____.

4 A: Matthew는 요리하는 것을 정말 즐겨.   B: 나도 그래. (I, do, so)

　→ A: Matthew enjoys cooking very much.

　　 B: _____.

GRAMMAR FOR WRITING

A 우리말과 일치하도록 ( ) 안의 말을 이용하여 문장을 완성하시오.

1 인생이 항상 신나는 일로 가득 찬 것은 아니다. (life)

→ _____ full of exciting things.

2 A: 나는 애완동물을 기르지 않아.　B: 나도 그래. (neither)

→ A: I don't have any pets.

　 B: _____ .

3 나는 요즘 콜라를 거의 마시지 않는다. (cola)

→ Hardly _____ these days.

4 길모퉁이를 돈 곳에 몇 개의 은행이 있다. (be, several)

→ Just around the corner _____ .

5 우리가 Tina와 저녁을 먹은 것은 바로 어제였다. (have dinner)

→ It _____ with Tina.

6 나는 내가 가수가 될 것이라고 결코 생각하지 못했다. (think)

→ Never _____ that I would become
a singer.

7 나는 다른 사람들을 가르치는 것과 새로운 것들을 배우는 것 둘 다 좋아한다. (others, learn)

→ I like both _____ new things.

B 우리말과 일치하도록 ( ) 안에 주어진 단어를 바르게 배열하시오.

1 모든 고양이가 혼자 놀기를 좋아하는 것은 아니다. (to, cat, likes, not, every, play)

→ _____ on its own.

2 내 여동생은 불어를 유창하게 하지만, 나는 할 수 없다. (speak, can't, French, can, but, I, fluently)

→ My sister _____ _____ .

3 Daniel은 운동을 하거나 보는 것 둘 다에 관심이 없다. (watching, playing, neither, nor, sports)

→ Daniel is interested in _____ .

4 나에게 봉사의 즐거움을 가르쳐준 사람은 바로 나의 선생님이셨다.

(was, teacher, taught, it, my, me, that)

→ _____ the joy of volunteering.

5 비록 영리하지만 Jay가 항상 현명한 결정을 내리지는 않는다. (smart, Jay, always, though, doesn't)

→ _____ make wise decisions.

6 나는 떡볶이를 만드는 법은 모르지만, 그것을 먹는 것은 정말 좋아한다. (eat, it, do, but, I, to, like)

→ I don't know how to make tteokbokki, _____ .

C 다음 문장을 ( ) 안의 지시대로 바꿔 쓰시오.

1 Ann is usually a joyful person, but she looks sad today. (look 강조)

→ _____

2 Frank sent flowers on my birthday. (Frank 강조)

→ _____

3 Big boxes and baskets were on the table. (on the table을 문두로)

→ _____

4 I bought the helmet at Kim's store. (at Kim's store 강조)

→ _____

5 When they are together, they look happier. (생략 가능한 부분 생략)

→ _____

6 This is my favorite painting by Van Gogh. It's called *Sunflowers*.
(my favorite painting by Van Gogh와 *Sunflowers*를 동격으로)

→ _____

D 그림을 보고 보기에서 알맞은 말을 골라 문장을 완성하시오. (단, 한 번씩만 쓸 것)

1  **2**  **3**

보기	not all of	none of	neither of

1 _____ the girls are wearing glasses.

2 Although it is late at night, _____ the children wants to go to bed.

3 _____ the boys played soccer during lunch break. Some of them played tennis.

REVIEW TEST

[1–5] 빈칸에 들어갈 알맞은 말을 고르시오.

1

| Never _____ to Boston. |

① I have been   ② I haven't been
③ have I been   ④ haven't I been
⑤ have been I

2

| I _____ send you a text message last night. |

① am   ② was
③ do   ④ does
⑤ did

3

| He likes animals, and _____. |

① so am I   ② so do I
③ so did I   ④ neither do I
⑤ neither did I

4

| Ron can neither speak nor _____ Chinese. |

① write   ② writes
③ wrote   ④ written
⑤ has written

5

| It was my science book _____ I lent to Ted last week. |

① what   ② when
③ where   ④ who
⑤ that

[6-7] 다음 중 어법상 틀린 것을 고르시오.

6 ① I do agree with you about this.
② Not all children learn the same way.
③ Jake, my old friend, lives near my house.
④ Little I knew what the movie was about.
⑤ It was a year ago that I started learning Chinese.

7 ① Forgiveness is not always easy.
② Though ill, I went to school as usual.
③ I am interested in both reading and writing articles.
④ I thought my mom was angry at me, but she wasn't.
⑤ Natasha is smart, pretty, and a sense of humor.

8 다음 중 문장을 우리말로 잘못 해석한 것은?

① It was you that cheered me up.
→ 날 힘이 나게 해 준 사람은 바로 너였어.

② Not all people like new things.
→ 모든 사람들은 새것을 좋아하지 않는다.

③ None of us knew the bridge was under construction.
→ 우리 중 아무도 다리가 공사 중인 것을 몰랐다.

④ Never have I been to a restaurant by myself.
→ 나는 혼자서 식당에 가 본 적이 없다.

⑤ It was France that won the World Cup trophy in 2018.
→ 2018년에 월드컵 트로피를 수상한 것은 프랑스였다.

[9-10] 다음 우리말을 영어로 바르게 옮긴 것을 고르시오.

9 그들 둘 다 돈에 대해서 말하는 것을 좋아하지 않는다.

① All of them like to talk about money.
② Both of them like to talk about money.
③ Not all of them likes to talk about money.
④ Neither of them likes to talk about money.
⑤ Not both of them like to talk about money.

10 일요일에 모든 가게가 문을 닫는 것은 아니다.

① Both shops are closed on Sundays.
② All shops are closed on Sundays.
③ Neither shops are closed on Sundays.
④ Not all shops are closed on Sundays.
⑤ None of the shops are closed on Sundays.

서술형

11 다음 문장에서 생략할 수 있는 부분을 찾아 쓰시오.

When I am in the library, I turn off my cell phone.

[12-13] 다음 대화의 빈칸에 들어갈 알맞은 말을 고르시오.

12
A: I watched a documentary about the environment last night.
B: _____.

① So am I   ② So do I
③ So did I   ④ Neither do I
⑤ Neither did I

13
A: I couldn't solve the math problem.
B: _____.

① So am I   ② So did I
③ So could I   ④ Neither did I
⑤ Neither could I

서술형 빈출

[14-16] 밑줄 친 부분을 강조하여 문장을 다시 쓰시오.

14 I found my ring <u>in the bathroom</u>.

→ _____
_____

15
A: Why didn't you tell me about the problem?
B: I <u>told</u> you yesterday.

→ B: _____

16 <u>When</u> did you decide to become a reporter?

→ _____
_____

17 다음 중 어법상 옳은 것은?

① Turn off the TV if you want to.
② Here the guest of today's show comes.
③ Rob did knew the score of the match.
④ Never he did ask about my personal interests.
⑤ That was Lucy that borrowed my sleeping bag yesterday.

서술형

[18-19] 우리말과 일치하도록 ( ) 안의 말을 이용하여 문장을 완성하시오.

18 내가 항상 내 직업에 만족하는 것은 아니다. (always)

→ I _____ happy with my job.

19 내 아내는 요리를 잘 못하고 나도 그렇다. (neither)

→ My wife is not good at cooking, and _____ .

서술형

[20-21] 다음 문장을 주어진 말로 시작할 때 빈칸에 알맞은 말을 쓰시오.

20 I have never seen such a great live concert before.

→ Never _____ _____ .

21 The important files are in the second drawer of my desk.

→ In the second drawer of my desk _____ .

서술형

[22-24] 우리말과 일치하도록 ( ) 안에 주어진 단어를 바르게 배열하시오.

22 Julia는 이 가게에서 가장 비싼 상품인 흰색 시계를 샀다. (most, the, shop, this, product, in, expensive, watch)

→ Julia bought a white _____ _____ .

23 나는 그 영화를 좋아하지 않았다. 그것은 지루했을 뿐만 아니라 비현실적이었다. (only, boring, also, not, unrealistic, but)

→ I didn't like the film. It was _____ _____ .

24 화가 날 때, 그는 그냥 운다. (he, cries, angry, just)

→ When _____ .

서술형

25 우리말과 일치하도록 주어진 조건에 맞게 문장을 완성하시오.

나는 요즘 밤에 잠을 거의 잘 수가 없다.

〈조건〉 1. Hardly로 시작할 것
2. can, at night을 이용할 것

→ _____
these days.

170

26 다음 중 어법상 옳은 것을 모두 고르면?

① It does looks real, but it isn't.
② I like both making and drink coffee.
③ When free, you can call me anytime.
④ None of my friends knew about my plan.
⑤ Not all of the students want to wear school uniforms.

27 다음 중 어법상 옳은 것으로 바르게 짝지어진 것은?

> a. Hangang Park, a good place for a picnic, is near my house.
> b. Hardly I have met him since last year.
> c. He enjoys neither swimming nor play tennis.
> d. Who was it that swore to you?
> e. My parents want me to learn piano, but I don't want to.

① a, b, c
② a, b, e
③ a, d, e
④ b, c, d
⑤ b, c, e

28 다음 중 어법상 옳은 것의 개수는?

> • Not every legend is a myth.
> • Under the ocean lie natural resources.
> • I did try to make him laugh, but I couldn't.
> • It is you that I want to spend the rest of my life with.
> • My sister not only sings very well but also playing the piano well.

① 1개
② 2개
③ 3개
④ 4개
⑤ 5개

[29-31] 밑줄 친 부분이 어법상 옳은지 판단하고, 틀리면 바르게 고치시오.

29 <u>Never have I</u> seen such an intelligent student.

(O / X) _____

30 <u>That</u> was at the Olympics that she won a silver medal.

(O / X) _____

31 On top of the mountain <u>a famous temple is</u>.

(O / X) _____

[32-33] 어법상 틀린 부분을 찾아 바르게 고치시오.

32 Christopher doesn't like rainy days. Neither I do. (1개)

33 Here things are that you should know before you audition for a role on this show. First, we prefer someone who is good at acting and dance. (2개)

LET'S REVIEW

주요 예문을 다시 한번 확인하고, 우리말과 일치하도록 빈칸을 채우시오.

- I don't remember his name, but I **do** remember his face.
  나는 그의 이름은 기억하지 못하지만, 그의 얼굴은 분명 기억한다. **Unit 01 - A**

- ¹_____ Tom **that** saw Julie at the theater yesterday.
  어제 극장에서 Julie를 본 것은 바로 Tom이었다. **Unit 01 - A**

- **It was** at the theater **that** Tom saw Julie yesterday.
  어제 Tom이 Julie를 본 것은 바로 극장에서였다. **Unit 01 - A**

- Who **was it that** wrote the novel? 그 소설을 쓴 건 대체 누구지? **Unit 01 - A**

- ²_____ **all** of the members agreed to the new plan.
  모든 구성원이 새로운 계획에 동의한 것은 아니었다. **Unit 01 - B**

- ³_____ of the students were in the classroom. 학생 중 누구도 교실에 없었다. **Unit 01 - B**

- ⁴_____ of us can play the guitar. 우리 둘 중 아무도 기타를 치지 못한다. **Unit 01 - B**

- I like neither ⁵_____ books nor **watching** movies.
  나는 책을 읽는 것도 영화를 보는 것도 좋아하지 않는다. **Unit 01 - C**

- **In the Trevi Fountain** ⁶_____ **a lot of coins.** 트레비 분수에는 동전이 많았다. **Unit 02 - A**

- **Hardly** ⁷_____ seen such an exciting soccer game.
  나는 그렇게 흥미진진한 축구 경기를 본 적이 거의 없다. **Unit 02 - A**

- A: I am afraid of spiders. 나는 거미가 무서워.
  B: ⁸_____. 나도 그래. **Unit 02 - A**

- Please help me if you can (**help me**)! 나를 도울 수 있으면 제발 도와줘! **Unit 02 - B**

- Though (⁹_____) wrong, she didn't know it.
  비록 그녀가 틀렸지만, 그녀는 그것을 몰랐다. **Unit 02 - B**

- John, **my younger brother**, doesn't eat any meat.
  내 남동생인 John은 고기를 전혀 먹지 않는다. **Unit 02 - C**

🔍 **Answers**

¹ It was ² Not ³ None ⁴ Neither ⁵ reading ⁶ were ⁷ have I ⁸ So am I ⁹ she was

172

MEMO

MEMO

MEMO

지은이

NE능률 영어교육연구소

NE능률 영어교육연구소는 혁신적이며 효율적인 영어 교재를 개발하고
영어 학습의 질을 한 단계 높이고자 노력하는 NE능률의 연구조직입니다.

GRAMMAR Inside 〈Level 3〉

펴 낸 이	주민홍
펴 낸 곳	서울특별시 마포구 월드컵북로 396(상암동) 누리꿈스퀘어 비즈니스타워 10층
	㈜NE능률 (우편번호 03925)
펴 낸 날	2022년 1월 5일 개정판 제1쇄 발행
	2024년 9월 15일 제17쇄
전 화	02 2014 7114
팩 스	02 3142 0356
홈 페 이 지	www.neungyule.com
등 록 번 호	제1-68호
I S B N	979-11-253-3709-6 53740
정 가	15,500원

NE 능률

고객센터

교재 내용 문의: contact.nebooks.co.kr (별도의 가입 절차 없이 작성 가능)
제품 구매, 교환, 불량, 반품 문의: 02-2014-7114
☎ 전화문의는 본사 업무시간 중에만 가능합니다.

NE능률 교재 MAP

아래 교재 MAP을 참고하여 본인의 현재 혹은 목표 수준에 따라 교재를 선택하세요.
NE능률 교재들과 함께 영어실력을 쑥쑥~ 올려보세요!
MP3 등 교재 부가 학습 서비스 및 자세한 교재 정보는 www.nebooks.co.kr 에서 확인하세요.

문법
구문
서술형

초1-2

초3
그래머버디 1
초등영어 문법이 된다 Starter 1

초3-4
그래머버디 2
초등영어 문법이 된다 Starter 2
초등 Grammar Inside 1
초등 Grammar Inside 2

초4-5
그래머버디 3
Grammar Bean 1
Grammar Bean 2
초등영어 문법이 된다 1
초등 Grammar Inside 3
초등 Grammar Inside 4

초5-6
Grammar Bean 3
Grammar Bean 4
초등영어 문법이 된다 2
초등 Grammar Inside 5
초등 Grammar Inside 6

초6-예비중
능률중학영어 예비중
Grammar Inside Starter
원리를 더한 영문법 STARTER

중1
능률중학영어 중1
Grammar Zone 입문편
Grammar Zone 워크북 입문편
1316 Grammar 1
문제로 마스터하는 중학영문법 1
Grammar Inside 1
열중 16강 문법 1
쓰기로 마스터하는 중학서술형 1학년
중학 천문장 1

중1-2
능률중학영어 중2
1316 Grammar 2
문제로 마스터하는 중학영문법 2
Grammar Inside 2
열중 16강 문법 2
원리를 더한 영문법 1
중학영문법 총정리 모의고사 1
중학 천문장 2

중2-3
Grammar Zone 기초편
Grammar Zone 워크북 기초편
1316 Grammar 3
원리를 더한 영문법 2
중학영문법 총정리 모의고사 2
쓰기로 마스터하는 중학서술형 2학년
중학 천문장 3

중3
능률중학영어 중3
문제로 마스터하는 중학영문법 3
Grammar Inside 3
열중 16강 문법 3
중학영문법 총정리 모의고사 3
쓰기로 마스터하는 중학서술형 3학년

예비고-고1
문제로 마스터하는 고등영문법
올클 수능 어법 start
천문장 입문

고1
Grammar Zone 기본편 1
Grammar Zone 워크북 기본편 1
Grammar Zone 기본편 2
Grammar Zone 워크북 기본편 2
필히 통하는 고등 영문법 기본편
필히 통하는 고등 서술형 기본편
천문장 기본

고1-2
필히 통하는 고등 영문법 실력편
필히 통하는 고등 서술형 실전편
TEPS BY STEP G+R Basic

고2-3
Grammar Zone 종합편
Grammar Zone 워크북 종합편
올클 수능 어법 완성
천문장 완성

고3

수능 이상/
토플 80-89·
텝스 600-699점

수능 이상/
토플 90-99·
텝스 700-799점

수능 이상/
토플 100·
텝스 800점 이상

TEPS BY STEP G+R 1

TEPS BY STEP G+R 2

TEPS BY STEP G+R 3

workbook

GRAMMAR Inside

LEVEL 3

A 4-level grammar course
with abundant writing practice

NE_ Neungyul

CONTENTS

GRAMMAR BASICS

01 문장의 성분

A 밑줄 친 부분의 문장성분을 보기에서 골라 쓰시오.

보기	주어	동사	목적어	보어	수식어

1 I want you to stay here.

2 The movie ends at 9:00 p.m.

3 He wants to see you again.

4 Dad will prepare dinner for us.

5 My teacher gave me good advice.

6 The Korean War broke out in 1950.

7 Getting an A in math is difficult for me.

8 Fortunately, all the students passed the exam.

9 I believe that our team can win the final match.

10 Sam and I were best friends in elementary school.

B 다음 문장에서 밑줄 친 부분이 목적어이면 O로, 보어이면 C로 표시하시오.

1 He just sat smiling.

2 I like to play computer games.

3 Susan became a famous artist.

4 My goal is to be a great writer.

5 He taught me how to swim.

6 My boyfriend gave me beautiful flowers.

7 I think that it's fun to learn a foreign language.

8 We wanted to make the world a better place.

9 The doctor told me to drink more water.

10 Jason helped me do my homework.

02 문장의 형식

A '/' 표시에 유의하여 문장을 해석하고 문장의 형식을 쓰시오.

1 The boy / laughed.

2 He / told / me / to get up.

3 Maria / became / a doctor.

4 You / look / beautiful / today.

5 James / sent / you / an email.

6 I / take / a bus / to go to school.

7 My mother / let / me / play outside.

8 My daughter / sings / like an angel.

9 Dad / gave / me / a Christmas present.

10 My younger brother / doesn't have / a smartphone.

B ( ) 안에서 알맞은 말을 고르시오.

1 Please stay (calm, calmly).

2 He showed (me, to me) the map.

3 There (is, are) a girl on the bench.

4 James likes (play, playing) soccer.

5 Mom bought a skirt (for, of) me.

6 She doesn't look (happy, happily) today.

7 I consider the town (beautiful, beautifully).

8 My teacher (went, entered) the classroom.

9 Let me (finish, to finish) my homework first.

10 We will leave home when the sun (rises, raises).

03 구와 절

A 밑줄 친 부분이 구인지 또는 절인지 쓰시오.

1 Susie is <u>a professional dancer</u>.

2 I bought <u>a new smartphone</u>.

3 I felt tired, so <u>I drank a cup of coffee</u>.

4 Jack likes playing the piano <u>very much</u>.

5 My sister likes Chinese food, but <u>I don't</u>.

6 When I was young, I lived <u>in a small town</u>.

7 We should wait here <u>until it stops raining</u>.

8 The child <u>on the playground</u> looks happy.

9 I remember the day <u>when we first met</u>.

10 It made me sad <u>that Sam left me</u>.

B 밑줄 친 부분이 명사, 형용사, 부사 중 어느 역할을 하는지 쓰시오.

1 My hobby is <u>playing tennis</u>.

2 My grandparents live <u>in Jeonju</u>.

3 I like him <u>because he is so kind</u>.

4 I think <u>Jimmy broke the window</u>.

5 My dream is <u>to travel around the world</u>.

6 <u>Not feeling well</u>, I went to the hospital.

7 Korea is a country <u>that has a long history</u>.

8 The child <u>in the picture</u> is my sister.

9 Close the window <u>before you leave</u>.

10 John is a boy <u>whose dream is to be an actor</u>.

UNIT 01

현재완료

Answer Key p.24

A ( ) 안에서 알맞은 말을 고르시오.

1 I (take, have taken) ballet lessons since I was eight.

2 He (was working, has been working) on the problem since yesterday.

3 I (broke, have broken) Grandma's crystal bowl a few days ago.

4 I (never have, have never had) my own room before.

5 His condition has improved a lot (for, since) last week.

6 This huge tree (is, has been) here for more than one hundred years.

7 He (is reading, has been reading) for an hour.

8 She (reserved, has reserved) a seat at the restaurant last week.

9 My uncle has played the violin in the orchestra (since, for) five years.

10 I (lose, have lost) my phone. I can't call him now.

B 밑줄 친 부분을 어법에 맞게 고치시오.

1 Sara has bought a new summer dress yesterday.

2 He worked as a firefighter since he was twenty-five.

3 I have been a big fan of the actor for I was young.

4 It was raining since last Saturday.

5 I think I have talked with you too much last night.

6 Dan has been to Australia, so he doesn't live with us now.

7 My parents have been married since fifteen years.

8 Nancy lives here for about five years now.

9 They have seen the musical a few days ago.

10 Have you ever gone to France before?

C 다음을 완료형 또는 완료진행형 문장으로 바꿀 때, 빈칸에 알맞은 말을 쓰시오.

1 My dad went to Shanghai. He's not at home now.

→ My dad _____ _____ _____ Shanghai.

2 Jake and I first became friends when we were ten. We are still friends.

→ Jake and I _____ _____ friends since we were ten.

3 It started snowing the day before yesterday. It's still snowing now.

→ It _____ _____ _____ for three days.

4 I lost my pearl earrings. I don't have them now.

→ I _____ _____ my pearl earrings.

5 The author worked on the novel last year. He is still working on it.

→ The author _____ _____ _____ on the novel since last year.

D 밑줄 친 부분에 유의하여 문장을 우리말로 해석하시오.

1 <u>Have you seen</u> his new music video?

2 He <u>has helped</u> the poor since his twenties.

3 I <u>have seen</u> the animated movie *Frozen* several times.

4 He <u>has been sleeping</u> on the sofa for more than an hour.

5 I <u>have just taken</u> a shower.

6 They <u>have been learning</u> Chinese for ten years.

7 She <u>has lost</u> her science textbook.

8 They <u>have already finished</u> their meal.

9 <u>Have you ever eaten</u> Vietnamese noodle soup?

10 Dad <u>has fixed</u> my bike, so I can ride it.

WRITING PRACTICE

Answer Key p.24

A 우리말과 일치하도록 ( ) 안의 말을 이용하여 문장을 완성하시오.

1 엄마가 막 쿠키를 구우셨다. (just, bake)

→ Mom _____ some cookies.

2 내 여동생은 어제 시험에 떨어졌다. (fail, the exam)

→ My sister _____ yesterday.

3 Jason은 지난 여름부터 수영 강습을 받고 있다. (take swimming lessons)

→ Jason _____ last summer.

4 그 노부인은 40년 동안 그 집에서 살고 있다. (live in the house)

→ The old lady _____ forty years.

5 그들은 전에 한 번 서로 만난 적이 있다. (meet, each other)

→ They _____ once before.

6 너는 파리에 가 본 적이 있니? (ever, be)

→ _____ Paris?

B 우리말과 일치하도록 ( ) 안에 주어진 단어를 바르게 배열하시오.

1 나는 중학교 때부터 태권도를 배워 왔다. (been, have, taekwondo, since, learning)

→ I _____ middle school.

2 아빠는 아침부터 지하실에서 일하시는 중이다. (has, since, working, been, in the basement)

→ Dad _____ this morning.

3 그 비행기는 벌써 이륙했다. (off, already, taken, has, the airplane)

→ _____.

4 그가 라면을 너무 오래 익혀서 맛이 없다. (the ramen, overcooked, has, he)

→ _____, so it isn't tasty.

5 Jimmy는 아직 그의 숙제를 마치지 않았다. (finished, not, homework, has, his)

→ Jimmy _____ yet.

6 그녀는 전에 그 소프트웨어를 사용해 본 적이 전혀 없다. (before, has, the software, used, never)

→ She _____.

UNIT 02 과거완료, 미래완료

A

( ) 안에서 알맞은 말을 고르시오.

1 I (have never heard, had never heard) about the artist before I met him.

2 In five minutes, I (had been waiting, will have been waiting) an hour for him.

3 He (has been, had been) on the team for five years before he quit.

4 I (had never skied, will have never skied) before I took ski lessons.

5 Kate (has finished, will have finished) her project by tomorrow night.

6 It (had been raining, will have been raining) for a week if it rains tomorrow.

7 He (has not done, had not done) his work yet when I asked him for it.

8 We (have built, will have built) the bridge by next year.

9 I (have been swimming, had been swimming) in the river when I heard someone shouting.

10 I (had never taken, will have never taken) Spanish classes before I went to high school.

B

( ) 안에 주어진 단어를 알맞은 완료형으로 고쳐 쓰시오.

1 She _____ fencing before she started skating. (learn)

2 I _____ the girl three times when I see her again. (see)

3 I _____ in this town for five years next year. (live)

4 The school _____ for fifty years before I entered it. (exist)

5 By the time my mom comes, I _____ the house. (clean)

6 The glass _____ before it was delivered. (be broken)

7 Next year, the country _____ independent for forty years. (be)

8 The movie _____ by the time we get to the cinema. (start)

9 I _____ about it before you told me. (never, hear)

10 They _____ lunch by the time I brought sandwiches for them. (already, eat)

C   밑줄 친 부분을 어법에 맞게 고치시오.

1   I have climbed Mt. Jiri three times if I climb it again next week.

2   He has already heard the news before I told him.

3   I have never been to the concert hall before I went to IU's concert.

4   I have been working on the paper for two months next month.

5   She has spent all her money, so she couldn't buy anything else.

6   By next year, I have lived in the US for three years.

7   I have lived in Busan before I moved here last month.

8   We have been waiting here for one hour when you arrived.

9   I have been thinking of calling you before you called me.

10   I have gone up the stairs already by the time someone knocked on the door.

D   밑줄 친 부분에 유의하여 문장을 우리말로 해석하시오.

1   You will have learned a lot by the time you finish this book.

2   He had been trying to fix it before the repairman came.

3   It will have been snowing for more than one week by tomorrow.

4   He had worked as a comedian before he became a musical actor.

5   He had lost his map, so he asked strangers for directions.

6   She had just stopped playing the piano when I entered the room.

7   The band had been popular even before their first album came out.

8   The thief had already disappeared when the police turned the corner.

9   I had deleted the files on the computer, so I typed everything again.

10   He had been searching for his mother for ten years before he met her.

WRITING PRACTICE

Answer Key p.25

A 우리말과 일치하도록 ( ) 안의 말을 이용하여 문장을 완성하시오.

1 버스가 막 떠나 버려서 나는 택시를 타야만 했다. (just, leave)

→ The bus _____, so I had to take a taxi.

2 우리는 그 개가 죽기 전에 10년을 같이 살았었다. (live)

→ We _____ with the dog for ten years before it died.

3 나는 다음 주면 그녀가 마음을 바꾸었을 것이라고 생각한다. (change)

→ I think she _____ her mind by next week.

4 나는 비가 내리기 시작하기 전에 한 시간째 농구를 하고 있었다. (play)

→ I _____ basketball for an hour before it started raining.

5 내년이면 그녀가 캘리포니아에서 5년 동안 공부하는 셈이 된다. (study)

→ By next year, she _____ in California for five years.

6 그는 18살이 되기 전에 자동차를 운전해 본 적이 전혀 없었다. (never, drive)

→ He _____ a car before he turned eighteen years old.

B 우리말과 일치하도록 ( ) 안에 주어진 단어를 바르게 배열하시오.

1 그는 저녁 식사 때까지 집에 돌아와 있을 것이다. (will, he, home, have, returned)

→ _____ by dinner.

2 내가 그의 집에 전화를 했을 때 그는 이미 그 체육관으로 가고 없었다.
(had, to, the gym, gone, already)

→ He _____ when I called his house.

3 그는 내년이면 첼로를 10년 동안 배운 셈이 된다.
(ten years, will, the cello, have, learning, for, he, been)

→ _____ by next year.

4 나의 삼촌은 퇴직하실 때 30년 동안 그 회사에서 일하셨다.
(thirty years, at the company, had, worked, for)

→ My uncle _____ when he retired.

5 내가 집에 도착했을 때 내 남동생의 생일 파티는 이미 끝나 버렸다.
(birthday party, ended, had, already, my brother's)

→ _____ when I got home.

6 전화벨이 울렸을 때 그는 정원에서 일하고 있었다.
(had, when, been, in the garden, the phone, working, rang)

→ He _____.

REVIEW TEST

Q Answer Key p.25

[1-4] 빈칸에 들어갈 알맞은 말을 고르시오.

1

| Isabella _____ four books about the Second World War since 2015. |

① writes   ② wrote
③ has written   ④ will have written
⑤ will have been writing

2

| I _____ that watch for two years before I sold it. |

① wear   ② am wearing
③ have worn   ④ had worn
⑤ will have worn

3

| Tony _____ the famous model at a party last week. |

① meets   ② met
③ has met   ④ had met
⑤ will have met

4

| My sister _____ Michael by next spring. |

① marries   ② married
③ has married   ④ had married
⑤ will have married

서술형

[5-7] 다음을 완료형 또는 완료진행형 문장으로 바꿀 때, 빈칸에 알맞은 말을 쓰시오.

5

Ava lost her necklace, so she doesn't have it now.

→ Ava _____ _____ her necklace.

6

I started doing my homework three hours ago. I'm still doing it.

→ I _____ _____ _____ my homework for three hours.

7

Chris started to play golf five years ago. Next year will be his sixth year.

→ Chris _____ _____ _____ _____ golf for six years by next year.

[8-9] 다음 중 어법상 틀린 것을 고르시오.

8 ① I have never taken Russian classes.
② She has been busy since last week.
③ We will have been living in this house for ten years next month.
④ Alex has just finished his presentation when you arrived.
⑤ When I came home, I realized that I had left my gloves in the taxi.

9
① Ted has gone to Hungary with his wife.
② We had been watching TV when it started to rain.
③ She has been playing the flute for two hours.
④ If he calls again, he had called me eight times.
⑤ Emily will have been working for the company for ten years on April 5.

13
> A: Does Bill live here?
> B: No, he _____ to New York.

① moves　　　　② was moving
③ has moved　　④ has been moving
⑤ will have moved

[10-11] 우리말과 일치하도록 할 때, 빈칸에 들어갈 알맞은 말을 고르시오.

10
> Betty는 세 시간 동인 컴퓨터 게임을 하고 있나.
> → Betty _____ a computer game for three hours.

① plays　　　　　　② was playing
③ had played　　　 ④ has been playing
⑤ will have been playing

[14-16] 밑줄 친 부분의 쓰임이 나머지 넷과 다른 것을 고르시오.

14
① He has never ridden a horse.
② I haven't made up my mind yet.
③ I have been to Germany three times.
④ Have you ever visited the museum?
⑤ This is the best poem I've ever read.

11
> 우리는 그 과제를 내일 오후 6시까지는 끝냈을 것이다.
> → We _____ the project by 6:00 p.m. tomorrow.

① finish　　　　　② were finishing
③ have finished　 ④ had finished
⑤ will have finished

15
① It has snowed heavily for three days.
② I have loved him since I was a child.
③ Sophia has lost her bracelet.
④ She has been sick since last Monday.
⑤ She has worked as a sales manager for five years.

[12-13] 다음 대화의 빈칸에 들어갈 알맞은 말을 고르시오.

12
> A: How long _____ Cindy?
> B: Since last year.

① do you know　　② are you knowing
③ have you known　④ did you know
⑤ had you known

16
① She has lost her bag at the station.
② I have left my car key at my office.
③ He has never driven a car before.
④ Jay has quit his job, and he regrets it.
⑤ As she has broken her leg, she can't take part in the game.

[17-18] 밑줄 친 부분을 어법에 맞게 고치시오.

17 I <u>have had</u> a car accident a year ago.

18 Wendy <u>played</u> tennis every evening since last July.

[19-21] 우리말과 일치하도록 ( ) 안에 주어진 단어를 바르게 배열하시오.

19 그가 전화했을 때 나는 두 시간 동안 그 잡지를 읽고 있었다. (been, the magazine, two hours, I, reading, had, for)

→ _____

_____ when he called.

20 우리는 7시까지는 저녁을 다 먹었을 것이다. (finished, have, we, dinner, eating, will)

→ _____

_____ by seven o'clock.

21 나는 그녀의 결혼 소식을 방금 들었다. (just, her, the news, I, marriage, have, of, heard)

→ _____

_____.

[22-23] 우리말과 일치하도록 ( ) 안의 말을 이용하여 문장을 완성하시오.

22 그는 이전에 Houston까지 차를 몰고 간 적이 한 번도 없다. (never, drive)

→ _____

a car to Houston before.

23 내가 거기에 도착했을 때 이미 1부가 시작했다. (already, start)

→ When I got there, the first part _____

_____.

[24-25] 어법상 **틀린** 부분을 찾아 바르게 고치시오.

24 I have studied hard for my finals until yesterday. I have just finished my last exam! (1개)

25 Today is my parents' 19th wedding anniversary. Next year, they will be married for twenty years. (1개)

UNIT 01

can, may, must, should

A

( ) 안에서 알맞은 말을 고르시오.

1 May I (close, closing) the window? It's raining outside.

2 You (can, must) go out to swim if you want.

3 You (must not, don't have to) use your cell phone during exams.

4 (May, Should) I borrow your book, please?

5 Ellie didn't answer my phone call. She (cannot, might) be busy.

6 I'm sorry, but I (cannot, may not) fix your computer.

7 Are you able to (see, seeing) the man over there? He's my boyfriend.

8 Josh (can, could) ride a bike when he was a kid.

9 You (have to, are able to) follow several rules in this school.

10 (Should, Could) you help me with my homework? I can't do it myself.

B

두 문장의 의미가 같도록 빈칸에 알맞은 말을 쓰시오.

1 You may go to the restroom during a break.

→ You _____ go to the restroom during a break.

2 You must come back home before ten o'clock.

→ You _____ _____ come back home before ten o'clock.

3 Even Mark couldn't solve the math problem.

→ Even Mark _____ _____ _____ solve the math problem.

4 Owen can speak Chinese well.

→ Owen _____ _____ _____ speak Chinese well.

5 You need not wake up early. Tomorrow is a holiday.

→ You _____ _____ _____ wake up early. Tomorrow is a holiday.

C 우리말과 일치하도록 밑줄 친 부분을 어법에 맞게 고치시오.

1 Ben은 곧 새로운 직업을 찾을 수 있을 것이다.

→ Ben <u>will can find</u> a new job soon.

2 너는 면허증 없이 운전해서는 안 된다.

→ You <u>must don't drive</u> without a license.

3 그녀는 혼자 있고 싶을지도 모른다.

→ She <u>can want</u> to be alone.

4 Clara는 막 이곳으로 이사했다. 그녀가 많은 사람들을 알 리가 없다.

→ Clara has just moved here. She <u>doesn't have to know</u> many people.

5 너는 내일 점심을 싸 올 필요가 없다.

→ You <u>must not bring</u> your lunch tomorrow.

6 Mark만이 그 문제를 풀었다. 그는 영리한 것이 틀림없다.

→ Only Mark solved the problem. He <u>can be</u> smart.

D 보기에서 알맞은 말을 골라 문장을 완성하시오.

[1-3]

보기	must be very hungry　　　　　　　might snow during the night may drink some water from the refrigerator

1 Are you thirsty? You _____.

2 Don't wash your car. It _____.

3 You _____. You haven't eaten anything today.

[4-6]

보기	should turn it down　　　　　　　must not make any noise can speak Spanish

4 Let's ask Joe to help us. He _____.

5 The music is too loud. You _____.

6 The baby is sleeping. We _____.

WRITING PRACTICE

Answer Key p.25

Ⓐ 우리말과 일치하도록 조동사와 ( ) 안의 말을 이용하여 문장을 완성하시오.

1 그 식당은 오늘 닫았을지도 모른다. 너는 그곳에 전화를 해 봐야 한다. (be)

→ The restaurant _____ closed today. You should call them.

2 Amy는 네 살에 읽을 수 있었다. (read)

→ Amy _____ at the age of four.

3 너는 이 문제를 우리와 의논할 필요가 없다. (have, discuss)

→ You _____ this problem with us.

4 Tina는 클래식 음악에 관심이 있는 것이 틀림없다. (be interested in)

→ Tina _____ classical music.

5 그의 대답이 사실일 리가 없다. (true)

→ His answer _____.

6 엄마, 저 지금 Jimmy의 생일 파티에 가도 돼요? (go)

→ Mom, _____ to Jimmy's birthday party now?

Ⓑ 우리말과 일치하도록 ( ) 안에 주어진 단어를 바르게 배열하시오.

1 너는 내 비밀을 다른 사람한테 말해서는 안 된다. (tell, you, not, secret, must, my)

→ _____ to others.

2 제가 당신의 신분증을 좀 봐도 될까요? (ID card, see, may, I, your)

→ _____?

3 저에게 소금을 건네주시겠어요? (you, the salt, could, pass, me)

→ _____?

4 나는 다음 주에 자원봉사를 할 수 있을 것이다. (I, the volunteer work, be, to, will, able, do)

→ _____ next week.

5 너는 너의 친구들에게 솔직해야 한다. (should, honest, your, you, friends, be, with)

→ _____.

6 Jerry는 Mina와 사랑에 빠질지도 모른다. (might, in, fall, love, Jerry)

→ _____ with Mina.

UNIT 02

🔍 Answer Key p.26

had better, ought to, used to, 조동사 + have v-ed

A ( ) 안에서 알맞은 말을 고르시오.

1 You (had better, used to) keep your promise this time.

2 We ought to (turn, turning) off the lights during the daytime.

3 Eli (should have been, must have been) there yesterday. I saw his car parked nearby.

4 We (used to, ought to) hang out together when we were young.

5 I shouldn't (buy, have bought) this expensive dress last week.

6 There (would, used to) be a flower shop here.

7 I used (to eat, to eating) sandwiches for lunch.

8 You (ought not to, ought to not) eat more ice cream now.

9 He (can't have told, must have told) a lie to me. He's very honest.

10 This room is too dirty. You (had not better, had better not) sleep here.

B 어법상 틀린 곳을 찾아 바르게 고치시오.

1 He has better pack his luggage tonight.

2 I used to playing football in middle school.

3 You ought to not eat too much late at night.

4 I'm late again. I must have gotten up earlier.

5 There was used to be a big tree in this garden.

6 Brian might read your novel already.

7 You had not better start right now.

8 He can't have going to the meeting yesterday.

9 Matthew ought to knowing about the history of his nation.

10 There would be a large bookstore here when I was young.

C 빈칸에 알맞은 말을 보기에서 골라 쓰시오. (단, 한 번씩만 쓸 것)

[1-3]

보기	used to	ought to	had better not

1 Dad _____ have a big farm truck when I was a little boy.

2 You _____ go outside. It's pouring now.

3 This news is very important. You _____ read it more carefully.

[4-6]

보기	shouldn't	must	can't

4 Paul _____ have heard us. He was far away from us.

5 I _____ have played computer games until midnight. I'm so tired now.

6 Ella got a good grade on her exam. She _____ have studied very hard.

D 보기에서 알맞은 말을 골라 문장을 완성하시오.

[1-3]

보기	had better go to see a doctor	ought to say sorry to him
	used to be very shy	

1 I _____, but now I am sociable.

2 You don't look good today. You _____.

3 You lost Jackson's camera. You _____.

[4-6]

보기	must have forgotten	may have seen him
	should have arrived here	

4 That boy looks familiar to me. I _____ before.

5 I have missed my train. I _____ earlier.

6 He got up late this morning. He _____ to set his alarm clock.

18

WRITING PRACTICE

Answer Key p.26

A 우리말과 일치하도록 ( ) 안의 말을 이용하여 문장을 완성하시오.

1 우리는 우리의 부모님을 존경해야 한다. (ought, respect)

→ We _____ our parents.

2 Eric이 네 생일을 잊었을 리가 없다. (forget)

→ Eric _____ your birthday.

3 Jason은 그의 어머니로부터 요리하는 것을 배웠던 게 틀림없다. (learn)

→ Jason _____ to cook from his mother.

4 너는 자러 가기 전에 아무것도 먹지 않는 게 좋겠다. (had, eat)

→ Before you go to bed, you _____ anything.

5 나는 겨울마다 스키를 타러 가곤 했다. (used, go skiing)

→ I _____ every winter.

6 나는 매일 친구들과 온라인으로 채팅을 하곤 했다. (used, chat online)

→ I _____ with my friends every day.

B 우리말과 일치하도록 ( ) 안에 주어진 단어를 바르게 배열하시오.

1 Jay는 그의 지갑을 찾았을지도 모른다. (have, Jay, wallet, might, found, his)

→ _____.

2 Sue는 그의 조언을 따르지 않는 게 좋겠다. (had, advice, his, Sue, not, better, follow)

→ _____.

3 너는 너무 늦게까지 밖에 있어서는 안 된다. (ought, to, stay, not, you, out)

→ _____ so late.

4 나의 아버지께서는 나에게 재미있는 이야기를 해 주시곤 했다. (me, father, tell, to, used, my)

→ _____ interesting stories.

5 나는 TV를 보면서 시간을 낭비하지 말았어야 했다. (wasted, I, have, time, shouldn't)

→ _____ watching TV.

6 Brad는 귀신을 무서워하곤 했다. (afraid, used, Brad, to, of, be, ghosts)

→ _____.

REVIEW TEST

[1-4] 빈칸에 들어갈 알맞은 말을 고르시오.

1

> You had better _____ a taxi here.

① take ② took
③ takes ④ taking
⑤ to take

2

> He looks just like Jake. He _____ be Jake's brother.

① can't ② must
③ had better ④ used to
⑤ doesn't have to

3

> I broke a vase on the table. I _____ more careful.

① don't have to be ② may have been
③ must have been ④ should have been
⑤ can't have been

4

> I _____ like detective stories when I was young.

① should ② had better
③ used to ④ ought to
⑤ must not

[5-6] 다음 중 어법상 <u>틀린</u> 것을 고르시오.

5 ① You don't have to hurry.
② May I open the front door?
③ You should take this chance.
④ She can't have lied to me.
⑤ You had not better change your job.

6 ① I used to play the violin with my sister.
② You must not enter the room.
③ If we hurry, we might get there on time.
④ He would to go for walks when he was angry.
⑤ We will be able to meet Tony tonight.

[7-9] 다음 우리말을 영어로 바르게 옮긴 것을 고르시오.

7

> 그녀가 병원에 입원 중일 리가 없다.

① She can't be in the hospital.
② She may not be in the hospital.
③ She doesn't have to be in the hospital.
④ She ought not to be in the hospital.
⑤ She must have been in the hospital.

8

> 나는 내 지갑을 그 버스에 두고 내렸던 게 틀림없다.

① I may leave my wallet on the bus.
② I can leave my wallet on the bus.
③ I may have left my wallet on the bus.
④ I must have left my wallet on the bus.
⑤ I should have left my wallet on the bus.

9 너는 그녀에게 사과할 필요가 없다.

① You can't apologize to her.
② You don't have to apologize to her.
③ You must not apologize to her.
④ You may not apologize to her.
⑤ You had better not apologize to her.

13 다음 중 어법상 옳은 것은?

① This might being good news for you.
② She won't able to come here.
③ You ought not to break your promise.
④ You had better seeing a doctor.
⑤ Alex used go climbing on Sundays.

서술형

[10-11] 빈칸에 공통으로 들어갈 말을 쓰시오.

10 • Sorry, but I _____ help you now.
• The rumor about Bob _____ be true. I trust him.

서술형

[14-16] 주어진 문장과 의미가 통하도록 빈칸에 알맞은 말을 쓰시오.

14 Emily is certainly not a liar.

→ Emily _____ _____ a liar.

11 • I may _____ said something wrong. She looks angry with me.
• You _____ to turn off your cell phone while the movie is playing.

15 I lived in an apartment, but now I don't anymore.

→ I _____ _____ _____ in an apartment.

빈출

12 밑줄 친 부분의 의미가 나머지 넷과 다른 것은?

① Roy <u>may</u> be a pianist.
② It <u>may</u> snow a lot tomorrow.
③ Tim <u>may</u> not be at home now.
④ You <u>may</u> stay here until tomorrow.
⑤ Jenny <u>may</u> not like my idea.

16 I'm sorry that I didn't wait for you yesterday.

→ I _____ _____ _____ for you yesterday.

17 다음 중 보기의 밑줄 친 부분과 의미가 같은 것은?

| 보기 | He <u>must</u> be very sick today. |

① You <u>must</u> be hungry now.
② You <u>must</u> be quiet in the class.
③ The child <u>must</u> not act like that.
④ You <u>must</u> save money for the future.
⑤ We <u>must</u> take his class this semester.

서술형

[18-19] 우리말과 일치하도록 ( ) 안의 말을 이용하여 문장을 완성하시오.

18 나는 그 회의에 참석할 수 있을 것이다. (attend)

→ _____

the meeting.

19 나는 그가 많이 그립다. 나는 그와 함께 스페인으로 떠났어야 했다. (leave)

→ I miss him a lot. _____
for Spain with him.

서술형

[20-21] 빈칸에 알맞은 조동사를 써서 대화를 완성하시오.

20 A: Must I fix this copy machine?
B: No, you _____ _____
_____. Peter will fix it.

21 A: How are you so good at soccer?
B: I _____ _____ play
soccer after school.

서술형

[22-23] 우리말과 일치하도록 ( ) 안에 주어진 단어를 바르게 배열하시오.

22 너는 이 방에서 어떤 것도 만져서는 안 된다.
(not, anything, you, ought, touch, to)

→ _____

in this room.

23 그는 그 역에서 그의 가방을 잃어버렸을지도 모른다.
(at the station, he, bag, have, his, may, lost)

→ _____

_____ .

서술형 고난도

[24-25] 어법상 틀린 부분을 찾아 바르게 고치시오.

24 Do you have a sore throat? You had better drinking some hot tea. (1개)

25 Kelly and Peter might fight yesterday. They didn't say anything to each other all day. (1개)

UNIT 01

수동태의 의미와 형태

🔍 Answer Key p.26

A ( ) 안에서 알맞은 말을 고르시오.

1 The meeting (canceled, was canceled) by our boss.

2 Portuguese (speaks, is spoken) in Brazil.

3 My brother (repaired, was repaired) my laptop.

4 The man (appeared, was appeared) in a movie last year.

5 The violin (was being played, was be played) in the hall.

6 The sisters (resemble, are resembled) each other.

7 His kindness (will be remember, will be remembered) forever.

8 Employees (are paying, are being paid) for their work.

9 Her strange behavior (cannot explained, cannot be explained) easily.

10 This essay (has been reviewed, has been reviewing) several times.

B 밑줄 친 부분을 어법에 맞게 고치시오.

1 Your bike can be store here for a month.

2 Jimmy's car is washing now.

3 Jack has talent but is lacked patience.

4 The flight to Jeju Island had be delayed due to the weather.

5 All the trouble caused by the boys.

6 The talk show will not be showing tonight.

7 Many people have be killed in car accidents.

8 Oil prices will be risen by ten percent next year.

9 The first modern Olympic Games were hold in Greece.

10 *The Little Prince* has be translated into many languages.

C 다음 문장을 수동태로 바꿔 쓰시오. (단, 행위자를 생략하지 말 것)

1 I booked my flight ticket three months ago.

→ _____ three months ago.

2 Jim has already solved the math problem.

→ The math problem _____ .

3 They will deliver the package to you on time.

→ The package _____ on time.

4 We must take this issue seriously.

→ This issue _____ .

5 My father is painting the old fence.

→ The old fence _____ .

6 Mr. Brown wrote the novel in 2019.

→ _____ in 2019.

7 We clean the toilets in our school every day.

→ The toilets in our school _____ every day.

8 We can use computers in various ways.

→ _____ in various ways.

9 The police officer was watching the woman.

→ The woman _____ .

10 My little brother has broken my tablet PC.

→ My tablet PC _____ .

11 They have to repair my car by Friday.

→ _____ by Friday.

12 Someone stole my wallet from my back pocket.

→ My wallet _____ .

13 The hotel staff is carrying our luggage.

→ Our luggage _____ .

14 The police arrested the killer yesterday.

→ _____ yesterday.

WRITING PRACTICE

Q Answer Key p.26

A 우리말과 일치하도록 ( ) 안의 말을 이용하여 문장을 완성하시오.

1 오늘 학교에서 재미있는 일이 일어났다. (happen)

→ A funny thing _____ at school today.

2 나는 나의 어머니를 닮았다. (resemble)

→ I _____ .

3 그 문은 나의 아버지에 의해 고쳐졌다. (fix)

→ The door _____ .

4 이 문제는 그 회의에서 논의될 것이다. (will, discuss)

→ This problem _____ at the meeting.

5 너의 차는 수리되고 있는 중이다. (repair)

→ Your car _____ .

6 우리 부모님은 17년간 결혼 생활을 해오셨다. (marry)

→ My parents _____ for seventeen years.

B 우리말과 일치하도록 ( ) 안에 주어진 단어를 바르게 배열하시오.

1 이 영화는 유명한 감독에 의해 만들어졌다. (a, by, made, famous, director, was)

→ This film _____ .

2 내 스마트폰이 그 버스에서 사라졌다. (my, bus, disappeared, on, smartphone, the)

→ _____ .

3 이 프로젝트는 다음 주 월요일까지 끝마쳐져야 한다. (project, be, this, finished, must)

→ _____ by next Monday.

4 그 벽은 다시 페인트칠이 되어야 한다. (should, wall, repainted, be, the)

→ _____ .

5 이 도시는 쓰나미에 의해 피해를 입었다. (has, damaged, a tsunami, this, by, city, been)

→ _____ .

6 그 행사는 뉴스팀에 의해 촬영되고 있다. (is, the, being, event, by, filmed)

→ _____ the news crew.

UNIT 02

4형식, 5형식 문장의 수동태

A ( ) 안에서 알맞은 말을 고르시오.

1 $5,000 was given (to, for) the photographer for his pictures.

2 Your school report will be shown (to, of) your parents.

3 A new desk was bought (to, for) him by his parents.

4 No one is allowed (enter, to enter) this room.

5 The wind was heard (blow, blowing) outside.

6 I was made (to stay, staying) home during the weekend.

7 The dog was named (Buddy, be Buddy) by me.

8 Most Korean students are made (wear, to wear) their school uniforms.

9 In the concert, my brother will be seen (play, playing) the piano.

10 Charlie was made (to help, helping) sick people.

B 어법상 틀린 부분을 찾아 바르게 고치시오.

1 A box of chocolates was given Scott on Valentine's Day.

2 This parcel was sent for me by my sister.

3 This medicine was made to those with headaches.

4 These headphones were bought of me by my brother.

5 This city was made to popular by its unique buildings.

6 The robber was seen break into a bank.

7 The staff at this restaurant are made smile all the time.

8 The heater was heard made a strange noise.

9 A bunch of flowers were given for Jinju.

10 The employees are made turn off their computers before they leave.

C 다음 문장을 수동태로 바꿔 쓰시오. (단, 행위자를 생략하지 말 것)

1 My uncle bought me this jacket.

→ This jacket _____.

2 His teacher made Ron stay after school.

→ Ron _____.

3 One of my neighbors saw a strange man enter my house.

→ A strange man _____.

4 The movie made this music popular.

→ This music _____.

5 They consider Dr. Kim to be an expert in this field.

→ Dr. Kim _____.

6 Mr. Flores taught us Spanish last year.

→ Spanish _____.

→ We _____.

7 They gave the artist the Best Singer Award.

→ The artist _____.

→ The Best Singer Award _____.

8 I bought my brother the comic books.

→ The comic books _____.

9 I heard the baby crying at midnight.

→ The baby _____.

10 My boyfriend made me a large snowman.

→ A large snowman _____.

11 We elected Jenny the leader of the project.

→ Jenny _____.

12 I will show you the new schedule.

→ You _____.

→ The new schedule _____.

WRITING PRACTICE

🔍 Answer Key p·27

A 우리말과 일치하도록 ( ) 안의 말을 이용하여 문장을 완성하시오.

1 내 사진이 스마트폰으로 나의 아버지께 전송되었다. (send)

→ My photo _____ with my smartphone.

2 이 새 치마는 나의 어머니를 위해 구매되었다. (buy)

→ This new skirt _____.

3 그는 국가적 영웅이라고 불렸다. (a national hero)

→ He _____.

4 그녀가 내 이름을 부르는 것이 들렸다. (hear)

→ She _____ _____.

5 Danny는 그의 고향을 떠나게 되었다. (make, leave)

→ Danny _____ his hometown.

6 십 대들은 술을 사는 것이 허락되지 않는다. (allow, buy)

→ Teenagers _____ alcohol.

B 우리말과 일치하도록 ( ) 안에 주어진 단어를 바르게 배열하시오.

1 나는 내 친구에게서 파일을 받았다. (given, my, by, friend, a file, was)

→ I _____.

2 할인을 받기 위해서는 그 점원에게 이 쿠폰이 보여져야 한다. (the, shown, be, should, to, clerk)

→ This coupon _____ to get a discount.

3 여러 개의 공원이 대중을 위해 지어졌다. (for, been, built, have, public, the)

→ Several parks _____.

4 이 인형의 집은 내 여동생들을 위해 만들어졌다. (my, for, made, sisters, was)

→ This doll house _____.

5 그가 해변에 누워 있는 것이 보였다. (on, lying, he, seen, beach, the, was)

→ _____.

6 Matt는 규칙적으로 운동을 하라고 조언받았다. (was, Matt, regularly, exercise, advised, to)

→ _____.

UNIT 03

주의해야 할 수동태

🔍 Answer Key p-27

A ( ) 안에서 알맞은 말을 고르시오.

1 This store is always crowded (with, for) customers.

2 Politicians are often (made fun of, made fun of by) comedians.

3 Your future will be filled (of, with) joy.

4 My desk is covered (with, from) ink.

5 Many kids are reported (be, to be) addicted to computer games.

6 We are really worried (in, about) climate change.

7 Women are (looked by down on, looked down on by) men in some countries.

8 It is said (to, that) different countries have different ways of greeting people.

9 Are you satisfied (with, at) the musical?

10 It (believes, is believed) that Shakespeare used about 3,000 new words in his works.

B 밑줄 친 부분을 어법에 맞게 고치시오.

1 Babies should be looked after <u>their parents</u> all day long.

2 Hundreds of animals <u>run over</u> by cars on highways last year.

3 This book says that paper <u>invented</u> by a Chinese man.

4 Kimchi is believed <u>being</u> one of the healthiest foods in the world.

5 It <u>believes</u> that it took ten years to build this statue.

6 It is <u>report</u> that the number of overweight children is increasing.

7 The committee is <u>composed by</u> three professors and three governors.

8 *Nanta* is well <u>known as</u> foreigners.

9 Watch this movie. You won't be <u>disappointed to</u> it.

10 You may be <u>surprised with</u> his success.

C 다음 문장을 수동태로 바꿔 쓰시오.

1 The elephant stepped on some flowers.

→ Some flowers _____.

2 His bad behavior disappointed everyone.

→ Everyone _____.

3 Ice dancing interests my cousin.

→ My cousin _____.

4 A lot of people looked up to the politician.

→ The politician _____.

5 They report that a lot of animals are killed by hunters.

→ It _____.

→ A lot of animals _____.

6 The math test score surprised Susie.

→ Susie _____.

7 People believe that exercising regularly is good for health.

→ It _____.

→ Exercising regularly _____.

8 People think that harmful insects are disgusting.

→ It _____.

→ Harmful insects _____.

9 The government should take care of public education.

→ Public education _____.

10 My progress pleased my parents.

→ My parents _____.

11 People say that John is a very selfish person.

→ It _____.

→ John _____.

WRITING PRACTICE

🔍 Answer Key p.27

A 우리말과 일치하도록 (   ) 안의 말을 이용하여 문장을 완성하시오.

1 나의 집은 한 도둑에 의해 침입당했다. (break into, thief)

→ My house _____ .

2 나의 억양은 내 친구들에게 놀림을 받았다. (make fun of)

→ My accent _____ .

3 그녀가 직업을 바꿀 것이라고 말해진다. (say)

→ It _____ she will change her job.

4 귀신이 이 집에 산다고 여겨진다. (live)

→ A ghost is believed _____ .

5 네 코트가 먼지로 뒤덮여 있다. (cover, dust)

→ Your coat _____ .

6 나는 그 소식에 놀랐다. (surprise, news)

→ I _____ .

B 우리말과 일치하도록 (   ) 안에 주어진 단어를 바르게 배열하시오.

1 네 잎 클로버는 행운을 가져온다고 여겨진다. (bring, is, luck, to, believed)

→ A four-leaf clover _____ .

2 여자가 남자보다 더 오래 사는 것으로 보고된다. (reported, women, than, that, is, longer, men, live)

→ It _____ .

3 그 나무들은 나의 할아버지에 의해서 보살핌을 받는다. (my, are, grandfather, taken, of, care, by)

→ The trees _____ .

4 저는 당신의 서비스에 만족했습니다. (service, I, your, was, with, satisfied)

→ _____ .

5 이 공책은 재활용된 종이로 만들어졌다. (from, paper, this, was, notebook, recycled, made)

→ _____ .

6 그는 한국 최고의 화가라고 말해진다. (said, be, he, to, best, the, is, painter)

→ _____ in Korea.

REVIEW TEST

[1–5] 빈칸에 들어갈 알맞은 말을 고르시오.

1

| Peter was made _____ the story by his mother. |

① repeat
② repeated
③ repeating
④ to repeat
⑤ to be repeated

2

| A pair of sunglasses were bought _____ me by my sister. |

① to
② of
③ in
④ for
⑤ with

3

| An interesting film script _____ by Jennifer soon. |

① was written
② will write
③ will be written
④ will being written
⑤ will have written

4

| The main hall was filled _____ little boys and girls. |

① in
② to
③ for
④ at
⑤ with

5

| The restroom _____ by a cleaning lady now. |

① cleans
② was cleaned
③ is cleaning
④ will clean
⑤ is being cleaned

[6–8] 다음 중 어법상 틀린 것을 고르시오.

6
① I was taught how to drive by Dad.
② She was seen sit under a tall tree.
③ The job must be done properly.
④ I'm worried about the result of the entrance exam.
⑤ It is said that his next movie will be released in October.

7
① A smartphone was given to him by his girlfriend.
② The poor dog was run over by a bus.
③ I'm satisfied with the car that I bought last week.
④ The shipment has already sent to your customer.
⑤ Her ID card was shown to the police officer by her.

8
① Jackson was surprised at the loud music downstairs.
② The presidential election will not be delayed.
③ Her grandmother was resembled by Emily.
④ Details of the accident were made public by a reporter.
⑤ My wedding ring had been stolen.

[9-10] 빈칸에 공통으로 들어갈 말을 고르시오.

9

> • I was very disappointed _____ my son's behavior.
> • His garden was covered _____ colorful flowers.

① for   ② to   ③ at
④ about   ⑤ with

10

> • This country is composed _____ two big islands.
> • His black wallet was made _____ soft leather.

① by   ② to   ③ at
④ of   ⑤ with

서술형

[11-13] ( ) 안의 말을 이용하여 문장을 완성하시오.

11 His idea will _____ by all the people in the room. (laugh at)

12 Amy was made _____ by her mother. (set the table)

13 The broken copy machine _____ _____ yesterday. (fix)

14 두 문장의 의미가 같도록 할 때, 빈칸에 들어갈 말은?

> I saw monkeys eat bananas in the zoo.
> → Monkeys were seen _____ bananas in the zoo.

① eat   ② eaten
③ eating   ④ being eaten
⑤ to be eaten

서술형 빈출

[15-17] 다음 문장을 주어진 말로 시작할 때 빈칸에 알맞은 말을 쓰시오.

15 His friends call him big brother.

→ He _____ by his friends.

16 He lent me his new bike.

→ His new bike _____ by him.

17 They said that Susan earned a lot of money dishonestly.

→ Susan _____ a lot of money dishonestly.

18 다음 우리말을 영어로 바르게 옮긴 것은?

> 에세이는 모든 학생에 의해 제출되어야 한다.

① An essay should hand in by every student.
② An essay should handed in by every student.
③ An essay should be handed in every student.
④ An essay should be handed in by every student.
⑤ An essay should be handed by in every student.

서술형

[19-20] 우리말과 일치하도록 ( ) 안의 말을 이용하여 문장을 완성하시오.

19 그 장비는 지금 엔지니어에 의해 검사되고 있는 중이다. (test)

→ That equipment _____
by the engineer now.

20 내 친구 중 한 명은 자원봉사 활동에 관심이 있다. (interest)

→ One of my friends _____
volunteer activities.

21 다음 중 어법상 옳은 것은?

① Lunch is being preparing now.
② His artistic talent is known with us.
③ Milk cartons can use as paper when recycled.
④ The concert ticket will be sent at her by mail.
⑤ She was told not to hang out with Linda by her mother.

서술형

[22-23] 우리말과 일치하도록 ( ) 안에 주어진 단어를 바르게 배열하시오.

22 이 테이블은 한 숙녀분에 의해 예약되었다.
(by, lady, reserved, has, table, a, been)

→ This _____
_____.

23 양파는 고혈압을 예방하는 데 좋다고 여겨진다.
(good, for, to, onions, believed, be, are)

→ _____
preventing high blood pressure.

서술형 고난도

[24-25] 어법상 틀린 부분을 찾아 바르게 고치시오.

24 Yesterday was my birthday. A delicious chocolate cake was made to me by my brother. (1개)

25 My sister has decided not to go to college. My parents are not pleased at her decision. (1개)

CHAPTER 04 부정사

명사적 용법의 to부정사

🔍 Answer Key p.28

A ( ) 안에서 알맞은 말을 고르시오.

1 I need (talk, to talk) to you right now.

2 Dad promised (buy, to buy) me a bike as a birthday present.

3 It takes a lot of effort (learn, to learn) a foreign language.

4 (It, That) was very fun to ride a snowboard.

5 Harry wanted (meet, to meet) her again.

6 We found (it, that) impossible to go to the finals.

7 I think it wrong (cheat, to cheat) on an exam.

8 (Wear, To wear) a scarf helps keep you warm.

9 He knows how (win, to win) the game.

10 His dream is (buy, to buy) a house in a quiet neighborhood.

B ( ) 안의 말을 이용하여 빈칸에 알맞은 말을 쓰시오.

1 Farmers know when _____. (sow)

2 _____ a lot is not good for your health. (eat)

3 I don't know whom _____. (believe)

4 I plan _____ this work by next week. (finish)

5 My favorite part is _____ out the candles to make a wish. (blow)

6 The rich man made it possible _____ the public library. (build)

7 His favorite hobby is _____ short films. (create)

8 It is healthy _____ your teeth after meals. (brush)

9 My little brother wants _____ shopping for toys. (go)

10 She found it very hard _____ many things at the same time. (do)

C 두 문장의 의미가 같도록 빈칸에 알맞은 말을 쓰시오.

1 To meet you will be a great pleasure.

→ _____ _____ _____ _____ _____ _____ to meet you.

2 To get up early in the morning is a good habit.

→ _____ _____ _____ _____ _____ to get up early in the morning.

3 To see the stars in the sky is not easy these days.

→ It is not easy _____ _____ _____ _____ _____ _____ _____ these days.

4 My teacher didn't tell me what I should do.

→ My teacher didn't tell me _____ _____ _____.

5 Please tell me where I should get off.

→ Please tell me _____ _____ _____ _____.

6 We don't know when we should start.

→ We don't know _____ _____ _____.

D 보기에서 알맞은 말을 골라 ( ) 안의 의문사와 to부정사를 함께 써서 문장을 완성하시오.

[1-3]

보기	go play eat

1 Can you tell me _____ this board game? (how)

2 I've been here many times before, so I know exactly _____. (where)

3 There are a lot of things to eat here. Let's decide _____. (what)

[4-6]

보기	find wear leave

4 He still hasn't decided _____ for the interview. (what)

5 Please let me know _____ a good used desk. (where)

6 A: Do you know _____ for the airport? (when)

B: Yes. Our flight is at 7:00 p.m., so we'll leave at four.

36

WRITING PRACTICE

Answer Key p-28

A 우리말과 일치하도록 to부정사와 ( ) 안의 말을 이용하여 문장을 완성하시오.

1 영어로 일기를 쓰는 것은 쉽지 않다. (easy, keep)

→ _____ a diary in English.

2 내 계획은 미국에서 의학을 공부하는 것이다. (study, medicine)

→ My plan is _____ in the US.

3 그는 그의 여름 휴가 동안 해외에 가지 않기로 결심했다. (decide, go)

→ He _____ abroad during his summer vacation.

4 나는 주말에 혼자 집에 있는 것이 외롭다는 것을 알았다. (lonely, stay home)

→ I found _____ alone on the weekend.

5 나는 언제 그 소식을 말해야 할지 몰랐다. (tell the news)

→ I didn't know _____.

6 무엇을 입을지 고르느라 시간을 너무 많이 보내지 말아라. (wear)

→ Don't spend too much time choosing _____.

B 우리말과 일치하도록 ( ) 안에 주어진 단어를 바르게 배열하시오.

1 중요한 것은 네 꿈을 포기하지 않는 것이다. (important, the, is, to, thing, up, give, not)

→ _____ on your dreams.

2 지금 새 잉크 카트리지를 주문하는 것은 좋은 생각이다. (order, to, it, a, good, is, idea)

→ _____ new ink cartridges now.

3 나는 박물관에서 시끄럽게 구는 것이 무례하다고 생각한다. (make, to, think, noise, rude, it)

→ I _____ in the museum.

4 그녀는 부모님을 위해 무엇을 해야 할지 몰랐다. (for, what, know, do, to, her parents)

→ She didn't _____.

5 궂은 날씨가 야외 활동 하는 것을 어렵게 만들었다. (made, bad, to, the, hard, it, weather, do)

→ _____ outdoor activities.

6 다음 단계는 피자에 치즈를 뿌리는 것이다. (sprinkle, the, step, cheese, is, next, to)

→ _____ on the pizza.

UNIT 02 형용사적 용법, 부사적 용법의 to부정사

A

( ) 안에서 알맞은 것을 고르시오.

1 He must be kind (to do, done) this for me.

2 I'm so sorry (disturb, to disturb) you.

3 The old woman needed someone (to talk, to talk to).

4 Spring is the best time (go, to go) on a picnic.

5 (See, To see) her big house on the hill, you would believe she was rich.

6 We are (wait, to wait) until Mary comes.

7 Diana and Charles (are, are to be) married next Sunday.

8 Do you have anything else (to talk, to talk about)?

9 Let's turn off the lights (to save, saved) energy.

10 Brad grew up (being, to be) a famous scientist.

B

밑줄 친 부분을 어법에 맞게 고치시오.

1 I have a lot of work <u>doing</u> by the weekend.

2 She has a puppy <u>to take care</u>.

3 My daughter just got a new bike <u>riding</u>.

4 Don't forget that you have your friends <u>to rely</u>.

5 If this plan is <u>succeed</u>, we must work together.

6 My parents worked hard <u>sent</u> me to college.

7 Japanese is easier <u>learning</u> than Chinese for me.

8 The family left Austria, never <u>return</u>.

9 I have a long list of people <u>inviting</u>.

10 He must be out of his mind <u>spent</u> all of his money on shoes.

C 밑줄 친 부분에 유의하여 문장을 우리말로 해석하시오.

1 There was nothing <u>to eat</u> on the table.

2 He <u>was to return</u> to his family after all.

3 No water <u>was to be found</u> nearby.

4 She woke up <u>to find</u> she was late for school.

5 The weather is fantastic <u>to go on a picnic</u>.

6 He must be sick <u>not to show up</u> today.

7 He is looking for <u>someone to ask for directions</u>.

8 There is nobody <u>to bother me</u> here.

9 I have many <u>friends to hang out with</u>.

10 He was very careful <u>not to fall on the ice</u>.

D 두 문장의 의미가 같도록 빈칸에 알맞은 말을 쓰시오.

1 I exercise regularly in order to keep my body in shape.

→ I exercise regularly _____ _____ my body in shape.

2 The company is going to release a new version of the application.

→ The company is _____ _____ a new version of the application.

3 They were destined to see each other again.

→ They were _____ _____ each other again.

4 Ron has to finish the work by tomorrow.

→ Ron is _____ _____ the work by tomorrow.

5 If you intend to pass the exam, study hard.

→ If you are _____ _____ the exam, study hard.

WRITING PRACTICE

Q Answer Key p.28

A 우리말과 일치하도록 to부정사와 ( ) 안의 말을 이용하여 문장을 완성하시오.

1 그 문제를 매우 빨리 푸는 것을 보니 그는 똑똑한 것임에 틀림없다. (solve, problem)

→ He must be smart _____ so fast.

2 그들을 보면 너는 그들이 결혼을 했다고 생각할 것이다. (see)

→ _____, you would think they were married.

3 그 소설은 이해하기 어렵다. (difficult, understand)

→ The novel is _____.

4 그는 내년에 새 영화를 감독할 예정이다. (be, direct)

→ He _____ a new movie next year.

5 우리 형은 내가 그의 새 청바지를 입었던 것을 알면 화를 낼 것이다. (angry, know)

→ My brother will be _____ that I wore his new jeans.

6 쉽게 잠들도록 따뜻한 우유를 한 잔 마시는 게 어떠니? (fall asleep, easily)

→ How about drinking a cup of warm milk _____?

B 우리말과 일치하도록 ( ) 안에 주어진 단어를 바르게 배열하시오.

1 연체료를 내지 않도록 반납일을 잊지 마라. (late fees, to, pay, not)

→ Don't forget the due date in order _____.

2 지금이 비행기 표를 예약하기에 가장 좋은 시기이다. (the, a flight, best, to, book, time)

→ Now is _____.

3 필기할 만한 것을 빌릴 수 있을까요? (to, something, write, with, borrow)

→ Can I _____?

4 그녀는 그녀의 이모를 그 역에서 만날 예정이었다. (at the station, her aunt, to, was, meet)

→ She _____.

5 그 왕은 살아서 100세가 되었다. (be, old, hundred, to, years, a)

→ The king lived _____.

6 그 영화의 리메이크작은 성공하게 되어 있었다.

(to, a success, was, the remake, the movie, of, be)

→ _____.

to부정사의 의미상의 주어, 시제, 태

🔍 Answer Key p.28

A ( ) 안에서 알맞은 말을 고르시오.

1 It is important (for you, of you) to review what you learned.

2 It was brave (for him, of him) to save the kid from the fire.

3 He doesn't seem (to know, knowing) how to use the machine.

4 The battery seems (to have run out, having run out) of power.

5 Jenny seems (to learn, to have learned) taekwondo when she was young.

6 It is difficult (for me, of me) to read a book in an hour.

7 I hate (to call, to be called) by the teacher during class.

8 A baby needs (to take care of, to be taken care of) by his or her parents.

9 Jamie seems (to have eaten, to have been eaten) my cake.

10 It isn't wise (to you, of you) to compare yourself with someone else.

  밑줄 친 부분을 어법에 맞게 고치시오.

1 It is easy <u>of her</u> to fix the computer.

2 It is kind <u>for him</u> to open the door for others.

3 There seemed <u>being</u> many tourists at the park.

4 This project needs <u>to do</u> by next week.

5 It was very generous <u>for her</u> to donate her entire wealth.

6 The old man seems <u>to be</u> a pianist when he was young.

7 The dead woman seems <u>to have shot</u> by someone.

8 It is impossible <u>of the old lady</u> to climb the mountain by herself.

9 It was very careless <u>for you</u> to trust the stranger.

10 The batteries need <u>to be replacing</u> at least twice a year.

( ) 안의 말을 이용하여 문장을 완성하시오.

1 It was careless _____ to lose her wedding ring again. (she)

2 It is necessary _____ to bring your passport. (you)

3 It took a long time _____ to get to my hometown. (I)

4 It was foolish _____ to cheat on the exam. (he)

5 It was kind _____ to take the lost child to the police. (they)

6 It is not easy _____ to make time to exercise. (I)

7 It was silly _____ to leave his bag on the bus. (he)

8 It is natural _____ to get angry in unfair situations. (she)

9 It was very rude _____ to leave the party like that. (you)

10 It is important _____ to pass the entrance exam. (he)

D

두 문장의 의미가 같도록 빈칸에 알맞은 말을 쓰시오.

1 It seems that the cello is fairly expensive.

→ The cello seems _____ fairly expensive.

2 It seems that no one has walked this path.

→ No one seems _____ this path.

3 It appears that the plant has been well cared for.

→ The plant appears _____ .

4 It seemed that the thief had stolen the diamond.

→ The thief seemed _____ the diamond.

5 It seemed that the doctor had a lot of work to do.

→ The doctor seemed _____ a lot of work to do.

6 It seems that he was adopted from a foreign country.

→ He seems _____ from a foreign country.

WRITING PRACTICE

Answer Key p.28

A 우리말과 일치하도록 to부정사와 ( ) 안의 말을 이용하여 문장을 완성하시오.

1 그 시는 그 아이가 이해하기 쉽지 않다. (child, understand)

→ The poem is not easy _____.

2 그 나무는 매우 오래돼 보인다. (seem, be)

→ The tree _____ very old.

3 박물관의 그 그림은 도난당했던 것으로 밝혀졌다. (steal)

→ The picture in the museum was found _____.

4 진실을 말하다니 너는 용감하다. (brave, tell)

→ It is _____ the truth.

5 이 약은 효과가 있어 보이지 않는다. (seem, work)

→ This medicine doesn't _____.

6 그 쇼는 매우 인기 있는 것처럼 보였다. (very popular)

→ The show appeared _____.

B 우리말과 일치하도록 ( ) 안에 주어진 단어를 바르게 배열하시오.

1 그 계획은 실패했던 것으로 보인다. (failed, have, to, seems)

→ The plan _____.

2 김치를 만드는 것은 내게 어렵다. (kimchi, make, for, hard, me, to)

→ It is _____.

3 당신의 발목이 부러진 것 같군요. (broken, seems, ankle, be, your, to)

→ _____.

4 너에게 먼저 사과하지 않다니 그는 매우 무례하다. (apologize, of, rude, not, very, to, him)

→ It is _____ to you first.

5 그 파이는 냉장 보관되어야 한다. (be, needs, refrigerated, to)

→ The pie _____.

6 이 책은 여성에 의해 쓰인 것으로 보인다. (to, seems, written, been, have)

→ This book _____ by a woman.

UNIT 04

목적격 보어로 쓰이는 부정사

A ( ) 안에서 알맞은 말을 고르시오.

1 I watched the chef (make, to make) sushi.

2 Her baby made her (smile, smiled).

3 I wanted my friend (stay, to stay) longer.

4 She smelled gas (leaking, to leak) in the kitchen.

5 The new bed let her (sleep, sleeping) better.

6 My son watched me (fix, to fix) the bike.

7 She heard someone (knocking, knocked) on the door.

8 The judge ordered him (pay, to pay) for the damages.

9 Taking a rest helped her (recover, recovered) from the disease.

10 He let us (start, to start) the meal after his long prayer.

B ( ) 안의 말을 이용하여 문장을 완성하시오.

1 The woman felt her head _____. (hurt)

2 Internet banking allows us _____ money easily. (transfer)

3 He asked me _____ basketball. (play)

4 I had the new table set _____ to my new house. (deliver)

5 The soldier heard a plane _____ loudly overhead. (fly)

6 The strange noise made him _____ scared. (feel)

7 I smelled the soup _____ on the stove. (burn)

8 The part time job helped him _____ a new computer. (buy)

9 The rich soil got the crops _____ faster. (grow)

10 I saw some of the police officers _____ the building. (enter)

C 밑줄 친 부분을 어법에 맞게 고치시오.

1 The teacher told the students <u>be</u> quiet.

2 I heard the kids <u>to play</u> outside.

3 My parents didn't let me <u>to download</u> the new game.

4 I had the files on the computer <u>to delete</u> permanently.

5 I saw my friend <u>to stand</u> by the bus stop.

6 I asked the shop owner <u>giving</u> me a discount.

7 The appointment got her <u>wake up</u> earlier than usual.

8 How can I make him <u>to exercise</u> regularly?

9 Mom got me <u>do</u> the dishes.

10 Why don't you have her <u>to take</u> a break for a while?

D 빈칸에 알맞은 말을 보기에서 골라 적절한 형태로 바꿔 쓰시오.

[1-4]

보기	speak	quit	finish	bite

1 The doctor advised him _____ smoking.

2 Don't let them _____ ill of you.

3 She saw a mosquito _____ her leg.

4 Her teacher got her _____ the work after class.

[5-8]

보기	waste	cut	hurt	arrive

5 She had her hair _____ by her favorite hairdresser.

6 We don't expect him _____ on time.

7 David felt his back _____ a lot.

8 I won't let her _____ my time.

WRITING PRACTICE

Q Answer Key p-29

A 우리말과 일치하도록 ( ) 안의 말을 이용하여 문장을 완성하시오.

1 그 판매원은 내가 모자를 써보도록 했다. (let, try)

→ The salesclerk _____ the hat on.

2 나는 추위에 내 몸이 떨리는 것을 느꼈다. (feel, shiver)

→ I _____ from the cold.

3 나의 어머니는 그 더러운 옷들이 세탁되게 하셨다. (dirty clothes, wash)

→ My mother had _____.

4 그녀는 지하실에서 이상한 소리가 나는 것을 들었다. (a strange sound, come)

→ She heard _____ from the basement.

5 그 경험이 그가 작가가 되게 하였다. (make, become)

→ The experience _____ a writer.

6 소방관들은 그들이 건물에서 탈출하도록 도왔다. (help, escape)

→ The firefighters _____ from the building.

B 우리말과 일치하도록 ( ) 안에 주어진 단어를 바르게 배열하시오.

1 엄마는 내가 매일 채소를 먹게 하신다. (every day, eat, gets, me, to, vegetables)

→ Mom _____.

2 보청기는 그가 더 잘 들을 수 있게 도와준다. (to, him, helps, hear, better)

→ The hearing aid _____.

3 그는 누군가가 빵을 굽는 냄새를 맡았다. (smelled, baking, someone, bread)

→ He _____.

4 그녀는 그녀의 딸에게 다양한 책들을 읽게 했다. (her, made, books, daughter, read, a variety of)

→ She _____.

5 경찰관이 그 운전자에게 속도를 낮추라고 경고했다. (lower, the, warned, to, driver)

→ The police officer _____ his speed.

6 그는 어젯밤에 하늘에서 별 하나가 떨어지는 것을 보았다. (star, from, a, falling, the sky, saw)

→ He _____ last night.

UNIT 05

to부정사 구문, 독립부정사

🔍 Answer Key p.29

A

( ) 안에서 알맞은 말을 고르시오.

1 Alaska is too far (to go, going) to from here.

2 (Tell, To tell) the truth, I didn't like her from the beginning.

3 I felt (enough warm, warm enough) to turn off the heater.

4 The house was cheap enough for him (to buy, buying).

5 This pizza is too salty for me (to eat, eating).

6 Their voices were loud (enough, too) to get people's attention.

7 Strange (to say, said), but he looks a lot like her.

8 (To make, Making) matters worse, their teacher appeared when they were fighting.

9 The internet speed was fast enough (download, to download) the file in a minute.

10 (Make, To make) a long story short, this is one of the greatest inventions of all time.

B

밑줄 친 부분을 어법에 맞게 고치시오.

1 I was too sleepy staying awake during the class.

2 He has a responsibility, so speak.

3 The old lady has lived long enough see her great-granddaughter.

4 The Spanish team was strong enough going to the finals.

5 Strange saying, I don't like to watch TV.

6 Make matters worse, he lost all his money.

7 His son was enough cute to be chosen as a baby model.

8 Being frank with you, I wasn't sure what to do.

9 This room is quiet enough for us study in.

10 The bench in the park was too hot sit on.

C   밑줄 친 부분에 유의하여 문장을 우리말로 해석하시오.

1   The house is <u>too old to live in</u>.

2   <u>To begin with</u>, let me explain why I am here today.

3   The couch was <u>comfortable enough for him to sleep on</u>.

4   It is <u>too cold for us to swim</u> in the sea.

5   <u>To tell the truth</u>, this sofa isn't as expensive as you might think.

6   The movie was <u>funny enough to make people laugh</u> a lot.

7   <u>Strange to say</u>, I think she is hiding something now.

8   The dog was <u>smart cnough to remember</u> his previous owner.

9   <u>To make a long story short</u>, he lived life for his family.

10   Bob was <u>too tired to go</u> shopping with his girlfriend.

D   두 문장의 의미가 같도록 빈칸에 알맞은 말을 쓰시오.

1   It was so cold that I could see my breath.

     → It was _____.

2   The dress is so small that she can't wear it.

     → The dress is _____.

3   The laptop battery is so strong that it can last more than fifteen hours.

     → The laptop battery is _____.

4   Emily is so busy that she can't go home early.

     → Emily is _____.

5   She was so fast that she could set a world record at the Olympics.

     → She was _____.

6   The airplane ticket to Europe is so expensive that I can't buy it.

     → The airplane ticket to Europe is _____.

WRITING PRACTICE

🔍 Answer Key p.29

A 우리말과 일치하도록 to부정사와 ( ) 안의 말을 이용하여 문장을 완성하시오.

1 이 컴퓨터는 너무 느려서 게임을 할 수 없다. (slow, play games)

→ This computer is _____.

2 이 약은 아이들이 먹을 만큼 충분히 안전하다. (safe, children, take)

→ This medicine is _____.

3 이상한 이야기지만, 나는 가끔 똑같은 꿈을 꾼다. (strange, say)

→ _____, sometimes I have the same dream.

4 그는 너무 멀리 와서 돌아갈 수가 없다. (far, turn back)

→ He has come _____.

5 설상가상으로, 그의 자동차 연료가 거의 떨어졌다. (make, matters)

→ _____, his car almost ran out of fuel.

6 Dean은 혼자서 그 상자들을 옮길 수 있을 만큼 힘이 세다. (strong, move)

→ Dean is _____ the boxes by himself.

B 우리말과 일치하도록 ( ) 안에 주어진 단어를 바르게 배열하시오.

1 이 스마트폰은 너무 복잡해서 사용할 수가 없다. (complicated, use, to, too)

→ This smartphone is _____.

2 그는 올해 최고의 모델이 될 만큼 충분히 잘생겼다. (enough, be, handsome, to, the best model)

→ He is _____ this year.

3 우선 너는 교통 법규를 지켜야 한다. (should, begin, to, with, follow, you)

→ _____ the traffic rules.

4 사실대로 말하면, 그가 그 돈을 훔친 게 아니었다. (tell, he, the truth, steal, didn't, to)

→ _____ the money.

5 그는 너무 가난해서 빵을 살 수조차 없었다. (couldn't, he, that, poor, so)

→ He was _____ even buy bread.

6 그 산은 너무 높아서 올라갈 수가 없다. (climb, is, too, to, the mountain, high)

→ _____.

REVIEW TEST

[1-4] 빈칸에 들어갈 알맞은 말을 고르시오.

1

I will do my best _____ my goal.

① achieve
② achieved
③ achieving
④ to achieve
⑤ to be achieved

2

The doctor told her _____ more water.

① drink
② drank
③ drinking
④ being drunken
⑤ to drink

3

My father made me _____ the importance of being on time.

① realize
② realizing
③ realized
④ to realize
⑤ to be realized

4

It was kind _____ him to show me around the city.

① to
② as
③ of
④ in
⑤ from

빈출

[5-6] 다음 중 보기의 밑줄 친 부분과 쓰임이 같은 것을 고르시오.

5

보기   I found a place to park my car.

① His dream is to own a bakery.
② I went shopping to buy a jacket.
③ This is my first time to visit Sydney.
④ I'm so glad to receive your postcard.
⑤ She loves to take a walk after lunch.

6

보기   We went to the airport to see Jenny off.

① I'm sorry to arrive too late.
② She must be angry to say nothing at all.
③ I would be happy to win the lottery.
④ He woke to find himself lying on a bench.
⑤ We stayed up all night to finish the project.

7 빈칸에 들어갈 말이 순서대로 바르게 짝지어진 것은?

• She found _____ interesting to play chess.
• Strange _____, I have seen an alien.

① too – say
② that – saying
③ it – saying
④ it – to say
⑤ that – to say

[8-9] 다음 중 어법상 틀린 것을 고르시오.

8 ① It is unusual for her to get up early.
② Her sister seems to be a teacher.
③ I saw him to enter the grocery store.
④ To be sure, he didn't break the mirror.
⑤ I don't know where to put this lamp.

9 ① Tim got me to wash his dirty car.
② I found it hard to learn Korean.
③ Cathy grew up being an architect.
④ Paul is to visit his parents next week.
⑤ He told me to practice the piano harder.

[10-11] 두 문장의 의미가 같도록 할 때, 빈칸에 들어갈 알맞은 말을 고르시오.

10
This soup is so salty that I can't eat it.
→ This soup is _____ to eat.

① salty ② so salty
③ salty enough ④ too salty
⑤ enough to salty

11
It seems that Eli gained some weight.
→ Eli seems _____ some weight.

① gain ② gained
③ to gain ④ having gained
⑤ to have gained

12 다음 중 밑줄 친 부분을 잘못 고친 것은?

① He helped me carrying the heavy box.
→ carry
② I didn't expect the meeting to cancel.
→ to be canceled
③ His brother is not enough mature to get married. → mature enough
④ My father had me cleaning my room.
→ to clean
⑤ It was rude to her to treat me like that.
→ of

서술형

[13-15] ( ) 안의 말을 이용하여 문장을 완성하시오.

13 She wanted me _____ her new mystery novel. (read)

14 I heard Edwin _____ to himself. (talk)

15 My mother didn't let me _____ to the party. (go)

[16-17] 다음 중 밑줄 친 부분이 어법상 옳은 것을 고르시오.

16 ① She had no pencil to write with.
② It is not easy challenge new things.
③ He seems to been to Paris several times.
④ Let's decide when go back to Germany.
⑤ You must be a genius knowing such things.

17 ① It's unusual of him to go to church.
② He told me taking a rest for a while.
③ I decided to be joined the drama club.
④ I watched her to dance with her dad.
⑤ The little girl was to be a Nobel Prize winner.

서술형
[21-23] 우리말과 일치하도록 ( ) 안에 주어진 단어를 바르게 배열하시오.

21 그녀는 너무 바빠서 이메일을 확인할 수 없었다.
(busy, she, to, was, too, check)

→ _____

_____ her email.

서술형
[18-19] 우리말과 일치하도록 ( ) 안의 말을 이용하여 문장을 완성하시오.

18 Alex는 인테리어 디자인을 공부하기 위해 프랑스에 가기로 결심했다. (go, study)

→ Alex decided _____ to France _____ interior design.

22 사실대로 말하면, 우리는 서로 싫어한다.
(each, tell, the, we, other, to, truth, dislike)

→ _____

_____ .

23 Jude는 이탈리아에서 태어난 것처럼 보인다.
(have, seems, born, been, to, Italy, in)

→ Jude _____

_____ .

19 그는 어제 내가 그 보고서를 작성하는 것을 도와주었다.
(help, make)

→ He _____ the report yesterday.

서술형 고난도
[24-25] 어법상 틀린 부분을 찾아 바르게 고치시오.

24 Tim and Emily seem to be very close when they were in elementary school. But they seldom talk to each other nowadays. (1개)

서술형
20 두 문장의 의미가 같도록 빈칸에 알맞은 말을 쓰시오.

Luke is smart enough to speak four different languages.

→ Luke is _____ that he _____ four different languages.

25 We are pleased inviting you to our Halloween party. Celebrate Halloween, we have prepared lots of fun activities for you. (2개)

UNIT 01

동명사의 역할

Answer Key p.30

A ( ) 안에서 알맞은 말을 고르시오.

1 (Smoke, Smoking) cigarettes is bad for health.

2 He kept (wonder, wondering) why Brian left early.

3 Thank you for (tell, telling) me the truth.

4 James hated (travel, traveling) in hot weather.

5 He doesn't like (I, me) visiting his office.

6 I was afraid of (not finding, finding not) the true answer.

7 She was upset about (be treated, being treated) unfairly.

8 I am proud of (have studied, having studied) hard when I was a student.

9 I can't understand (she, her) being late again.

10 His favorite hobby is (repair, repairing) electrical goods.

B ( ) 안의 말을 이용하여 문장을 완성하시오.

1 Anthony likes _____ novels when he has time. (read)

2 _____ a walk with my dog is my favorite thing. (take)

3 One of my hobbies is _____ documentary films. (watch)

4 People don't like _____ by others. (ignore)

5 Instead of _____ to Paris, they agreed to go to New York. (go)

6 He is ashamed of _____ the money. (steal)

7 My job was _____ care of the garden. (take)

8 _____ on a stool for a long time hurts my back. (sit)

9 _____ model planes is one of his favorite activities. (build)

10 Kate needs to study without _____. (disturb)

C 밑줄 친 부분을 어법에 맞게 고치시오.

1 Mom gave me some tips for <u>pack</u> a suitcase.

2 I'm happy about <u>accepting</u> by Oxford University.

3 <u>Pull</u> out unused power cords can save energy.

4 He was satisfied with <u>she</u> playing the piano.

5 They were opposed to <u>build</u> fences around the park.

6 <u>Sleep</u> well is a good way to recover when you catch a cold.

7 I thought of <u>going not</u> to school yesterday.

8 The clerk was partly responsible for <u>have been</u> robbed.

9 My son's favorite activity is <u>go fishing</u> with me.

10 I would like to relax on the beach without <u>be bothered</u>.

D 두 문장의 의미가 같도록 빈칸에 알맞은 말을 쓰시오.

1 Julia was angry that he was late.

→ Julia was angry at _____ _____ _____.

2 Ian was excited that he was given the prize.

→ Ian was excited about _____ _____ _____ _____.

3 I am sorry that I didn't call you back.

→ I am sorry for _____ _____ _____ you back.

4 We were worried that she drove on icy roads.

→ We were worried about _____ _____ on icy roads.

5 My mother is proud that I work hard.

→ My mother is proud of _____ _____ _____.

6 Would you mind if I borrowed your pen?

→ Would you mind _____ _____ your pen?

7 I was sure that he had done the work.

→ I was sure of _____ _____ _____ the work.

WRITING PRACTICE

Answer Key p.30

A 우리말과 일치하도록 ( ) 안의 말을 이용하여 문장을 완성하시오.

1 좋은 친구들을 갖는 것은 인생에서 매우 중요하다. (good friends)

→ _____ is very important in life.

2 그는 오늘 체육관에 가지 않을 생각이다. (go to the gym)

→ He is thinking about _____ today.

3 그의 습관은 긴장하면 입술을 깨무는 것이다. (habit, bite)

→ _____ his lips when he is nervous.

4 나의 엄마는 내가 혼자 외국에 가는 것을 걱정하셨다. (go)

→ My mom worried about _____ to a foreign country alone.

5 그녀는 쇼핑하러 가는 것을 좋아하지 않는다. (go shopping)

→ She doesn't like _____.

6 Leo는 그의 엄마에게 거짓말을 했던 것을 부끄러워했다. (lie)

→ Leo was ashamed of _____ to his mom.

B 우리말과 일치하도록 ( ) 안에 주어진 단어를 바르게 배열하시오.

1 교통 법규를 따르지 않는 것은 위험하다. (traffic, following, is, rules, not, dangerous)

→ _____.

2 그는 그 팀에서 쫓겨났던 것으로 알려졌다. (having, kicked, been, off)

→ He was known for _____ the team.

3 나의 개는 자고 있을 때 쓰다듬어 주는 것을 좋아하지 않는다. (doesn't, being, like, patted)

→ My dog _____ when he is sleeping.

4 나는 길게 줄 서서 기다리는 것을 싫어한다. (long, in, hate, waiting, lines)

→ I _____.

5 내 여동생은 아이들을 잘 돌본다. (good, children, at, is, of, taking, care)

→ My sister _____.

6 나는 그 클럽의 회원인 것이 자랑스러웠다. (of, proud, was, a member, being)

→ I _____ of the club.

UNIT 02 동명사 vs. to부정사

Ⓐ ( ) 안에서 알맞은 말을 고르시오.

1 I feel like (drinking, to drink) coffee when I am sleepy.

2 They refused (talking, to talk) with us.

3 Do you mind (putting, to put) away these boxes?

4 It stopped (snowing, to snow) in the late afternoon yesterday.

5 On (enter, entering) the house, I turned on the light.

6 There is no (knowing, to know) where she is now.

7 Don't expect (seeing, to see) me during this week.

8 He was used to (make, making) a presentation in front of many people.

9 Don't forget (taking, to take) your umbrella when you go out.

10 Remember (sending, to send) him an email tomorrow.

Ⓑ ( ) 안의 말을 이용하여 문장을 완성하시오.

1 They continued _____ about their jobs. (talk)

2 I began _____ Spanish when I was seven years old. (learn)

3 He remembers _____ his ring at the hotel yesterday. (leave)

4 He has already spent two hours _____ on this report. (work)

5 He wishes _____ a brand-new cell phone. (buy)

6 The man denied _____ the building that night. (enter)

7 My uncle decided _____ his own company. (start)

8 The police prevented cars from _____ the bridge. (cross)

9 You can avoid _____ the exam by studying hard. (fail)

10 My parents want _____ a bigger house. (buy)

C 밑줄 친 부분을 어법에 맞게 고치시오.

1　My mom enjoys <u>to read</u> the newspaper every morning.

2　I'm planning <u>completing</u> this part by tomorrow.

3　Both schools agreed <u>sharing</u> the gym.

4　She couldn't help <u>shut</u> the door because it was too noisy outside.

5　Don't forget <u>calling</u> him tonight.

6　I am considering <u>to go</u> to Spain on vacation.

7　The heavy rain kept us from <u>climb</u> the mountain.

8　We are looking forward to <u>work</u> with you.

9　Sara quit <u>to drink</u> after she got heart disease.

10　This topic is worth <u>to talk</u> about.

D 두 문장의 의미가 같도록 빈칸에 알맞은 말을 쓰시오.

1　I remember that I met the movie star six months ago.

　→ I remember ＿＿＿＿＿＿＿＿ the movie star six months ago.

2　Don't forget that you should turn off the stove after using it.

　→ Don't forget ＿＿＿＿＿＿＿＿ the stove after using it.

3　Please remember that you should call Anthony when you get there.

　→ Please remember ＿＿＿＿＿＿＿＿ Anthony when you get there.

4　I don't like to ask for help.

　→ I don't like ＿＿＿＿＿＿＿＿ for help.

5　My sister loves chatting online with her friends.

　→ My sister loves ＿＿＿＿＿＿＿＿ online with her friends.

6　The rain started to pour after school.

　→ The rain started ＿＿＿＿＿＿＿＿ after school.

WRITING PRACTICE

Q Answer Key p.30

A 우리말과 일치하도록 ( ) 안의 말을 이용하여 문장을 완성하시오.

1 그의 부모님은 그에게 차를 사주기로 동의하셨다. (agree, buy)

→ His parents _____ him a car.

2 그녀는 시험 삼아 그 큰 트럭을 운전해 보았다. (try, drive)

→ She _____ the big truck.

3 나는 내 친구에게 그 책을 빌려준 것을 잊어버렸다. (lend)

→ I _____ the book to my friend.

4 그 영화가 너무 감동적이어서 나는 울지 않을 수 없었다. (help, cry)

→ I _____ because the movie was so touching.

5 Jimmy는 캠핑을 위해 가방을 싸는 것을 마쳤다. (finish, pack)

→ Jimmy _____ his bags for camping.

6 일주일에 세 번 이상 운동하려고 노력해라. (try, exercise)

→ _____ more than three times a week.

B 우리말과 일치하도록 ( ) 안에 주어진 단어를 바르게 배열하시오.

1 그녀는 여름에 수상 스키 타는 것을 좋아한다. (likes, the, water skiing, summer, in)

→ She _____ .

2 표가 너무 비싸서 나는 기차 타는 것을 포기했다. (taking, the, gave, train, up)

→ I _____ because the tickets were too expensive.

3 요즘 버스 요금이 계속 오르고 있다. (fares, going, keep, bus, up)

→ _____ these days.

4 Bill은 지금 빨래하느라 바쁘다. (doing, laundry, is, busy)

→ Bill _____ now.

5 경찰을 보자마자 그는 달아났다. (away, seeing, ran, he, the, police)

→ On _____ .

6 그 판매자는 내일까지 그 가구를 배달할 것을 약속했다. (promised, deliver, to, furniture, the)

→ The seller _____ by tomorrow.

REVIEW TEST

Answer Key p.30

[1-4] 빈칸에 들어갈 알맞은 말을 고르시오.

1

This novel is worth _____ .

① read
② reading
③ to read
④ to be reading
⑤ to be read

2

I expect _____ you in London.

① see
② seeing
③ saw
④ being seen
⑤ to see

3

I hate _____ by my mother.

① punish
② punishing
③ to punish
④ be punished
⑤ being punished

4

Do you mind _____ on the air conditioner?

① turn
② to turn
③ turning
④ turned
⑤ to be turned

[5-6] 다음 중 어법상 옳은 것을 고르시오.

5
① He enjoys to watch documentaries.
② I have no doubt of he being honest.
③ I wish traveling abroad someday.
④ Upon see him, she burst into tears.
⑤ His job is treating patients in a hospital.

6
① Bill decided quitting his job.
② Josh gave up going on a diet.
③ He is proud of be Spanish.
④ I finished to write a letter to my brother.
⑤ She is afraid of criticized by others.

[7-8] 다음 우리말을 영어로 바르게 옮긴 것을 고르시오.

7

나는 내가 간호사였던 것이 자랑스럽다.

① I'm proud of be a nurse.
② I'm proud of not being a nurse.
③ I'm proud of to have been a nurse.
④ I'm proud of having been a nurse.
⑤ I'm proud of my have been a nurse.

8

나는 그가 1등으로 입상할 것을 확신한다.

① I'm sure of winning first prize.
② I'm sure of he winning first prize.
③ I'm sure of his winning first prize.
④ I'm sure of his being won first prize.
⑤ I'm sure of him having won first prize.

9 빈칸에 들어갈 말로 알맞지 <u>않은</u> 것은?

> We _____ to have a cute dog.

① wanted   ② decided

③ considered   ④ agreed

⑤ planned

[10-11] 빈칸에 들어갈 말이 순서대로 바르게 짝지어진 것을 고르시오.

10

> • I could not help _____ yes.
> • The heavy rain prevented me from _____ hiking.

① to say – to go

② to say – going

③ saying – to go

④ saying – going

⑤ to saying – going

11

> • He is afraid of _____ in the pool.
> • Kelly hates _____ what she should do.

① swim – telling

② swimming – being telling

③ swim – to tell

④ swimming – to be told

⑤ to swim – being told

[12-13] 다음 중 어법상 <u>틀린</u> 것을 고르시오.

12 ① Exercising is good for your health.

② I tried to contact him several times.

③ I look forward to going to the concert.

④ She avoided mentioning the accident.

⑤ She didn't forgive me for telling not her the truth.

13 ① I'm scared of watching horror movies.

② She regrets not having studied harder.

③ He loves to take pictures of flowers.

④ I spent two years to traveling around the world.

⑤ Sally remembers putting her earrings on the desk.

[14-16] 우리말과 일치하도록 ( ) 안의 말을 이용하여 문장을 완성하시오.

14 나는 너와 함께 여행한 것을 결코 잊지 않을 것이다. (travel)

→ I will never _____ _____ with you.

15 그녀는 세 명의 아이를 돌보느라 바쁘다. (take care of)

→ She _____ _____ _____ _____ _____ three children.

16 그는 그 비밀을 다른 사람들에게 말했던 것을 부인했다. (deny, tell)

→ He _____ _____ _____ the secret to others.

17 다음 중 밑줄 친 부분을 바르게 고친 것은?

① I refused join his basketball team.
→ joining

② I'm sorry for break the window.
→ broke

③ He finished paint the kitchen wall.
→ being painted

④ Joe began prepare a special dinner.
→ to prepare

⑤ My sister is not used stay up late.
→ to stay

서술형

[18-19] 우리말과 일치하도록 ( ) 안에 주어진 단어를 바르게 배열하시오.

18 더 일찍 전화 드리지 않은 것을 양해해 주십시오.
(for, earlier, me, not, excuse, calling, you)

→ _____ .

19 나는 내일 스쿠버 다이빙을 하러 가고 싶다.
(scuba diving, feel, going, I, like)

→ _____
tomorrow.

서술형

[20-21] 두 문장의 의미가 같도록 빈칸에 알맞은 말을 쓰시오.

20 I'm sure that he will get the job.

→ I'm sure of _____ _____ the job.

21 She is ashamed that she lied to her best friend.

→ She is ashamed of _____ _____ to her best friend.

서술형

[22-23] 우리말과 일치하도록 ( ) 안의 말을 이용하여 문장을 완성하시오.

22 오늘 숙제하는 것을 잊지 말아라. (forget, do)

→ _____
your homework today.

23 나는 시험 삼아 그 낡은 바이올린을 켜 보았다.
(try, play)

→ _____ the old violin.

서술형 고난도

[24-25] 어법상 틀린 부분을 찾아 바르게 고치시오.

24 I will have the midterm exam next week. My classmate Danny suggested to study together. (1개)

25 If you want to improve your writing skills, keep to write essays. Also, remember focusing on one subject when you write. (2개)

CHAPTER 06 분사

현재분사 vs. 과거분사

A ( ) 안에서 알맞은 말을 고르시오.

1 The old town and its (surrounding, surrounded) area will be developed.

2 I couldn't open the (locking, locked) door of my car.

3 You can easily see the house (painting, painted) in green on the hill.

4 He said that he saw a strange (flying, flown) object in the sky.

5 My sister is (baking, baked) oatmeal cookies now.

6 He sat (watching, watch) other people pass by.

7 The ending of the movie was (satisfying, satisfied).

8 The (exciting, excited) soccer fans were screaming.

9 A mother tried to calm her (crying, cried) baby.

10 He felt (embarrassing, embarrassed) when his car stopped in the middle of the road.

B ( ) 안의 말을 이용하여 문장을 완성하시오.

1 His presentation was _____. (bore)

2 The reporters asked him _____ questions. (embarrass)

3 It is difficult for him to read the book _____ in Chinese. (write)

4 The two boys stood _____ each other. (face)

5 Mom kept me _____ for more than one hour at the station. (wait)

6 The people _____ in the accident were rushed to a hospital. (wound)

7 They make the bread using flour _____ in Korea. (produce)

8 She has not _____ her car since last month. (wash)

9 His explanation was very _____. (confuse)

10 He heard his sister _____ in her room. (sing)

C 밑줄 친 부분을 어법에 맞게 고치시오.

1 The customers were satisfying with their service.

2 The car was stopping by the police.

3 We were amazing to see the Grand Canyon.

4 He had his car fixing yesterday.

5 My trip to Europe was very satisfied.

6 My father looked tiring after a long day of work.

7 Try to read books writing in English as often as possible.

8 The girl stood in the front row is my sister.

9 I read an amused comic.

10 I saw the police chased after a car.

D 주어진 문맥과 일치하도록 빈칸에 알맞은 말을 쓰시오.

1 The show amazed us.

a. We were _____ by the show.

b. The show was _____ to us.

2 His lecture bored me.

a. His lecture was _____ to me.

b. I was _____ with his lecture.

3 The festival disappointed them.

a. The festival was _____ to them.

b. They were _____ with the festival.

4 The result of the soccer game surprised us.

a. We were _____ at the result of the soccer game.

b. The result of the soccer game was _____ to us.

5 This hopeless situation depressed me.

a. This hopeless situation was _____ to me.

b. I was _____ by this hopeless situation.

WRITING PRACTICE

Answer Key p.31

A 우리말과 일치하도록 분사와 ( ) 안의 말을 이용하여 문장을 완성하시오.

1 그는 수학과 과학에 흥미가 있다. (interest)

→ He _____ in math and science.

2 그는 록 음악을 들으며 서 있었다. (stand, listen to)

→ He _____ rock music.

3 그는 나에게 그 깨진 창문을 만지지 말라고 말했다. (break)

→ He told me not to touch _____.

4 오빠는 에펠탑이 실망스러운 관광지라고 말했다. (disappoint, tourist spot)

→ My brother said the Eiffel Tower was _____.

5 사람들은 유기농으로 재배된 채소를 좋아한다. (vegetables, grow)

→ People like _____ organically.

6 그 개는 지난주에 한 가족에게 입양되었다. (adopt, by a family)

→ The dog was _____ last week.

B 우리말과 일치하도록 ( ) 안에 주어진 단어를 바르게 배열하시오.

1 그들은 나를 밖에서 오랫동안 기다리게 했다. (kept, time, they, me, long, a, waiting, for)

→ _____ outside.

2 나는 그 게임에 빨리 싫증이 났다. (bored, with, the, got, game)

→ I _____ quickly.

3 그는 그 연설자가 그의 이름을 부르는 것을 들었다. (heard, he, the, calling, speaker, his name)

→ _____.

4 놀라울 정도로 많은 사람들이 마라톤에 참가했다. (people, number, surprising, of, participated, a)

→ _____ in the marathon.

5 오후 2시에 떠나는 기차가 한 대 있다. (a, is, leaving, there, at, train)

→ _____ 2:00 p.m.

6 Olivia는 그녀의 사진이 찍히도록 했다. (taken, photograph, had, Olivia, her)

→ _____.

UNIT 02 분사구문

🔍 Answer Key p.31

( ) 안에서 알맞은 말을 고르시오.

1 (Put, Putting) down the book, she turned off the lamp.

2 (Listening, Listened) to the radio, my mom prepared dinner.

3 (Being, Be) very sensitive to noise, I was not able to concentrate.

4 I just stood there (not knowing, no knowing) what to do next.

5 (Play, Playing) in the living room, we made a mess.

6 (Came, Coming) from the northern part of the country, he spoke with an accent.

7 (Hoped, Hoping) to see Santa Claus, I waited beside the Christmas tree.

8 (Not brushing, Brushing not) regularly, he has unhealthy teeth.

9 (Be, Being) busy raising her four kids, she had to give up her job.

10 Although (live, living) near his house, I have rarely seen him.

올바른 분사구문이 되도록 밑줄 친 부분을 어법에 맞게 고치시오.

1 <u>Plug</u> in the device, you should be careful to avoid electric shock.

2 <u>Not had</u> any worries, I feel very happy these days.

3 <u>Fall</u> on hard times, he became pessimistic.

4 <u>Turn</u> left, you will find the bus stop.

5 I had a talk with a travel agent, <u>explained</u> my vacation plans.

6 <u>Wait</u> for her friend, she shopped for some clothes.

7 <u>Be</u> sleepy, I stopped reading the novel.

8 <u>Listen</u> to music, my brother studied for a math test.

9 <u>Talk</u> on the phone, she watered the flowers.

10 <u>Knowing not</u> the meaning of a word, I looked it up in a dictionary.

C 밑줄 친 부분을 분사구문으로 바꿔 쓰시오.

1 As he doesn't enjoy sushi, he rarely goes to Japanese restaurants.

→ _____, he rarely goes to Japanese restaurants.

2 If you think positively, you will see more opportunities.

→ _____, you will see more opportunities.

3 Because he was very sick, he couldn't complete the work.

→ _____, he couldn't complete the work.

4 Because he didn't know what to do, he called the police.

→ _____, he called the police.

5 When you jog in the dark, you should wear bright clothes.

→ _____, you should wear bright clothes.

6 As I grew up in the country, I learned much about various insects.

→ _____, I learned much about various insects.

7 While he walked in the park, he listened to the birds singing.

→ _____, he listened to the birds singing.

D 보기의 접속사를 이용하여, 밑줄 친 부분을 「접속사 + 주어 + 동사」의 형태로 바꿔 쓰시오. (단, 한 번씩만 쓸 것)

보기	when	because	after	if

1 Looking out the window, I saw Jim.

→ _____, I saw Jim.

2 Finishing my homework, I went outside to meet James.

→ _____, I went outside to meet James.

3 Not knowing his name, I called him "the gentleman."

→ _____, I called him "the gentleman."

4 Looking closely, you will notice the difference.

→ _____, you will notice the difference.

WRITING PRACTICE

🔍 Answer Key p.31

A 우리말과 일치하도록 ( ) 안의 말을 이용하여 분사구문을 만드시오.

1 그 대도시가 싫어서 우리는 작은 마을로 이사를 갔다. (like, big city)

→ _____, we moved to a small town.

2 외국에 사는 동안 그녀는 항상 모국을 그리워했다. (live, overseas)

→ _____, she always missed her home country.

3 이 지도를 따라가면 그들은 집에 안전하게 도착할 것이다. (follow, map)

→ _____, they'll get home safely.

4 샤워를 하면서 그는 노래를 불렀다. (take a shower)

→ _____, he sang a song.

5 과체중이기 때문에 그는 기름진 음식을 피한다. (be, overweight)

→ _____, he avoids fatty food.

6 몸이 좋지 않아서, 그는 진료를 예약했다. (feel well)

→ _____, he made an appointment with his doctor.

B 우리말과 일치하도록 ( ) 안에 주어진 단어를 바르게 배열하시오.

1 배가 불러서 나는 점심을 먹지 않았다. (full, I, being, eat, didn't)

→ _____ lunch.

2 해변에 앉아서 그들은 노을을 보았다. (watched, they, on, sitting, the beach)

→ _____ the sunset.

3 늦어서 나는 시험을 칠 수 없었다. (I, being, able, not, was, to, late)

→ _____ take the exam.

4 작별 인사를 하면서 그녀는 친구들에게 손을 흔들었다. (goodbye, she, saying, waved)

→ _____ to her friends.

5 불을 켜면서 나는 그 방에 들어갔다. (light, switching, the, on)

→ _____, I entered the room.

6 그 비행기는 8시에 도쿄를 떠나 서울에 10시에 도착했다. (at, arriving, Seoul, in, ten)

→ The plane left Tokyo at eight, _____.

UNIT 03

여러 가지 분사구문

A ( ) 안에서 알맞은 말을 고르시오.

1 Jay stood with his hair (blowing, blown) in the wind.

2 After (finish, finishing) my homework, I will visit Jenny.

3 (Strictly speak, Strictly speaking), he is not a good singer.

4 (Having been given, Having given) the prize, she was very happy.

5 With the stove (turning, turned) on, she went outside.

6 (Judge from, Judging from) the smell, Mom is baking cakes.

7 (Being, It being) Sunday, the restaurant is closed.

8 (Having been raised, To have raised) in Korea, Tony eats kimchi.

9 (Generally speaking, Generally spoken), the people in the village are kind.

10 (Learn, Having learned) German in my childhood, I can speak German fairly well now.

B 밑줄 친 부분을 어법에 맞게 고치시오.

1 <u>Writing</u> by a famous writer, the book became a bestseller.

2 After <u>finish</u> breakfast quickly, I left home for work.

3 <u>Rejecting</u> by the college, she was very disappointed.

4 There <u>be</u> a big tree right in front of the window, the room was dark.

5 <u>Spoken of</u> Italian food, why don't we have some for dinner?

6 When <u>eat</u> meat, it is good to eat vegetables too.

7 <u>Frankly speak</u>, I was jealous of my younger brother.

8 Nari sleeps better with music <u>played</u>.

9 He sat down with his arms <u>crossing</u>.

10 <u>Considered</u> his inexperience, he did a very good job.

🔍 **Answer Key p-31**

C 밑줄 친 부분을 분사구문으로 바꿔 쓰시오.

1 <u>Because I was born in this country,</u> I have citizenship here.

→ _____ _____ _____ in this country, I have citizenship here.

2 <u>As it was fairly hot,</u> he turned on the air conditioner.

→ _____ _____ _____ _____, he turned on the air conditioner.

3 <u>As he was adopted,</u> he doesn't know his birth parents.

→ _____ _____ _____, he doesn't know his birth parents.

4 <u>Because I was asked to help her,</u> I carried some of the boxes.

→ _____ _____ _____ _____, I carried some of the boxes.

5 <u>After I finish this work,</u> I will help you.

→ _____ _____ _____ _____, I will help you.

6 <u>Because it was too dark outside,</u> I couldn't go out.

→ _____ _____ _____ _____ _____, I couldn't go out.

D 우리말과 일치하도록 밑줄 친 부분을 어법에 맞게 고치시오.

1 그 책을 이전에 읽었기 때문에 나는 결말을 기억한다.

→ <u>Reading</u> the book before, I remember the ending.

2 운동을 하라는 충고를 듣고 나는 체육관에 등록했다.

→ <u>Advising</u> to exercise, I enrolled in a gym.

3 그 음식을 전에 먹은 적이 있어서 이번에는 다른 것을 먹을 거야.

→ <u>Trying</u> the dish before, I'll have a different one this time.

4 버스에 남은 자리가 없어서 나는 학교 가는 길 내내 서 있었다.

→ <u>Being</u> no seats left on the bus, I stood all the way to school.

5 밖에 오랜 시간 두어서 그 우유는 상했다.

→ <u>Keeping</u> outside for a long time, the milk went bad.

WRITING PRACTICE

Q Answer Key p.31

A 우리말과 일치하도록 ( ) 안의 말을 이용하여 분사구문을 완성하시오.

1 솔직히 말해서 그 음식은 안 좋았다. (frankly, speak)

→ _____, the food was bad.

2 그 영화를 봐서 나는 그것을 다시 보고 싶지 않다. (watch, the movie)

→ _____, I don't want to see it again.

3 일반적으로 말해서, 외국어를 배우는 것은 쉽지 않다. (generally, speak)

→ _____, learning a foreign language is not easy.

4 그녀는 두 눈을 감은 채로 누워 있었다. (with, close)

→ She was lying _____.

5 그의 묘사로 판단하건대, 그 섬은 매우 아름다운 게 틀림없다. (judge, description)

→ _____, the island must be very beautiful.

6 집에 설탕이 없어서 나는 나의 이웃에게서 조금 빌렸다. (There, be)

→ _____ no sugar at home, I borrowed some from my neighbor.

B 우리말과 일치하도록 ( ) 안에 주어진 단어를 바르게 배열하시오.

1 남은 시간을 고려하면 우리는 서둘러야 한다. (the, considering, time, remaining)

→ _____, we have to hurry.

2 먹고 나면 그녀는 항상 이를 닦는다. (she, after, always, eating, brushes)

→ _____ her teeth.

3 폭풍 속에서 밖에 놓여 있었기 때문에 내 신발이 모두 젖었다.
(storm, in, having, outside, the, left, been)

→ _____, my shoes were all wet.

4 전에 시간을 허비해서 나는 지금 더 열심히 일해야 한다. (before, having, time, wasted)

→ _____, I have to work harder now.

5 숙제를 제출하지 않아서 그는 나쁜 성적을 받았다. (not, homework, having, his, submitted)

→ _____, he received poor grades.

6 세계사 이야기가 나와서 말인데, 내가 가장 좋아하는 부분은 고대 로마 시대이다.
(world history, of, speaking)

→ _____, my favorite part is the ancient Roman era.

REVIEW TEST

Answer Key p-31

[1-4] 빈칸에 들어갈 알맞은 말을 고르시오.

1
> The end of the musical was a little _____.

① disappoint　　② disappointed
③ disappointing　④ to disappointing
⑤ having been disappointed

2
> Do you think you can fix the _____ TV?

① break　　② breaking
③ broken　　④ to break
⑤ to breaking

3
> Who is the little boy _____ a snowman?

① builds　　② built
③ to build　④ building
⑤ being built

4
> _____ at the train station, I called Nancy.

① Arrive　　② Arriving
③ Arrived　④ Being Arrived
⑤ Having been arrived

[5-6] 다음 중 어법상 옳은 것을 고르시오.

5
① The police found the stealing jewelry.
② I am not satisfying with my salary.
③ The woman wore a red cap is my mom.
④ Frankly spoken, this cell phone is not good enough.
⑤ Going straight, you will find a hospital on your right.

6
① Irritating by the noise, we closed the door.
② I woke up because of the barked dog.
③ The library being closed, she couldn't borrow books.
④ He had a cup of coffee with his legs crossing.
⑤ Judged from his appearance, he is tired.

[7-8] 보기의 밑줄 친 부분과 분사구문 용법이 같은 것을 고르시오.

7
보기	Watching TV, Diana blow-dried her hair.

① Being hungry, we ordered pizza.
② Feeling tired, I went to bed early.
③ Walking down the street, I saw a cute dog.
④ Not knowing his phone number, I couldn't contact him.
⑤ Coming late, you won't get a seat.

8

Knowing little about the issues, he didn't say anything.

① Listening to music, I prepared dinner.
② Reading a novel, I waited for him.
③ She sat at the window, knitting a hat.
④ Swimming at the beach yesterday, I wore a swimsuit.
⑤ Being clever, he understood exactly what I wanted to say.

빈출

9 밑줄 친 부분의 쓰임이 나머지 넷과 다른 것은?

① I found her drinking my juice without permission.
② He sat reading a poem in his room.
③ Look at the candle burning on the desk.
④ Eva has a sister working as a model.
⑤ David enjoys chatting with his friends.

[10-11] 다음 중 어법상 틀린 것을 고르시오.

10 ① The boy looked very confused.
② She is looking for her lost child.
③ Studying not hard, I failed the exam.
④ Frankly speaking, he is not my type.
⑤ The actor sat with his arms folded.

11 ① Eaten so much lunch, he is still full.
② Can you open the locked door?
③ After finishing my report, I watched TV.
④ Listening to the news, she changed her clothes.
⑤ The fireman saved people from the burning house.

서술형

[12-14] ( ) 안의 말을 이용하여 문장을 완성하시오.

12 I was very _____ to hear that you would marry Jack. (surprise)

13 The black car _____ illegally is Amy's. (park)

14 _____ a cold, he sneezed several times. (have)

서술형

[15-17] 밑줄 친 부분을 분사구문으로 바꿔 쓰시오.
(단, 접속사는 생략할 것)

15 As he sang a song, Jay washed the dishes.

→ _____,
Jay washed the dishes.

16 Because I was his close friend, I know him well.

→ _____,
I know him well.

17 If you leave your house now, you won't be late.

→ _____,
you won't be late.

72

[18-19] 빈칸에 들어갈 말이 순서대로 바르게 짝지어진 것을 고르시오.

18
> • This math problem is _____ .
> • My brother got _____ about going to Disneyland.

① confuse – exciting
② confused – excited
③ confused – exciting
④ confusing – excited
⑤ confusing – exciting

19
> • I saw him _____ on the sofa.
> • _____ tennis, Joel suddenly fell down.

① lied – Played
② lied – Playing
③ lying – Playing
④ lying – Played
⑤ lied – Having played

서술형

[20-21] 두 문장의 의미가 같도록 빈칸에 알맞은 말을 쓰시오.

20 Because it was cold, I drank a cup of hot water.

→ _____ _____ cold, I drank a cup of hot water.

21 After she changed schools, she has to ride the bus two hours a day.

→ _____ _____ _____ , she has to ride the bus two hours a day.

서술형

[22-23] 우리말과 일치하도록 ( ) 안에 주어진 단어를 바르게 배열하시오.

22 TV가 켜진 채로 나는 아침을 먹었다.
(with, TV, turned, the, on)

→ I had breakfast _____

_____ .

23 스페인에서 3년을 살았기 때문에 나는 그 나라를 잘 안다. (three years, having, for, Spain, lived in)

→ _____ ,

I know the country well.

서술형 고난도

[24-25] 어법상 틀린 부분을 찾아 바르게 고치시오.

24 While worked at the company, my mom met my dad. (1개)

25 Although Janet had studied hard for the exam, the results were not satisfied. She was very disappointing, so she decided to study even harder. (2개)

UNIT 01

원급, 비교급, 최상급

A ( ) 안에서 알맞은 말을 고르시오.

1 She cooks as (well, better) as her mother.

2 My dog can dig a hole (deeper, deepest) than this.

3 Central Park is not the (bigger, biggest) park in New York City.

4 This is the (more delicious, most delicious) pizza I have ever eaten.

5 The bread feels as (soft, softer) as silk.

6 The gas prices are (very, even) more expensive than they were last year.

7 The comedy show was not as (funny, funnier) as we expected.

8 The game was (more difficult, most difficult) than they thought it would be.

9 The weather was as (good, better) as he had predicted.

10 This company's customer service is the (better, best) of all.

B ( ) 안의 말을 이용하여 문장을 완성하시오.

1 Silk is _____ than cotton. (soft)

2 Kevin is the _____ of all the team members. (old)

3 Their products sold out as _____ as before. (fast)

4 I like Beethoven _____ than Mozart. (much)

5 I believe he is the _____ comedian in our country. (funny)

6 Sapphires were once as _____ as gold. (expensive)

7 His second album was _____ than his debut album. (popular)

8 The event grew _____ than they had planned. (big)

9 This is the _____ mistake I have ever made. (foolish)

10 He is the _____ of all his friends. (tall)

C 밑줄 친 부분을 어법에 맞게 고치시오.

1 Gina was paid so much as she wanted.

2 I think dogs are intelligent than chimpanzees.

3 I like vanilla ice cream the more out of all the ice cream flavors.

4 He is strongest man I have ever seen.

5 They couldn't come home as earliest as they had hoped.

6 The new smartphone is even advanced than the old one.

7 That airline sells the cheaper tickets in the country.

8 The edited video is far good than we imagined it would be.

9 He wants to be the faster runner in the world.

10 Haiti was as hotter as the state of Arizona two days ago.

D 주어진 문장과 의미가 통하도록 ( ) 안의 말을 이용하여 빈칸에 알맞은 말을 쓰시오.

1 Maggie looks more than fifty years old.
His elder sister looks like she's about forty years old.

→ Maggie looks _____ _____ her elder sister. (old)

2 He drinks coffee once a day.
His wife drinks coffee three times a day.

→ He doesn't drink coffee _____ _____ _____ his wife. (often)

3 This room is seven hundred square feet.
The room on the second floor is eight hundred square feet.

→ This room is _____ _____ the one on the second floor. (small)

4 He can only say a few words in Chinese.
His sister speaks Chinese fluently.

→ He can't speak Chinese _____ _____ _____ his sister. (well)

5 The old battery lasts only two hours.
The new battery lasts more than five hours.

→ The new battery lasts _____ _____ the old one. (long)

WRITING PRACTICE

🔍 Answer Key p.32

A 우리말과 일치하도록 ( ) 안의 말을 이용하여 문장을 완성하시오.

1 그 쇼핑몰은 우리가 그럴 거라 예상했던 것만큼 컸다. (big, expect)

→ The shopping mall was _____ it would be.

2 그 상황은 우리가 처음 생각했던 것보다 더 심각했다. (bad)

→ The situation was _____ we first thought.

3 그것은 우리가 본 것 중 최고의 오페라다. (good, opera, ever, see)

→ It is _____.

4 다이아몬드는 모든 보석 중에서 가장 단단하다. (hard)

→ Diamonds are _____ all jewels.

5 그 탑은 우리 도시에서 가장 인기 있는 관광지이다. (popular, tourist spot)

→ The tower is _____ our city.

6 그녀는 내가 생각했던 것보다 훨씬 더 바빴다. (a lot, busy, think)

→ She was _____.

B 우리말과 일치하도록 ( ) 안에 주어진 단어를 바르게 배열하시오.

1 그 상처는 내가 생각했던 것만큼 심하지 않았다. (I, not, bad, as, thought, as)

→ The wound was _____.

2 Ellen은 우리 팀에서 그 일을 할 최적의 사람이다. (team, the, on, person, our, best)

→ Ellen is _____ to do the work.

3 그 노트북 컴퓨터는 판매자가 광고하는 것만큼 속도가 빠르다. (seller, fast, as, the, advertises, as)

→ The laptop works _____.

4 그 영화의 리메이크는 원작보다 훨씬 더 좋았다. (one, than, far, original, the, better)

→ The remake of the movie was _____.

5 그는 내가 그를 처음 봤을 때보다 지금 더 멋있어 보인다. (when, than, handsome, more, I, now)

→ He looks _____ first saw him.

6 나는 Katherine이 내 모든 딸들 중에서 가장 근면하다고 생각한다.
(daughters, the, my, hardworking, of, all, most)

→ I think Katherine is _____.

UNIT 02

여러 가지 비교구문

🔍 Answer Key p.32

A ( ) 안에서 알맞은 말을 고르시오.

1 A firefighter is one of the (more dangerous, most dangerous) jobs in the world.

2 This airplane is (twice as fast as, two faster than) the others.

3 The clouds in the sky are getting (dark and dark, darker and darker).

4 The more she worked, (the good, the better) she could do her job.

5 The polar bear is one of the most endangered (animal, animals) in the world.

6 The hole in my shirt is getting (big and big, bigger and bigger).

7 Open the door as wide as (possible, you possible).

8 The less you exercise, (the easily, the more easily) you will get tired.

9 The hotel rates in the high season are almost (three, three times) as expensive as in the off-season.

10 You are going to see houses (little and little, less and less) as you go deeper into the woods.

B 밑줄 친 부분을 어법에 맞게 고치시오.

1 Broccoli is one of <u>the most nutritious vegetable</u>.

2 My computer works almost <u>two</u> as fast as yours.

3 Walk as quietly as <u>can</u> so as not to wake the baby.

4 I want to know how I can live <u>as best as</u> I can.

5 The situation in the village was getting <u>bad and bad</u>.

6 The more you listen to his songs, <u>much</u> you will love him.

7 This line is three times longer <u>as</u> that one.

8 The book gets <u>more and much</u> interesting with each page.

9 <u>The light</u> laptop computers become, the easier they are to carry around.

10 This model is one of <u>the most popular car</u> made by our company.

C 두 문장의 의미가 같도록 빈칸에 알맞은 말을 쓰시오.

1 Let's spend as little as we can to save for a trip.

→ Let's spend _____ to save for a trip.

2 As we learn more about nature, we understand it better.

→ _____ we learn about nature, _____ we understand it.

3 Express your love to your family as often as you can.

→ Express your love to your family _____.

4 As you love others more, you'll be loved more.

→ _____ you love others, _____ you'll be loved.

D 보기의 문장과 의미가 같도록 빈칸에 알맞은 말을 쓰시오.

보기	Mount Kilimanjaro is the highest mountain in Africa.

1 Mount Kilimanjaro is _____ _____ _____ _____ in Africa.

2 No other mountain in Africa is _____ _____ _____ Mount Kilimanjaro.

3 No other mountain in Africa is _____ _____ Mount Kilimanjaro.

보기	World history is the most interesting subject to me.

4 World history is _____ _____ _____ _____ _____ _____ to me.

5 No other subject is _____ _____ _____ world history to me.

6 No other subject is _____ _____ than world history to me.

보기	Alaska is the largest state in the United States.

7 Alaska is _____ _____ _____ _____ _____ in the United States.

8 No other state in the United States is _____ _____ _____ _____.

9 No other state in the United States is _____ _____ _____.

WRITING PRACTICE

Answer Key p-32

A 우리말과 일치하도록 ( ) 안의 말을 이용하여 문장을 완성하시오.

1 지난해의 거의 두 배만큼 비가 내렸다. (much)

→ It rained nearly _____ as it had the previous year.

2 우리 도시의 건물들이 점점 높아지고 있다. (get, high)

→ The buildings in our city are _____.

3 이것은 중국에서 가장 유명한 사원 중 하나이다. (famous, temple)

→ This is _____ in China.

4 Tommy는 그의 팀에서 가장 빠른 주자 중 한 명이다. (fast, runner)

→ Tommy is _____ on his team.

5 가능한 한 빨리 그것을 배달해 주세요. (soon, possible)

→ Please deliver it _____.

6 너는 땀을 더 많이 흘릴수록 물을 더 많이 마실 필요가 있다. (much, sweat)

→ _____, the more water you need to drink.

B 우리말과 일치하도록 ( ) 안에 주어진 단어를 바르게 배열하시오.

1 그녀의 자동차는 내 것보다 세 배 더 비싸다. (times, expensive, three, as, mine, as)

→ Her car is _____.

2 기계에서 나는 소음이 점점 더 커지고 있었다. (louder, was, louder, getting, and)

→ The noise from the machine _____.

3 소리를 최대한 낮춰 주십시오. (low, turn down, as, possible, the volume, as)

→ Please _____.

4 우리 학교의 어떤 선생님도 장 선생님만큼 인기가 있지 않다.
(school, in, as, other, teacher, as, popular, no, our, is)

→ _____ Ms. Jang.

5 네가 더욱 감사할수록 너의 삶은 더 행복해질 것이다.
(thankful, the, you, happier, the, more, are)

→ _____ your life will be.

6 프라하는 유럽에서 가장 아름다운 도시 중 하나이다.
(cities, Europe, one, in, most, the, of, beautiful)

→ Prague is _____.

REVIEW TEST

[1-5] 빈칸에 들어갈 알맞은 말을 고르시오.

1

| He is not as _____ as his brother. |

① brave ② braver
③ bravest ④ more brave
⑤ most brave

2

| The chicken pasta was _____ than I expected. |

① bad ② more bad
③ worse ④ more worse
⑤ the worst

3

| Penny is _____ clerk in the shop. |

① kind ② kinder
③ the kindest ④ more kind
⑤ as kind

4

| _____ other boy in my class is friendlier than Peter. |

① All ② As
③ No ④ So
⑤ More

5

| This is _____ car I've ever driven. |

① safer ② more safe
③ the safer ④ the safest
⑤ most safe

[6-7] 다음 중 어법상 틀린 것을 고르시오.

6 ① Wendy is not as intelligent as Linda.
② He is the slowest runner on the team.
③ The actor became more and more famous.
④ Your garden is more beautiful than mine.
⑤ This necklace is two as expensive as that one.

7 ① My bicycle is a lot heavier than yours.
② The older he got, the richer he became.
③ Ted is one of the smartest boy in my class.
④ She practiced the piano as much as she could.
⑤ No store in this town is as crowded with people as Joe's.

8 다음 우리말을 영어로 바르게 옮긴 것은?

| 날씨가 더 더워질수록 사람들은 아이스크림을 더 많이 먹는다. |

① The hot it gets, the much ice cream people eat.
② It gets hotter, people eat ice cream more.
③ The hottest it gets, the most ice cream people eat.
④ Hotter it gets, more ice cream people eat.
⑤ The hotter it gets, the more ice cream people eat.

9 다음 중 어법상 옳은 것은?

① This is the larger bank in Asia.

② Her house is twice as larger as mine.

③ The patient is getting the better and the better.

④ Betty goes shopping more often than I do.

⑤ His car is expensive than any other car in the parking lot.

서술형 빈출

[14-16] 주어진 문장과 의미가 통하도록 (   ) 안의 말을 이용하여 문장을 완성하시오.

14
- It takes five minutes to go there by bus.
- It takes eight minutes to go there by subway.

→ It is _____ to go there by bus _____ by subway. (fast)

서술형

[10-12] 두 문장의 의미가 같도록 빈칸에 알맞은 말을 쓰시오.

10 Colchester is the oldest town in Britain.

→ No town in Britain is _____ _____ _____ Colchester.

15
- The blue T-shirt is $10.
- The red T-shirt is $15.
- The yellow T-shirt is $22.

→ No other T-shirt of the three is

_____ _____ _____

the yellow T-shirt. (expensive)

11 The thieves ran as far as they could.

→ The thieves ran _____ _____ _____ _____.

16
- Robert is twelve years old.
- Nate is thirty-six years old.

→ Nate is _____ _____ _____ _____ as Robert. (old)

12 Nothing is more important than love.

→ Love is _____ _____ _____ thing.

17 다음 중 밑줄 친 부분을 잘못 고친 것은?

① Bill is the taller of the brothers.
   → tallest

② He is one of more famous writers in the world.   → the most famous

③ This bag is very lighter than that one.
   → even

④ She is not as friendly so her sister.
   → as

⑤ The more junk food you eat, the high your cholesterol levels become.
   → highest

13 빈칸에 공통으로 들어갈 말은?

- You can have as _____ as you like.
- My grades were _____ worse than I expected.

① much   ② better   ③ even
④ very   ⑤ many

18 다음 우리말을 영어로 잘못 옮긴 것은?

> 이것이 그 빵집에서 가장 맛있는 케이크다.

① This is the most delicious cake in the bakery.
② Any cake in the bakery is more delicious than this.
③ This is more delicious than any other cake in the bakery.
④ No cake in the bakery is as delicious as this.
⑤ No cake in the bakery is more delicious than this.

19 다음 중 두 문장의 의미가 같지 <u>않은</u> 것은?

① The model is shorter than Cathy.
  → Cathy is taller than the model.
② *Jane Eyre* is the oldest book on my bookshelf.
  → *Jane Eyre* is older than any other book on my bookshelf.
③ Sarah doesn't drive as fast as Chris.
  → Sarah drives slower than Chris.
④ No student in the class is more diligent than Roy.
  → Roy is one of the diligent students in the class.
⑤ He is the richest man in the world.
  → No other man in the world is as rich as him.

서술형

[20-21] 우리말과 일치하도록 (   ) 안의 말을 이용하여 문장을 완성하시오.

20 그의 작문 실력은 점점 더 좋아지고 있다.
(get, good)

→ His writing skills are _____
_____.

21 Cats는 내가 지금까지 본 것 중 가장 흥미로운 뮤지컬이다. (ever, watch)

→ *Cats* is the most exciting musical
_____.

서술형

[22-23] 우리말과 일치하도록 (   ) 안에 주어진 단어를 바르게 배열하시오.

22 그녀의 손은 내 손보다 훨씬 더 크다.
(than, hands, a lot, her, bigger, mine, are)

→ _____
_____.

23 더 많은 돈을 저축할수록 너는 더 부유해진다.
(you, save, become, the, you, richer, money, more, the)

→ _____
_____.

서술형 고난도

[24-25] 어법상 <u>틀린</u> 부분을 찾아 바르게 고치시오.

24 I bought new sneakers, but they were not more comfortable as I expected.
(1개)

25 The Empire State Building is one of the most famous building in New York. It is nearly twice as tallest as the 63 Building. (2개)

UNIT 01

종속 접속사

Answer Key p.32

( ) 안에서 알맞은 말을 고르시오.

1 I hope to see you as soon as I (arrive, will arrive) there.

2 Where were you going (when, if) we met yesterday?

3 Listen carefully (while, until) Eric reads his essay.

4 (Each time, Unless) I use my computer, I come across a lot of ads.

5 Please wait here (until, though) my boss comes back.

6 Jeremy has been interested in music (since, as) he entered middle school.

7 I couldn't go to the concert (because, although) I lost my ticket.

8 (When, Though) he loves her, he doesn't want to marry her.

9 (If, Unless) you see a foreigner in your hometown, offer some help.

10 I'm looking for a part-time job, (as, while) I need some money.

B

밑줄 친 부분을 어법에 맞게 고치시오.

1 I will keep in touch with you through email while I <u>will be</u> on vacation.

2 Mason called me several times while I <u>am</u> sleeping.

3 You should stay with your parents until you <u>will enter</u> university.

4 Ava has never felt happy <u>until</u> she left her hometown.

5 Let's go for lunch as soon as we <u>will finish</u> this class.

6 <u>Unless</u> you don't have any questions, you may leave now.

7 Every time I <u>will go</u> to the beach, I feel refreshed.

8 Jacob lost his job <u>although</u> he told a lie to his boss.

9 <u>Because</u> we don't see each other often, we are still very good friends.

10 If you <u>will tell</u> me the truth, I will keep it secret.

C 빈칸에 알맞은 말을 보기에서 골라 쓰시오. (단, 한 번씩만 쓸 것)

[1-4]

보기	although	because	unless	when

1 _____ I arrive at the airport, I'll call you.

2 _____ I love you so much, I'll be with you forever.

3 I can't hear you _____ you turn down the TV.

4 _____ her background was impressive, she didn't get the job.

[5-8]

보기	since	even if	until	as

5 Darren has lived alone _____ he was twenty.

6 _____ time passes, marine pollution will get worse.

7 You must follow the rules _____ you think that they are unfair.

8 Don't hurry. I'll wait _____ you finish your meal.

[9-12]

보기	though	if	as	while

9 _____ you don't bring your membership card, you won't be able to get in the room.

10 _____ yoga makes me feel calm, I like it.

11 _____ she was ill, she always looked happy.

12 I first met my boyfriend _____ I was traveling around Europe.

[13-16]

보기	every time	since	as soon as	unless

13 _____ I hadn't eaten anything all day, I was hungry.

14 _____ you study hard, you will fail the exam.

15 _____ you read this email, please reply to it.

16 _____ I try to visit her, she isn't home.

WRITING PRACTICE

Answer Key p.33

A 우리말과 일치하도록 ( ) 안의 말을 이용하여 문장을 완성하시오.

1 그 영화가 끝날 때까지 나는 여기서 기다리겠다. (movie, over)

→ I'll wait here _____.

2 시간이 지남에 따라 그는 더 관대해진다. (go by)

→ _____, he becomes more generous.

3 Ben은 그가 독일에 온 이후로 은행에서 일을 하고 있다. (come, Germany)

→ Ben has been working for a bank _____.

4 네가 외국에 있는 동안 내가 너의 개를 돌봐줄게. (be, abroad)

→ I'll take care of your dog _____.

5 건강해지고 싶다면 너는 규칙적으로 운동을 해야 한다. (want, be, healthy)

→ _____, you should exercise regularly.

6 내일 비가 오지 않으면 우리는 현장 학습을 떠날 것이다. (rain)

→ _____, we will go on a field trip.

B 우리말과 일치하도록 ( ) 안에 주어진 단어를 바르게 배열하시오.

1 나는 대학을 졸업하자마자 내 회사를 설립했다. (as, graduated, I, as, university, from, soon)

→ _____, I founded my own company.

2 그녀는 가난한 가정 출신이어서 고등 교육을 받을 수 없었다. (as, family, a, from, she, came, poor)

→ _____, she couldn't receive a higher education.

3 칼을 사용할 때는 조심해라. (when, knife, you, use, a)

→ Be careful _____.

4 내가 Suji에게 전화를 걸 때마다 그녀는 전화를 받지 않는다. (every, call, Suji, time, I)

→ _____, she doesn't answer the phone.

5 Jeremy가 많은 책을 읽긴 했지만 모든 것을 알지는 못한다.
(read, books, many, has, though, Jeremy)

→ _____, he doesn't know everything.

6 네가 오페라를 좋아하지 않는다고 하더라도, 그녀의 목소리에 감명받게 될 것이다.
(opera, if, even, you, like, don't)

→ _____, you will be impressed by her voice.

UNIT 02 짝으로 이루어진 접속사, 간접의문문

A ( ) 안에서 알맞은 말을 고르시오.

1 I'll join (both, either) the movie club or the book club.

2 She (either, neither) slept nor ate anything.

3 He stopped (both, neither) smoking and drinking alcohol.

4 I didn't know whether (he wanted, did he want) to eat out for lunch.

5 You should either help me (or, nor) go home.

6 Both the mother (or, and) her child are smiling beautifully.

7 I wonder (if she would, if would she) marry him.

8 I don't know (who will win, will who win) the prize.

9 Sunmi speaks (not only, only) Chinese but also Japanese.

10 (Why do you guess, Do you guess why) he was absent from school?

B 밑줄 친 부분을 어법에 맞게 고치시오.

1 Both the movie <u>or</u> the play were good.

2 Can you tell me where <u>is the convenience store</u>?

3 My mom doesn't know where <u>was I</u> last night.

4 <u>Do you think who</u> will win the singing contest?

5 <u>Either</u> you and Jessica can leave now.

6 I'm not sure <u>if will he visit</u> me.

7 <u>Either</u> Eric nor Emily enjoys jogging.

8 <u>Neither</u> my brother or I should clean the bathroom.

9 I don't know who <u>is the girl with red hair</u>.

10 This drug is not only expensive <u>and also</u> dangerous.

C 다음 문장을 ( ) 안의 접속사를 이용하여 한 문장으로 쓰시오.

1 Josh can leave today, or he can leave tomorrow.

→ Josh can leave _____. (either ~ or)

2 I don't have money, and I don't have time either.

→ I have _____. (neither ~ nor)

3 The actress is very famous in Korea, and she is very famous abroad too.

→ The actress _____. (both ~ and)

4 Justin Timberlake is a singer, and he is also an actor.

→ Justin Timberlake is _____. (not only ~ but also)

5 They gave food to the homeless. They also gave clothes to the homeless.

→ They gave _____ to the homeless. (as well as)

D 다음 두 문장을 한 문장으로 쓰시오.

1 I don't know. + Where was he going?

→ _____

2 I'm not sure. + Do you want to stay with us?

→ _____

3 Tell me. + Why do you hate Logan?

→ _____

4 I want to know. + Who saved my life?

→ _____

5 Do you think? + What will you be in the future?

→ _____

6 I wonder. + Did he finish the project successfully?

→ _____

WRITING PRACTICE

Q Answer Key p.33

A 우리말과 일치하도록 ( ) 안의 말을 이용하여 문장을 완성하시오.

1 누가 그 창문을 깼는지 나에게 말해라. (break, window)

→ Tell me _____.

2 너는 프랑스어와 독일어 둘 중 하나는 배워야 한다. (French, German)

→ You must learn _____.

3 너는 내가 너를 얼마나 사랑하는지 모른다. (how much)

→ You don't know _____.

4 나는 그가 나를 아는지 확신할 수 없다. (know)

→ I'm not sure _____.

5 이 의자는 비쌀 뿐만 아니라 실용적이지 않다. (expensive)

→ This chair is _____ impractical.

6 나는 영화를 보는 것과 게임을 하는 것 둘 다 즐긴다. (watch movies)

→ I enjoy _____ playing games.

B 우리말과 일치하도록 ( ) 안에 주어진 단어를 바르게 배열하시오.

1 Betty도 너도 틀리지 않다. (you, neither, wrong, Betty, nor, are)

→ _____.

2 그는 영리할 뿐만 아니라 정직하기도 하다. (smart, as, he, honest, as, well, is)

→ _____.

3 너는 그녀가 왜 여기 왔는지 아니? (why, here, came, do, you, she, know)

→ _____?

4 기술은 좋고 나쁜 면을 둘 다 가지고 있다. (and, both, technology, bad, sides, good, has)

→ _____.

5 무엇이 너를 행복하게 하는지 나에게 말해봐라. (happy, tell, you, me, what, makes)

→ _____.

6 너는 누가 우리의 지도자가 되어야 한다고 믿니? (you, our, who, believe, should, do, be, leader)

→ _____?

REVIEW TEST

Answer Key p.33

[1-4] 빈칸에 들어갈 알맞은 말을 고르시오.

1

| Eli can _____ swim nor water ski. |

① if   ② either
③ neither   ④ both
⑤ as well as

2

| I've loved singing songs _____ I was a child. |

① as   ② if
③ when   ④ since
⑤ though

3

| Sam is a movie director _____ a screenwriter. |

① both   ② unless
③ neither   ④ either
⑤ as well as

4

| _____ you or Elijah is going to Mexico with me. |

① Both   ② Either
③ Neither   ④ Not only
⑤ If

[5-6] 다음 중 어법상 틀린 것을 고르시오.

5 ① Neither Sue nor I was late for school.
② Unless you work harder, you'll be fired.
③ In her forties, she achieved both fame or wealth.
④ Though she was sick, she came to my birthday party.
⑤ As soon as I got on the bus, my cell phone rang.

6 ① You can have either cake or cookies.
② As I was thirsty, I drank a whole bottle of water.
③ Not only I but also he speak French.
④ Every time they meet, they go to the coffee shop.
⑤ I found this ring while I was cleaning my room.

7 다음 두 문장을 한 문장으로 바꾼 것 중 잘못된 것은?

① I know. + Where is the grocery store?
   → I know where the grocery store is.
② I wonder. + What time is it now?
   → I wonder what time it is now.
③ I'm curious. + Is she your classmate?
   → I'm curious whether she is your classmate.
④ Do you think? + What does he do for a living?
   → Do you think what he does for a living?
⑤ Do you know? + Is he going to buy that house?
   → Do you know if he is going to buy that house?

[8-10] 밑줄 친 접속사의 의미가 나머지 넷과 <u>다른</u> 것을 고르시오.

8
① As it gets dark, it becomes colder.
② As he grew older, he became wise.
③ As the car was very expensive, we couldn't buy it.
④ As we climbed higher, the wind got stronger.
⑤ As time passed, many buildings were built in my town.

9
① I feel tired <u>since</u> I played tennis for three hours.
② I don't like him <u>since</u> he is always too serious.
③ She was late for school <u>since</u> she woke up late.
④ He is in the hospital <u>since</u> he has a stomach problem.
⑤ We have been good friends <u>since</u> we were ten years old.

10
① <u>If</u> you win the race, I'll buy you a laptop.
② I'm not sure <u>if</u> Max is from England.
③ <u>If</u> you don't leave now, I'll call the police.
④ He'll be punished <u>if</u> he does such a thing.
⑤ Just let me know <u>if</u> you have any problems.

서술형 빈출

[11-13] 두 문장의 의미가 같도록 빈칸에 알맞은 말을 쓰시오.

11
Unless you accept his offer, you will regret it later.

→ _____ ,
you will regret it later.

12
Every time I go shopping, I spend lots of money.

→ _____ ,
I spend lots of money.

13
I don't want to wear this red dress, and I don't want to wear that white dress either.

→ I want to wear _____ this red dress _____ that white dress.

서술형

[14-15] 우리말과 일치하도록 빈칸에 알맞은 접속사를 쓰시오.

14 이 샐러드는 신선할 뿐 아니라 맛있다.

→ This salad is delicious _____
_____ _____ fresh.

15 그녀가 돌아올 때까지 나는 그녀의 아이를 돌볼 것이다.

→ I'll take care of her child _____
she returns.

16 다음 중 어법상 옳은 것은?

① I'm not sure when did she leave.
② Do you know where lives Wyatt?
③ As I have a musical ticket, I can't watch it.
④ He wants to be either a pilot nor a doctor.
⑤ Since I love you, I will do anything you want.

[17-19] 다음 두 문장을 간접의문문을 이용하여 한 문장으로 쓰시오.

17 I wonder. + Where did they have their wedding?

→ _____

their wedding.

18 Do you believe? + What will change our society?

→ _____

will change our society?

19 I don't know. + Is it good to change my job now?

→ _____

to change my job now.

서술형

[20-21] 빈칸에 공통으로 들어갈 접속사를 쓰시오.

20 • _____ you come home early, I'll make your favorite pizza.
• Even _____ you are very busy, you should make time for your kids.

21 • I will hire him _____ he is very creative.
• I've met many good neighbors _____ I moved to this village.

서술형

[22-23] 우리말과 일치하도록 ( ) 안에 주어진 단어를 바르게 배열하시오.

22 정크 푸드는 염분이 많을 뿐 아니라 칼로리도 높다.
(also, only, high in calories, but, not, salty)

→ Junk food is _____

_____ .

23 그녀는 나를 보자마자 기뻐서 폴짝폴짝 뛰었다.
(as, saw, soon, me, as, she)

→ _____ ,

she leaped with joy.

서술형 고난도

[24-25] 어법상 틀린 부분을 찾아 바르게 고치시오.

24 Luke loves Mia very much. I wonder when will he propose to her. (1개)

25 My sister and I are planning to travel to Europe for vacation. We haven't decided where to go yet, but we will choose either Spain nor Portugal. (1개)

UNIT 01

관계대명사

Ⓐ ( ) 안에서 알맞은 말을 고르시오.

1 Soccer is a sport (that, what) a lot of people all around the world like.

2 (Which, What) he said last night was not true.

3 Is there a country (whose, whom) population is less than 500,000?

4 This is the chair (what, which) I bought at the secondhand store.

5 His brother was the only person (that, which) understood him.

6 We had dinner at a restaurant (whose, which) service was great.

7 Dylan is a teacher (who, whom) understands his students very well.

8 (That, What) you eat now will decide your health in the future.

9 There is a new movie (who, which) you might like.

10 (That, What) made me feel terrible was seeing the starving kids in Africa.

Ⓑ 빈칸에 알맞은 말을 보기에서 골라 쓰시오.

보기	what	whose	who	which

1 _____ I want most now is to take a break.

2 That is the house _____ my family will move into.

3 People _____ have positive attitudes tend to have higher self-esteem.

4 He is the pianist _____ I have liked since my childhood.

5 He is a successful businessman _____ company is very big.

6 I want a computer _____ has a lot of memory.

7 Barry Nelson was the first actor _____ played James Bond.

8 That was an embarrassing moment _____ I can't forget.

9 I saw a car _____ windows were broken.

10 I ordered _____ the waiter recommended.

C 다음 두 문장을 관계대명사를 이용하여 한 문장으로 쓰시오.

1 She met the author. She followed him on Twitter.

→ _____

2 He will give me a desk. He does not use it any longer.

→ _____

3 She went to the gallery. Its collection was very impressive.

→ _____

4 This is the pencil case. I have used it since elementary school.

→ _____

5 I have a friend. He traveled around the world.

→ _____

6 This store sells vases. Their colors are very unique.

→ _____

D 밑줄 친 부분을 어법에 맞게 고쳐 쓰시오.

1 They are great artists <u>whom</u> inspired many others.

2 Is there anything <u>what</u> I can help you with?

3 He wrote novels <u>what</u> are very popular.

4 <u>That</u> he didn't expect was that they had already left.

5 Think again before doing anything <u>what</u> you might regret.

6 The boy and the dog <u>what</u> are running down the path look excited.

7 She is a famous glass artist <u>which</u> works are very expensive.

8 Italy was the second country <u>whom</u> the president visited.

9 I met many great people <u>whose</u> I could have as role models.

10 We did all the work <u>what</u> my teacher asked us to do.

WRITING PRACTICE

Q Answer Key p.34

A 우리말과 일치하도록 관계대명사와 ( ) 안의 말을 이용하여 문장을 완성하시오.

1 그녀는 경험 많은 의사를 찾고 있다. (a lot of, experience)

→ She is looking for a doctor _____ .

2 나는 아버지가 미용사인 한 소년을 안다. (hairdresser)

→ I know a boy _____ .

3 당신이 가르친 학생은 시험에 합격했나요? (teach)

→ Did the student _____ pass the exam?

4 지금 중요한 것은 더 많은 생명을 구하는 것이다. (matter)

→ _____ is to save more lives.

5 너를 돕기 위해 내가 할 수 있는 일이 있을까? (anything, can)

→ Is there _____ to help you?

6 이것은 내가 가지고 놀았던 로봇이다. (play)

→ This is the robot _____ with.

B 우리말과 일치하도록 ( ) 안에 주어진 단어를 바르게 배열하시오.

1 그는 일정이 약속으로 가득 찬 바쁜 사람이다. (filled, busy, whose, is, a, man, schedule)

→ He is _____ with appointments.

2 잘 들어주는 친구가 되어라. (friend, a, listens, who, well)

→ Be _____ .

3 그는 그의 아들이 그에게 말하고자 하는 것을 이해했다. (what, son, understood, his, trying, was)

→ He _____ to say to him.

4 그는 내가 신뢰할 수 있는 유일한 사람이다. (I, that, person, trust, only, the, can)

→ He is _____ .

5 그녀는 청중이 요청한 그 음악을 연주했다. (the, requested, the, which, music, audience)

→ She played _____ .

6 이것은 우리 엄마가 차고 세일에서 구입하신 바로 그 램프이다. (my, the, that, very, mom, lamp)

→ This is _____ bought at a garage sale.

UNIT 02 관계부사

🔍 Answer Key p.34

A

( ) 안에서 알맞은 말을 고르시오.

1 He still remembers the place (when, where) his first concert was held.

2 That's (how, the way how) she met her husband.

3 My family moved to Canada in the year (when, at when) I was born.

4 That's (how, where) I got an A on the test!

5 The reason (how, why) I don't help you is that I want you to do it on your own.

6 This is a time (when, where) you can show off your talents.

7 My home is the only place (where, why) I can be by myself.

8 I don't understand (why, where) he was so rude to me.

9 The program showed (which, how) she became such a great golfer.

10 This store is a place (where, why) you can get some great deals.

B

빈칸에 알맞은 말을 보기에서 골라 쓰시오.

보기	when	where	why	how

1 Do you remember the day _____ we saw Tom Cruise?

2 Can you tell me _____ you made this spaghetti?

3 The reason _____ she performs so well is that she practices a lot.

4 This is a café _____ teenagers like to hang out.

5 I am lost. Can you tell me _____ I can get to the library?

6 The place _____ you want to have the party is too far from the town.

7 Dad always talks about the day _____ he first met Mom.

8 I don't understand the reason _____ you are always late.

9 Now is the time _____ we should leave.

10 I like _____ he looks in the photo.

C 두 문장의 의미가 같도록 빈칸에 알맞은 관계부사를 쓰시오.

1 This is the way she knitted the sweater.

→ This is _____ she knitted the sweater.

2 The reason for which I'm moving out of the house is that it is too cold.

→ The reason _____ I'm moving out of the house is that it is too cold.

3 Summer is the time during which we can enjoy various water sports.

→ Summer is the time _____ we can enjoy various water sports.

4 People say this is the house in which a ghost used to appear.

→ People say this is the house _____ a ghost used to appear.

5 He explained to the police the way he hacked into the computers.

→ He explained to the police _____ he hacked into the computers.

6 We want it to be a place in which you can feel at home.

→ We want it to be a place _____ you can feel at home.

D 다음 두 문장을 관계부사를 이용하여 한 문장으로 쓰시오. (단, 선행사나 관계부사를 생략하지 말 것)

1 Carnegie Hall is a place. Musicians want to perform there.

→ _____

2 The year was 1988. The Olympics were held in Korea at that time.

→ _____

3 The square is the place. Artists gather there.

→ _____

4 Twelve o'clock is the time. He should take the medicine then.

→ _____

5 This is the way. I cut my electricity bill in half in this way.

→ _____

6 The salesperson explained the reason. The car would be good for me for that reason.

→ _____

WRITING PRACTICE

🔍 Answer Key p.34

A 우리말과 일치하도록 관계부사와 ( ) 안의 말을 이용하여 문장을 완성하시오.

1 너는 그녀가 나타나지 않았던 이유를 아니? (show up)

→ Do you know the reason _____ ?

2 그 절은 내가 자주 명상을 하는 장소이다. (often, meditate)

→ The temple is the place _____ .

3 편찮으신 어머니가 그가 집으로 돌아온 이유였다. (come back)

→ His ill mother was the reason _____ .

4 이것이 그녀가 부유해진 방법이다. (become)

→ This is _____ .

5 이곳이 내가 수영을 하곤 했던 그 강이다. (used to)

→ This is the river _____ .

6 지금이 교통이 가장 혼잡한 시간이다. (the traffic, the heaviest)

→ This is the time _____ .

B 우리말과 일치하도록 ( ) 안에 주어진 단어를 바르게 배열하시오.

1 너는 우리가 해변에 갔던 때를 기억하니? (when, the beach, the time, we, to, went)

→ Do you remember _____ ?

2 이것이 그가 그 퍼즐을 푼 방법이다. (he, the puzzle, is, solved, the way)

→ This _____ .

3 이곳은 와인을 위한 포도가 재배되는 마을이다. (where, are, grapes for wine, a town, grown)

→ This is _____ .

4 그녀가 가족과 함께 떠나지 않았던 이유가 무엇이니? (didn't, the reason, leave, she, why)

→ What is _____ with her family?

5 그 의사는 내가 한 달 만에 10kg를 감량한 방법을 물었다. (I, how, 10 kg, lost, in a month)

→ The doctor asked me _____ .

6 여러분이 휴식을 취하고 재충전할 수 있는 곳에 오신 것을 환영합니다.

(you, a place, relax and recharge, can, where)

→ Welcome to _____ .

UNIT 03 주의해야 할 관계사

A ( ) 안에서 알맞은 말을 고르시오.

1 The boy (standing, is standing) next to the mailbox is Nathan.

2 Let me introduce a new employee with (that, whom) you will work.

3 I was guided by the mayor, (who, that) was born and raised in the village.

4 This is the house (which, in which) the famous writer lives.

5 The man donated a lot of money, (which, what) was used to help people.

6 She is the friend (whose, that) I share the apartment with.

7 He got married to Sofia, (that, which) surprised everybody.

8 She likes going to the park, (when, where) there are many trees.

9 I often sing, (what, which) relaxes me.

10 I woke up at seven o'clock, (when, where) the alarm rang.

B 다음 문장에서 생략할 수 있는 부분을 ( )로 묶으시오. (생략할 수 있는 부분이 없으면 X표 하시오.)

1 I saw the dog for which you were looking.

2 The food which was served that night was not bad.

3 Tolstoy is the writer whom I like the most.

4 The helicopter which was flying above us made a loud noise.

5 I have a friend whose major is English literature.

6 I saw the pictures that you sent to me yesterday.

7 The movie which was shown at the festival was great.

8 China is one of the biggest countries with which Korea trades.

9 Look at the man who my sister will get married to.

10 He finished writing the book, which later became a huge bestseller.

C 밑줄 친 부분을 어법에 맞게 고치시오.

1   Steve, <u>that</u> is a firefighter, works very hard.

2   I used to make flower bouquets, <u>that</u> eventually became my job.

3   He brushes his teeth after every meal, <u>what</u> keeps his teeth healthy.

4   Brian, <u>whom</u> runs very fast, caught the thief.

5   Let's meet at the café, <u>when</u> we can talk and use a laptop.

6   We stayed at the Southern Hotel, <u>what</u> there is a very nice pool.

7   The old lady <u>was selling</u> vegetables on the street looked tired.

8   Ellie was the last person <u>to who</u> I spoke.

9   The room in <u>that</u> we stayed for three nights was clean and nice.

10   Mt. Seorak is beautiful in the fall, <u>where</u> the mountain is covered with colorful leaves.

D 두 문장의 의미가 같도록 빈칸에 알맞은 말을 쓰시오.

1   My brother found my dad's guitar. It had been in the attic for many years.
    → My brother found my dad's guitar, _____.

2   He didn't come to class. That made his teacher worried.
    → He didn't come to class, _____.

3   Eat almonds. They contain healthy omega-3 fatty acids.
    → Eat almonds, _____.

4   She often goes to bookstores. Doing so makes her happy.
    → She often goes to bookstores, _____.

5   She met her favorite singer. He has sold more than three million albums.
    → She met her favorite singer, _____.

6   Madison visited Silicon Valley. She had worked there the previous year.
    → Madison visited Silicon Valley, _____.

7   I met Jenny in 2019. I was fifteen years old at that time.
    → I met Jenny in 2019, _____.

WRITING PRACTICE

Q Answer Key p.34

A 우리말과 일치하도록 관계사와 ( ) 안의 말을 이용하여 문장을 완성하시오.

1 엄마가 자두를 좀 사오셨는데, 그것들은 너무 시었다. (too, sour)

→ Mom bought some plums, _____.

2 나는 그가 이야기하고 있는 영화에 관심이 없었다. (talk about)

→ I wasn't interested in the movies _____.

3 Benjamin은 오래된 친구인데, 영화배우가 되었다. (an old friend)

→ Benjamin, _____, became a movie star.

4 Kevin은 열심히 공부했고, 이것은 그가 시험에 합격하게끔 도왔다. (help, pass the exam)

→ Kevin studied hard, _____.

5 그가 내가 전에 이야기했던 반 친구이다. (talk about, before)

→ He is the classmate _____.

6 나는 파리에 갔는데, 그곳에서 일주일을 머물렀다. (stay for a week)

→ I went to Paris, _____.

B 우리말과 일치하도록 ( ) 안에 주어진 단어를 바르게 배열하시오.

1 나는 엄마께 생신 케이크를 만들어 드렸는데, 이것이 엄마를 놀라게 했다. (surprised, which, her)

→ I made Mom a birthday cake, _____.

2 이곳이 당신이 전에 말했던 그 식당입니까? (restaurant, talked, you, about, the, that, before)

→ Is this _____ _____?

3 그는 보통 이른 아침에 공부를 하는데, 이때는 매우 조용하다. (quiet, when, it, very, is)

→ He usually studies early in the morning, ____ _____.

4 이 사람이 Victoria가 그 파티에서 함께 춤추었던 소년이다. (the, danced, boy, with, Victoria)

→ This is _____ at the party.

5 저쪽에서 물을 마시고 있는 남자는 우리 선생님이시다. (drinking, over, man, there, the, water)

→ _____ is my teacher.

6 미술관에서 도난당한 그 그림은 매우 가치 있다. (the, stolen, the, picture, gallery, from)

→ _____ is very valuable.

100

UNIT 04 복합관계사

🔍 Answer Key p.34

A ( ) 안에서 알맞은 말을 고르시오.

1 They'll give the free gift to (whenever, whoever) comes first.

2 (Wherever, Whichever) place we go, I will be happy with you.

3 (Whatever, However) strong the army is, it can still be defeated.

4 I am reminded of my aunt (whenever, whatever) I see Angelina.

5 (However, Wherever) you go, let's keep in touch.

6 (Whenever, However) I call customer service, the line is busy.

7 (Whatever, However) happens, she will not be surprised.

8 (Whoever, Whomever) does the work, it needs to be finished by tomorrow.

9 (How, However) nice your neighbor is, he will get angry about all this noise.

10 (Wherever, Whatever) happens, he will complete his mission.

B 두 문장의 의미가 같도록 빈칸에 알맞은 복합관계사를 쓰시오.

1 No matter when you ask me, I am ready to help you.

→ _____ you ask me, I am ready to help you.

2 He is a generous person. He helps anyone who is in need.

→ He is a generous person. He helps _____ is in need.

3 Anything that he wrote became a hit.

→ _____ he wrote became a hit.

4 No matter which challenge he selects, he will complete it successfully.

→ _____ challenge he selects, he will complete it successfully.

5 No matter where the wild bear goes, the device will help scientists find it.

→ _____ the wild bear goes, the device will help scientists find it.

6 No matter how noisy it was, the baby slept well.

→ _____ noisy it was, the baby slept well.

C 빈칸에 알맞은 말을 보기에서 골라 쓰시오. (단, 한 번씩만 쓸 것)

[1-4]

보기	whenever	however	whoever	whatever

1 _____ sees the picture will love it.

2 _____ I went to the shop, it was closed.

3 _____ happens, he won't give up on his goal.

4 _____ much money you have, you can't buy happiness.

[5-8]

보기	whichever	wherever	whomever	however

5 Please invite _____ you want.

6 You can choose _____ you prefer.

7 _____ angry he is, he doesn't yell.

8 They'll deliver this parcel to him _____ he is.

D 우리말과 일치하도록 빈칸에 알맞은 복합관계사를 쓰시오.

1 네가 좋아하는 것은 무엇이든지 내가 요리해 줄 것이다.

→ I will cook _____ you like.

2 우리가 그 식당에 갈 때마다, 그곳은 매우 붐빈다.

→ _____ we go to the restaurant, it is very crowded.

3 누구든 마지막에 나가는 사람은 불을 꺼주세요.

→ _____ leaves last, please turn off the lights.

4 그들은 어디에 살더라도 그들만의 문화를 지켰다.

→ They kept their own culture _____ they lived.

5 저 차가 아무리 비싸더라도, 사람들은 그것을 사고 싶어할 것이다.

→ _____ expensive that car is, people will want to buy it.

102

WRITING PRACTICE

Q Answer Key p.35

A 우리말과 일치하도록 복합관계사와 ( ) 안의 말을 이용하여 문장을 완성하시오.

1 그 가수는 어디를 가든지 팬이 많다. (singer, go)

→ _____, he has lots of fans.

2 그것이 아무리 어렵다 하더라도 우리는 함께 해낼 수 있다. (hard)

→ _____, we can make it through together.

3 나는 이곳에 언제 오더라도 편안함을 느낀다. (come here)

→ _____, I feel comfortable.

4 네가 어느 경로를 선택하든 그곳에 도착하는 데 많은 시간이 걸릴 것이다. (route, choose)

→ _____, it will take a long time to get there.

5 우리는 그 선거에서 승리하는 누구든 지지할 것이다. (support, win)

→ We'll _____ the election.

6 당신이 좋아하는 것은 무엇이든 가져도 좋다. (have, like)

→ You may _____.

B 우리말과 일치하도록 ( ) 안에 주어진 단어를 바르게 배열하시오.

1 아무리 피곤해도 그녀는 숙제를 할 것이다. (tired, she, is, will, however, she, do)

→ _____ her homework.

2 나는 당신이 추천하는 누구든 신뢰할 것이다. (trust, you, whomever, will, recommend)

→ I _____.

3 당신이 뭘 하든 그들은 생각을 바꾸지 않을 것이다. (they, you, will, whatever, change, not, do)

→ _____ their minds.

4 나는 네가 나에게 전화할 때마다 잘 들리지 않는다. (very, whenever, call, you, me, well)

→ I can't hear you _____.

5 당신이 있는 어디에서라도 인터넷에 접속할 수 있다. (wherever, the internet, are, access, you)

→ You can _____.

6 누가 이기더라도 사람들은 노래 대회의 결과에 대해 실망할 것이다.
(people, be, whoever, disappointed, wins, will, with)

→ _____ the results of the singing contest.

REVIEW TEST

1

I know a man _____ dream is to run a pizza shop.

① who   ② that
③ which   ④ what
⑤ whose

2

I believe _____ he's just said.

① who   ② that
③ which   ④ whom
⑤ what

3

_____ tired we are, we should finish the project by 7:00 p.m.

① That   ② Which
③ Whenever   ④ However
⑤ Whichever

4

This is the town _____ Mozart was born.

① whose   ② which
③ why   ④ when
⑤ where

5

_____ loves to play tennis can join our club.

① Who   ② What
③ Whoever   ④ Whenever
⑤ Whatever

[6–7] 다음 중 어법상 틀린 것을 고르시오.

6   ① Whenever I hear her songs, I think of my hometown.
② This is the French restaurant where I often eat.
③ They went to a coffee shop, which was very crowded.
④ She asked me the way how she could use the washing machine.
⑤ The spaghetti that he made was too salty for me.

7   ① The girl whom you met is Donovan's younger sister.
② This is the parking lot where the thief was last seen.
③ Ray is the man with that I went on a date last Friday.
④ Whatever you buy in this shop, you will not be satisfied with it.
⑤ I remember the day when I went on a picnic with you.

8   다음 밑줄 친 부분과 바꿔 쓸 수 있는 것은?

Tomorrow, Kurt will leave the country in which he has lived for twenty years.

① which   ② when
③ what   ④ where
⑤ however

빈출

9 빈칸에 들어갈 말이 순서대로 바르게 짝지어진 것은?

> - Sam remembers the day _____ he proposed to his wife.
> - Tell me _____ you know about the event.

① when – what   ② how – that

③ where – that   ④ when – which

⑤ which – what

서술형

[10-11] 다음 문장에서 생략할 수 있는 부분을 찾아 쓰시오.

10 Mr. Stone is a teacher whom all the students in my school respect.

11 This is one of the most famous pictures that was painted by Monet.

12 다음 중 어법상 옳은 것은?

① She is the lawyer which I met at the conference.

② I go to the lake whatever I visit this town.

③ I couldn't tell them the reason why I quit my previous job.

④ He traveled to Houston, when he met his old friend.

⑤ Jacob wrote this book, that became a bestseller.

서술형

[13-16] 두 문장의 의미가 같도록 빈칸에 알맞은 관계사를 쓰시오.

13 I live with Chloe, and she is active and humorous.

→ I live with Chloe, _____ is active and humorous.

14 The thing that made me happy was his small gift.

→ _____ made me happy was his small gift.

15 Anyone who breaks the company rules will be fired.

→ _____ breaks the company rules will be fired.

16 Choose anything that you want from the list.

→ Choose _____ you want from the list.

서술형

[17-18] 다음 두 문장을 관계사를 이용하여 한 문장으로 쓰시오.

17 My father bought me a laptop. Its color is white.

→ _____

_____

18 Anne should be responsible for the thing. She did the thing yesterday.

→ _____
  _____

[19-20] 우리말과 일치하도록 ( ) 안의 말을 이용하여 문장을 완성하시오.

19 Jay는 어디를 가든 그의 개를 데리고 간다. (go)

→ Jay takes his dog with him _____
  _____ _____.

20 네가 아무리 똑똑하다고 해도, 이 수수께끼는 풀 수 없을 것이다. (smart)

→ _____
  _____, you won't be able to solve this riddle.

21 다음 중 밑줄 친 부분을 생략할 수 <u>없는</u> 것은?

① I bought a TV <u>that was</u> made in Japan.
② I saw the movie <u>that</u> you recommended.
③ I met the man to <u>whom</u> Ava will get married.
④ Do you know the girl <u>who is</u> waving at us?
⑤ This is the bracelet <u>which</u> Mason gave me as a Christmas gift.

[22-23] 우리말과 일치하도록 ( ) 안에 주어진 단어를 바르게 배열하시오.

22 누구든 정답을 맞추는 사람이 이 상을 받을 것이다. (the, whoever, answer, correct, gets)

→ _____
  will receive this prize.

23 내가 알고 싶은 것은 그 차 사고가 언제 났는지이다. (know, what, want, is, I, to)

→ _____
  when the car accident happened.

[24-25] 어법상 틀린 부분을 찾아 바르게 고치시오.

24 Let's go to the beach next Saturday, where you are less busy. (1개)

25 I know someone who password is her surname and birthday. Whatever I tell her to change her password, she says that it will be all right. (2개)

UNIT 01

가정법 과거, 가정법 과거완료, 혼합 가정법

Q Answer Key p.35

A ( ) 안에서 알맞은 말을 고르시오.

1 If I (am, were) rich, I could buy that house.

2 If he (hasn't, didn't) like butter, he might not be overweight.

3 What (will, would) you do if your friend cheated on an exam?

4 If I had read this book before, I (can, could) answer your question now.

5 If she (had, has) left yesterday, she might have seen him.

6 If she hadn't worked so hard, she wouldn't (be, have been) famous now.

7 If she (ate, had eaten) the food, she might have been sick.

8 My mother would have been mad if I (didn't clean, hadn't cleaned) my room.

9 If I hadn't learned English, I couldn't (apply, have applied) for my current job.

10 If I had majored in computer science, I would (be, have been) a computer programmer now.

B 밑줄 친 부분을 어법에 맞게 고치시오.

1 If you exercised regularly, you might have felt better.

2 More people will vote for him if he were honest.

3 If it were not so hot, I would have gone trekking with you.

4 If I didn't have to work today, I would have gone to pick you up.

5 If our team practiced harder, we could have won the game.

6 If you had stayed there longer, you could meet her.

7 I would buy everything in the store if I am rich.

8 If I hadn't taken his English class, I will be poor at English now.

9 If the rain hadn't stopped, we won't be here now.

10 If we didn't book our tickets last month, we would have to wait for the next plane now.

C 빈칸에 알맞은 말을 보기에서 골라 쓰시오. (단, 한 번씩만 쓸 것)

[1-3]

보기	could have finished	had read your email	won the lottery

1 If I _____, I would help children in need.

2 If I _____, I would have replied to it.

3 If he had not been sick, he _____ writing the book.

[4-6]

보기	would not be alive	knew how to drive	would participate

4 If I _____, I would take you to the airport.

5 If I were good at singing, I _____ in the concert.

6 If he hadn't gone to the hospital in time, he _____ now.

D 주어진 문장과 의미가 통하도록 빈칸에 알맞은 말을 쓰시오.

1 As I don't have my cell phone, I can't call you right now.

→ If _____, I could call you right now.

2 As you didn't help me with the work, I couldn't finish it on time.

→ If _____, I could have finished it on time.

3 As I didn't answer the question correctly, I couldn't get the job.

→ If _____, I could have gotten the job.

4 As my son didn't take my advice, he couldn't get into the college.

→ If my son had taken my advice, _____.

5 As I didn't sleep well last night, I can't concentrate.

→ If _____, I would be able to concentrate.

6 As she didn't drink coffee this morning, she isn't awake now.

→ If she had drunk coffee this morning, _____.

WRITING PRACTICE

Answer Key p.35

A 우리말과 일치하도록 ( ) 안의 말을 이용하여 문장을 완성하시오.

1 만약 내가 피곤하지 않다면, 해변에 갈 텐데. (tired)

→ _____, I would go to the beach.

2 만약 그녀가 돈을 낭비하지 않았다면, 이 자동차를 살 수 있을 텐데. (waste, her money)

→ _____, she could buy this car.

3 만약 Liv가 그 소식을 알았다면, 그녀는 나에게 그것에 대해 말했을지도 모른다. (tell)

→ If Liv had known the news, _____ about it.

4 만약 내가 그렇게 훌륭한 선생님을 만나지 않았다면, 나는 지금 이 자리에 없을 것이다. (in this place)

→ If I had not met such a great teacher, _____

5 만약 그녀가 여기 있다면, 나는 행복할 텐데. (happy)

→ _____ if she were here.

6 만약 그가 정답을 알았다면, 그는 나에게 알려줬을 텐데. (know)

→ _____, he would have let me know.

B 우리말과 일치하도록 ( ) 안에 주어진 단어를 바르게 배열하시오.

1 내게 시간이 더 많다면, 나는 너와 함께 시간을 보낼 텐데. (had, time, if, I, more, I, spend, would)

→ _____ it with you.

2 네가 메시지를 남겼다면, 내가 너에게 다시 전화를 했을 텐데.
(had, a message, you, left, if, have, I, would, called)

→ _____ you back.

3 만약 그가 담배를 더 일찍 끊었다면, 그는 지금 더 건강할 텐데.
(if, earlier, he, healthier, be, would, he, quit, had, smoking)

→ _____ now.

4 만약 그가 그의 꿈을 포기하지 않았다면, 그는 지금 영화감독일지도 모른다.
(his, a film director, might, he, be, given up, hadn't, if, he, dream)

→ _____ now.

5 그가 너의 고민을 그때 알았다면 그는 너를 도울 수 있었을 텐데.
(helped, he, have, you, could, known, he, had, if)

→ _____ your worries then.

6 내가 너를 보지 못했다면 나는 실망했을 텐데.
(if, disappointed, seen, I, have, would, been, I, hadn't)

→ _____ you.

UNIT 02

I wish, as if, It's time + 가정법

A ( ) 안에서 알맞은 말을 고르시오.

1 That boy is my classmate, but he acts as if he (don't, didn't) know me.

2 I wish I (can, could) read your mind right now.

3 It's time my boss (will pay, paid) my salary.

4 I wish I (know, knew) how to stop smoking.

5 She dances as if she (were, had been) a dancer when she was young.

6 I wish I (don't, didn't) have to go to school on Fridays.

7 It's time we (will find, found) other energy sources.

8 The taxi driver drives as if he (are, were) drunk.

9 I wish I (knew, had known) that the book was on sale.

10 She seems as if she (isn't, hadn't been) sick yesterday.

B ( ) 안의 말을 이용하여 가정법 문장을 완성하시오.

1 I wish I _____ more popular now. (be)

2 She talks as if she _____ the novel before. (read)

3 He is very lazy. It's time you _____ him. (fire)

4 The concert is sold out. I wish I _____ a ticket earlier. (buy)

5 It's sunny. I wish I _____ at the beach. (be)

6 It's 7:00 p.m. It's time I _____ home. (go)

7 I can't trust you. I wish you _____ honest with me now. (be)

8 I didn't do well in the piano competition. I wish I _____ more. (practice)

9 She always talks to me as if I _____ her student. (be)

10 I think it's time you _____ a solution. (find)

C 빈칸에 알맞은 말을 보기에서 골라 쓰시오.

[1-3]

| 보기 | had dinner | were my boss | had come with me |

1 The show was very good. I wish you _____.

2 I'm so hungry. It's time I _____.

3 I don't like working with Jeremy. He acts as if he _____.

[4-6]

| 보기 | were cheaper | gave it back to me | had gone there earlier |

4 The shop was closed. I wish I _____.

5 These shoes are too expensive. I wish they _____.

6 You borrowed my bag last month. It's time you _____.

D 주어진 문장과 의미가 통하도록 빈칸에 알맞은 말을 쓰시오.

1 In fact, he is not from China.

→ He speaks Chinese as if _____.

2 I'm sorry that she didn't keep her promise.

→ _____ her promise.

3 In fact, my sister didn't travel to Hong Kong.

→ My sister talks as if _____.

4 I'm sorry that I don't have my own car.

→ _____ my own car.

5 I'm sorry that I didn't meet him earlier.

→ _____ him earlier.

6 In fact, Thomas doesn't know the truth.

→ Thomas looks as if _____.

7 I'm sorry that there are so many mosquitoes in the summer.

→ _____ in the summer.

WRITING PRACTICE

Answer Key p-36

A 우리말과 일치하도록 ( ) 안의 말을 이용하여 문장을 완성하시오.

1 내 머리카락이 더 길면 좋을 텐데. (hair, long)

→ I wish _____.

2 늦었어! 내가 지하철을 탔더라면 좋을 텐데. (take, the subway)

→ I'm late! I wish _____.

3 내가 그에게 투표를 하지 않았다면 좋을 텐데. (vote for)

→ _____.

4 그 개는 마치 죽은 것처럼 보인다. (it, dead)

→ The dog looks _____.

5 그는 마치 전에 그 영화를 봤던 것처럼 말한다. (see the movie)

→ He talks _____ before.

6 이제 네가 샤워를 해야 할 때이다. (take a shower)

→ It's time _____.

B 우리말과 일치하도록 ( ) 안에 주어진 단어를 바르게 배열하시오.

1 네가 이 마을에 살면 좋을 텐데. (you, this, I, lived, town, wish, in)

→ _____.

2 우리 아빠가 내 자전거를 고치셨더라면 좋을 텐데. (my, I, my, had, dad, wish, fixed, bike)

→ _____.

3 경찰관이 거기에 제때 도착했더라면 좋을 텐데. (police officer, wish, I, had, arrived, the)

→ _____ there in time.

4 Daniel은 그가 변호사인 것처럼 행동한다. (a, Daniel, as, acts, were, he, lawyer, if)

→ _____.

5 나는 마치 아무 일도 일어나지 않았던 것처럼 행동할 수 없다. (happened, nothing, if, as, had)

→ I cannot act _____.

6 이제 정부가 선택을 할 때이다. (made, the, time, is, a choice, government, it)

→ _____.

UNIT 03

주의해야 할 가정법

🔍 Answer Key p.36

A ( ) 안에서 알맞은 말을 고르시오.

1 (Without, But) his paintings, no one would remember the artist.

2 (Without, With) his fingerprints, the police couldn't have caught the robber.

3 (Had, Have) it not been for your note, I wouldn't have known where you were.

4 I would be relieved (talk, to talk) with the counselor.

5 (My son had, Had my son) listened to me, he wouldn't have been in trouble.

6 (But, But for) the news, I wouldn't have invested my money in the company.

7 (She were, Were she) a millionaire, she would be happy.

8 If (you were, were you) a good listener, you would have more friends.

9 (With, Without) hope, I would have given up my dreams.

10 (He were, Were he) a great leader, he would make practical policies.

B 밑줄 친 부분을 어법에 맞게 고치시오.

1 But the movie, the actor could not have become famous.

2 If it have not been for the doctor's advice, he would not have lost weight.

3 It had not been for this program, you could not have solved the problem.

4 If were I in your shoes, I would participate in the competition.

5 Were Jodie here, she will help you with your homework.

6 You had seen the movie, you would have been touched.

7 He would be satisfied take this course.

8 I were to live for a thousand years, I would try hundreds of jobs.

9 If it were not for his luck, he would have lost all his money in gambling.

10 You would be upset hear what she said.

C 빈칸에 알맞은 말을 보기에서 골라 쓰시오. (단, 한 번씩만 쓸 것)

[1-3]

보기	without the light	if it were not for the internet	were I a robot

1 _____, I wouldn't feel sadness.

2 _____, I could not study at night.

3 _____, it wouldn't be easy to share information.

[4-6]

보기	had I left earlier	with good service	to read my report

4 _____, I wouldn't have been late.

5 My professor would be disappointed _____.

6 _____, the restaurant could attract many customers.

D 주어진 문장과 의미가 통하도록 빈칸에 알맞은 말을 쓰시오.

1 If Edison were alive today, what would he invent?

→ _____ _____ _____ _____, what would he invent?

2 You would be surprised if you saw the skyscraper.

→ You would be surprised _____ _____ _____ _____.

3 If you helped him, he would easily find the place.

→ _____ _____ _____, he would easily find the place.

4 If she had taken the pill, she could have slept well.

→ _____ _____ _____ _____ _____, she could have slept well.

5 If it had not been for the loud noises, I would have been able to concentrate better.

→ _____ _____ _____ _____, I would have been able to concentrate better.

6 If it had not been for my math teacher's help, I couldn't have graduated from high school.

→ _____ _____ _____ _____ _____, I couldn't have graduated from high school.

114

WRITING PRACTICE

🔍 Answer Key p.36

A 우리말과 일치하도록 ( ) 안의 말을 이용하여 if가 <u>없는</u> 가정법 문장을 완성하시오.

1 내가 너의 문자 메시지를 읽었다면, 너에게 전화했을 텐데. (text message)

→ _____, I would have called you.

2 좋은 학생이라면 시험에서 부정행위를 하지 않을 것이다. (good, cheat)

→ _____ on the exam.

3 우리 감독이 없었다면, 우리 축구 팀은 경기에서 졌을 것이다. (coach)

→ _____, our soccer team would have lost the game.

4 내가 그 회사 회장이라면, 너를 고용할 것이다. (the president)

→ _____ of the company, I would hire you.

5 햇빛이 없다면, 식물은 자랄 수 없을 것이다. (sunlight)

→ _____, plants could not grow.

6 그녀의 노고가 없었다면, 그녀는 금메달을 따지 못했을 것이다. (hard work)

→ _____, she couldn't have won the gold medal.

B 우리말과 일치하도록 ( ) 안에 주어진 단어를 바르게 배열하시오.

1 네가 이 차를 선택했더라면, 너는 만족했을 텐데. (you, chosen, car, had, this)

→ _____, you would have been satisfied.

2 시간이 조금만 더 있었다면, 그가 그녀를 따라잡았을 텐데. (a little, with, time, more)

→ _____, he would have caught up to her.

3 네가 내일 죽는다면, 너는 오늘 무엇을 하겠는가? (to, you, were, tomorrow, die)

→ _____, what would you do today?

4 좋은 시민이라면 법을 어기지 않을 것이다. (the law, a, wouldn't, citizen, good, break)

→ _____.

5 그 개가 아니었다면, 그 도둑은 잡히지 않았을 것이다. (had, the, it, if, not, for, been, dog)

→ _____, the thief would not have been caught.

6 물이 없다면, 지구상에 생명이 존재하지 못할 것이다. (life, for, exist, but, water, not, could)

→ _____ on Earth.

REVIEW TEST

[1–5] 빈칸에 들어갈 알맞은 말을 고르시오.

1

| If I _____ more time, I would have gone hiking with you. |

① have
② had
③ have had
④ had had
⑤ would have had

2

| I wish I _____ how to make potato pizza before I left home. |

① learn
② learned
③ have learned
④ had learned
⑤ would have learned

3

| If it _____ not snowing, we would go for a walk in the park. |

① is
② were
③ had be
④ would be
⑤ will be

4

| _____ your good advice, I wouldn't be successful as an interior designer. |

① If
② With
③ Without
④ Were to
⑤ But

5

| He talks as if he _____ everything, but he doesn't. |

① knew
② know
③ had known
④ would know
⑤ would have known

[6–7] 다음 중 어법상 틀린 것을 고르시오.

6
① Jen acts as if she were my mother.
② It is time you washed the dishes.
③ You would be surprised to hear Sandra sing.
④ I had practiced more, I could have passed the driving test.
⑤ If I met Emily again, I would tell her I love her.

7
① If I had not gained weight, I could have worn this sweater.
② A good singer would not make such a mistake on stage.
③ I wish I could take a picture with the famous musician.
④ If he had not taken the flight, he would have been alive now.
⑤ If it had not been for your help, I couldn't have arrived at the airport on time.

8 우리말과 일치하도록 할 때, 빈칸에 들어갈 알맞은 말은?

| 지도가 있었다면, 우리는 길을 잃지 않았을 텐데. |
| → _____ a map, we would not have gotten lost. |

① With
② But
③ But for
④ Without
⑤ Without for

빈출

[9-10] 다음 우리말을 영어로 바르게 옮긴 것을 고르시오.

9 만약 내가 기타를 더 잘 치면, 그 오디션에 참가할 텐데.

① If I played the guitar better, I took part in the audition.

② If I played the guitar better, I would take part in the audition.

③ If I play the guitar better, I would have taken part in the audition.

④ If I had played the guitar better, I would have taken part in the audition.

⑤ If I had played the guitar better, I would had taken part in the audition.

10 그녀는 마치 내게 뭔가 할 말이 있는 것처럼 보인다.

① She looks as if she have something to tell me.

② She looks as if she had something to tell me.

③ She looks as if she has had something to tell me.

④ She looks as if she had had something to tell me.

⑤ She looks as if she would have something to tell me.

[11-13] 두 문장의 의미가 같도록 할 때, 빈칸에 들어갈 알맞은 말을 고르시오.

11 I'm sorry I can't speak French fluently.
→ ＿＿＿＿＿＿＿ French fluently.

① I wish I can speak

② I wished I could speak

③ I wish I could speak

④ I wish I could not speak

⑤ I wish I had spoken

12 If she had heard the bad news, she would have been shocked.
→ ＿＿＿＿＿＿＿ the bad news, she would have been shocked.

① She had heard　　② Have heard she

③ Had heard she　　④ Had she heard

⑤ She would have heard

13 Without my dog, I would have been very lonely on the island.
→ ＿＿＿＿＿＿＿ my dog, I would have been very lonely on the island.

① With　　　　　　② Even if

③ So for　　　　　④ If it were not for

⑤ If it had not been for

서술형

[14-17] 우리말과 일치하도록 ( ) 안의 말을 이용하여 문장을 완성하시오.

14 내가 우리 조부모님을 더 자주 볼 수 있다면, 나는 행복할 텐데. (happy)

→ If I could see my grandparents more often, ＿＿＿＿＿＿＿.

15 그녀가 약속이 없었다면, 나와 함께 쇼핑을 갔을 텐데. (go shopping)

→ If she had not had an appointment, she ＿＿＿＿＿＿＿ with me.

16 그녀는 나에게 관심이 없는 것처럼 말한다. (interest)

→ She talks as if she _____
me.

17 현명한 사람이라면 행동하기 전에 재차 생각할 텐데.
(think twice)

→ A wise person _____
before taking action.

서술형

[18-20] 다음 문장을 가정법으로 바꿀 때, 빈칸에 알맞은 말을
쓰시오.

18 It is time you should say goodbye to
your friends.

→ It is time you _____
to your friends.

19 I'm sorry I didn't lend my umbrella to
Connor.

→ _____
my umbrella to Connor.

20 As I didn't take the subway, I arrived
late for the job interview.

→ If I _____ the subway, I
_____ late for the
job interview.

서술형

[21-23] 우리말과 일치하도록 ( ) 안에 주어진 단어를 바르게
배열하시오.

21 네가 도와주었다면, 저렴한 항공권을 구할 수 있었을 텐
데. (gotten, could, your help, I, with, have)

→ _____
a cheap airline ticket.

22 내가 억만장자라면, 돈을 쓰는 것에 대해 걱정할 필요
가 없을 텐데. (would, billionaire, I, to, were,
not, I, a, have)

→ _____
worry about spending money.

23 내가 이를 잘 닦았다면, 나는 지금 치과에 가지 않아도
될 텐데. (I, my, not, would, brushed, if, have,
go, teeth, to, I, had)

→ _____ well,
_____ to the dentist now.

서술형 고난도

[24-25] 어법상 틀린 부분을 찾아 바르게 고치시오.

24 My younger sister always wishes that
she will be better looking. But I think
she is very pretty. (1개)

25 I wish I could go back to my teenage
days. If I went back to those days, I
would had been a better son. (1개)

UNIT 01 수의 일치

🔍 Answer Key p.36

A ( ) 안에서 알맞은 말을 고르시오.

1 Each person (has, have) his or her strong points.

2 Five days (is, are) not enough time to visit another continent.

3 Physics (is, are) the study of nature.

4 Ten dollars (is, are) not expensive for this hat.

5 Listening to classical music (make, makes) me sleepy.

6 When these buildings were built (is, are) unknown.

7 The number of unemployed (is, are) increasing.

8 Both you and Chris (has, have) to come to my office after school.

9 The old (has, have) different values from the young.

10 A number of my friends (is, are) going to a summer camp.

B 어법상 틀린 부분을 찾아 바르게 고치시오.

1 Everyone have the right to freedom.

2 Nobody were making noise in the classroom.

3 Mathematics are the subject that I like the most.

4 Two hours are enough time for me to clean this house.

5 The sick in this country is supported by the government.

6 Helping children in Ghana were the best experience in my life.

7 What you did last night are not important.

8 John and Bart enjoys playing football together.

9 The number of natural disasters have increased recently.

10 Both my mother and my sister likes chocolate cake.

C ( ) 안의 말을 이용하여 문장을 완성하시오. (단, 현재형으로 쓸 것)

1 No one _____ forever. (live)

2 Nowadays the young _____ difficulty in getting jobs. (have)

3 Driving in a snow storm _____ very dangerous. (be)

4 Both my father and my brother _____ blond hair. (have)

5 Looking at these pictures _____ me of my childhood. (remind)

6 _____ anyone seen my dog? (have)

7 Twenty kilograms _____ too heavy for me to lift. (be)

8 The United States _____ the largest producer of corn. (be)

9 Every student _____ to get good grades. (want)

10 A number of trees _____ cut down every year. (be)

D 빈칸에 알맞은 말을 보기에서 골라 쓰시오. (단, 한 번씩만 쓸 것)

[1-3]

보기	needs to be cleaned helps relieve my stress teaches us about the history of people

1 Every room _____.

2 Social studies _____.

3 Chatting with friends _____.

[4-6]

보기	die of hunger are dairy products is a short distance to drive

4 Two kilometers _____.

5 Cheese and yogurt _____.

6 A number of children _____ every year.

120

WRITING PRACTICE

🔍 Answer Key p.36

A 우리말과 일치하도록 ( ) 안의 말을 이용하여 문장을 완성하시오.

1 아무도 정답을 모른다. (nobody)

→ _____ the answer.

2 세 시간은 쇼핑하기에 짧은 시간이다. (hour)

→ _____ a short time for shopping.

3 나쁜 습관을 없애는 것은 쉽지 않다. (break, habits)

→ _____ not easy.

4 너와 나는 둘 다 옳다. (both)

→ _____ right.

5 부자들은 더 많은 세금을 낸다. (the rich, pay)

→ _____ more taxes.

6 많은 동물들이 위험에 처해 있다. (number)

→ _____ in danger.

B 우리말과 일치하도록 ( ) 안에 주어진 단어를 바르게 배열하시오.

1 누구도 너보다 더 아름답지 않다. (than, no, you, is, beautiful, one, more)

→ _____ .

2 수학은 내가 가장 좋아하는 과목이다. (my, subject, is, favorite, mathematics)

→ _____ .

3 30달러가 이 치마를 사는 데 지불되었다. (this, paid, thirty, for, was, dollars, skirt)

→ _____ .

4 따뜻한 목욕을 하는 것은 내가 긴장을 풀도록 돕는다. (helps, a, taking, me, warm, to, relax, bath)

→ _____ .

5 그가 왜 여기 왔는지는 비밀이다. (a secret, why, here, came, he, is)

→ _____ .

6 나의 아버지와 어머니 둘 다 안경을 끼신다. (wear, my father, both, and, glasses, my mother)

→ _____ .

UNIT 02

시제의 일치

A

( ) 안에서 알맞은 말을 고르시오.

1 She said that the area (have, had) been flooded last week.

2 It is reported that the castle (is, was) built in 1700.

3 My teacher said that Ahn Ik-tae (composed, composes) the Korean anthem.

4 Jenny told me that her printer (doesn't, didn't) work, so I fixed it.

5 She said she (doesn't eat, hadn't eaten) anything for a few days.

6 It is said that the pen (is, was) mightier than the sword.

7 I learned that light (travels, traveled) faster than sound.

8 He said that black rhinos (had been, are) an endangered species now.

9 Did you say that you (haven't, hadn't) gone to school until last week?

10 Mark is very funny, so I thought you (will, would) like him.

B

밑줄 친 부분을 어법에 맞게 고치시오.

1 I read that whales <u>were</u> not fish.

2 It is believed that babies <u>were</u> good language learners.

3 I didn't know you lived here. I thought you <u>are</u> a stranger.

4 My mother always said that two heads <u>were</u> better than one.

5 It is believed that the first practical car <u>is</u> invented by Karl Benz.

6 Did you know that the Wright brothers <u>invent</u> the first plane?

7 My daughter said that she <u>wants</u> to be a vet, but she became a teacher.

8 I thought he <u>is</u> a vegetarian, but he wasn't.

9 It is said that the glue stick <u>is</u> invented in 1969.

10 I heard that my professor <u>wins</u> the Nobel Prize the previous year.

C   ( ) 안의 말을 이용하여 문장을 완성하시오.

1   My teacher said that paper _____ invented in 105 AD. (be)

2   He believes that hard work _____ to success. (lead)

3   I heard that headphones _____ invented by Nathaniel Baldwin. (be)

4   He believed that a friend in need _____ a friend indeed. (be)

5   I read in my textbook that there _____ no air in space. (be)

6   I learned that the Second World War _____ in 1939. (begin)

7   I found out that the cuckoo _____ its eggs in other birds' nests. (lay)

8   Jake said he _____ for me. (will wait)

9   It is believed that the first submarine _____ used for military purposes. (be)

10   I thought that I _____ something burning when I entered the house. (smell)

D   문장의 주절을 과거시제로 바꿀 때, 빈칸에 알맞은 말을 쓰시오.

1   My parents say that they have lived here for twenty years.
→ My parents said that _____.

2   I learn that a female emperor penguin lays one egg a year.
→ I learned that _____.

3   My mom doesn't know that I had a car accident.
→ My mom didn't know _____.

4   The boy learns that a shrimp's heart is in its head.
→ The boy learned _____.

5   She says that she will star in the drama.
→ She said _____.

6   It is said that the professor retired.
→ It was said _____.

7   I think my brother will go hiking with me.
→ I thought _____.

WRITING PRACTICE

🔍 Answer Key p.37

A 우리말과 일치하도록 ( ) 안의 말을 이용하여 문장을 완성하시오.

1 워털루 전투는 1815년에 일어났다고 한다. (the Battle of Waterloo, occur)

→ It is said that _____ in 1815.

2 Nora는 커피가 건강에 해롭다고 생각한다. (harmful)

→ Nora thinks that _____ to health.

3 너에게 편지를 보내지 않아서 미안하다. (send)

→ I'm sorry that _____ a letter.

4 나는 그 신발이 편하다고 생각했다. (shoes, comfortable)

→ I thought _____.

5 나는 히틀러가 1939년에 폴란드를 침공한 것을 알았다. (Hitler, invade)

→ I knew that _____ Poland in 1939.

6 엄마는 언제나 일찍 일어나는 새가 벌레를 잡는다고 말하셨다. (the early bird, catch)

→ Mom always said that _____ the worm.

B 우리말과 일치하도록 ( ) 안에 주어진 단어를 바르게 배열하시오.

1 너를 화나게 해서 미안해. (made, sorry, I, am, you, I, upset)

→ _____.

2 나는 그가 그 시를 썼다고 믿었다. (believed, that, the, I, he, poem, wrote)

→ _____.

3 나는 네가 그 수업을 들었다고 생각했다. (the, you, I, had, course, taken, thought)

→ _____.

4 그 소녀는 모기를 싫어한다고 말했다. (mosquitoes, the, said, girl, hated, she)

→ _____.

5 나는 지구가 점점 더워지고 있다고 들었다. (heard, the, getting, I, earth, is, warmer)

→ _____.

6 Mac은 자신이 과학을 전공한다고 말했다. (said, in, science, majored, he, Mac, that)

→ _____.

UNIT
03

화법

🔍 Answer Key p.37

Ⓐ ( ) 안에서 알맞은 말을 고르시오.

1 You said that you (need, needed) to borrow some money.

2 He (said, told) me that he couldn't meet the deadline.

3 Jeremy told me that he (will, would) not forgive me for lying.

4 The doctor asked me what symptoms (I had, did I have).

5 The foreigner asked me (if, that) I could speak English.

6 My neighbors asked us (be, to be) quiet at night.

7 The waiter asked me if I (am, was) ready to order.

8 The police officer asked me if (had I seen, I had seen) any strangers.

9 The nurse advised me (not eat, not to eat) for a while.

10 The police officer ordered me (to show, show) him my ID card.

Ⓑ 밑줄 친 부분을 어법에 맞게 고치시오.

1 Last weekend, Jerry <u>told</u> that he was busy.

2 She <u>said</u> me that she had bought a new dress.

3 My aunt asked me <u>that</u> I would visit her.

4 Laura <u>said</u> me that she was lonely.

5 She asked him if <u>did he want</u> to go out for dinner with her.

6 My mom asked me if <u>had I had</u> lunch.

7 He asked me where <u>did I live</u>.

8 My parents always ask me <u>if</u> I want to be in the future.

9 I told my father <u>not worry</u> about me.

10 My teacher advised me <u>apply</u> for college.

다음을 간접화법으로 바꿀 때, 빈칸에 알맞은 말을 쓰시오.

1 She said to me, "I run my own business."

→ She told _____.

2 He said, "I will apply for the job."

→ He said _____.

3 I said to him, "What are you eating?"

→ I asked _____.

4 Benjamin said to me, "How can I get to the theater?"

→ Benjamin _____.

5 Morgan said to me, "Do you know who I am?"

→ Morgan _____.

6 My doctor said to me, "Eat more vegetables."

→ My doctor _____.

7 My mother said to me, "Don't put your dirty clothes on the sofa."

→ My mother _____.

D

다음을 직접화법으로 바꿔 쓰시오.

1 My mom told me that I needed to stay at home.

→ _____

2 My father asked me what I wanted to eat.

→ _____

3 She asked me if I would stay at her home longer.

→ _____

4 My boss asked me if I had broken my computer.

→ _____

5 Dennis told me to take him to the festival.

→ _____

6 The dentist advised me not to eat candy.

→ _____

WRITING PRACTICE

🔍 Answer Key p.37

A 우리말과 일치하도록 ( ) 안의 말을 이용하여 문장을 완성하시오.

1 나의 친구들은 내가 훌륭한 간호사가 될 거라고 내게 말했다. (tell, become)

→ My friends _____ a good nurse.

2 그 사진사는 나에게 내가 결혼했는지 물어보았다. (ask, be married)

→ The photographer _____.

3 내 여동생은 내가 무엇을 찾고 있는지 내게 물어보았다. (ask, look for)

→ My sister _____.

4 그들은 내가 주변에서 야생 동물을 본 적이 있는지 내게 물어보았다. (ask, see)

→ They _____ any wild animals around.

5 엄마는 내게 내 방을 청소하라고 명령하셨다. (order, clean)

→ Mom _____ my room.

6 Rebecca는 나에게 캠핑에 가지 말라고 충고했다. (advise, go)

→ Rebecca _____ camping.

B 우리말과 일치하도록 ( ) 안에 주어진 단어를 바르게 배열하시오.

1 그는 여름 스포츠를 즐긴다고 말한다. (he, sports, he, says, enjoys, summer, that)

→ _____.

2 그녀는 내게 복도에서 뛰지 말라고 지시했다. (in, ordered, not, she, run, the, me, to, hallway)

→ _____.

3 Michael은 나에게 내가 신을 믿는지 물어보았다. (if, God, Michael, me, in, I, asked, believed)

→ _____.

4 나는 점원에게 그 드레스가 할인 판매 중인지 물어보았다.
(asked, was, if, I, the clerk, on, sale, the dress)

→ _____.

5 나의 어머니는 나에게 여동생을 돌보라고 말씀하셨다.
(my, care, sister, mother, told, of, my, take, me, to)

→ _____.

6 Nicole은 내게 그녀가 자신의 기차를 놓쳤다고 말했다.
(her, that, Nicole, told, had, train, me, she, missed)

→ _____.

REVIEW TEST

[1–5] 빈칸에 들어갈 알맞은 말을 고르시오.

1

> She asked me what time I _____ home the previous night.

① come ② to come
③ coming ④ has come
⑤ had come

2

> The inventor always said that necessity _____ the mother of invention.

① be ② is
③ was ④ has been
⑤ had been

3

> Elizabeth asked me _____ I was going to attend tomorrow's meeting.

① if ② that
③ which ④ what
⑤ unless

4

> Do you know that Einstein _____ in 1955 at the age of seventy-six?

① die ② dies
③ died ④ has died
⑤ to die

5

> Aiden told me _____ to her for keeping her waiting.

① apologize ② apologized
③ apologizing ④ to apologize
⑤ being apologized

[6–7] 다음 중 어법상 틀린 것을 고르시오.

6 ① Both Smith and Jill have never been to Mexico.
② Sophie said that she always eats breakfast at 7:00 a.m.
③ The wounded was transferred to the nearest hospital.
④ I knew that they would fall in love with each other.
⑤ A number of people were lined up to enter the stadium.

7 ① Physics is not an easy subject for me.
② I believe that Jay stole my watch yesterday.
③ I ordered the boy to get out of the room quickly.
④ Every person has his or her strengths and weaknesses.
⑤ The number of employees in the company have increased greatly.

빈출

8 다음을 간접화법으로 바르게 전환한 것은?

> Chloe said to me, "I didn't mean to hurt you."

① Chloe said me that she didn't mean to hurt me.
② Chloe told me that I didn't mean to hurt you.
③ Chloe told me that she hadn't meant to hurt me.
④ Chloe said me that I hadn't meant to hurt you.
⑤ Chloe told me if she hadn't meant to hurt me.

빈출

[9-11] 빈칸에 들어갈 말이 순서대로 바르게 짝지어진 것을
고르시오.

9

- Each student _____ writing an essay about the Cold War.
- Thirty minutes _____ not enough time to finish this job.

① is – is   ② is – are
③ are – is   ④ are – are
⑤ be – are

10

- Watching American soap operas _____ fun.
- Both Steve and I _____ going to visit Spain next year.

① is – is   ② is – are
③ are – is   ④ are – are
⑤ be – are

11

- A number of white birds _____ singing in the tall tree.
- The homeless _____ more likely to have diseases.

① is – is   ② is – are
③ are – is   ④ are – are
⑤ be – are

서술형

[12-14] 우리말과 일치하도록 ( ) 안의 말을 이용하여 문장을
완성하시오.

12 Kate는 내게 남자 친구가 있는지 물었다.
(have, boyfriend)

→ Kate asked me _____.

13 Gary와 나는 둘 다 캐주얼을 즐겨 입는다. (enjoy)

→ Both _____ wearing casual clothes.

14 그 학생들은 나무들이 산소를 생성한다는 것을 배웠다.
(learn, produce)

→ The students _____ oxygen.

15 다음 중 어법상 옳은 것은?

① My mom told me not go to bed too late.
② He thought that Amy will be elected as the MVP of the year.
③ Joseph said that he has two sons and one daughter.
④ Two kilometers were a long distance for me to run.
⑤ Betty said that the First World War breaks out in 1914.

서술형

[16-18] 다음을 간접화법으로 바꿀 때, 빈칸에 알맞은 말을 쓰
시오.

16 Jason said to me, "What time does the movie start?"

→ Jason _____

_____.

17 Rachel said to her brother, "Don't bother me."

→ Rachel _____
_____ .

18 The man said to me, "Have you seen a pink dolphin?"

→ _____
a pink dolphin.

서술형

[19-21] ( ) 안의 말을 이용하여 문장을 완성하시오.
(단, 현재시제로 쓸 것)

19 Playing baseball with my close friends _____ very exciting. (be)

20 I think that mathematics _____ the science of patterns and relationships. (be)

21 Every player on the team _____ their coach. (respect)

서술형

[22-23] 우리말과 일치하도록 ( ) 안에 주어진 단어를 바르게 배열하시오.

22 그녀는 내게 어떤 티셔츠가 그녀에게 더 잘 어울리는지 물었다.
(her, T-shirt, better, which, looked, on)

→ She asked me _____
_____ .

23 그 경찰은 그에게 손을 들라고 명령했다.
(him, ordered, to, his hands, raise)

→ The police _____
_____ .

서술형 고난도

[24-25] 어법상 틀린 부분을 찾아 바르게 고치시오.

24 I ran into an old friend of mine a few days ago. She told that she was running a restaurant with her sister. (1개)

25 Last night, I watched a documentary about Australia. I learned that the country had summer in December. I also learned that the country has a big desert in its center. (1개)

UNIT 01

강조, 부정구문, 병렬

🔍 Answer Key p.38

Ⓐ ( ) 안에서 알맞은 말을 고르시오.

1 You did (save, saved) my life.

2 He did (wait, waiting) for you for two hours.

3 (It, She) was Bridget that became the student president.

4 It was a serious flu (who, that) Jenny suffered from.

5 (All not, Not all) mosquitoes bite you.

6 I enjoy not only swimming but also (jogging, to jog).

7 It was very quiet. (All, None) of the birds were singing.

8 Jerry (do, does) always make fun of Tom.

9 (Both, Neither) of these dishes can be eaten. They are made of clay!

10 I play the piano to make money and (expressing, to express) my feelings.

Ⓑ 밑줄 친 부분을 어법에 맞게 고치시오.

1 I did <u>called</u> you several times.

2 Matthew doesn't like kimchi, but he does <u>likes</u> kimchijjigae.

3 <u>This</u> was my father that sent me the package.

4 Who <u>it was</u> that moved my chair?

5 I <u>haven't</u> been to none of these places.

6 <u>All not</u> kids like hamburgers.

7 I <u>do</u> call you last night, but you didn't answer.

8 No one <u>wouldn't</u> buy the painting.

9 In the morning, I have breakfast and <u>brushing</u> my teeth.

10 You need to take this medicine and <u>getting</u> some rest.

C 주어진 문장과 의미가 통하도록 빈칸에 알맞은 말을 보기에서 골라 쓰시오.

보기	not	no	neither

1 Most mammals live on land, but some of them don't.

→ _____ all mammals live on land.

2 My daughter often goes to bed at 10:00 p.m., but sometimes she doesn't.

→ My daughter does _____ always go to bed at 10:00 p.m.

3 My father doesn't like cola, and I don't either.

→ _____ my father nor I like cola.

4 Most of his stories are fictional, but some aren't.

→ _____ all of his stories are fictional.

5 I don't own any of the jewels in this room.

→ _____ jewels in this room are owned by me.

D 밑줄 친 부분을 강조하여 쓸 때, 빈칸에 알맞은 말을 쓰시오.

1 I studied for the exam, but I didn't get good grades.

→ I _____ for the exam, but I didn't get good grades.

2 He lied to me, but I forgave him.

→ He _____ to me, but I forgave him.

3 I hope you will achieve your dream.

→ I _____ you will achieve your dream.

4 She forgot everything else, but she remembers what you said.

→ She forgot everything else, but she _____ what you said.

5 I lost my cat last month.

→ _____.

6 Who did you go to Paris with?

→ _____?

7 A fan of mine sends me letters every week.

→ _____.

WRITING PRACTICE

🔍 Answer Key p.38

A 우리말과 일치하도록 ( ) 안의 말을 이용하여 문장을 완성하시오.

1 나는 오페라는 좋아하지 않지만, 뮤지컬은 정말 좋아한다. (do, musicals)

→ I don't like operas, but _____.

2 내가 George를 본 곳은 우체국이었다. (at the post office, see)

→ It was _____.

3 그 배우를 유명하게 만든 것은 이 영화였다. (film, make)

→ _____ the actor famous.

4 너희들 모두 시험에 통과하지 못했다. (none)

→ _____ passed the exam.

5 모든 채식주의자들이 두유를 마시는 것은 아니다. (all, vegetarian)

→ _____ soy milk.

6 나는 이 의견 둘 중 어느 쪽도 마음에 들지 않는다. (neither, these opinions)

→ I like _____.

B 우리말과 일치하도록 ( ) 안에 주어진 단어를 바르게 배열하시오.

1 나는 내 부모님과 그 문제에 대해 의논을 하긴 했다. (discuss, the problem, with, I, did)

→ _____ my parents.

2 내가 마시고 싶은 것은 녹차이다. (to, that, it, green tea, I, drink, is, want)

→ _____.

3 그는 독서와 음악 듣는 것을 좋아한다. (he, reading, to, listening, likes, music, and)

→ _____.

4 인터넷상의 모든 정보가 유용한 것은 아니다. (information, on, is, not, the internet, useful, all)

→ _____.

5 모든 발명품이 우리에게 도움이 되지는 않는다. (not, helpful, all, are, to, inventions, us)

→ _____.

6 우리 둘 중 누구도 영어를 하지 못한다. (of, English, neither, speak, us, can)

→ _____.

UNIT 02

도치, 생략, 동격

Ⓐ ( ) 안에서 알맞은 말을 고르시오.

1 Right over the building (a plane passed, passed a plane).

2 Here (comes my daughter, my daughter comes).

3 Rarely (my teacher remembers, does my teacher remember) our names.

4 BTS, (a Korean boy band, is a Korean boy band), is popular around the world.

5 A: Why don't you join us?
   B: Sure, I'd like (to, do).

6 While (wait, waiting) for the bus, he read a newspaper.

7 I want to help her if I (can, do).

8 A: I was really tired after the race.
   B: So (I was, was I).

9 A: I didn't expect Joy to come on time.
   B: (Neither, So) did I.

Ⓑ 밑줄 친 부분을 어법에 맞게 고치시오.

1 Near the river my house was.

2 Around the corner my ex-boyfriend stood.

3 Emma wore Hanbok Korean traditional clothes.

4 Little I thought of being a teacher.

5 A: Maggie updated her homepage.   B: So I did.

6 A: I'm not satisfied with my test results.   B: So am I.

7 A: I can't read Spanish.   B: Neither do I.

8 Hardly I drank water after eating.

9 Little he realized how important his health was to him.

10 Never I have heard such a strange song.

C 다음 문장에서 생략할 수 있는 부분을 ( )로 묶으시오.

1 You may use my computer if you need to use it.

2 The weather isn't as good as it was last month.

3 Please draw my portrait if you can draw it.

4 I will learn Spanish if I have to learn Spanish.

5 I don't drink now, but I used to drink.

6 Though he was hungry, he didn't eat dinner.

7 You can start when you are ready.

8 You can see him today, but you can't see him tomorrow.

9 Though he is young, he supports his family.

10 A: Were they busy yesterday?
 B: Yes, they were busy.

D 다음 문장을 주어진 말로 시작할 때 빈칸에 알맞은 말을 쓰시오.

1 My parents live in the countryside.

→ In the countryside _____.

2 The pianist sat beside me.

→ Beside me _____.

3 A tall building stands across from my house.

→ Across from my house _____.

4 He hardly eats fast food.

→ Hardly _____.

5 She has little dreamed of becoming this famous.

→ Little _____.

6 Jeremy could hardly breathe in the water.

→ Hardly _____.

7 I have never seen such a lovely baby.

→ Never _____.

WRITING PRACTICE

🔍 Answer Key p.38

A 우리말과 일치하도록 ( ) 안의 말을 이용하여 문장을 완성하시오.

1 이 터널을 통해 그 버스가 지나간다. (tunnel, go)

→ Through _____ .

2 나는 충분히 잠을 잘 수가 없었다. (get, enough sleep)

→ Never _____ .

3 그녀는 그의 목소리를 거의 들을 수 없었다. (hear, voice)

→ Hardly _____ .

4 할 수 있다면 네 조부모님을 방문해라. (grandparents, if)

→ Visit _____ .

5 A: 난 온천에 가고 싶어. B: 나도 그래. (so)

→ A: I want to go to the spa.

B: _____ .

6 A: 나는 아직 그 동호회에 가입하지 않았어. B: 나도 그래. (neither)

→ A: I didn't sign up for the club yet.

B: _____ .

B 우리말과 일치하도록 ( ) 안에 주어진 단어를 바르게 배열하시오.

1 그 다리 아래에 여우 가족이 산다. (foxes, the, lives, family, a, bridge, of)

→ Under _____ .

2 나는 팝콘을 먹으면서 영화를 보는 것을 좋아한다. (watching, eating, I, while, like, movies)

→ _____ popcorn.

3 내 친구는 TV를 거의 보지 않는다. (friend, TV, does, my, little, watch)

→ _____ .

4 그녀는 자신이 해 보고 싶은 것은 무엇이든지 해 본다. (to, whatever, tries, she, wants, she)

→ _____ .

5 위대한 피아니스트인 쇼팽은 많은 클래식 음악을 작곡했다.

(classical, pianist, music, of, great, lots, the, wrote)

→ Chopin, _____ .

6 너는 지루할 때 무엇을 하니? (bored, you, when, do, do)

→ What _____ ?

REVIEW TEST

Q Answer Key p.38

[1-5] 빈칸에 들어갈 알맞은 말을 고르시오.

1
In front of the blackboard _____.

① Jake stood ② stood Jake
③ did Jake stand ④ Jake did stand
⑤ does Jake stand

2
Mia doesn't want to go bungee jumping, and _____.

① so am I ② so do I
③ neither will I ④ neither do I
⑤ neither am I

3
It was yesterday _____ I went to the amusement park with Nate.

① what ② how
③ whom ④ where
⑤ that

4
He didn't call me. He _____ send me an email, though.

① is ② was
③ does ④ did
⑤ had

5
Hardly _____ to the school library.

① she goes ② goes she
③ does she go ④ does she goes
⑤ did she goes

[6-7] 다음 중 어법상 틀린 것을 고르시오.

6
① Never I have seen such a cute cat.
② Last night, I watched *Soul*, an animated movie.
③ It was Hudson that I ran into on the street.
④ None of the students wanted to see the horror movie.
⑤ Though tired, he finished the work on his own.

7
① Turn down the music if you want to.
② Not all my employees like my idea.
③ On the bench a homeless man slept.
④ I attended the marketing conference, and so did Mark.
⑤ Neither of my friends has experience in management.

8 밑줄 친 부분의 쓰임이 나머지 넷과 다른 것은?

① The speeding car did run over a cat.
② She does hate wearing a uniform.
③ I did persuade him to join our club.
④ Zoe did tell me that the rumor was true.
⑤ Jacob did his best to win the hundred-meter race.

9 다음 우리말을 영어로 바르게 옮긴 것은?

> 그 소녀들 중 누구도 만리장성에 가 본 적이 없다.

① One of the girls has been to the Great Wall.
② All the girls have been to the Great Wall.
③ None of the girls have been to the Great Wall.
④ Not all the girls have been to the Great Wall.
⑤ Neither of the girls has been to the Great Wall.

서술형
[10-11] 다음 문장에서 생략할 수 있는 부분을 찾아 쓰시오.

10 She sang songs while she was taking a shower.

11 Amber doesn't like to go on business trips, but she must go on business trips.

[12-13] 다음 대화의 빈칸에 들어갈 알맞은 말을 고르시오.

12
> A: I am very excited about going to Paris this Friday.
> B: _____.

① So am I
② So do I
③ So did I
④ Neither am I
⑤ Neither do I

13
> A: I won't get married until I'm thirty.
> B: _____.

① So do I
② So will I
③ Neither am I
④ Neither do I
⑤ Neither will I

서술형 빈출
[14-16] 밑줄 친 부분을 강조하여 문장을 다시 쓰시오.

14 I forgot to bring a copy of my ID card.

→ _____

_____

15 I witnessed a car accident on my way to work.

→ _____

_____

16 She little dreamed that she would meet her favorite actor.

→ _____

_____

17 다음 중 어법상 옳은 것은?

① He doesn't always tell you the truth.
② This car our newest product is an electric car.
③ The design of this dress is excellent, and so the color is.
④ Never she could believe that Jenna betrayed her.
⑤ You should either fix the phone or bought a new one.

서술형

18 우리말과 일치하도록 빈칸에 알맞은 말을 쓰시오.

나는 때때로 학교 버스를 놓치는데, 그도 그렇다.

→ I sometimes miss the school bus, and

_____ _____ _____ .

서술형

19 밑줄 친 부분이 동격 관계가 되도록 한 문장으로 쓰시오.

J. K. Rowling wrote *Harry Potter*.
She's a British author.

→ J. K. Rowling, _____

_____ .

서술형

[20-21] 다음 문장을 주어진 말로 시작할 때 빈칸에 알맞은
말을 쓰시오.

20 I hardly imagined that Anne would be
a fashion model.

→ Hardly _____

_____ .

21 His office is on the second floor of
this building.

→ On the second floor of this building

_____ .

서술형

[22-23] 우리말과 일치하도록 ( ) 안에 주어진 단어를 바르
게 배열하시오.

22 우리 둘 다 그 결과에 만족하지 못했다. (was,
result, of, satisfied, neither, us, with, the)

→ _____

_____ .

23 모든 소년이 액션 영화 보는 걸 즐기는 것은 아니다.
(every, watching, action movies, not,
enjoys, boy)

→ _____

_____ .

서술형 고난도

[24-25] 어법상 틀린 부분을 찾아 바르게 고치시오.

24 On the grass an enormous dog sat.
Never I had seen such a big dog. (2개)

25 I didn't know what I wanted to do
when young. That was my father that
encouraged me to play the guitar. (1개)

MEMO

MEMO

MEMO

MEMO

MEMO

GRAMMAR Inside

workbook

A 4-level grammar course
with abundant writing practice

Compact and concise English grammar
간결하고 정확한 문법 설명

Extensive practice in sentence writing
다양한 유형의 영어 문장 쓰기

Full preparation for middle school tests
최신 완벽 대비

- Workbook with additional exercises
풍부한 양의 추가 문제

Answer Key

GRAMMAR Inside

LEVEL 3

A 4-level grammar course
with abundant writing practice

NE Neungyule

GRAMMAR Inside

LEVEL 3

UNIT 01 현재완료

CHECK UP p.12

1. ⓑ **2.** ⓑ **3.** ⓒ

PRACTICE p.13

STEP 1	**1.** had **2.** have lost **3.** for **4.** heard **5.** has been living
STEP 2	**1.** ate **2.** has gone **3.** have been playing / have played
STEP 3	**1.** have had a toothache **2.** have left **3.** has been to
STEP 4	**1.** has known her since **2.** Have you ever been to **3.** joined the dance club **4.** has already read **5.** have been listening to

UNIT 02 과거완료, 미래완료

CHECK UP p.14

1. ⓑ **2.** ⓑ **3.** ⓒ **4.** ⓒ

PRACTICE p.15

STEP 1	**1.** had been **2.** will have finished **3.** will have been living **4.** had been watching
STEP 2	**1.** had finished **2.** will have watched **3.** will have been **4.** had waited / had been waiting
STEP 3	**1.** had been chatting **2.** will have been learning
STEP 4	**1.** had been living **2.** had already left **3.** will have been **4.** had saved **5.** will have been working

GRAMMAR FOR WRITING pp.16-17

A **1.** has just arrived **2.** has never met
3. has liked him since **4.** traveled Europe
5. had left my purse **6.** will have rained /
will have been raining **7.** had never eaten

B **1.** Diana has just recovered from her illness
2. after he had saved the file **3.** She has
been a lawyer for three years **4.** He has
been reading that book for two hours
5. She will have been running the store
6. he had been sleeping for eight hours

C **1.** have forgotten my aunt's address **2.** had
never ridden a roller coaster **3.** will have
snowed / will have been snowing **4.** has
been crying / has cried **5.** will have read the
book four times **6.** had worked for the shop
for two years

D **1.** met, have known **2.** got, will have been

REVIEW TEST pp.18-21

1. ③ **2.** ④ **3.** ④ **4.** ⑤ **5.** ④ **6.** ③ **7.** ③ **8.** ⑤
9. ② **10.** ④ **11.** ② **12.** Have you ever seen
13. ③ **14.** have spent **15.** has been cooking
16. will have stayed / will have been staying
17. has gone → had gone **18.** have seen → will
have seen **19.** Have you ever cooked spaghetti
before **20.** I have been wearing glasses since
21. She had been looking for her purse **22.** ②,
④ **23.** has been to Brazil **24.** will have broken
down four times **25.** had already started when
we arrived / had started already when we arrived
26. ③, ④, ⑤ **27.** ④ **28.** ③ **29.** X, will have left
30. O **31.** X, had just finished **32.** for → since,
have mastered → will have mastered **33.** have
played → had played, will play → will have played
/ will have been playing

1 과거부터 현재까지 계속되는 일은 현재완료로 나타낸다.
2 결과를 나타내는 현재완료 용법이다.
3 과거의 한 시점보다 더 이전의 일은 과거완료로 나타낸다.
4 미래의 특정 시점까지 진행되고 있을 일은 미래완료 진행형으로
나타낸다.
5 since + 기준 시점: ~ 이래로 / for + 기간: ~ 동안
6 ③ 미래의 특정 시점까지 진행되고 있을 일은 미래완료 진행형
으로 나타낸다. (has been studying → will have been
studying)

7 과거부터 현재까지의 경험은 현재완료로 나타낸다.

8 과거의 한 시점보다 더 이전의 일은 과거완료로 나타낸다.

9 과거에서 현재까지 계속 진행되고 있는 동작은 현재완료 진행형으로 나타낸다.

10 보기와 ④는 현재완료의 〈경험〉을 나타낸다. ①은 〈결과〉, ②, ⑤는 〈계속〉, ③은 〈완료〉를 나타낸다.

11 보기와 ②는 현재완료의 〈계속〉을 나타낸다. ①은 〈결과〉, ③, ⑤는 〈완료〉, ④는 〈경험〉을 나타낸다.

12 경험을 나타내는 현재완료 용법이다.

13 ③ 과거를 나타내는 부사구(three days ago)가 있으므로 과거시제가 와야 한다. (have fixed → fixed)

14 현재까지 영향을 미치는 과거의 일은 현재완료로 나타낸다.

15 과거에서 현재까지 계속 진행되고 있는 동작은 현재완료 진행형으로 나타낸다.

16 미래의 특정 시점까지 지속될 상태는 미래완료로 나타낸다.

17 과거의 한 시점보다 더 이전의 일은 과거완료로 나타낸다.

18 미래의 특정 시점까지 완료될 동작이나 지속될 상태는 미래완료로 나타낸다.

19 경험을 나타내는 현재완료 용법이다.

20 과거에서 현재까지 계속 진행되고 있는 동작은 현재완료 진행형으로 나타낸다.

21 과거 이전에 시작하여 과거의 한 시점까지 진행되었던 일은 과거완료 진행형으로 나타낸다.

22 ① was → have been ③ have seen → saw
⑤ has been → had been

23 과거부터 현재까지의 경험은 현재완료로 나타낸다.

24 미래의 특정 시점까지 완료될 동작이나 지속될 상태는 미래완료로 나타낸다.

25 과거의 한 시점보다 더 이전의 일은 과거완료로 나타낸다.

26 ① has been raining → rained[was raining]
② have eaten → had been eating / was eating

27 a. has lost → had lost
d. has been teaching → will have been teaching / will have taught

28 ・had seen → saw ・has lived → had lived

29 미래의 특정 시점까지 완료될 동작이나 지속될 상태는 미래완료로 나타낸다.

30 과거의 한 시점보다 더 이전의 일은 과거완료로 나타낸다.

31 과거의 한 시점보다 더 이전의 일은 과거완료로 나타낸다.

32 since + 기준 시점: ~ 이래로 / for + 기간: ~ 동안
미래의 특정 시점까지 완료될 동작이나 지속될 상태는 미래완료로 나타낸다.

33 과거의 한 시점보다 더 이전의 일은 과거완료로 나타낸다. / 미래의 특정 시점까지 완료될 동작이나 지속될 상태는 미래완료로 나타낸다.

UNIT 01 can, may, must, should

CHECK UP   p.24

1. ⓐ **2.** ⓐ **3.** ⓒ

PRACTICE   p.25

STEP 1	**1.** should **2.** must **3.** might **4.** Could
STEP 2	**1.** May[Could] **2.** can't[cannot] fly **3.** has to
STEP 3	**1.** must not → don't have[need] to / need not **2.** should not → can't [cannot] **3.** can → should[must, have to]
STEP 4	**1.** is able to ride **2.** You have to fasten **3.** may[might] come **4.** must[should, may] not tell anyone

UNIT 02 had better, ought to, used to, 조동사 + have v-ed

CHECK UP   p.26

1. ⓐ **2.** ⓒ **3.** ⓐ

PRACTICE   p.27

STEP 1	**1.** memorize **2.** had better not **3.** may have gone **4.** to go
STEP 2	**1.** used to **2.** had better **3.** ought to
STEP 3	**1.** can → can't[cannot] **2.** would → used to **3.** ought to not → ought not to **4.** should → may[might]
STEP 4	**1.** ought not to miss **2.** used to have **3.** should have brought **4.** had better take his advice

GRAMMAR FOR WRITING
pp.28-29

A 1. This smartphone must be 2. may[might] have gone home 3. can't[cannot] have bought 4. should have gone 5. had better not drink 6. don't have to finish 7. will be able to save

B 1. She must have been ill yesterday 2. You should wear your seat belt 3. The store might be open 4. Could you recommend a good restaurant 5. I used to watch baseball games 6. You ought not to make loud noises

C 1. had better rest 2. be able to do 3. can't be 4. May I go 5. must have caught 6. should have left 7. can't have seen 8. would play

D 1. Can you carry 2. have to turn right 3. shouldn't[should not] have eaten

REVIEW TEST
pp.30-33

1. ② 2. ④ 3. ① 4. ③ 5. ⑤ 6. ② 7. ④ 8. ①
9. ④ 10. must 11. used to 12. ④ 13. ④
14. must have forgotten 15. used to 16. ③
17. ③ 18. used to be 19. may[might] have taken
20. don't have[need] to hurry / need not hurry
21. have to / had better, ought to 22. can't
23. I should have listened to my parents 24. You had better not play outside 25. You ought not to talk loudly 26. ①, ③, ⑤ 27. ① 28. ② 29. X, ought not to 30. O 31. X, had better 32. eat → have eaten 33. dress → have dressed

1 ought to + 동사원형: ~해야 한다

2 must have v-ed: ~이었음에 틀림없다(과거의 일에 대한 강한 추측)

3 can't[cannot] + 동사원형: ~일 리가 없다(강한 부정적 추측)

4 used to + 동사원형: ~하곤 했다(과거의 습관) / ~이었다(과거의 상태)

5 ⑤ 두 개의 조동사는 연이어 쓸 수 없으므로, 조동사 다음에는 be able to를 쓴다. (will can → will be able to)

6 ② had better의 부정형: had better not (had not better → had better not)

7 must not: ~해서는 안 된다(금지) / don't have to: ~할 필요가 없다(= don't need to, need not)

8 can't have v-ed: ~이었을 리가 없다(과거의 일에 대한 강한 의심)

9 don't have to: ~할 필요가 없다(= don't need to, need not)

10 must + 동사원형: ~임에 틀림없다(강한 추측) / ~해야 한다(의무)

11 used to + 동사원형: ~하곤 했다(과거의 습관) / ~이었다(과거의 상태)

12 ①, ②, ③, ⑤는 '~해야 한다(의무)'의 의미이고, ④는 '~임에 틀림없다(강한 추측)'의 의미이다.

13 ① is → be ② working → work ③ are not able → are not able to ⑤ have to → has to

14 must have v-ed: ~이었음에 틀림없다(과거의 일에 대한 강한 추측)

15 used to + 동사원형: ~이었다(과거의 상태)

16 ⓐ may, might ⓑ should ⓒ can't

17 보기와 ③은 '~일지도 모른다(약한 추측)'의 의미이고, ①, ②, ④, ⑤는 '~해도 된다(허가)'의 의미이다.

18 used to + 동사원형: ~이었다(과거의 상태)

19 may[might] have v-ed: ~이었을지도 모른다(과거의 일에 대한 약한 추측)

20 don't have to: ~할 필요가 없다(= don't need to, need not)

21 have to + 동사원형: ~해야 한다 / had better + 동사원형: ~하는 게 좋겠다 / ought to + 동사원형: ~해야 한다

22 can't have v-ed: ~이었을 리가 없다(과거의 일에 대한 강한 의심)

23 should have v-ed: ~했어야 했다(과거의 일에 대한 후회나 유감)

24 had better의 부정형: had better not

25 ought to의 부정형: ought not to

26 ② could be able to → could[was able to]
④ have not to → don't have to

27 d. wear → have worn e. would → used to

28 • won't able → won't be able
• had not better → had better not
• must be → must have been

29 ought to의 부정형: ought not to

30 must not: ~해서는 안 된다(금지)

31 had better + 동사원형: ~하는 게 좋겠다

32 must have v-ed: ~이었음에 틀림없다(과거의 일에 대한 강한 추측)

33 should have v-ed: ~했어야 했다(과거의 일에 대한 후회나 유감)

CHAPTER 03 수동태

UNIT 01 수동태의 의미와 형태

CHECK UP p.36

1. ⓒ 2. ⓑ 3. ⓑ

PRACTICE p.37

STEP 1	1. was invented 2. resembles 3. made 4. being shown 5. been suggested
STEP 2	1. being discussed 2. disappeared [has disappeared] 3. be shown 4. was punished
STEP 3	1. is played by people all around the world 2. will be delivered within three days (by them) 3. is being destroyed by tourists
STEP 4	1. was taken 2. was being built 3. has been done 4. can be bought

UNIT 02 4형식, 5형식 문장의 수동태

CHECK UP p.38

1. ⓐ 2. ⓑ

PRACTICE p.39

STEP 1	1. to 2. for 3. playing 4. to work
STEP 2	1. shouting[to shout] 2. for me 3. to him 4. to stand
STEP 3	1. was made angry by the boy's rude attitude 2. was seen painting[to paint] the beautiful scenery (by me) 3. was made to help my brother with his homework by my mom 4. was taught to me by my grandfather, was taught Chinese by my grandfather
STEP 4	1. is called Lucky 2. were made to read 3. was bought for me 4. were heard laughing

UNIT 03 주의해야 할 수동태

CHECK UP p.40

1. ⓒ 2. ⓒ 3. ⓑ

PRACTICE p.41

STEP 1	1. was laughed at 2. with 3. with 4. are taken care of
STEP 2	1. was reported that the police arrested the murderer 2. was run over by the speeding truck 3. is believed to affect personality by some people
STEP 3	1. of 2. to 3. with 4. about
STEP 4	1. is composed of 2. It is said that 3. is looked up to by 4. was disappointed with[at]

GRAMMAR FOR WRITING pp.42-43

A 1. was created by 2. must be kept 3. is being updated 4. was seen entering[to enter] 5. was made to learn 6. was made for my dad 7. is believed to earn

B 1. The puzzle has not been solved 2. were given the new textbooks 3. Bill will be elected our class president 4. Dan is satisfied with his new position 5. My puppies were taken care of by my sister 6. This ring was given to me by my boyfriend

C 1. has been influenced 2. was put off (by him) 3. was made to bring 4. is being built (by them) 5. will be given to you (by me) 6. should be baked (by you) 7. is said that

D 1. is composed of 2. is interested in 3. is filled with

REVIEW TEST pp.44-47

1. ④ 2. ② 3. ③ 4. ③ 5. ② 6. ② 7. ② 8. ④
9. ② 10. ⑤ 11. is being built 12. to be
13. fighting[to fight] 14. ④ 15. was made for me
16. hasn't[has not] been fixed (by them) 17. was

given to me **18.** ①, ⑤ **19.** were made to pick
up **20.** will be released **21.** is filled with **22.** ③
23. The deer was run over by the truck **24.** your
password should be changed **25.** It is said that
yoga is good **26.** ③, ④, ⑤ **27.** ⑤ **28.** ③
29. X, was given to **30.** X, were surprised at
31. X, was seen helping[to help] **32.** enjoy →
enjoyed **33.** saying → to say

1 야구 경기가 취소된 것이므로 수동태를 써야 한다.

2 조동사가 있는 문장의 수동태: 조동사 + be + v-ed

3 사역동사의 목적격 보어로 쓰인 동사원형은 수동태 문장에서 to
부정사로 바뀐다.

4 직접목적어가 문장의 주어가 될 때 수여동사 make는 간접목적
어 앞에 for를 쓴다.

5 be known to: ~에게 알려지다

6 ② 타동사 resemble은 수동태로 쓰지 않는다.

7 ② 지각동사의 목적격 보어로 쓰인 동사원형은 수동태 문장에
서 현재분사나 to부정사로 바뀐다. (enter → entering[to
enter])

8 ④ be crowded with: ~로 붐비다 (to → with)

9 직접목적어가 문장의 주어가 될 때 수여동사 show는 간접목적
어 앞에 to를 쓴다. / 사역동사의 목적격 보어로 쓰인 동사원형
은 수동태 문장에서 to부정사로 바뀐다.

10 be pleased with: ~로 기뻐하다 / be satisfied with:
~에 만족하다

11 진행형의 수동태: be동사 + being + v-ed

12 that절의 주어를 수동태 문장의 주어로 할 때, that절의 동사
는 to부정사로 바뀐다.

13 지각동사의 목적격 보어로 쓰인 동사원형은 수동태 문장에서 현
재분사나 to부정사로 바뀐다.

14 목적어가 that절인 문장의 수동태: It + be동사 + v-ed +
that ~

15 직접목적어가 문장의 주어가 될 때 수여동사 make는 간접목적
어 앞에 for를 쓴다.

16 완료형의 수동태: have[has, had] been + v-ed

17 직접목적어가 문장의 주어가 될 때 수여동사 give는 간접목적
어 앞에 to를 쓴다.

18 목적어가 that절인 문장의 수동태는 「It + be동사 + v-ed +
that ~」의 형태로 쓴다. that절의 주어를 수동태 문장의 주어
로 할 때, that절의 동사는 to부정사로 바뀐다.

19 사역동사의 목적격 보어로 쓰인 동사원형은 수동태 문장에서 to
부정사로 바뀐다.

20 미래시제의 수동태: will be + v-ed

21 be filled with: ~로 가득 차다

22 ① that is → to be ② is → was ④ jog → jogging[to
jog] ⑤ Sam → for Sam

23 동사구는 수동태로 바꿀 때 하나의 동사처럼 취급한다.

24 조동사가 있는 문장의 수동태: 조동사 + be + v-ed

25 It으로 시작해야 하므로, 목적어가 that절인 문장의 수동태인
「It + be동사 + v-ed + that ~」의 형태로 쓴다.

26 ① building → built ② sign → signed

27 a. repair → repaired c. cleaning → to clean

28 • 소유를 나타내는 타동사 have는 수동태로 쓰지 않는다.
• bought to → bought for

29 직접목적어가 문장의 주어가 될 때 수여동사 give는 간접목적
어 앞에 to를 쓴다.

30 be surprised at: ~에 놀라다

31 지각동사의 목적격 보어로 쓰인 동사원형은 수동태 문장에서 현
재분사나 to부정사로 바뀐다.

32 경기가 즐겨진 것이므로 수동태를 써야 한다.

33 사역동사의 목적격 보어로 쓰인 동사원형은 수동태 문장에서 to
부정사로 바뀐다.

CHAPTER 04 부정사

UNIT 01 명사적 용법의 to부정사

CHECK UP p.50

1. © **2.** ⓑ **3.** ⓐ **4.** ⓑ

PRACTICE p.51

STEP 1	1. to travel 2. it 3. to wear 4. to exercise
STEP 2	1. It, to learn 2. when to start 3. It, to clean
STEP 3	1. what to do 2. how to cook 3. where to go
STEP 4	1. is to be an architect 2. was fun to go 3. when to finish 4. it impossible to arrive

UNIT 02 형용사적 용법, 부사적 용법의
to부정사

CHECK UP p.52

1. © **2.** © **3.** ©

PRACTICE
p.53

STEP 1	1. to live in 2. to become 3. to wake 4. are to make
STEP 2	1. to play → to play with 2. doing → to do 3. know → to know 4. to seeing → to see
STEP 3	1. 그 배우는 매우 유명해져서 행복하다. 2. 우 리는 사랑은 살 수 없다는 것을 안다. 3. 지금이 네 부모님께 전화드릴 가장 좋은 시간이다. 4. 세계를 혼자 여행하다니 Jenny는 용감한 것 이 틀림없다.
STEP 4	1. many reasons to read 2. is to arrive in 3. to hear from him 4. was very happy to hear

UNIT 03 to부정사의 의미상의 주어, 시제, 태

CHECK UP
p.54

1. ⓑ 2. ⓒ 3. ⓑ

PRACTICE
p.55

STEP 1	1. for us 2. of him 3. to have lost 4. to be punished
STEP 2	1. for him 2. of you 3. of her 4. for me
STEP 3	1. to have made 2. to be invited 3. to be disappointed 4. to have been told
STEP 4	1. to be paid 2. polite of him to apologize 3. important for us to finish 4. seems to have been

UNIT 04 목적격 보어로 쓰이는 부정사

CHECK UP
p.56

1. ⓒ 2. ⓐ 3. ⓐ

PRACTICE
p.57

STEP 1	1. to wear 2. dance 3. write 4. painted 5. spoken
STEP 2	1. buy 2. to stay 3. play[playing] 4. to become 5. pulled

STEP 3	1. to hit → hit[hitting] 2. renovating → renovated 3. choosing → choose[to choose] 4. change → to change 5. to give up → give up
STEP 4	1. heard them make[making] noises 2. helped me find 3. didn't let me have 4. told me to bring

UNIT 05 to부정사 구문, 독립부정사

CHECK UP
p.58

1. ⓑ 2. ⓒ 3. ⓒ

PRACTICE
p.59

STEP 1	1. To tell 2. To be 3. to answer 4. good enough
STEP 2	1. to cook 2. too 3. good enough 4. to say
STEP 3	1. too bitter for me to drink 2. smart enough to guide 3. too old to drive on the highway 4. interesting enough for adults to enjoy
STEP 4	1. To be sure 2. smart enough to pass 3. To make matters worse 4. too dangerous to go

GRAMMAR FOR WRITING
pp.60-61

A 1. saw her ride[riding] a bike 2. wise of him
to accept 3. someone to depend on
4. To tell the truth 5. needs to be repaired
6. is believed to have been built 7. seems
to have thought

B 1. difficult for him to make her laugh 2. it
impossible to change his mind 3. told me
not to eat fast food 4. The couple is to be
married 5. We will decide where to stay
6. My parents were very pleased to know

C 1. him to move the heavy boxes 2. you to
go there instead of me 3. me to put on
sunscreen 4. (to) paint the wall 5. me cry
a lot 6. me wear his new jacket 7. to give
him a birthday present

D **1.** how to train dogs **2.** hot enough to wear shorts **3.** too sick to get out of bed

---

REVIEW TEST

pp.62-65

1. ③ **2.** ⑤ **3.** ③ **4.** ① **5.** ⑤ **6.** ④ **7.** ④ **8.** ③
9. ③ **10.** ③ **11.** ⑤ **12.** to have gotten **13.** ②
14. sing[singing] **15.** reserve **16.** to be trained
17. ④ **18.** ④ **19.** let me have **20.** seems to have been poor **21.** too hot to take a bath
22. ④ **23.** It is impossible for me to beat him
24. The restaurant is large enough to hold
25. Mom told me not to touch **26.** ②, ③ **27.** ②
28. ③ **29.** X, to be asked **30.** X, decide **31.** O
32. using → to use **33.** enough warm → warm enough, come → to come

1 to부정사가 주어로 쓰일 경우 보통 가주어 it을 쓰고 to부정사는 뒤로 보낸다.

2 형용사적 용법의 to부정사 / 수식 받는 명사가 to부정사 속의 동사에 이어지는 전치사의 의미상 목적어가 될 때는 전치사를 반드시 같이 쓴다.

3 advise는 to부정사를 목적격 보어로 취하는 동사이다.

4 지각동사(watch)는 동사원형이나 분사를 목적격 보어로 취한다.

5 사람에 대한 주관적 평가를 나타내는 형용사와 함께 쓰이면 to부정사의 의미상의 주어로 「of + 목적격」을 쓴다.

6 get은 to부정사를 목적격 보어로 취하는 동사이다.

7 ④ to부정사가 주어로 쓰일 경우 보통 가주어 it을 쓰고 to부정사는 뒤로 보낸다. (reply → to reply)

8 ③ 사역동사(have)는 동사원형을 목적격 보어로 취한다. (to bring → bring)

9 보기와 ③은 명사적 용법, ①, ②, ⑤는 부사적 용법, ④는 형용사적 용법의 to부정사이다.

10 ③ to부정사의 시제가 문장의 시제보다 앞설 때 「to have v-ed(완료부정사)」를 쓴다. (to wait → to have waited)

11 ⑤ 그녀는 너무 어려서 이 영화를 볼 수 없다.

12 to부정사의 시제가 문장의 시제보다 앞설 때 「to have v-ed(완료부정사)」를 쓴다.

13 ② get은 to부정사를 목적격 보어로 취하는 동사이다. (bringing → to bring)

14 지각동사(hear)는 동사원형이나 분사를 목적격 보어로 취한다.

15 사역동사(have)는 동사원형을 목적격 보어로 취한다.

16 to부정사의 수동태(단순형): to be v-ed

17 ① → to receive ② → to be repaired
③ → too shy to ask ⑤ → well enough to leave

18 ① → to sit on ② → to be ③ → to play
⑤ → to have

19 사역동사(let) + 목적어 + 원형부정사: ~가 …하게 하다

20 to부정사의 시제가 문장의 시제보다 앞설 때 「to have v-ed(완료부정사)」를 쓴다.

21 too ~ to-v: 너무 ~해서 …할 수 없다

22 ④ 사람에 대한 주관적 평가를 나타내는 형용사와 함께 쓰이면 to부정사의 의미상의 주어로 「of + 목적격」을 쓴다.

23 to부정사가 주어로 쓰일 경우 보통 가주어 it을 쓰고 to부정사는 뒤로 보낸다.

24 ~ enough to-v: …할 만큼 충분히 ~하다

25 tell은 to부정사를 목적격 보어로 취하는 동사이다.

26 ② talk → to talk ③ eat → to eat

27 c. crossing → cross[to cross]
d. laugh → to laugh

28 · to shout → shout[shouting]
· watch → to watch

29 to부정사의 수동태(단순형): to be v-ed

30 사역동사(make)는 동사원형을 목적격 보어로 취한다.

31 to make a long story short: 간단히 말해서

32 부사적 용법의 to부정사(형용사 수식)

33 ~ enough to-v: …할 만큼 충분히 ~하다 / 명사적 용법의 to부정사(목적어)

CHAPTER 05 동명사

UNIT 01 동명사의 역할

CHECK UP p.68

1. ⓑ **2.** ⓑ **3.** ⓒ

PRACTICE p.69

STEP 1	**1.** Drinking **2.** his **3.** drinking **4.** not telling **5.** being elected
STEP 2	**1.** being invited / having been invited **2.** Eating[To eat] **3.** visiting[having visited] **4.** not keeping / not having kept
STEP 3	**1.** having missed **2.** my[me] closing **3.** being involved
STEP 4	**1.** Losing weight was **2.** not going **3.** his[him] being sick **4.** having been treated

UNIT 02 동명사 vs. to부정사

CHECK UP p.70

1. ⓑ 2. ⓒ

PRACTICE p.71

STEP 1	1. running 2. meeting 3. hearing 4. to change 5. to turn
STEP 2	1. complaining[to complain] 2. to answer 3. seeing 4. watching
STEP 3	1. listening 2. starting 3. to become 4. hearing
STEP 4	1. stopped buying 2. Try to eat 3. is worth visiting 4. remembers returning the book 5. prevented him from going

GRAMMAR FOR WRITING pp.72-73

A 1. I don't mind his[him] coming
2. remembers borrowing money
3. forgot watering 4. promised to help
5. was afraid of being punished
6. stopped playing 7. try drinking tea

B 1. He could not help laughing at
2. Predicting the weather is difficult
3. worried about not finishing my homework
4. All people like being loved by others
5. He denied having cheated on the exam
6. Mark is proud of having been raised

C 1. forgot to visit
2. enjoy going to the cinema
3. refused to take a walk
4. her spending too much time
5. prevent, making

D 1. singing or speaking loudly
2. to lock the door
3. Having pets / To have pets

REVIEW TEST pp.74-77

1. ④ 2. ② 3. ④ 4. ② 5. ⑤ 6. ① 7. ④ 8. her
9. not being invited / not having been invited
10. ⑤ 11. ④ 12. ③ 13. ⑤ 14. to bring
15. staying 16. playing 17. ⑤ 18. angry about my being late again 19. Giving up old habits is difficult 20. denied having stolen the money
21. his[him] being 22. ④ 23. was afraid of being arrested 24. Remember to meet 25. try using 26. ①, ③ 27. ⑤ 28. ④ 29. O 30. X, hoped to receive 31. X, to hearing 32. turning → to turn 33. to see → seeing

1 decide는 to부정사만 목적어로 취하는 동사이다.

2 avoid는 동명사만 목적어로 취하는 동사이다.

3 동명사가 수동의 의미이고 시제가 문장의 시제와 같을 때 단순형 수동태(being v-ed)를 쓴다.

4 keep + 목적어 + from v-ing: ~가 …하는 것을 막다

5 ① Shop → Shopping[To shop] ② to stand → standing ③ he → his[him] ④ to watch → watching

6 ② play → playing ③ to use → using ④ to eat → eating ⑤ calling → being[to be] called

7 try not to-v: ~하지 않으려고 노력하다

8 동명사의 의미상의 주어는 동명사 앞에 소유격 또는 목적격을 써서 나타낸다.

9 초대받는 것이므로 동명사의 수동태를 써야 한다.

10 consider는 동명사만 목적어로 취하는 동사이다.

11 want는 to부정사만 목적어로 취하는 동사이다.

12 ③ remember to-v: ~할 것을 기억하다 (calling → to call)

13 ⑤ 동명사의 부정은 동명사 바로 앞에 not을 붙인다. (changing not → not changing)

14 forget to-v: ~할 것을 잊다

15 feel like v-ing: ~하고 싶어지다

16 stop v-ing: ~하는 것을 멈추다

17 expect는 to부정사만 목적어로 취하는 동사이다. / be used to v-ing: ~하는 것에 익숙하다

18 전치사의 목적어로 동명사를 쓰고 동명사의 의미상의 주어는 동명사 앞에 소유격 또는 목적격을 써서 나타낸다.

19 주어 역할을 하는 동명사이다.

20 동명사의 시제가 문장의 시제보다 앞설 때 완료형(having v-ed)을 쓴다.

21 동명사의 의미상의 주어는 동명사 앞에 소유격 또는 목적격을 써서 나타낸다.

22 ④ mind는 동명사만 목적어로 취하는 동사이다. (turn → turning)

23 동명사가 수동의 의미이고 시제가 문장의 시제와 같을 때 단순형 수동태(being v-ed)를 쓴다.

24 remember to-v: ~할 것을 기억하다

25 try v-ing: (시험 삼아) ~해 보다

26 ② to clean → cleaning ④ buy → buying

⑤ ask → asking

27 a. ride → riding c. to have → having

28 ・ to meet → meeting

29 suggest는 동명사만 목적어로 취하는 동사이다.

30 hope는 to부정사만 목적어로 취하는 동사이다.

31 look forward to v-ing: ~하기를 고대하다

32 forget to-v: ~할 것을 잊다

33 be worth v-ing: ~할 가치가 있다

CHAPTER
06 분사

UNIT 01 현재분사 vs. 과거분사

CHECK UP   p.80

1. ⓒ **2.** ⓑ **3.** ⓑ

PRACTICE   p.81

STEP 1	**1.** boiling **2.** rented **3.** smiling **4.** shouting
STEP 2	**1.** painted **2.** sleeping **3.** running **4.** depressed
STEP 3	**1.** bored **2.** amazing **3.** locked
STEP 4	**1.** an interesting book **2.** some people interested **3.** looked disappointed **4.** their car covered

UNIT 02 분사구문

CHECK UP   p.82

1. ⓐ **2.** ⓒ **3.** ⓑ

PRACTICE   p.83

STEP 1	**1.** Feeling **2.** waiting **3.** Not being **4.** Turning off
STEP 2	**1.** Taking this bus **2.** Falling down the stairs **3.** Not knowing what to buy

STEP 3	**1.** If you turn left **2.** While I traveled in Europe **3.** Because she didn't[did not] have enough time
STEP 4	**1.** Drinking coffee **2.** Being hungry **3.** Visiting our website **4.** Not finishing his work

UNIT 03 여러 가지 분사구문

CHECK UP   p.84

1. ⓑ **2.** ⓒ

PRACTICE   p.85

STEP 1	**1.** Weather permitting **2.** Judging **3.** Accepted
STEP 2	**1.** There being a lot of snow **2.** (Being) Chosen to be the team captain **3.** (Having been) Run over by a car
STEP 3	**1.** (Having been / Being) Left **2.** finishing[she finished] **3.** Generally speaking **4.** with the lights turned off
STEP 4	**1.** Considering his age **2.** with her legs crossed **3.** Having lost

---

GRAMMAR FOR WRITING   pp.86-87

A **1.** boiling water **2.** He wasn't[was not] satisfied **3.** Having studied **4.** Turning left **5.** with his eyes closed **6.** Not having any money **7.** (Being) Written

B **1.** saw a man taking a walk **2.** It being cold, I turned **3.** Judging from his accent **4.** While playing football, he got **5.** an email written by his father **6.** Having finished my homework, I went out

C **1.** a. disappointing b. disappointed
 2. a. exciting b. excited
 3. a. amused b. amusing
 4. a. interested b. interesting
 5. a. satisfied b. satisfying

D **1.** playing on a swing **2.** Lying on the bed
 3. his arms folded

REVIEW TEST

REVIEW TEST pp.88-91

1. ② 2. ③ 3. ② 4. ② 5. ⑤ 6. ③ 7. ② 8. ⑤
9. ⑤ 10. ④ 11. parked 12. surrounded
13. playing 14. Judged from → Judging from
15. ③ 16. Not knowing where to get a taxi
17. (Having been) Given lots of homework
18. ③ 19. Having made the mistake 20. found the restaurant closed 21. Taking this medicine
22. ③ 23. The red car parked outside 24. I felt something hitting my leg 25. It being too cold outside 26. ③, ⑤ 27. ③ 28. ③ 29. X, connecting 30. X, (Having been) Cooked
31. X, Finishing[Having finished] 32. crossing → crossed 33. damaging → damaged, Be → Being

1 '손을 흔들고 있는'이라는 능동, 진행의 의미이므로 현재분사를 써야 한다.

2 그들이 '놀란' 감정을 느끼는 것이므로 과거분사를 써야 한다.

3 액션 영화의 결말이 '충격적인' 감정을 느끼게 하는 것이므로 현재분사를 써야 한다.

4 이유를 나타내는 분사구문

5 완료형 분사구문(having v-ed)

6 ①, ②, ④, ⑤는 현재분사이고, ③은 동명사이다.

7 ①, ③, ④, ⑤는 현재분사이고, ②는 동명사이다.

8 ⑤ '도난당한'이라는 수동의 의미이므로 과거분사를 써야 한다. (stealing → stolen)

9 ⑤ 수동 분사구문(having been v-ed)을 써야 한다. (Having raised → (Having been) Raised)

10 ① interesting → interested ② surprised → surprising ③ stood → standing ⑤ satisfying → satisfied

11 '(차가) 주차된 채'라는 수동의 의미이므로 과거분사를 써야 한다.

12 '~에 둘러싸여'라는 수동의 의미이므로 과거분사를 써야 한다.

13 '(농구를) 하고 있는'이라는 능동, 진행의 의미이므로 현재분사를 써야 한다.

14 judging from: ~로 판단하건대

15 이유를 나타내는 분사구문

16 분사구문의 부정은 분사 앞에 not을 붙인다.

17 수동 분사구문(having been v-ed)으로, having been은 생략 가능하다.

18 ③ 문두에 Having been이 생략된 수동 분사구문이다. (→ Because it was placed in the fridge)

19 부사절의 시제가 주절의 시제보다 앞선 경우 완료형 분사구문(having v-ed)을 쓴다.

20 '닫힌'은 수동의 의미이므로 과거분사를 쓴다.

21 조건을 나타내는 분사구문

22 boring: 지루한 / bored: 지루해하는

23 분사가 다른 어구와 함께 쓰여 길어질 경우 명사 뒤에서 수식한다.

24 목적격 보어 역할을 하는 현재분사

25 부사절의 주어가 주절의 주어와 다르므로 분사 앞에 주어를 남겨둔다.

26 ③ Be nervous → Being nervous ⑤ run → running

27 a. amused → amusing e. taking → taken

28 · bored → boring · Knowing not → Not knowing

29 '연결하는'이라는 능동의 의미로 현재분사를 써야 한다.

30 수동 분사구문(having been v-ed)을 써야 한다.

31 분사구문(v-ing)이나 완료형 분사구문(having v-ed)을 써야 한다.

32 '꼬아진'이라는 수동의 의미로 과거분사 crossed를 써야 한다. cross one's fingers: 행운을 빌다

33 '피해를 입은'이라는 수동의 의미로 과거분사 damaged를 써야 한다. / 분사구문이므로 Being을 써야 한다.

CHAPTER 07 비교

UNIT 01 원급, 비교급, 최상급

CHECK UP p.94

1. ⓐ 2. ⓑ 3. ⓐ 4. ⓒ

PRACTICE p.95

STEP 1	1. soft 2. even 3. more 4. most boring
STEP 2	1. more careful than 2. much[even, far, a lot] 3. the youngest 4. not as difficult
STEP 3	1. not as heavy 2. more expensive than 3. the strongest of
STEP 4	1. as many books as 2. far heavier than 3. more comfortable than 4. the biggest city in 5. the scariest movie I have ever seen / the scariest movie that I've ever seen

UNIT 02 여러 가지 비교구문

CHECK UP p.96

1. ⓑ 2. ⓒ 3. ⓑ 4. ⓒ

PRACTICE p.97

STEP 1	1. twice 2. cities 3. the better 4. More and more 5. as early as possible
STEP 2	1. as hard as possible 2. The more, the better 3. braver than any other man
STEP 3	1. funnier than any other boy 2. as funny as 3. funnier than
STEP 4	1. three times heavier than 2. The more, the more tired 3. more and more exciting 4. one of the biggest temples

GRAMMAR FOR WRITING pp.98-99

A 1. faster than any other train 2. The more, the better 3. as soon as possible 4. three times as thick as / three times thicker than 5. one of the most dangerous sports 6. the coldest month of 7. more and more confident

B 1. go fishing as much as I do 2. The hotel was not as comfortable as my home 3. My cat is getting heavier and heavier 4. The laptop was a lot cheaper than I thought 5. No boy in his school runs faster than Junho 6. the funniest teacher I have ever met

C 1. more difficult 2. three times as long 3. busier, any other day, as busy, busier 4. larger, any other dog, No (other) dog, as large, No (other) dog, larger

D 1. as heavy as 2. the fastest 3. lighter than any other 4. as short as / shorter than 5. (he is) younger than 6. as tall as / taller than

REVIEW TEST pp.100-103

1. ① 2. ⑤ 3. ④ 4. ④ 5. ⑤ 6. ① 7. ④ 8. ③ 9. ③ 10. ③ 11. the most beautiful 12. The more, the more 13. possible 14. ④ 15. as fast as 16. earlier than 17. ② 18. ③ 19. one of the hottest days 20. more and more useful 21. even harder than 22. ② 23. finish the work

as soon as possible 24. the most delicious cake I have ever had 25. The more you practice, the better 26. ②, ③, ⑤ 27. ③ 28. ③ 29. X, one of the most famous teenage actors 30. O 31. X, better than any other dish 32. bigger as bigger → bigger and bigger, biggest → big 33. most crowded → more crowded

1 as + 원급 + as: ~만큼 …한[하게]
2 the + 최상급 + in: ~에서 가장 …한[하게]
3 the + 비교급, the + 비교급: 더 ~할수록 더 …하다
4 부정 주어 ~ 비교급 + than
5 배수사 + as + 원급 + as: ~의 몇 배로 …한[하게]
6 ① much, even, far, a lot 등은 비교급 앞에서 '훨씬'의 의미로 쓰여 비교급을 강조한다. (so more than → much[a lot, even, far] more than)
7 ④ one of the + 최상급 + 복수명사: 가장 ~한 … 중 하나 (friend → friends)
8 Oliver가 Ethan보다 키가 더 크므로, ③은 표의 내용과 일치하지 않는다.
9 ① three → three times ② bad and bad → worse and worse ④ very → much[even, far, a lot] ⑤ day → days
10 ③ 비교급 + and + 비교급: 점점 더 ~한[하게] (heavy and heavy → heavier and heavier)
11 the + 최상급 + in: ~에서 가장 …한[하게]
12 the + 비교급, the + 비교급: 더 ~할수록 더 …하다
13 as + 원급 + as + 주어 + can = as + 원급 + as possible
14 much, even, far, a lot 등은 비교급 앞에서 '훨씬'의 의미로 쓰여 비교급을 강조한다.
15 A not as ~ as B: A는 B만큼 ~하지 않다
16 Sam이 셋 중에서 가장 먼저 일어난다.
17 ⓐ more ⓑ most ⓒ the ⓓ in
18 ①, ②, ④, ⑤는 모두 최상급의 의미이다.
19 one of the + 최상급 + 복수명사: 가장 ~한 … 중 하나
20 비교급 + and + 비교급: 점점 더 ~한[하게]
21 much, even, far, a lot 등은 비교급 앞에서 '훨씬'의 의미로 쓰여 비교급을 강조한다.
22 ② 첫 번째 문장은 '나의 개는 너의 개만큼 무겁지 않다'의 의미이고, 두 번째 문장은 '나의 개가 너의 개보다 더 무겁다'의 의미이다.
23 as + 원급 + as possible: 가능한 한 ~한[하게]
24 the + 최상급 + (that +) 주어 + have ever v-ed: 지금까지 ~한 것 중 가장 …한
25 the + 비교급, the + 비교급: 더 ~할수록 더 …하다
26 ② smart → smarter ③ as not → not as ⑤ the more easy → the easier
27 b. bigger → big d. very → much[even, far, a lot]
28 · most happy → happier · funnier → funny
29 -ous로 끝나는 단어는 앞에 most를 붙여 최상급을 만든다.

12

30 배수사 + as + 원급 + as: ~의 몇 배로 …한[하게]

31 the + 최상급 = 비교급 + than any other + 단수명사

32 비교급 + and + 비교급: 점점 더 ~한[하게]

배수사 + as + 원급 + as: ~의 몇 배로 …한[하게]

33 비교급 + than: ~보다 더 …한[하게]

CHAPTER 08 접속사

UNIT 01 종속 접속사

CHECK UP   p.106

1. ⓑ **2.** ⓐ

PRACTICE   p.107

STEP 1	**1.** hears **2.** until **3.** As **4.** when
STEP 2	**1.** since **2.** says **3.** If
STEP 3	**1.** As **2.** while **3.** Though **4.** If
STEP 4	**1.** until[till] she tells me **2.** Every[Each] time he hears **3.** Even if he doesn't come **4.** Though[Although] he had little time **5.** As soon as the show starts

UNIT 02 짝으로 이루어진 접속사, 간접의문문

CHECK UP   p.108

1. ⓑ **2.** ⓑ **3.** ⓐ

PRACTICE   p.109

STEP 1	**1.** Both **2.** or **3.** but also **4.** the movie starts
STEP 2	**1.** Both, and **2.** neither, nor **3.** either, or
STEP 3	**1.** Who do you think will be the next president? **2.** Can you tell me how much this hat is? **3.** Do you know who lives next door? **4.** I'd like to know if[whether] Harry has a girlfriend.

STEP 4	**1.** Both Liam and I wear **2.** as well as delicious **3.** Why do you think he stole

---

GRAMMAR FOR WRITING   pp.110-111

A **1.** what her email address is
2. While I was cleaning the living room
3. Both the facilities and the teachers
4. I as well as Andy want to be **5.** who sent this parcel **6.** neither big nor crowded
7. Unless you come / If you don't come

B **1.** What do you think is the key
2. Since I didn't have any money
3. As soon as you pass the bank
4. Though he was angry
5. either in her room or in the kitchen
6. If you want to read my books

C **1.** either kung fu or taekwondo
2. when she wrote her first novel
3. Since it rained heavily
4. Although he was very tired
5. if the restaurant is open on Sundays
6. Both Zoey and I like to learn new languages
7. neither in my room nor in the living room

D **1.** because we were hungry **2.** not only pizza but also hamburgers / not only hamburgers but also pizza **3.** if we wanted something to drink **4.** while we waited[were waiting] for the food

---

REVIEW TEST   pp.112-115

1. ② **2.** ⑤ **3.** ① **4.** ③ **5.** ③ **6.** ① **7.** ⑤ **8.** ④
9. ① **10.** Unless **11.** not only, but also **12.** ④
13. either ice cream or cake **14.** what happened to him **15.** As soon as you get home **16.** ⑤
17. ④ **18.** Who do you think knows
19. if[whether] Carl has a pet **20.** when I can visit Korea **21.** since **22.** if[If] **23.** As
24. Neither Mom nor I like to go shopping
25. Nobody knows who stole **26.** ②, ③ **27.** ③
28. ③ **29.** O **30.** X, rains **31.** O **32.** am → are
33. where will he visit → where he will visit

---

1 either A or B: A와 B 둘 중 하나

2	though: 비록 ~하지만
3	의문사가 없는 경우의 간접의문문: if[whether] + 주어 + 동사
4	if: 만일 ~라면 / unless: ~하지 않으면
5	① is he → he is ② Do you guess when → When do you guess ④ who the window broke → who broke the window ⑤ Where can you tell me → Can you tell me where
6	② Either → Neither　③ and → nor ④ and also → but also　⑤ but → and
7	⑤ → I wonder if[whether] he is interested in art.
8	①, ②, ③, ⑤는 '만일 ~라면'의 의미이고, ④는 '~인지 아닌지'의 의미이다.
9	②, ③, ④, ⑤는 '~ 때문에'의 의미이고, ①은 '~한 이래로'의 의미이다.
10	unless: ~하지 않으면(= if ~ not)
11	not only A but also B: A뿐만 아니라 B도(= B as well as A)
12	보기와 ④는 '~함에 따라'의 의미이고, ①, ③은 '~할 때', ②, ⑤는 '~ 때문에'의 의미이다.
13	either A or B: A와 B 둘 중 하나
14	의문사가 있는 간접의문문에서 의문사가 주어일 때는 「의문사 + 동사」의 어순으로 쓴다.
15	as soon as: ~하자마자
16	whenever: ~할 때마다
17	④ unless: ~하지 않으면(= if ~ not) (Unless → If)
18	주절의 동사가 think, believe, guess, suppose 등인 경우 의문사를 맨 앞에 둔다.
19	의문사가 없는 경우의 간접의문문: if[whether] + 주어 + 동사
20	의문사가 있는 경우의 간접의문문: 의문사 + 주어 + 동사
21	since: ~ 때문에 / since: ~한 이래로
22	if: ~인지 아닌지 / if: 만일 ~라면
23	as: ~ 때문에 / as: ~함에 따라
24	neither A nor B: A도 B도 아닌
25	의문사가 있는 간접의문문에서 의문사가 주어일 때는 「의문사 + 동사」의 어순으로 쓴다.
26	② as → since　③ when I'll arrive → when I arrive
27	a. was → were　e. have → has
28	・ is he → he is　・ though → because[since, as]
29	B as well as A에서 B에 동사의 수를 일치시킨다.
30	조건을 나타내는 부사절에서는 현재시제로 미래를 나타낸다.
31	although: 비록 ~하지만
32	both A and B는 복수 취급한다.
33	의문사가 있는 경우의 간접의문문: 의문사 + 주어 + 동사

CHAPTER
09 관계사

UNIT 01 관계대명사

CHECK UP　　　　　　　　　　　　p.118

1. ⓐ　**2.** ⓑ　**3.** ⓒ

PRACTICE　　　　　　　　　　　　p.119

STEP 1	**1.** What　**2.** that　**3.** which **4.** whose　**5.** whom
STEP 2	**1.** who → whose **2.** what → which[that] **3.** that → what / the things that[which] **4.** which → who[that]
STEP 3	**1.** I have a parrot whose feathers are very colorful and attractive.　**2.** The newspaper which[that] was delivered this morning was wet.　**3.** The reporter interviewed a woman who[that] won first prize in a contest.
STEP 4	**1.** a boyfriend whose hobby is the same　**2.** the first man that walked on the moon　**3.** The website which compares the prices

---

UNIT 02 관계부사

CHECK UP　　　　　　　　　　　　p.120

1. ⓐ　**2.** ⓑ　**3.** ⓑ

PRACTICE　　　　　　　　　　　　p.121

STEP 1	**1.** when　**2.** how　**3.** where　**4.** why
STEP 2	**1.** where　**2.** how　**3.** when　**4.** why
STEP 3	**1.** Tomorrow is the day when the shopping mall will start its big sale. **2.** I don't know the reason why my grades are lower than I expected. **3.** The video clip shows how rice cakes are cooked.
STEP 4	**1.** the reason why　**2.** how you fixed **3.** the day when　**4.** the store where

주의해야 할 관계사

CHECK UP   p.122

1. ⓐ   2. ⓑ

PRACTICE   p.123

STEP 1	1. which 2. sitting 3. which 4. where
STEP 2	1. X 2. which were 3. that 4. that are 5. X
STEP 3	1. who didn't[did not] reply 2. where we slept for one night 3. which are still loved by many children
STEP 4	1. a teacher everyone 2. made of[from] cotton 3. whom you talked 4. where I met

---

UNIT 04   복합관계사

CHECK UP   p.124

1. ⓑ   2. ⓒ   3. ⓑ

PRACTICE   p.125

STEP 1	1. Wherever 2. whomever 3. However 4. Whichever
STEP 2	1. However 2. whenever 3. whoever
STEP 3	1. Wherever 2. whenever 3. whoever 4. whatever
STEP 4	1. Whoever auditions 2. Whatever happens 3. However angry you are 4. Whenever I meet Ben

---

GRAMMAR FOR WRITING   pp.126-127

A   1. whom Noah is talking   2. what I bought for her   3. which made the bread softer 4. Whatever she says   5. However hard I tried   6. how the artist painted   7. where I enjoyed surfing

B   1. Einstein is the scientist I admire
2. a man whose dream was to make films
3. a company that makes LED monitors
4. that you told me about yesterday
5. is the time when you should think about
6. The girls standing in front of the airport

C   1. why he is upset with me   2. where I used to play soccer with friends   3. when we went on a field trip   4. that is interested in politics   5. whose ambition is to win the championship   6. how his company makes money

D   1. where[in which] we spent the last weekend
2. who[that] is grilling some meat
3. whose hat is purple
4. which[that] I am holding

REVIEW TEST   pp.128-131

1. ② 2. ④ 3. ④ 4. ② 5. ① 6. ⑤ 7. ① 8. ①
9. ④ 10. ⑤ 11. which 12. that are 13. ②
14. where 15. What 16. Whenever 17. which
18. The store which[that] sells my favorite type of bags is closed today.   19. They didn't say the reason why[for which] the game was canceled.
20. I saw a building whose roof collapsed.
21. However fast I ran 22. Whenever she meets her friends 23. ③ 24. anything that you will regret later 25. where I met an old friend of mine
26. ①, ②, ④ 27. ③ 28. ④ 29. X, What[The thing that[which]] 30. O 31. X, why[for which]
32. that → which 33. what → which[that], who → which

1   사람이 선행사일 때 주격 관계대명사는 that, who이다.
2   사람이 선행사인 목적격 관계대명사는 whom이다. / 전치사 바로 뒤에는 관계대명사 who나 that을 쓸 수 없다.
3   사물이 선행사인 주격 관계대명사는 which이다. / 관계대명사 that은 계속적 용법으로 쓸 수 없다.
4   장소가 선행사인 관계부사 where
5   whoever: ~하는 누구나
6   ⑤ Whatever: 무엇을[이] ~할지라도 (What → Whatever)
7   ① 선행사 the way와 관계부사 how는 함께 쓰지 않는다. (the way how → how[the way])
8   whoever: 누가 ~할지라도(양보의 부사절)
9   앞의 빈칸에는 소유격 관계대명사 whose, 뒤의 빈칸에는 앞 문장 전체를 선행사로 하는 계속적 용법의 관계대명사 which가 와야 한다.

10 사람이 선행사인 계속적 용법의 주격 관계대명사 who

11 목적격 관계대명사는 생략 가능하다.

12 「주격 관계대명사 + be동사」는 뒤에 형용사구[분사구]가 올 때 생략 가능하다.

13 ① → what ③ → which ④ → whom ⑤ → whose

14 장소가 선행사인 관계부사 where

15 선행사를 포함한 관계대명사 what

16 whenever: ~할 때마다

17 사물이 선행사인 계속적 용법의 주격 관계대명사 which

18 사물이 선행사인 주격 관계대명사 which, that

19 이유가 선행사인 관계부사 why(= for which)

20 소유격 관계대명사 whose

21 however: 아무리 ~하더라도(양보의 부사절)

22 whenever: ~할 때마다(시간의 부사절)

23 전치사가 관계대명사 앞에 쓰인 경우 관계대명사는 생략할 수 없다.

24 목적격 관계대명사 that

25 계속적 용법의 관계부사 where

26 ③ who → whom ⑤ that → who

27 b. which → where c. is talking → talking[who [that] is talking]

28 · that was → which was

29 선행사를 포함한 관계대명사 what

30 wherever: ~하는 곳은 어디든지

31 이유가 선행사인 관계부사 why(= for which)

32 that은 계속적 용법으로 쓸 수 없다. 앞 문장 전체를 선행사로 하는 계속적 용법의 관계대명사 which가 와야 한다.

33 사물이 선행사인 목적격 관계대명사 which[that] / 사물이 선행사인 계속적 용법의 주격 관계대명사 which

STEP 2	1. would you say 2. would have 3. would be 4. had not bought
STEP 3	1. lived, would see 2. had had, could have gone 3. hadn't[had not] done, couldn't[could not] play
STEP 4	1. were, would pay 2. had had, would have asked 3. had gone, wouldn't be

UNIT 02 I wish, as if, It's time + 가정법

CHECK UP   p.136

1. ⓒ 2. ⓐ 3. ⓑ

PRACTICE   p.137

STEP 1	1. were 2. had attended 3. had made 4. went
STEP 2	1. the weather were nice 2. I had listened to 3. she were an expert on the environment 4. it had been his fault
STEP 3	1. were 2. had saved 3. knew 4. hadn't[had not] eaten
STEP 4	1. I wish I had been more active 2. as if he were my father 3. It is time you stopped complaining

UNIT 03 주의해야 할 가정법

CHECK UP   p.138

1. ⓒ 2. ⓑ 3. ⓑ

CHAPTER 10 가정법

UNIT 01 가정법 과거, 가정법 과거완료, 혼합 가정법

CHECK UP   p.134

1. ⓑ 2. ⓒ 3. ⓑ

PRACTICE   p.135

| STEP 1 | 1. were 2. will 3. would be 4. hadn't told |

PRACTICE   p.139

STEP 1	1. But 2. Were it not for 3. to take a nap
STEP 2	1. Were it warmer 2. But for the internet 3. Without my teacher's advice
STEP 3	1. to make friends 2. A wise man 3. With my brother's help
STEP 4	1. Without my parents' support 2. Had it not been for his injury 3. A British person would not use that word

GRAMMAR FOR WRITING pp.140-141

A 1. were, could take 2. Without your phone call 3. With Stacy's help 4. had spoken, could have been 5. had not snowed, would go 6. as if she had had

B 1. talks as if he knew 2. It is time we took a break 3. Your family would not blame you 4. It would be nice to have 5. Were I a superhero, I could help 6. Had it not been for her beautiful voice

C 1. played, could join 2. had had, could have answered 3. I had been 4. had seen 5. hadn't[had not] played, wouldn't[would not] have won 6. I could speak

D 1. had an umbrella 2. could ride it 3. had studied harder

REVIEW TEST pp.142-145

1. ② 2. ⑤ 3. ④ 4. ③ 5. ④ 6. ④ 7. ⑤ 8. ②
9. ③ 10. ④ 11. ② 12. ② 13. ② 14. wish my house were 15. Were I you 16. Without the security camera 17. ① 18. had, could pick 19. hadn't[had not] fastened, would have been 20. I wish I had read a lot of books 21. An honest person would not say 22. Without a travel guide, I could not have found 23. It's time we went home 24. ⑤ 25. Had he asked me 26. ②, ④, ⑤ 27. ② 28. ④ 29. O 30. X, had not lost 31. O 32. go → went 33. showed → had shown

1 가정법 과거: If + 주어 + 동사의 과거형, 주어 + would[could, might] + 동사원형

2 가정법 과거완료: If + 주어 + had v-ed, 주어 + would[could, might] + have v-ed

3 혼합 가정법: If + 주어 + had v-ed, 주어 + would[could, might] + 동사원형

4 I wish + 가정법 과거완료: I wish + 주어 + had v-ed

5 if절의 동사가 were일 때 접속사 if를 생략할 수 있으며, 이때 주어와 동사의 위치가 바뀐다.

6 ④ if절의 동사가 had일 때 접속사 if를 생략할 수 있으며, 이때 주어와 동사의 위치가 바뀐다. (I had known → Had I known / If I had known)

7 ⑤ 혼합 가정법: If + 주어 + had v-ed, 주어 + would[could, might] + 동사원형 (would have had → would have)

8 without, but for, if it were not for, were it not for: ~가 없다면

9 혼합 가정법: If + 주어 + had v-ed, 주어 + would[could, might] + 동사원형

10 I wish + 가정법 과거완료: I wish + 주어 + had v-ed

11 as if + 가정법 과거: as if + 주어 + 동사의 과거형

12 부사구가 가정법의 if절을 대신해 쓰일 수 있다.

13 to부정사구가 가정법의 if절을 대신해 쓰일 수 있다.

14 I wish + 가정법 과거: I wish + 주어 + 동사의 과거형

15 if절의 동사가 were일 때 접속사 if를 생략할 수 있으며, 이때 주어와 동사의 위치가 바뀐다.

16 without: ~가 없었다면

17 without, but for, if it had not been for, had it not been for: ~가 없었다면

18 가정법 과거: If + 주어 + 동사의 과거형, 주어 + would[could, might] + 동사원형

19 가정법 과거완료: If + 주어 + had v-ed, 주어 + would[could, might] + have v-ed

20 I wish + 가정법 과거완료: I wish + 주어 + had v-ed

21 주어가 가정법의 if절을 대신해서 쓰일 수 있다. (= If he/she were an honest person, he/she ...)

22 without: ~가 없었다면

23 It's time + 가정법: It's time + 주어 + 동사의 과거형

24 ⓐ were ⓑ would ⓒ had ⓓ have

25 if절의 동사가 had일 때 접속사 if를 생략할 수 있으며, 이때 주어와 동사의 위치가 바뀐다.

26 ① Were I → Had I been / If I had been ③ know → had known

27 c. have had → had had d. meet → to meet

28 · woke → had woken

29 가정법 과거완료: If + 주어 + had v-ed, 주어 + would[could, might] + have v-ed

30 I wish + 가정법 과거완료: I wish + 주어 + had v-ed

31 부사구가 가정법의 if절을 대신해서 쓰일 수 있다.

32 It's time + 가정법: It's time + 주어 + 동사의 과거형

33 I wish + 가정법 과거완료: I wish + 주어 + had v-ed

UNIT 01 수의 일치

CHECK UP — p.148

1. ⓑ 2. ⓐ

PRACTICE — p.149

STEP 1	1. Is 2. is 3. were 4. come
STEP 2	1. are → is 2. were → was
	3. is → are 4. are → is
STEP 3	1. is 2. has 3. is 4. seems
STEP 4	1. Someone is sitting 2. Physics is
	3. What Connor said was
	4. Reading fantasy novels is

UNIT 02 시제의 일치

CHECK UP — p.150

1. ⓒ 2. ⓐ 3. ⓑ

PRACTICE — p.151

STEP 1	1. had lost 2. would study 3. is
	4. was
STEP 2	1. is 2. discovered 3. invented
	4. has
STEP 3	1. was 2. would attend 3. is
	4. was
STEP 4	1. water freezes 2. broke out
	3. practice makes 4. he would go

UNIT 03 화법

CHECK UP — p.152

1. ⓑ 2. ⓒ

PRACTICE — p.153

STEP 1	1. told 2. why he had called 3. if
	4. not to go
STEP 2	1. said (that) his business was
	2. told me (that) she had fallen in love
	with me 3. asked us if[whether] we
	had seen 4. told me (that) I would
	get 5. asked us who had broken the
	vase 6. advised[told] him to drink
	eight glasses 7. told[ordered] the
	children not to run
STEP 3	1. me when I would get 2. me to be
	3. if[whether] I was 4. Sarah where
	she had bought

GRAMMAR FOR WRITING — pp.154-155

A 1. Two hours is enough time 2. said (that) experience is 3. Sarah and Brad go
4. asked me why I was[had been] late
5. asked me if[whether] I liked 6. learned (that) water covers 7. was returned

B 1. Whether you like it or not is
2. Collecting home run balls is
3. They said that they wanted to change
4. I realized that I had left
5. My teacher ordered us not to make
6. the young run faster than the old

C 1. (that) life is short, but art is long
2. if[whether] I had medicine for a headache
3. (that) he had found his cell phone in the bathroom 4. not to blame him for the accident 5. (that) blue jeans were invented in America in 1873 6. (that) the earth rotates once a day 7. when I had seen the strange man with a moustache

D 1. Every seat was 2. Each player has
3. A number of fans are

REVIEW TEST — pp.156-159

1. ③ 2. ③ 3. ② 4. ⑤ 5. ④ 6. ④ 7. ⑤ 8. ⑤
9. ③ 10. ② 11. ① 12. ⑤ 13. expands
14. was 15. is 16. ④ 17. My secretary told me (that) someone had called me several times.
18. My professor advised[told] me to study

marketing abroad.   **19.** The waiter asked me how I liked my steak.   **20.** Every country has **21.** goes around the sun   **22.** asked me if [whether] I liked   **23.** I thought that he would be **24.** not to tell his secret   **25.** The sick are taken care of   **26.** ②, ⑤   **27.** ④   **28.** ③   **29.** X, has **30.** O   **31.** X, were   **32.** I liked → if[whether] I liked   **33.** don't be → not to be

1 주절의 시제가 과거인 경우 종속절에는 과거나 과거완료가 와야 한다. -one은 단수 취급한다.

2 역사적 사실은 항상 과거시제를 쓴다.

3 일반적 사실은 항상 현재시제를 쓴다.

4 의문사가 없는 의문문의 화법 전환에서 접속사는 whether나 if를 쓴다.

5 명령문의 간접화법 전환: tell[ask, order, advise, ...] + 목적어 + to-v

6 ④ 시간은 단수 취급한다. (are → is)

7 ⑤ 일반적 사실은 현재시제를 쓴다. (stayed → stay)

8 부정 명령문의 간접화법 전환: tell[ask, order, advise, ...] + 목적어 + not to-v

9 「a number of + 복수명사」(많은 ~)는 복수 취급하고, 「the number of + 복수명사」(~의 수)는 단수 취급한다.

10 동명사구가 주어인 경우 단수 취급하고, 「the + 형용사」(~한 사람들)는 복수 취급한다.

11 금액과 -one은 단수 취급한다.

12 ① don't touch → not to touch   ② am → are ③ was → is   ④ are → is

13 과학적 사실은 항상 현재시제를 쓴다.

14 역사적 사실은 항상 과거시제를 쓴다.

15 과목명은 단수 취급한다.

16 ④ 의문사가 없는 의문문의 간접화법 전환: ask (+ 목적어) + if[whether] + 주어 + 동사 (had anyone seen → anyone had seen)

17 평서문의 간접화법 전환: tell + 목적어 (+ that) + 주어 + 동사

18 명령문의 간접화법 전환: tell[ask, order, advise, ...] + 목적어 + to-v

19 의문사가 있는 의문문의 간접화법 전환: ask (+ 목적어) + 의문사 + 주어 + 동사

20 every는 단수 취급한다.

21 과학적 사실은 항상 현재시제를 쓴다.

22 의문사가 없는 의문문의 간접화법 전환: ask (+ 목적어) + if[whether] + 주어 + 동사

23 주절의 시제가 과거인 경우 종속절에는 과거나 과거완료가 와야 한다.

24 부정 명령문의 간접화법 전환: tell[ask, order, advise, ...] + 목적어 + not to-v

25 「the + 형용사」(~한 사람들)는 복수 취급한다.

26 ① have → has   ③ ends → ended   ④ are → is

27 a. does he support → he supports   e. are → is

28 · air was → air is
· the dead rises → the dead rise

29 국가명은 단수 취급한다.

30 주절의 시제가 현재일 때 종속절에는 모든 시제가 올 수 있다. 여기서는 과거의 일을 말하고 있으므로 과거시제를 쓴다.

31 「a number of + 복수명사」(많은 ~)는 복수 취급한다.

32 의문사가 없는 의문문의 간접화법 전환: ask (+ 목적어) + if[whether] + 주어 + 동사

33 부정 명령문의 간접화법 전환: tell[ask, order, advise, ...] + 목적어 + not to-v

CHAPTER 12 기타 구문

UNIT 01   강조, 부정구문, 병렬

CHECK UP   p.162

1. ⓐ   **2.** ⓐ   **3.** ©

PRACTICE   p.163

STEP 1	**1.** do know **2.** writing **3.** listening
STEP 2	**1.** did study **2.** was Brian that **3.** it that revealed
STEP 3	**1.** all **2.** Neither **3.** always
STEP 4	**1.** It was in the bathroom that **2.** None of us have been abroad **3.** Not every girl likes to play **4.** not only skiing but also snowboarding

UNIT 02   도치, 생략, 동격

CHECK UP   p.164

1. ©   **2.** ⓐ

PRACTICE   p.165

STEP 1	**1.** was a tree house **2.** do I **3.** could I understand
STEP 2	**1.** is a famous Italian restaurant **2.** does Caleb come **3.** have I seen

STEP 3	**1.** 뒤의 is an actor **2.** I was
	3. 뒤의 leave now **4.** she was
STEP 4	**1.** sat a butterfly **2.** did I dream of
	winning **3.** the tallest structure in
	Paris, is beautiful **4.** So do I

GRAMMAR FOR WRITING pp.166-167

A 1. Life is not always 2. Neither do I
3. do I drink cola 4. are several banks
5. was yesterday that we had dinner 6. did
I think 7. teaching[to teach] others and
learning[to learn]

B 1. Not every cat likes to play 2. can speak
French fluently, but I can't 3. neither playing
nor watching sports 4. It was my teacher
that taught me 5. Though smart, Jay
doesn't always 6. but I do like to eat it

C 1. Ann is usually a joyful person, but she
does look sad today. 2. It was Frank that
sent flowers on my birthday. 3. On the table
were big boxes and baskets. 4. It was at
Kim's store that I bought the helmet.
5. When together, they look happier.
6. This is my favorite painting by Van Gogh,
Sunflowers. / This is *Sunflowers*, my favorite
painting by Van Gogh.

D 1. None of 2. neither of 3. Not all of

REVIEW TEST pp.168-171

1. ③ 2. ⑤ 3. ② 4. ① 5. ⑤ 6. ④ 7. ⑤ 8. ②
9. ④ 10. ④ 11. I am 12. ③ 13. ⑤ 14. It was
in the bathroom that I found my ring. 15. I did
tell you yesterday. 16. When was it that you
decided to become a reporter? 17. ① 18. am
not always 19. neither am I 20. have I seen
such a great live concert before 21. are the
important files 22. watch, the most expensive
product in this shop 23. not only boring but also
unrealistic 24. angry, he just cries 25. Hardly
can I sleep at night 26. ③, ④, ⑤ 27. ③ 28. ④
29. O 30. X, It 31. X, is a famous temple 32. I
do → do I 33. things are → are things, dance →
dancing

1 부정의 부사가 앞에 나올 경우의 도치: 부정의 부사 + 조동사 + 주어

2 과거 동사를 강조할 때 「did + 동사원형」을 쓴다.

3 so + 동사 + 주어(긍정문 뒤): ~도 또한 그렇다

4 등위 접속사로 연결되는 말은 동일한 문법 형태와 구조를 가져야 한다.

5 「It is[was] ~ that ....」에 의한 강조: 강조하고자 하는 부분을 It is[was]와 that 사이에 놓는다.

6 ④ 부정의 부사가 앞에 나올 경우의 도치: 부정의 부사 + do[does, did] + 주어 + 동사원형 (I knew → did I know)

7 ⑤ 등위 접속사로 연결되는 말은 동일한 문법 형태와 구조를 가져야 한다. (a sense of humor → humorous)

8 not + all: 모두 ~인 것은 아니다(부분 부정)

9 neither: 둘 다 ~ 않다(전체 부정)

10 not + all: 모두 ~인 것은 아니다(부분 부정)

11 부사절과 주절의 주어가 같고 부사절의 동사가 be동사인 경우 「주어 + be동사」는 생략 가능하다.

12 so + 동사 + 주어(긍정문 뒤): ~도 또한 그렇다

13 neither + 동사 + 주어(부정문 뒤): ~도 또한 그렇지 않다

14 「It is[was] ~ that ....」에 의한 강조: 강조하고자 하는 부분을 It is[was]와 that 사이에 놓는다.

15 과거 동사를 강조할 때 「did + 동사원형」을 쓴다.

16 의문사 강조: 의문사 + is[was] + it + that ...

17 ② the guest of today's show comes → comes the guest of today's show ③ did knew → did know ④ he did ask → did he ask ⑤ That → It

18 not + always: 항상 ~인 것은 아니다(부분 부정)

19 neither + 동사 + 주어(부정문 뒤): ~도 또한 그렇지 않다

20 부정의 부사가 앞에 나올 경우의 도치: 부정의 부사 + 조동사 + 주어

21 장소의 부사(구)가 문장 앞으로 나오는 경우의 도치: 부사(구) + 동사 + 주어

22 a white watch의 의미를 보충하기 위해 동격이 쓰였다.

23 등위 접속사로 연결되는 말은 동일한 문법 형태와 구조를 가져야 한다.

24 부사절과 주절의 주어가 같고 부사절의 동사가 be동사인 경우 「주어 + be동사」는 생략 가능하다.

25 부정의 부사가 앞에 나올 경우의 도치: 부정의 부사 + 조동사 + 주어

26 ① does looks → does look ② drink → drinking

27 b. I have → have I c. play → playing

28 · playing → plays

29 부정의 부사가 앞에 나올 경우의 도치: 부정의 부사 + 조동사 + 주어

30 「It is[was] ~ that ....」에 의한 강조: 강조하고자 하는 부분을 It is[was]와 that 사이에 놓는다.

31 장소의 부사(구)가 문장 앞으로 나오는 경우의 도치: 부사(구) + 동사 + 주어

32 neither + 동사 + 주어(부정문 뒤): ~도 또한 그렇지 않다

33 장소의 부사(구)가 문장 앞으로 나오는 경우의 도치: 부사(구) + 동사 + 주어 / 등위 접속사로 연결되는 말은 동일한 문법 형태와 구조를 가져야 한다.

workbook
Answer Key

GRAMMAR
Inside

LEVEL 3

GRAMMAR BASICS

01 문장의 성분 p.2

A 1. 보어 2. 수식어 3. 목적어 4. 동사 5. 주어
6. 동사 7. 주어 8. 수식어 9. 목적어 10. 보어

B 1. C 2. O 3. C 4. C 5. O, O 6. O, O
7. O 8. O, C 9. O, C 10. O, C

02 문장의 형식 p.3

A 1. 그 소년이 웃었다. (1형식) 2. 그가 내게 일어나라고
말했다. (5형식) 3. Maria는 의사가 되었다. (2형식)
4. 너는 오늘 아름다워 보인다. (2형식) 5. James가 네
게 이메일을 보냈다. (4형식) 6. 나는 학교에 가기 위해
버스를 탄다. (3형식) 7. 나의 어머니는 나를 밖에서 놀게
하셨다. (5형식) 8. 내 딸은 천사처럼 노래한다. (1형식)
9. 아빠가 내게 크리스마스 선물을 주셨다. (4형식)
10. 내 남동생은 스마트폰을 가지고 있지 않다. (3형식)

B 1. calm 2. me 3. is 4. playing 5. for
6. happy 7. beautiful 8. entered 9. finish
10. rises

03 구와 절 p.4

A 1. 구 2. 구 3. 절 4. 구 5. 절 6. 구 7. 절
8. 구 9. 절 10. 절

B 1. 명사 2. 부사 3. 부사 4. 명사 5. 명사 6. 부사
7. 형용사 8. 형용사 9. 부사 10. 형용사

UNIT 01 현재완료 pp.5-6

A 1. have taken 2. has been working
3. broke 4. have never had 5. since
6. has been 7. has been reading
8. reserved 9. for 10. have lost

B 1. bought 2. has worked / has been working
3. since 4. has been raining / has rained
5. talked 6. has gone 7. for 8. has lived /
has been living 9. saw 10. been

C 1. has gone to 2. have been 3. has been
snowing 4. have lost 5. has been working

D 1. 너는 그의 새 뮤직비디오를 본 적이 있니? 2. 그는
20대 때부터 가난한 사람들을 도와 왔다. 3. 나는 애니메
이션 영화 Frozen을 여러 번 보았다. 4. 그는 한 시간
넘게 소파에서 잠을 자고 있다. 5. 나는 방금 샤워를 했
다. 6. 그들은 10년째 중국어를 배우고 있다. 7. 그녀
는 그녀의 과학 교과서를 잃어버렸다. 8. 그들은 이미 식
사를 마쳤다. 9. 너는 베트남 국수를 먹어 본 적이 있니?
10. 아빠가 내 자전거를 고쳐 주셔서 나는 그것을 탈 수 있
다.

WRITING PRACTICE p.7

A 1. has just baked 2. failed the exam
3. has taken swimming lessons since / has
been taking swimming lessons since
4. has lived in the house for / has been living
in the house for 5. have met each other
6. Have you ever been to

B 1. have been learning taekwondo since
2. has been working in the basement since
3. The airplane has already taken off
/ The airplane has taken off already
4. He has overcooked the ramen
5. has not finished his homework
6. has never used the software before

UNIT 02 과거완료, 미래완료 pp.8-9

A 1. had never heard 2. will have been waiting
3. had been 4. had never skied 5. will have
finished 6. will have been raining 7. had

not done **8.** will have built **9.** had been swimming **10.** had never taken

B **1.** had learned **2.** will have seen **3.** will have lived / will have been living **4.** had existed **5.** will have cleaned **6.** had been broken **7.** will have been **8.** will have started **9.** had never heard **10.** had already eaten

C **1.** will have climbed **2.** had already heard **3.** had never been **4.** will have been working / will have worked **5.** had spent **6.** will have lived / will have been living **7.** had lived / lived **8.** had been **9.** had been / was **10.** had gone

D **1.** 이 책을 끝낼 무렵이면 너는 많은 것을 배우게 되었을 것이다. **2.** 그는 수리공이 오기 전까지 그것을 고치려고 애쓰고 있었다. **3.** 내일이면 일주일 넘게 눈이 오는 것이다. **4.** 그는 뮤지컬 배우가 되기 전에 코미디언으로 일했었다. **5.** 그는 지도를 잃어버려서 낯선 사람들에게 길을 물었다. **6.** 내가 방에 들어갔을 때 그녀는 막 피아노 치는 것을 멈추었다. **7.** 그 밴드는 그들의 첫 번째 앨범이 나오기도 전에 인기가 많았다. **8.** 경찰이 모퉁이를 돌았을 때 그 도둑은 이미 사라졌다. **9.** 내가 그 컴퓨터에 있는 파일들을 지워버려서 나는 모든 것을 다시 입력했다. **10.** 그는 어머니를 만나기 전까지 10년간 그의 어머니를 찾고 있었다.

WRITING PRACTICE   p.10

A **1.** had just left **2.** had lived **3.** will have changed **4.** had been playing **5.** will have studied / will have been studying **6.** had never driven

B **1.** He will have returned home **2.** had already gone to the gym / had gone to the gym already **3.** He will have been learning the cello for ten years **4.** had worked at the company for thirty years **5.** My brother's birthday party had already ended / My brother's birthday party had ended already **6.** had been working in the garden when the phone rang

REVIEW TEST   pp.11-13

1. ③ **2.** ④ **3.** ② **4.** ⑤ **5.** has lost **6.** have been doing **7.** will have been playing **8.** ④

9. ④ **10.** ④ **11.** ⑤ **12.** ③ **13.** ③ **14.** ② **15.** ③ **16.** ③ **17.** had **18.** has played / has been playing **19.** I had been reading the magazine for two hours **20.** We will have finished eating dinner **21.** I have just heard the news of her marriage **22.** He has never driven **23.** had already started / had started already **24.** have studied → had studied / studied **25.** be → have been

CHAPTER
02 조동사

UNIT 01   can, may, must, should
pp.14-15

A **1.** close **2.** can **3.** must not **4.** May **5.** might **6.** cannot **7.** see **8.** could **9.** have to **10.** Could

B **1.** can **2.** have to **3.** wasn't able to **4.** is able to **5.** don't have[need] to

C **1.** will be able to find **2.** must not drive **3.** may[might] want **4.** can't[cannot] know **5.** don't have[need] to bring / need not bring **6.** must be

D **1.** may drink some water from the refrigerator **2.** might snow during the night **3.** must be very hungry **4.** can speak Spanish **5.** should turn it down **6.** must not make any noise

WRITING PRACTICE   p.16

A **1.** may[might] be **2.** could[was able to] read **3.** don't have to discuss **4.** must be interested in **5.** can't[cannot] be true **6.** can[may] I go

B **1.** You must not tell my secret **2.** May I see your ID card **3.** Could you pass me the salt **4.** I will be able to do the volunteer work **5.** You should be honest with your friends **6.** Jerry might fall in love

UNIT 02 had better, ought to, used to, 조동사 + have v-ed pp.17-18

A 1. had better 2. turn 3. must have been
4. used to 5. have bought 6. used to
7. to eat 8. ought not to 9. can't have told
10. had better not

B 1. has better → had better 2. playing →
play 3. ought to not → ought not to
4. must → should 5. was used to → used to
6. read → have read 7. had not better →
had better not 8. going → gone
9. knowing → know 10. would → used to

C 1. used to 2. had better not 3. ought to
4. can't 5. shouldn't 6. must

D 1. used to be very shy 2. had better go to
see a doctor 3. ought to say sorry to him
4. may have seen him 5. should have
arrived here 6. must have forgotten

WRITING PRACTICE p.19

A 1. ought to respect 2. can't have forgotten
3. must have learned 4. had better not eat
5. used to go skiing 6. used to chat online

B 1. Jay might have found his wallet 2. Sue
had better not follow his advice 3. You
ought not to stay out 4. My father used to
tell me 5. I shouldn't have wasted time
6. Brad used to be afraid of ghosts

REVIEW TEST pp.20-22

1. ① 2. ② 3. ④ 4. ③ 5. ⑤ 6. ④ 7. ① 8. ④
9. ② 10. can't[cannot] 11. have 12. ④ 13. ③
14. can't[cannot] be 15. used to live 16. should
have waited 17. ① 18. I will be able to attend
19. I should have left 20. don't have[need] to
21. used to 22. You ought not to touch anything
23. He may have lost his bag at the station
24. drinking → drink 25. fight → have fought

CHAPTER 03 수동태

UNIT 01 수동태의 의미와 형태 pp.23-24

A 1. was canceled 2. is spoken 3. repaired
4. appeared 5. was being played
6. resemble 7. will be remembered 8. are
being paid 9. cannot be explained 10. has
been reviewed

B 1. be stored 2. being washed 3. lacks[is
lacking] 4. been delayed 5. was caused
6. be shown 7. been killed 8. rise 9. held
10. been translated

C 1. My flight ticket was booked by me
2. has already been solved by Jim 3. will be
delivered to you by them 4. must be taken
seriously by us 5. is being painted by my
father 6. The novel was written by Mr. Brown
7. are cleaned by us 8. Computers can be
used by us 9. was being watched by the
police officer 10. has been broken by my
little brother 11. My car has to be repaired
by them 12. was stolen from my back
pocket by someone 13. is being carried by
the hotel staff 14. The killer was arrested
by the police

WRITING PRACTICE p.25

A 1. happened 2. resemble my mother
3. was fixed by my father 4. will be
discussed 5. is being repaired 6. have
been married

B 1. was made by a famous director 2. My
smartphone disappeared on the bus 3. This
project must be finished 4. The wall should
be repainted 5. This city has been damaged
by a tsunami 6. The event is being filmed by

UNIT 02 4형식, 5형식 문장의 수동태
pp.26-27

A 1. to 2. to 3. for 4. to enter 5. blowing
6. to stay 7. Buddy 8. to wear 9. playing

10. to help

B **1.** Scott → to Scott **2.** for → to **3.** to → for **4.** of → for **5.** to popular → popular **6.** break → breaking[to break] **7.** smile → to smile **8.** made → making[to make] **9.** for → to **10.** turn → to turn

C **1.** was bought for me by my uncle **2.** was made to stay after school by his teacher **3.** was seen entering[to enter] my house by one of my neighbors **4.** was made popular by the movie **5.** is considered to be an expert in this field by them **6.** was taught to us by Mr. Flores last year, were taught Spanish by Mr. Flores last year **7.** was given the Best Singer Award by them, was given to the artist by them **8.** were bought for my brother by me **9.** was heard crying[to cry] at midnight by me **10.** was made for me by my boyfriend **11.** was elected the leader of the project by us **12.** will be shown the new schedule by me, will be shown to you by me

WRITING PRACTICE   p.28

A **1.** was sent to my father **2.** was bought for my mother **3.** was called a national hero **4.** was heard calling[to call] my name **5.** was made to leave **6.** are not allowed to buy

B **1.** was given a file by my friend **2.** should be shown to the clerk **3.** have been built for the public **4.** was made for my sisters **5.** He was seen lying on the beach **6.** Matt was advised to exercise regularly

UNIT 03 주의해야 할 수동태   pp.29-30

A **1.** with **2.** made fun of by **3.** with **4.** with **5.** to be **6.** about **7.** looked down on by **8.** that **9.** with **10.** is believed

B **1.** by their parents **2.** were run over **3.** was invented **4.** to be **5.** is believed **6.** reported **7.** composed of **8.** known to **9.** disappointed with[at] **10.** surprised at

C **1.** were stepped on by the elephant

2. was disappointed with[at] his bad behavior **3.** is interested in ice dancing **4.** was looked up to by a lot of people **5.** is reported that a lot of animals are killed by hunters, are reported to be killed by hunters **6.** was surprised at the math test score **7.** is believed that exercising regularly is good for health, is believed to be good for health **8.** is thought that harmful insects are disgusting, are thought to be disgusting **9.** should be taken care of by the government **10.** were pleased with my progress **11.** is said that John is a very selfish person, is said to be a very selfish person

WRITING PRACTICE   p.31

A **1.** was broken into by a thief **2.** was made fun of by my friends **3.** is said that **4.** to live in this house **5.** is covered with dust **6.** was surprised at the news

B **1.** is believed to bring luck **2.** is reported that women live longer than men **3.** are taken care of by my grandfather **4.** I was satisfied with your service **5.** This notebook was made from recycled paper **6.** He is said to be the best painter

REVIEW TEST   pp.32-34

1. ④ **2.** ④ **3.** ③ **4.** ⑤ **5.** ⑤ **6.** ② **7.** ④ **8.** ③ **9.** ⑤ **10.** ④ **11.** be laughed at **12.** to set the table **13.** was fixed **14.** ③ **15.** is called big brother **16.** was lent to me **17.** was said to earn **18.** ④ **19.** is being tested **20.** is interested in **21.** ⑤ **22.** table has been reserved by a lady **23.** Onions are believed to be good for **24.** to → for **25.** at → with

CHAPTER 04 부정사

7. 그는 길을 물어볼 사람을 찾는 중이다. 8. 여기에는 나를 귀찮게 할 사람이 없다. 9. 나는 함께 어울릴 친구들이 많다. 10. 그는 얼음 위에서 넘어지지 않기 위해 매우 조심했다.

UNIT 01 명사적 용법의 to부정사   pp.35-36

A 1. to talk 2. to buy 3. to learn 4. It 5. to meet 6. it 7. to cheat 8. To wear 9. to win 10. to buy

B 1. to sow 2. To eat / Eating 3. to believe 4. to finish 5. to blow / blowing 6. to build 7. to create / creating 8. to brush 9. to go 10. to do

C 1. It will be a great pleasure 2. It is a good habit 3. to see the stars in the sky 4. what to do 5. where to get off 6. when to start

D 1. how to play 2. where to go 3. what to eat 4. what to wear 5. where to find 6. when to leave

WRITING PRACTICE   p.37

A 1. It is not easy to keep 2. to study medicine 3. decided not to go 4. it lonely to stay home 5. when to tell the news 6. what to wear

B 1. The important thing is not to give up 2. It is a good idea to order 3. think it rude to make noise 4. know what to do for her parents 5. The bad weather made it hard to do 6. The next step is to sprinkle cheese

UNIT 02 형용사적 용법, 부사적 용법의 to부정사   pp.38-39

A 1. to do 2. to disturb 3. to talk to 4. to go 5. To see 6. to wait 7. are to be 8. to talk about 9. to save 10. to be

B 1. to do 2. to take care of 3. to ride 4. to rely on 5. to succeed 6. to[in order to] send 7. to learn 8. to return 9. to invite 10. to spend

C 1. 식탁 위에 먹을 것이 아무것도 없었다. 2. 그는 결국 그의 가족에게 돌아오게 되어 있었다. 3. 근처에서 물을 찾을 수 없었다. 4. 그녀는 잠에서 깨자 학교에 늦었다는 걸 알았다. 5. 소풍을 가기에 날씨가 정말 좋다. 6. 오늘 나오지 않은 것을 보니 그는 아픈 것임에 틀림없다.

D 1. to keep 2. to release 3. to see 4. to finish 5. to pass

WRITING PRACTICE   p.40

A 1. to solve the problem 2. To see them 3. difficult to understand 4. is to direct 5. angry to know 6. to[in order to] fall asleep easily

B 1. not to pay late fees 2. the best time to book a flight 3. borrow something to write with 4. was to meet her aunt at the station 5. to be a hundred years old 6. The remake of the movie was to be a success

UNIT 03 to부정사의 의미상의 주어, 시제, 태   pp.41-42

A 1. for you 2. of him 3. to know 4. to have run out 5. to have learned 6. for me 7. to be called 8. to be taken care of 9. to have eaten 10. of you

B 1. for her 2. of him 3. to be 4. to be done 5. of her 6. to have been 7. to have been shot 8. for the old lady 9. of you 10. to be replaced

C 1. of her 2. for you 3. for me 4. of him 5. of them 6. for me 7. of him 8. for her 9. of you 10. for him

D 1. to be 2. to have walked 3. to have been well cared for 4. to have stolen 5. to have 6. to have been adopted

WRITING PRACTICE   p.43

A 1. for the child to understand 2. seems to be 3. to have been stolen 4. brave of you to tell 5. seem to work 6. to be very popular

B 1. seems to have failed 2. hard for me to make kimchi 3. Your ankle seems to be broken 4. very rude of him not to apologize 5. needs to be refrigerated 6. seems to have been written

UNIT 04 목적격 보어로 쓰이는 부정사
pp.44-45

A 1. make 2. smile 3. to stay 4. leaking
5. sleep 6. fix 7. knocking 8. to pay
9. recover 10. start

B 1. hurting[hurt] 2. to transfer 3. to play
4. delivered 5. flying[fly] 6. feel
7. burning[burn] 8. buy[to buy] 9. to grow
10. entering[enter]

C 1. to be 2. playing[play] 3. download
4. deleted 5. standing[stand] 6. to give
7. to wake up 8. exercise 9. to do 10. take

D 1. to quit 2. speak 3. biting[bite] 4. to
finish 5. cut 6. to arrive 7. hurting[hurt]
8. waste

WRITING PRACTICE
p.46

A 1. let me try 2. felt my body shivering
[shiver] 3. the dirty clothes washed
4. a strange sound coming[come] 5. made
him become 6. helped them escape[to
escape]

B 1. gets me to eat vegetables every day
2. helps him to hear better 3. smelled
someone baking bread 4. made her
daughter read a variety of books 5. warned
the driver to lower 6. saw a star falling from
the sky

UNIT 05 to부정사 구문, 독립부정사
pp.47-48

A 1. to go 2. To tell 3. warm enough
4. to buy 5. to eat 6. enough 7. to say
8. To make 9. to download 10. To make

B 1. to stay 2. so to speak 3. to see
4. enough to go 5. Strange to say
6. To make 7. cute enough 8. To be frank
9. to study 10. to sit

C 1. 그 집은 살기에 너무 오래되었다. 2. 우선, 제가 오늘
여기에 왜 있는지 설명하겠습니다. 3. 그 소파는 그가 잘
수 있을 만큼 충분히 편안했다. 4. 너무 추워서 우리는 바
다에서 수영할 수 없다. 5. 사실대로 말하면, 이 소파는
당신이 생각하는 것만큼 비싸지 않다. 6. 그 영화는 사람
들을 많이 웃게 할 정도로 충분히 재미있었다. 7. 이상한
이야기지만, 나는 그녀가 지금 무언가를 숨기고 있다고 생

각한다. 8. 그 개는 그의 전 주인을 기억할 만큼 충분히
똑똑했다. 9. 간단히 말해서, 그는 그의 가족을 위해 삶을
살았다. 10. Bob은 너무 피곤해서 그의 여자 친구와 쇼
핑을 갈 수 없었다.

D 1. cold enough for me to see my breath
2. too small for her to wear 3. strong
enough to last more than fifteen hours
4. too busy to go home early 5. fast enough
to set a world record at the Olympics 6. too
expensive for me to buy

WRITING PRACTICE
p.49

A 1. too slow to play games 2. safe enough
for children to take 3. Strange to say
4. too far to turn back 5. To make matters
worse 6. strong enough to move

B 1. too complicated to use 2. handsome
enough to be the best model 3. To begin
with, you should follow 4. To tell the truth,
he didn't steal 5. so poor that he couldn't
6. The mountain is too high to climb

REVIEW TEST
pp.50-52

1. ④ 2. ⑤ 3. ① 4. ③ 5. ③ 6. ⑤ 7. ④ 8. ③
9. ③ 10. ④ 11. ⑤ 12. ④ 13. to read
14. talking[talk] 15. go 16. ① 17. ⑤ 18. to
go, to[in order to] study 19. helped me make[to
make] 20. so smart, can speak 21. She was
too busy to check 22. To tell the truth, we
dislike each other 23. seems to have been born
in Italy 24. be → have been 25. inviting → to
invite, Celebrate → To[In order to] celebrate

05 동명사

UNIT 01 동명사의 역할 pp.53-54

A 1. Smoking 2. wondering 3. telling
4. traveling 5. me 6. not finding 7. being treated 8. having studied 9. her
10. repairing

B 1. reading[to read] 2. Taking[To take]
3. watching[to watch] 4. being ignored / to be ignored 5. going 6. stealing[having stolen] 7. taking[to take] 8. Sitting[To sit]
9. Building[To build] 10. being disturbed

C 1. packing 2. being accepted 3. Pulling[To pull] 4. her 5. building 6. Sleeping[To sleep] 7. not going 8. having been / being
9. going[to go] fishing 10. being bothered

D 1. his[him] being late 2. being given the prize 3. not having called 4. her driving
5. my[me] working hard 6. my[me] borrowing 7. his[him] having done

WRITING PRACTICE p.55

A 1. Having[To have] good friends 2. not going to the gym 3. His habit is biting[to bite] 4. my[me] going 5. going[to go] shopping 6. having lied / lying

B 1. Not following traffic rules is dangerous
2. having been kicked off 3. doesn't like being patted 4. hate waiting in long lines
5. is good at taking care of children 6. was proud of being a member

UNIT 02 동명사 vs. to부정사 pp.56-57

A 1. drinking 2. to talk 3. putting
4. snowing 5. entering 6. knowing
7. to see 8. making 9. to take 10. to send

B 1. talking[to talk] 2. learning[to learn]
3. leaving 4. working 5. to buy
6. entering[having entered] 7. to start
8. crossing 9. failing 10. to buy

C 1. reading 2. to complete 3. to share

4. shutting 5. to call 6. going 7. climbing
8. working 9. drinking 10. talking

D 1. meeting 2. to turn off 3. to call
4. asking 5. to chat 6. pouring

WRITING PRACTICE p.58

A 1. agreed to buy 2. tried driving 3. forgot lending 4. couldn't help crying 5. finished packing 6. Try to exercise

B 1. likes water skiing in the summer 2. gave up taking the train 3. Bus fares keep going up 4. is busy doing laundry 5. seeing the police, he ran away 6. promised to deliver the furniture

REVIEW TEST pp.59-61

1. ② 2. ⑤ 3. ⑤ 4. ③ 5. ⑤ 6. ② 7. ④ 8. ③
9. ③ 10. ④ 11. ④ 12. ⑤ 13. ④ 14. forget traveling 15. is busy taking care of 16. denied having told 17. ④ 18. Excuse me for not calling you earlier 19. I feel like going scuba diving 20. his[him] getting 21. having lied
22. Don't forget to do 23. I tried playing 24. to study → studying 25. to write → writing, focusing → to focus

06 분사

UNIT 01 현재분사 vs. 과거분사 pp.62-63

A 1. surrounding 2. locked 3. painted
4. flying 5. baking 6. watching
7. satisfying 8. excited 9. crying
10. embarrassed

B 1. boring 2. embarrassing 3. written
4. facing 5. waiting 6. wounded
7. produced 8. washed 9. confusing
10. singing[sing]

C 1. satisfied 2. stopped 3. amazed
4. fixed 5. satisfying 6. tired 7. written
8. standing 9. amusing 10. chasing[chase]

D 1. a. amazed b. amazing
2. a. boring b. bored
3. a. disappointing b. disappointed
4. a. surprised b. surprising
5. a. depressing b. depressed

WRITING PRACTICE
p.64

A 1. is interested 2. stood[was standing] listening to 3. the broken window 4. a disappointing tourist spot 5. vegetables grown 6. adopted by a family

B 1. They kept me waiting for a long time
2. got bored with the game 3. He heard the speaker calling his name 4. A surprising number of people participated 5. There is a train leaving at 6. Olivia had her photograph taken

UNIT 02 분사구문
pp.65-66

A 1. Putting 2. Listening 3. Being 4. not knowing 5. Playing 6. Coming 7. Hoping 8. Not brushing 9. Being 10. living

B 1. Plugging 2. Not having 3. Falling
4. Turning 5. explaining 6. Waiting
7. Being 8. Listening to 9. Talking
10. Not knowing

C 1. Not enjoying sushi 2. Thinking positively
3. Being very sick 4. Not knowing what to do 5. Jogging in the dark 6. Growing up in the country 7. Walking in the park

D 1. When I looked out the window 2. After I finished my homework 3. Because I didn't know his name 4. If you look closely

WRITING PRACTICE
p.67

A 1. Not liking the big city 2. Living overseas
3. Following this map 4. Taking a shower
5. Being overweight 6. Not feeling well

B 1. Being full, I didn't eat 2. Sitting on the beach, they watched 3. Being late, I was not able to 4. Saying goodbye, she waved

5. Switching on the light / Switching the light on 6. arriving in Seoul at ten

UNIT 03 여러 가지 분사구문
pp.68-69

A 1. blowing 2. finishing 3. Strictly speaking
4. Having been given 5. turned 6. Judging from 7. It being 8. Having been raised
9. Generally speaking 10. Having learned

B 1. (Having been) Written 2. finishing
3. (Having been) Rejected 4. being
5. Speaking of 6. eating 7. Frankly speaking 8. playing 9. crossed
10. Considering

C 1. Having been born 2. It being fairly hot
3. Having been adopted 4. Asked to help her 5. After finishing this work 6. It being too dark outside

D 1. Having read 2. (Having been) Advised
3. Having tried 4. There being
5. (Having been / Being) Kept

WRITING PRACTICE
p.70

A 1. Frankly speaking 2. Having watched the movie 3. Generally speaking 4. with her eyes closed 5. Judging from his description
6. There being

B 1. Considering the remaining time 2. After eating, she always brushes 3. Having been left outside in the storm 4. Having wasted time before 5. Not having submitted his homework 6. Speaking of world history

REVIEW TEST
pp.71-73

1. ③ 2. ③ 3. ④ 4. ② 5. ⑤ 6. ③ 7. ③ 8. ⑤
9. ⑤ 10. ③ 11. ① 12. surprised 13. parked
14. Having 15. Singing a song 16. Having been his close friend 17. Leaving your house now
18. ④ 19. ③ 20. It being 21. Having changed schools 22. with the TV turned on 23. Having lived in Spain for three years 24. worked → working 25. satisfied → satisfying, disappointing → disappointed

CHAPTER 07 비교

UNIT 01 원급, 비교급, 최상급   pp.74-75

A 1. well 2. deeper 3. biggest 4. most delicious 5. soft 6. even 7. funny **8.** more difficult 9. good 10. best

B 1. softer 2. oldest 3. fast 4. more **5.** funniest 6. expensive 7. more popular 8. bigger 9. most foolish 10. tallest

C 1. as 2. more intelligent 3. most 4. the strongest 5. early 6. more advanced **7.** cheapest 8. better 9. fastest 10. hot

D 1. older than 2. as often as / more often than 3. smaller than 4. as well as 5. longer than

WRITING PRACTICE   p.76

A 1. as big as we expected 2. worse than **3.** the best opera (that) we have ever seen **4.** the hardest of 5. the most popular tourist spot in 6. a lot busier than I thought

B 1. not as bad as I thought 2. the best person on our team 3. as fast as the seller advertises 4. far better than the original one 5. more handsome now than when I **6.** the most hardworking of all my daughters

UNIT 02 여러 가지 비교구문   pp.77-78

A 1. most dangerous 2. twice as fast as **3.** darker and darker 4. the better **5.** animals 6. bigger and bigger 7. possible 8. the more easily 9. three times 10. less and less

B 1. the most nutritious vegetables 2. twice [two times] 3. possible[you can] 4. as well as 5. worse and worse 6. the more **7.** than 8. more and more 9. The lighter 10. the most popular cars

C 1. as little as possible 2. The more, the better 3. as often as possible 4. The more, the more

D 1. higher than any other mountain 2. as

high as 3. higher than 4. more interesting than any other subject 5. as interesting as 6. more interesting 7. larger than any other state 8. as large as Alaska 9. larger than Alaska

WRITING PRACTICE   p.79

A 1. twice[two times] as much 2. getting higher and higher 3. one of the most famous temples 4. one of the fastest runners 5. as soon as possible 6. The more you sweat

B 1. three times as expensive as mine 2. was getting louder and louder 3. turn down the volume as low as possible 4. No other teacher in our school is as popular as **5.** The more thankful you are, the happier **6.** one of the most beautiful cities in Europe

REVIEW TEST   pp.80-82

1. ① **2.** ③ **3.** ③ **4.** ③ **5.** ④ **6.** ⑤ **7.** ③ **8.** ⑤ **9.** ④ **10.** as old as **11.** as far as possible **12.** the most important **13.** ① **14.** faster, than **15.** as expensive as / more expensive than **16.** three times as old **17.** ⑤ **18.** ② **19.** ④ **20.** getting better and better **21.** (that) I have ever watched **22.** Her hands are a lot bigger than mine **23.** The more money you save, the richer you become **24.** more → as 또는 as → than **25.** building → buildings, tallest → tall

CHAPTER 08 접속사

UNIT 01 종속 접속사   pp.83-84

A 1. arrive 2. when 3. while 4. Each time **5.** until 6. since 7. because 8. Though **9.** If 10. as

B 1. am 2. was 3. enter 4. since

5. finish 6. If 7. go 8. because[as, since]
9. Though[Although, Even though] 10. tell

C 1. When 2. Because 3. unless
4. Although 5. since 6. As 7. even if
8. until 9. If 10. As 11. Though
12. while 13. Since 14. Unless
15. As soon as 16. Every time

WRITING PRACTICE   p.85

A 1. until[till] the movie is over 2. As time
goes by 3. since he came to Germany
4. while you are abroad 5. If you want to be
healthy 6. Unless it rains tomorrow / If it
doesn't rain tomorrow

B 1. As soon as I graduated from university
2. As she came from a poor family 3. when
you use a knife 4. Every time I call Suji
5. Though Jeremy has read many books
6. Even if you don't like opera

UNIT 02 짝으로 이루어진 접속사, 간접의문문
pp.86-87

A 1. either 2. neither 3. both 4. he wanted
5. or 6. and 7. if she would 8. who will
win 9. not only 10. Why do you guess

B 1. and 2. the convenience store is
3. I was 4. Who do you think 5. Both
6. if he will visit 7. Neither 8. Either
9. the girl with red hair is 10. but also

C 1. either today or tomorrow 2. neither
money nor time 3. is very famous both in
Korea and abroad 4. not only a singer but
also an actor 5. clothes as well as food /
food as well as clothes

D 1. I don't know where he was going. 2. I'm
not sure if[whether] you want to stay with us.
3. Tell me why you hate Logan. 4. I want to
know who saved my life. 5. What do you
think you will be in the future? 6. I wonder
if[whether] he finished the project
successfully.

WRITING PRACTICE   p.88

A 1. who broke the window 2. either French
or German 3. how much I love you

4. if[whether] he knows me 5. not only
expensive but also 6. both watching movies
and

B 1. Neither Betty nor you are wrong 2. He is
honest as well as smart 3. Do you know
why she came here 4. Technology has both
good and bad sides 5. Tell me what makes
you happy 6. Who do you believe should
be our leader

REVIEW TEST   pp.89-91

1. ③ **2.** ④ **3.** ⑤ **4.** ② **5.** ③ **6.** ③ **7.** ④ **8.** ③
9. ⑤ **10.** ② **11.** If you don't accept his offer
12. Whenever[Each time] I go shopping
13. neither, nor **14.** as well as **15.** until[till]
16. ⑤ **17.** I wonder where they had **18.** What
do you believe **19.** I don't know if[whether] it is
good **20.** If[if] **21.** since **22.** not only salty but
also high in calories **23.** As soon as she saw me
24. will he → he will **25.** nor → or 또는 either →
neither

CHAPTER
09 관계사

UNIT 01 관계대명사   pp.92-93

A 1. that 2. What 3. whose 4. which
5. that 6. whose 7. who 8. What
9. which 10. What

B 1. What 2. which 3. who 4. who
5. whose 6. which 7. who 8. which
9. whose 10. what

C 1. She met the author who(m)[that] she
followed on Twitter. 2. He will give me a
desk which[that] he does not use any longer.
3. She went to the gallery whose collection
was very impressive. 4. This is the pencil
case which[that] I have used since
elementary school. 5. I have a friend

who[that] traveled around the world.
6. This store sells vases whose colors are very unique.

D 1. who[that] 2. that 3. which[that] 4. What [The thing that[which]] 5. that 6. that 7. whose 8. that 9. who(m)[that] 10. that

WRITING PRACTICE p.94

A 1. who[that] has a lot of experience
2. whose father is a hairdresser 3. who(m) [that] you taught 4. What[The thing that[which]] matters now 5. anything that I can do 6. which[that] I played

B 1. a busy man whose schedule is filled
2. a friend who listens well
3. understood what his son was trying
4. the only person that I can trust
5. the music which the audience requested
6. the very lamp that my mom

UNIT 02 관계부사 pp.95-96

A 1. where 2. how 3. when 4. how 5. why 6. when 7. where 8. why 9. how 10. where

B 1. when 2. how 3. why 4. where 5. how 6. where 7. when 8. why 9. when 10. how

C 1. how 2. why 3. when 4. where 5. how 6. where

D 1. Carnegie Hall is a place where musicians want to perform. 2. The year when the Olympics were held in Korea was 1988. 3. The square is the place where artists gather. 4. Twelve o'clock is the time when he should take the medicine. 5. This is how I cut my electricity bill in half. 6. The salesperson explained the reason why the car would be good for me.

WRITING PRACTICE p.97

A 1. why she didn't show up 2. where I often meditate 3. why he came back home 4. how she became rich 5. where I used to swim 6. when the traffic is the heaviest

B 1. the time when we went to the beach

2. is the way he solved the puzzle 3. a town where grapes for wine are grown 4. the reason why she didn't leave 5. how I lost 10 kg in a month 6. a place where you can relax and recharge

UNIT 03 주의해야 할 관계사 pp.98-99

A 1. standing 2. whom 3. who 4. in which 5. which 6. that 7. which 8. where 9. which 10. when

B 1. X 2. which was 3. whom 4. which was 5. X 6. that 7. which was 8. X 9. who 10. X

C 1. who 2. which 3. which 4. who 5. where 6. where 7. (who[that] was) selling 8. to whom 9. which 10. when

D 1. which had been in the attic for many years
2. which made his teacher worried 3. which contain healthy omega-3 fatty acids
4. which makes her happy 5. who has sold more than three million albums 6. where she had worked the previous year 7. when I was fifteen years old

WRITING PRACTICE p.100

A 1. which were too sour 2. which[that] he was talking about 3. who is an old friend
4. which helped him (to) pass the exam
5. who(m)[that] I talked about before
6. where I stayed for a week

B 1. which surprised her 2. the restaurant that you talked about before 3. when it is very quiet 4. the boy Victoria danced with
5. The man drinking water over there
6. The picture stolen from the gallery

UNIT 04 복합관계사 pp.101-102

A 1. whoever 2. Whichever 3. However 4. whenever 5. Wherever 6. Whenever 7. Whatever 8. Whoever 9. However 10. Whatever

B 1. Whenever 2. whoever 3. Whatever 4. Whichever 5. Wherever 6. However

C 1. Whoever 2. Whenever 3. Whatever
4. However 5. whomever 6. whichever
7. However 8. wherever

D 1. whatever 2. Whenever 3. Whoever
4. wherever 5. However

WRITING PRACTICE p.103

A 1. Wherever the singer goes 2. However
hard it is 3. Whenever I come here
4. Whichever route you choose 5. support
whoever wins 6. have whatever you like

B 1. However tired she is, she will do
2. will trust whomever you recommend
3. Whatever you do, they will not change
4. very well whenever you call me 5. access
the internet wherever you are 6. Whoever
wins, people will be disappointed with

REVIEW TEST pp.104-106

1. ⑤ 2. ⑤ 3. ④ 4. ⑤ 5. ③ 6. ④ 7. ③ 8. ④
9. ① 10. whom 11. that was 12. ③ 13. who
14. What 15. Whoever 16. whatever[whichever]
17. My father bought me a laptop whose color is
white. 18. Anne should be responsible for
what[the thing that[which]] she did yesterday.
19. wherever he goes 20. However smart you
are 21. ③ 22. Whoever gets the correct answer
23. What I want to know is 24. where → when
25. who → whose, Whatever → Whenever

CHAPTER 10 가정법

UNIT 01 가정법 과거, 가정법 과거완료, 혼합 가정법 pp.107-108

A 1. were 2. didn't 3. would 4. could
5. had 6. be 7. had eaten 8. hadn't
cleaned 9. have applied 10. be

B 1. feel 2. would vote 3. hadn't[had not]
been 4. would go 5. had practiced
6. could have met 7. were 8. would be
9. wouldn't[would not] be 10. hadn't[had
not] booked

C 1. won the lottery 2. had read your email
3. could have finished 4. knew how to drive
5. would participate 6. would not be alive

D 1. I had my cell phone 2. you had helped
me with the work 3. I had answered the
question correctly 4. he could have gotten
into the college 5. I had slept well last night
6. she would be awake now

WRITING PRACTICE p.109

A 1. If I weren't[were not] tired 2. If she
hadn't[had not] wasted her money 3. she
might have told me 4. I wouldn't[would not]
be in this place now 5. I would be happy
6. If he had known the answer

B 1. If I had more time, I would spend 2. If
you had left a message, I would have called
3. If he had quit smoking earlier, he would be
healthier 4. If he hadn't given up his dream,
he might be a film director 5. He could
have helped you if he had known 6. I would
have been disappointed if I hadn't seen

UNIT 02 I wish, as if, It's time + 가정법 pp.110-111

A 1. didn't 2. could 3. paid 4. knew 5. had
been 6. didn't 7. found 8. were 9. had
known 10. hadn't been

B 1. were 2. had read 3. fired 4. had
bought 5. were 6. went 7. were 8. had
practiced 9. were 10. found

C 1. had come with me 2. had dinner
3. were my boss 4. had gone there earlier
5. were cheaper 6. gave it back to me

D 1. he were from China 2. I wish she had
kept 3. she had traveled to Hong Kong
4. I wish I had 5. I wish I had met 6. he
knew the truth 7. I wish there weren't[were
not] so many mosquitoes

WRITING PRACTICE p.112

A
1. my hair were longer
2. I had taken the subway
3. I wish I hadn't[had not] voted for him
4. as if it were dead
5. as if he had seen the movie
6. you took a shower

B
1. I wish you lived in this town
2. I wish my dad had fixed my bike
3. I wish the police officer had arrived
4. Daniel acts as if he were a lawyer
5. as if nothing had happened
6. It is time the government made a choice

REVIEW TEST pp.116-118

1. ④ 2. ④ 3. ② 4. ③ 5. ① 6. ④ 7. ④ 8. ①
9. ② 10. ② 11. ③ 12. ④ 13. ⑤ 14. I would
be happy 15. would have gone shopping
16. weren't[were not] interested in 17. would
think twice 18. said goodbye 19. I wish I had
lent 20. had taken, wouldn't[would not] have
arrived 21. With your help, I could have gotten
22. Were I a billionaire, I would not have to
23. If I had brushed my teeth, I would not have to
go 24. will be → were 25. had been → be

UNIT 03 주의해야 할 가정법 pp.113-114

A
1. Without 2. Without 3. Had 4. to talk
5. Had my son 6. But for 7. Were she
8. you were 9. Without 10. Were he

B
1. But for / Without[If it had not been for,
Had it not been for] 2. had not been
3. Had it / If it had 4. If I were / Were I
5. would help 6. If you had / Had you 7. to
take / if he took 8. Were I / If I were 9. had
not been 10. to hear / if you heard

C
1. Were I a robot 2. Without the light 3. If
it were not for the internet 4. Had I left
earlier 5. to read my report 6. With good
service

D
1. Were Edison alive today 2. to see the
skyscraper 3. With your help 4. Had she
taken the pill 5. Without the loud noises
6. Without my math teacher's help

CHAPTER 11 일치와 화법

UNIT 01 수의 일치 pp.119-120

A
1. has 2. is 3. is 4. is 5. makes 6. is
7. is 8. have 9. have 10. are

B
1. have → has 2. were → was 3. are → is
4. are → is 5. is → are 6. were → was
7. are → is 8. enjoys → enjoy 9. have →
has 10. likes → like

C
1. lives 2. have 3. is 4. have 5. reminds
6. Has 7. is 8. is 9. wants 10. are

D
1. needs to be cleaned 2. teaches us about
the history of people 3. helps relieve my
stress 4. is a short distance to drive 5. are
dairy products 6. die of hunger

WRITING PRACTICE p.115

A
1. Had I read your text message 2. A good
student wouldn't[would not] cheat
3. Without[But for, Had it not been for] our
coach 4. Were I the president 5. Without
[But for, Were it not for] sunlight 6. Without
[But for, Had it not been for] her hard work

B
1. Had you chosen this car 2. With a little
more time 3. Were you to die tomorrow
4. A good citizen wouldn't break the law
5. If it had not been for the dog 6. But for
water, life could not exist

WRITING PRACTICE p.121

A
1. Nobody knows 2. Three hours is
3. Breaking[To break] bad habits is
4. Both you and I are 5. The rich pay
6. A number of animals are

B
1. No one is more beautiful than you
2. Mathematics is my favorite subject
3. Thirty dollars was paid for this skirt
4. Taking a warm bath helps me to relax
5. Why he came here is a secret
6. Both my father and my mother wear glasses

A   1. had   2. was   3. composed   4. didn't
    5. hadn't eaten   6. is   7. travels   8. are
    9. hadn't   10. would

B   1. are   2. are   3. were   4. are   5. was
    6. invented   7. wanted   8. was   9. was
    10. had won

C   1. was   2. leads   3. were   4. is   5. is
    6. began   7. lays   8. would wait   9. was
    10. smelled

D   1. they had lived here for twenty years
    2. a female emperor penguin lays one egg a
    year   3. that I had had a car accident
    4. that a shrimp's heart is in its head
    5. that she would star in the drama
    6. that the professor had retired
    7. my brother would go hiking with me

WRITING PRACTICE   p.124

A   1. the Battle of Waterloo occurred
    2. coffee is harmful   3. I didn't send you
    4. (that) the shoes were comfortable
    5. Hitler invaded   6. the early bird catches

B   1. I am sorry I made you upset
    2. I believed that he wrote the poem
    3. I thought you had taken the course
    4. The girl said she hated mosquitoes
    5. I heard the earth is getting warmer
    6. Mac said that he majored in science

A   1. needed   2. told   3. would   4. I had
    5. if   6. to be   7. was   8. I had seen
    9. not to eat   10. to show

B   1. said   2. told   3. if[whether]   4. told
    5. he wanted   6. I had had   7. I lived
    8. what   9. not to worry   10. to apply

C   1. me (that) she ran her own business
    2. (that) he would apply for the job   3. him
    what he was eating   4. asked me how he
    could get to the theater   5. asked me
    if[whether] I knew who he was
    6. told[advised] me to eat more vegetables
    7. told[ordered] me not to put my dirty
    clothes on the sofa

D   1. My mom said to me, "You need to stay
    at home."   2. My father said to me, "What
    do you want to eat?"   3. She said to me,
    "Will you stay at my home longer?"
    4. My boss said to me, "Did you break your
    computer?"   5. Dennis said to me, "Take me
    to the festival."   6. The dentist said to me,
    "Don't[Do not] eat candy."

WRITING PRACTICE   p.127

A   1. told me (that) I would become
    2. asked me if[whether] I was married
    3. asked me what I was looking for
    4. asked me if[whether] I had seen
    5. ordered me to clean
    6. advised me not to go

B   1. He says that he enjoys summer sports
    2. She ordered me not to run in the hallway
    3. Michael asked me if I believed in God
    4. I asked the clerk if the dress was on sale
    5. My mother told me to take care of my sister
    6. Nicole told me that she had missed her train

REVIEW TEST   pp.128-130

1. ⑤   2. ②   3. ①   4. ③   5. ④   6. ③   7. ⑤   8. ③
9. ①   10. ②   11. ④   12. if[whether] I had a
boyfriend   13. Gary and I enjoy   14. learned
(that) trees produce   15. ③   16. asked me what
time the movie started   17. told[asked] her
brother not to bother her   18. The man asked
me if[whether] I had seen   19. is   20. is
21. respects   22. which T-shirt looked better on
her   23. ordered him to raise his hands   24. told
→ said[told me]   25. had summer → has summer

12 기타 구문

UNIT 01 강조, 부정구문, 병렬   pp.131-132

A   1. save   2. wait   3. It   4. that   5. Not all
6. jogging   7. None   8. does   9. Neither
10. to express

B   1. call   2. like   3. It   4. was it   5. have
6. Not all   7. did   8. would   9. brush
10. get

C   1. Not   2. not   3. Neither   4. Not   5. No

D   1. did study   2. did lie   3. do hope   4. does
remember   5. It was last month that I lost
my cat   6. Who was it that you went to Paris
with   7. It is a fan of mine that sends me
letters every week

WRITING PRACTICE   p.133

A   1. I do like musicals   2. at the post office
that I saw George   3. It was this film that
made   4. None of you   5. Not all
vegetarians drink   6. neither of these
opinions

B   1. I did discuss the problem with   2. It is
green tea that I want to drink   3. He likes
reading and listening to music   4. Not all
information on the internet is useful   5. Not
all inventions are helpful to us   6. Neither of
us can speak English

UNIT 02 도치, 생략, 동격   pp.134-135

A   1. passed a plane   2. comes my daughter
3. does my teacher remember   4. a Korean
boy band   5. to   6. waiting   7. can
8. was I   9. Neither

B   1. was my house   2. stood my ex-boyfriend
3. Hanbok, Korean traditional clothes   4. did
I think   5. did I   6. Neither   7. can I   8. did I
drink   9. did he realize   10. have I heard

C   1. use it   2. it was   3. draw it   4. 뒤의 learn
Spanish   5. 뒤의 drink   6. he was   7. you are
8. 뒤의 see him   9. he is   10. B의 busy

D   1. live my parents   2. sat the pianist
3. stands a tall building   4. does he eat fast
food   5. has she dreamed of becoming this
famous   6. could Jeremy breathe in the
water   7. have I seen such a lovely baby

WRITING PRACTICE   p.136

A   1. this tunnel goes the bus   2. could I get
enough sleep   3. could she hear his voice
4. your grandparents if you can   5. So do I
6. Neither did I

B   1. the bridge lives a family of foxes   2. I like
watching movies while eating   3. Little does
my friend watch TV   4. She tries whatever
she wants to   5. the great pianist, wrote lots
of classical music   6. do you do when bored

REVIEW TEST   pp.137-139

1. ②   2. ④   3. ⑤   4. ④   5. ③   6. ①   7. ③   8. ⑤
9. ③   10. she was   11. 뒤의 go on business trips
12. ①   13. ⑤   14. I did forget to bring a copy of
my ID card.   15. It was a car accident that I
witnessed on my way to work.   16. Little did she
dream that she would meet her favorite actor.
17. ①   18. so does he   19. a British author,
wrote *Harry Potter*   20. did I imagine that Anne
would be a fashion model   21. is his office
22. Neither of us was satisfied with the result
23. Not every boy enjoys watching action movies
24. an enormous dog sat → sat an enormous
dog, I had → had I   25. That → It